The World's Top Photographers

Nudes

A RotoVision Book

Published and distributed by
RotoVision SA
Route Suisse 9
CH-1295 Mies
Switzerland

RotoVision SA
Sales and Editorial Office
Sheridan House
114 Western Road
Hove BN3 1DD
UK

Tel: +44 (0)1273 72 72 68
Fax: +44 (0)1273 72 72 69
www.rotovision.com

10 9 8 7 6 5 4 3 2 1

978-2-940378-27-2

Editor: Chris Middleton
Art Director: Luke Herriott
Design: Studio Ink

Cover image: *White Nudes*, R. J. Muna.

Reprographics in Singapore by ProVision Pte. Ltd
Tel: +65 6334 7720
Fax: +65 6334 7721

Printed in Singapore by Star Standard Pte (Ltd)

The World's Top Photographers

and the stories behind their greatest images

Nudes

Anthony LaSala

Contents

"If any thing is sacred, the human body is sacred."
Walt Whitman, I Sing the Body Electric, *(from* Leaves of Grass*)*

"Nakedness reveals itself. Nudity is placed on display .... The nude is condemned to never being naked. Nudity is a form of dress."
John Berger, Ways of Seeing

The study and recording of the nude human form, the physical essence of each and every person, has been the most revered, controversial, divisive, and hallowed subject in the history of art. From early classical sculptures and statues to the paintings of such artists as Peter Paul Rubens, Egon Schiele, and Pablo Picasso, the human body invites curiosity, dispute, divergence, and fascination from all corners of the creative realm.

After the invention of photographic techniques by, among others, Louis Jacques Mandé Daguerre in 1839, photography gradually became recognized as a creative medium equal to established art forms such as painting, drawing, and sculpting. However, the photographic image of the naked body, a subject that, more than 150 years later, is sometimes still taboo, continued for many years to be seen as an inferior imitation of traditional artistic creations.

In the early days, nude photography was mainly limited to being a visual aid for painters, or a tool for scientific and physiological research (in the case of Eadweard Muybridge's motion studies and realist painter Thomas Eakins's nude photographs). Beyond these limited uses there were the first titillating erotic postcards and pornography, and images in the overdone style of romantic impressionism.

Early photographers in the field, such as the Swedish-born Oscar Gustave Rejlander, Robert Demachy of France, and pictorialists Clarence H. White and Frank Eugene, created impressive portfolios of work that began to break down the barriers to nude photography's acceptance as a serious art form. However, their images mainly copied or complemented the works of painters. It took the efforts of two former pictorialists—an Illinois-born photographer named Edward Weston, and Alfred Stieglitz of New Jersey—to really begin to change things.

From the late teens in the 20th century, through the 1940s, Weston made hundreds of images of the nude form. "I am stimulated to work with the nude body, because of the infinite combination of lines which are present with every move," he wrote in his now famous *Daybooks*.

Concentrating mainly on the love interests of his life—Margrethe Mather, Tina Modotti, Sonya Noskowiak, and Charis Wilson—it was Weston's work, in addition to Stieglitz's brilliant studies of his own wife and muse Georgia O'Keeffe, that first presented the nude in an artistically beautiful and alluring manner, while also displaying an open desire for the subject. Stieglitz's images were stunning surveys of form and figure, while also being unguarded declarations of love and lust. Weston's nudes were radiant recordings of shape and structure, of contours and curves. They were, quite simply, revolutionary masterpieces that are still celebrated and imitated throughout the world.

In the wake of Weston and Stieglitz, many other photographers began to make their own marks on the history of the nude photograph. Imogen Cunningham's abstract images added a distinct sensuality. Man Ray's surreal creations, including his foray into darkroom techniques such as solarization, were groundbreaking and continue to influence artists today. Bill Brandt's *Perspective of Nudes* series in 1961 challenged viewers with haunting shapes, contrasting shadows, and extreme angles.

The harsh sexuality of Helmut Newton's photographs intimidated and entranced at the same time, while the super-realistic photography of Robert Mapplethorpe presented male nudes in a new and provocative light. Les Krims and Joel-Peter Witkin combined shock and humor. Jock Sturges and Sally Mann displayed innocence and beauty in the young, nude body, attracting both critical praise and controversy for their conceptions.

Today, the field of nude photography is burgeoning and healthy. Within every art and magazine section of every bookstore—and in every corner of the ever-expanding Internet, of course—the unclothed (usually female) figure is rife. Naturally, many of these images are considered more pornographic than artistic, but definitions shift dramatically through the years and fluctuate with each set of ethics and eyes. What is certain is that there is a staggering amount of inspired work being created.

Among the images showcased here are: the original and ever-shifting conceptions of Sam Haskins, including images from his celebrated book *Cowboy Kate* (Haskins Press, 1964); the rebellious visions of Bob Carlos Clarke; the twisted glamor of Guy Bourdin; the sensitivity and intimacy of Mona Kuhn; new perspectives on the male nude by Greg Gorman and Arthur Tress; the boldness of Rankin; the sensuality of Marc Baptiste, Andreas Bitesnich, and Barbara Bordnick; the fashionably stylistic images of Bettina Rheims; and the dark beauty of Robert Mapplethorpe's vision of the male.

You will also observe how technological advancements, including the explosion in use of digital tools, have impacted on nude photography. At the same time, you will see how the works of Weston still cast a long shadow many decades later—in the classic style of the legendary Ralph Gibson, for example, as well as in the images of Regina DeLuise and Nic Tucker.

As Weston himself said: "The camera should be used for a recording of life, for rendering the very substance and quintessence of the thing itself, whether it be polished steel or palpitating flesh." It is the latter, in all its glorious forms, that will captivate your eyes on the following pages.

Anthony La Sala, New York, 2005

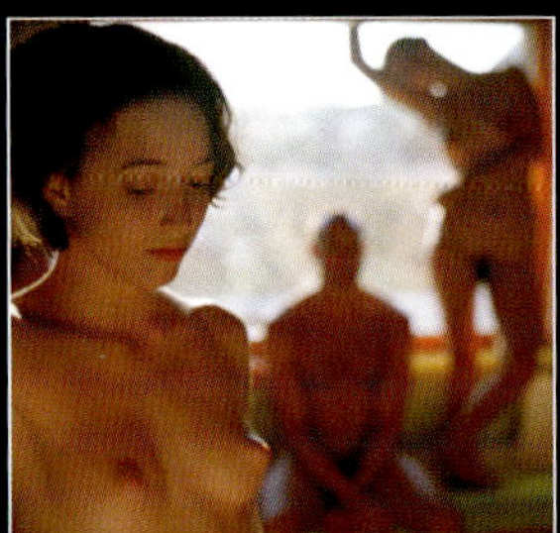

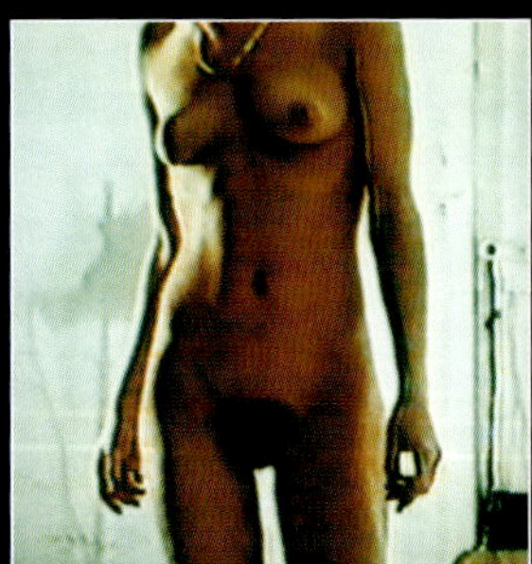

(Above) **Kolia, 2003** by Mona Kuhn

(Right) **Emma Video 577, 2003** by Marc Atkins

(Opposite) **Cheating the Ace, 1963** by Sam Haskins

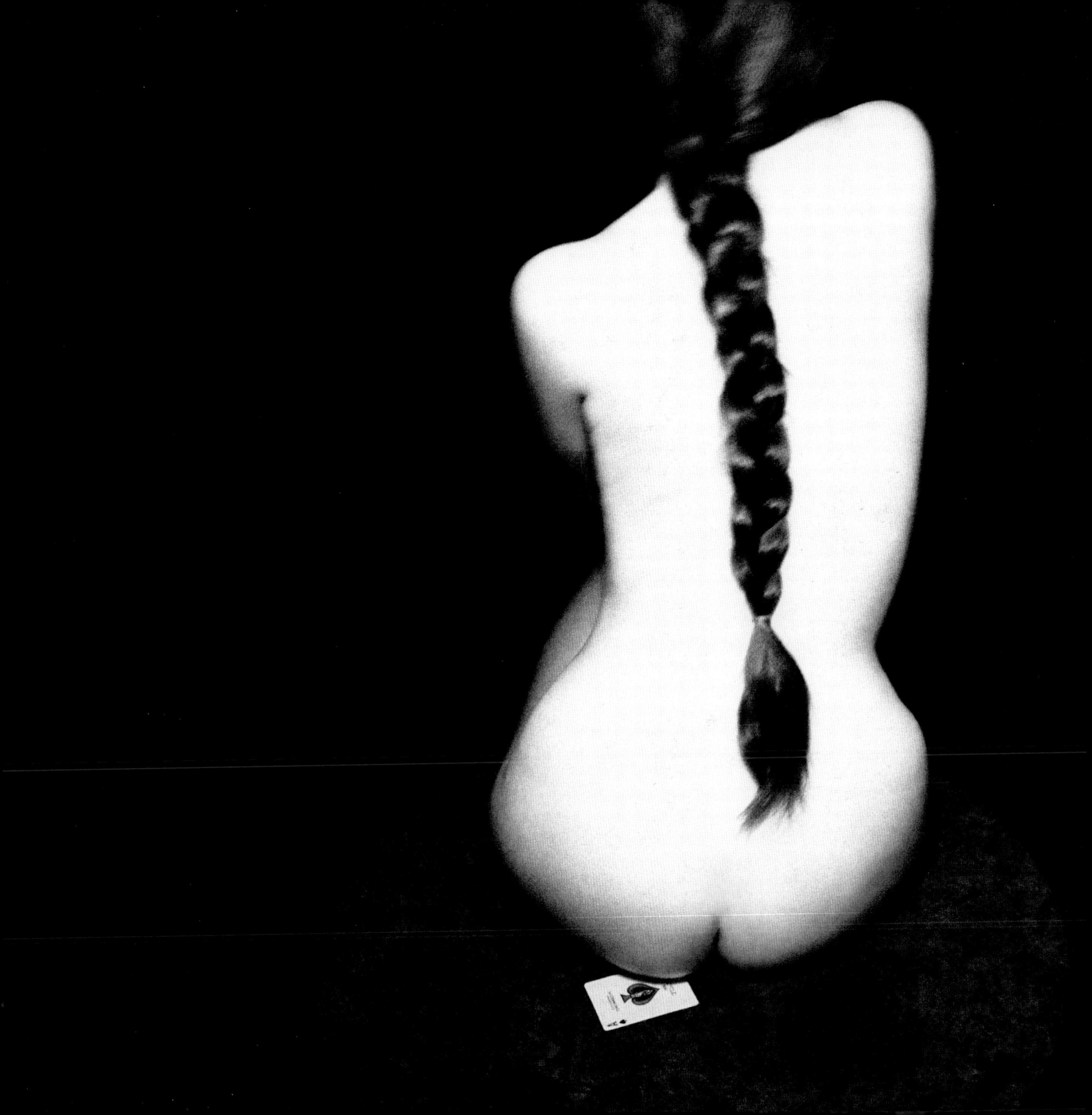

Guido Argentini

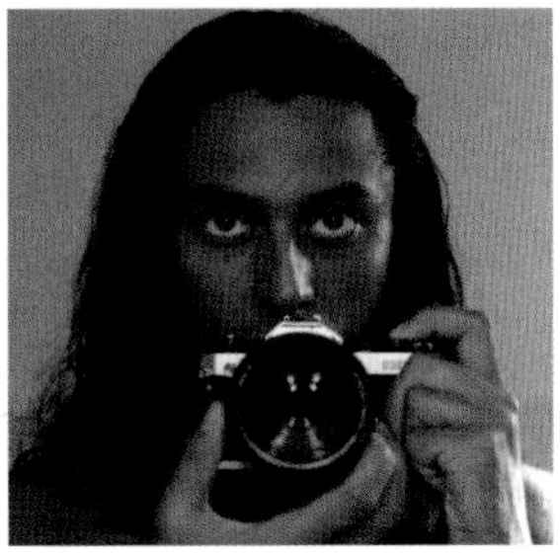

The photographs of Guido Argentini are like sculptures that have come to life. Women's bodies, dipped in silver, glisten and flash. Others blend with the natural environment, balanced on waves of sand, or beached on outcrops of granite.

Argentini has a passion for dance and for the sculpting of human forms in metal and stone. His images are a reflection of that. "I was heavily influenced by the art of Constantin Brancusi, whose primeval sculptures of polished bronze made me aware of the fascination of the absolute," he says. "That is why I used silver paint to emphasize the body form of my models."

Silvereye (teNeues, 2003) is a vibrant collection of images that took 12 years to make. As well as his studies of bodies covered in a metallic sheen, it is Argentini's geometric studies that set his work apart. Subjects interact with circles, squares, and triangles, twisting their bodies to harmonize with the shapes. The resulting compositions are homages to both form and flesh.

"In some cases, I have made use of certain structural elements that are based on a pattern of elementary geometric figures, such as the triangle and the square, which I used to confine a space. In other cases, I chose the desert or the sea. These two aspects are not contradictory, since in both cases I wanted to convey a sense of the infinite," he explains. "In the first case, I resorted to a rather abstract, mathematical approach; in the second, I made use of a landscape that is authentic, but not subject to temporal limitations."

Born in 1966 in Florence, Italy, Argentini originally studied medicine at the University of Florence. Although he always loved photography (his first photo session was with his girlfriend at the age of 17), it wasn't until he was 23 that he focused his attention on it as a career. Inspired by Helmut Newton's and Guy Bourdin's success in "creating a new way to look at women," Argentini moved to the United States and began a career that has seen him shooting for dozens of major magazines, including *Vogue*, *Maxim*, *Playboy*, *Men's Health*, and *Marie Claire*. He now splits his time between Los Angeles, Miami, and his original home in Florence.

His devotion to nude photography stems from his love and dreams of women. "The women I portray represent the abstraction of beauty to a far greater extent than reflecting traditional aesthetic values that the world of fashion takes so much to heart," he says.

"The energy that flows between me and my model is stronger and more intense when I am alone with the model. The personal relationship that develops between the photographer and the model is of decisive importance and the basis of the

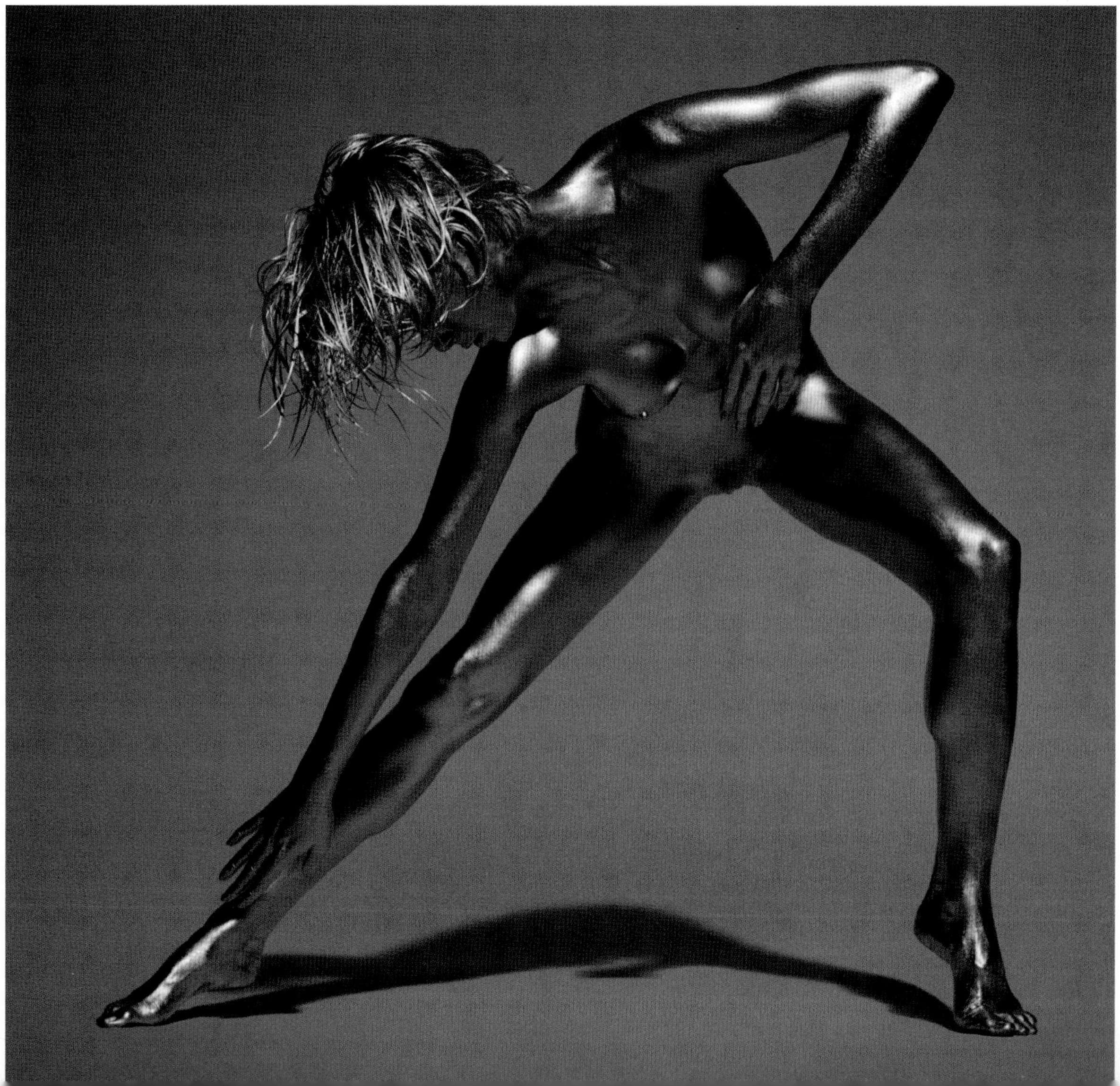

Both images: Silver Girl, 2003 (*right, opposite*)
"If my book dealt with eroticism, then the look would be most significant, but in the present case, sensuality is transferred to the body. That is why the model's face is almost never visible, and when it is, the eyes never look into the camera. The women I portray represent the abstraction of beauty to a far greater extent than reflecting traditional aesthetic values that the world of fashion takes so much to heart."

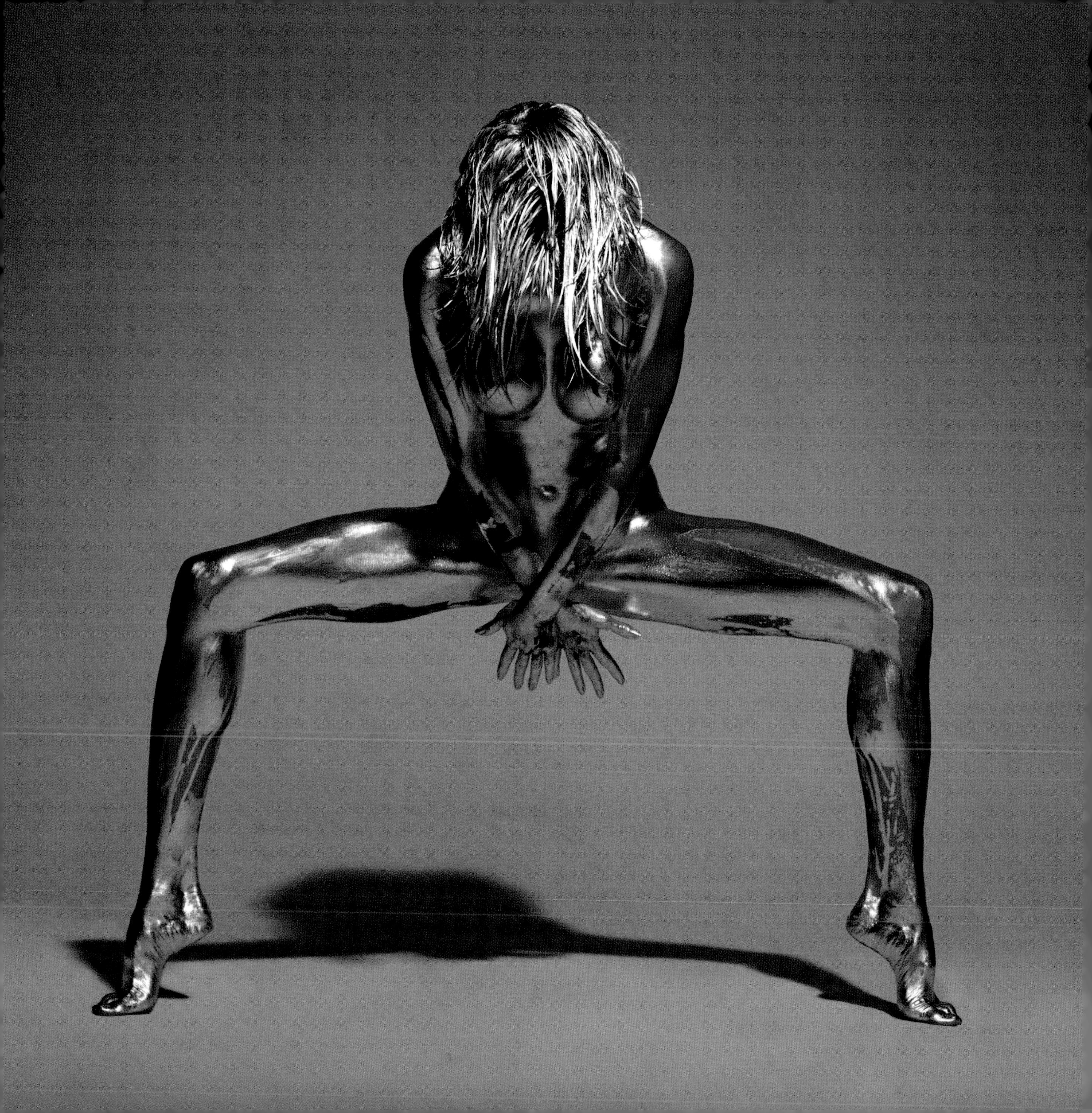

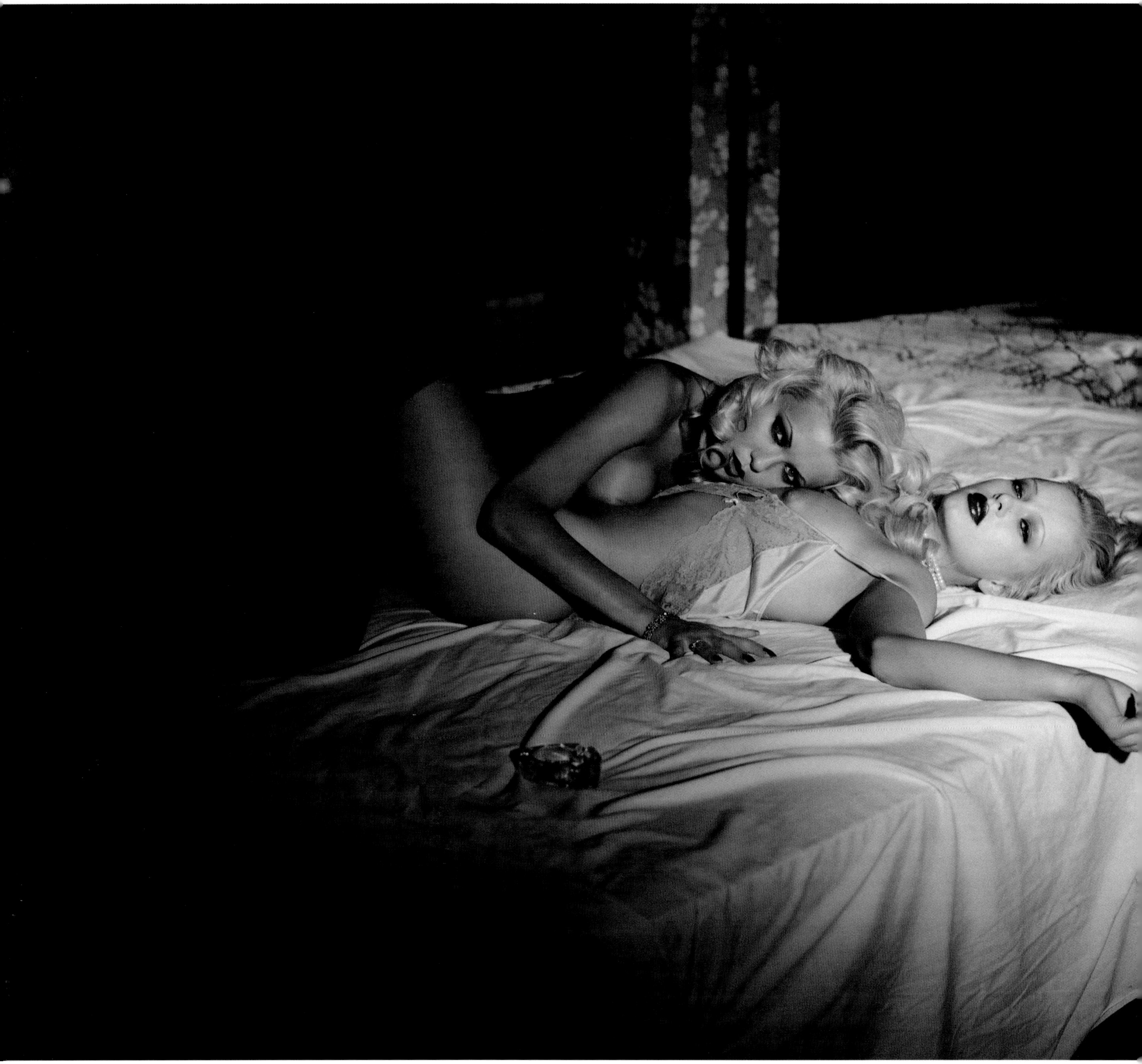

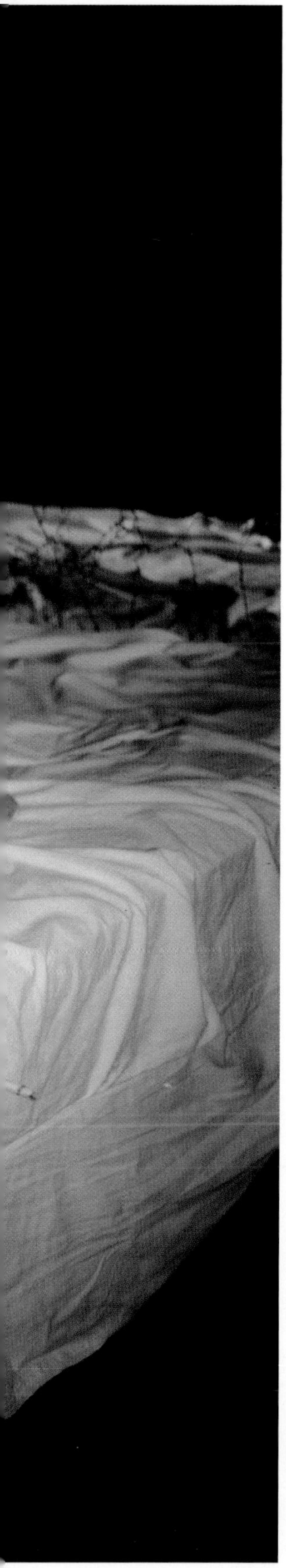

final result. And because that is so, I am prepared to wait a long time until I find the right subject for a particular idea.

"I have seen how strongly the model's attitude depends on the personality of the photographer and on the type of attraction that unfolds between the two, and that there is an interdependence that necessarily has to do with sexuality. Just think of Helmut Newton's and Bettina Rheims's photographs in comparison with those of Herb Ritts and Bruce Weber."

Still using the same camera that he has had since he was 20 years old—a Hasselblad—Argentini has continued his study of the nude with a "more erotic" follow-up to *Silvereye*.

"Nude photography is a difficult subject, probably the most difficult of all," he explains, "but for this very reason it is also the most stimulating—it is a continual challenge. It is a walk on a tightrope requiring a steady gait, for it carries the risk of plummeting into pornography on the one hand or plunging into banality on the other.

"Some photographs of nudes have been so heavily retouched by computer that the bodies look as though they are made of plastic," he continues. "Do I insult anyone by saying that some photographers just betray their lack of self-confidence that way? My understanding of the quest for perfection is not the battle against scars or other blemishes, which is conducted with such vehemence that it annihilates the energy contained in the picture. For me, perfection is truth and vitality."

Jana & Milena, Los Angeles, 1997 *(left)*

Two Girls, Silver, 2003 *(below)*
"Every form of art, whether it manifests itself in a painting, a sculpture, a poem, or a photograph, is always interpreted according to the personal sensitivity and culture of the viewer. My message—if anyone cares to look for a message in my photographs at all—does not in any way seek to exert force or compulsion, but only to arouse emotions."

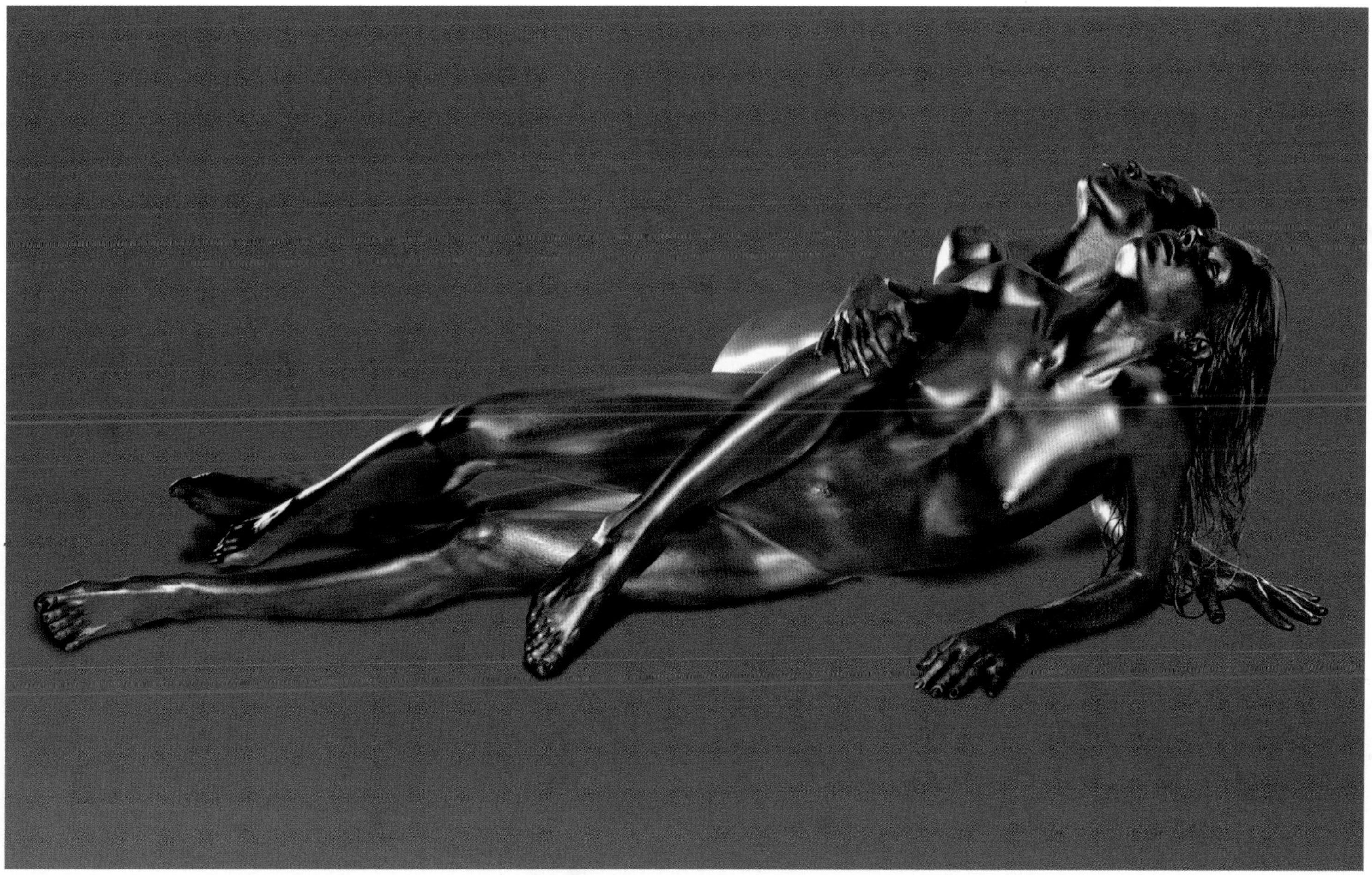

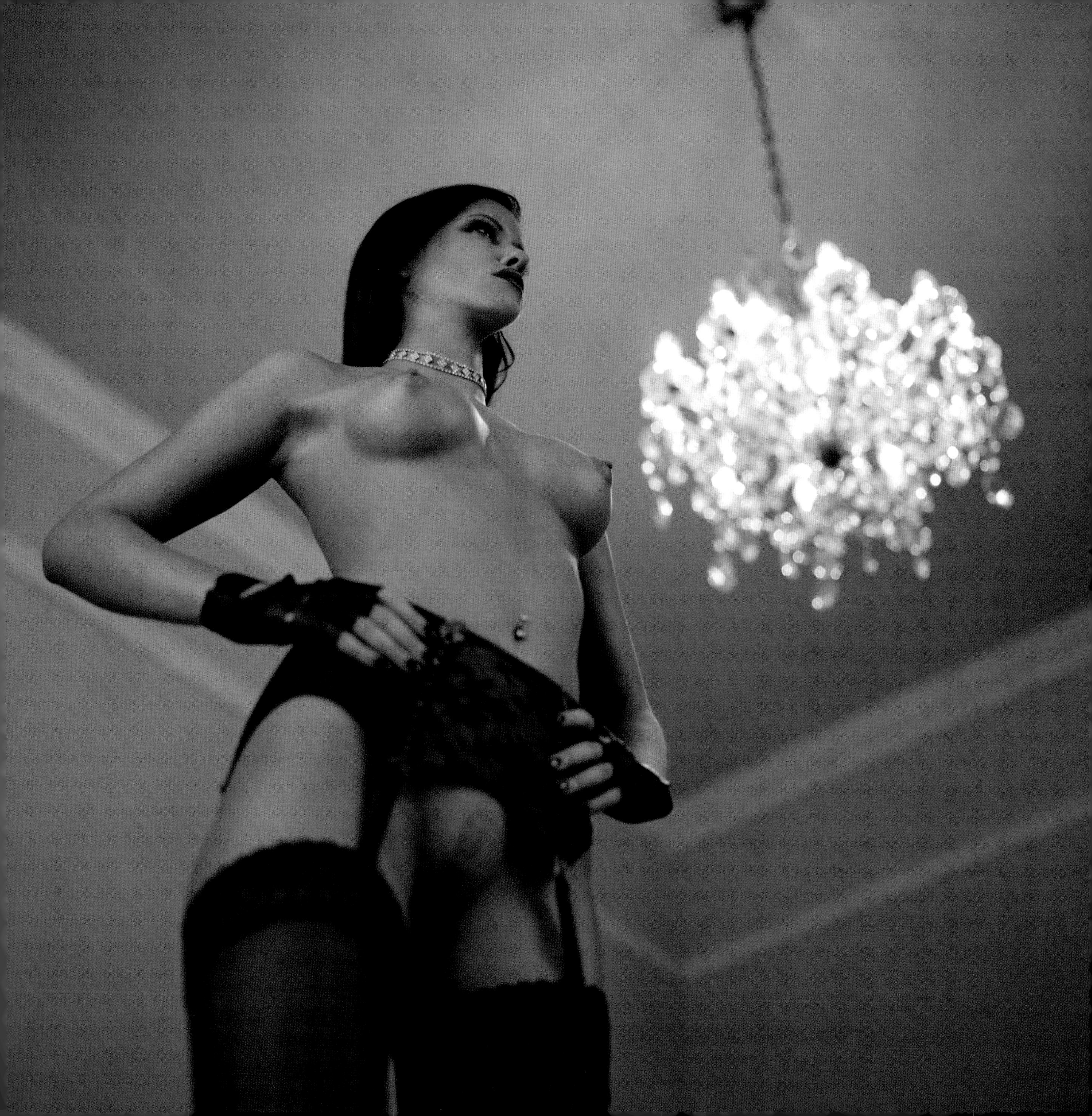

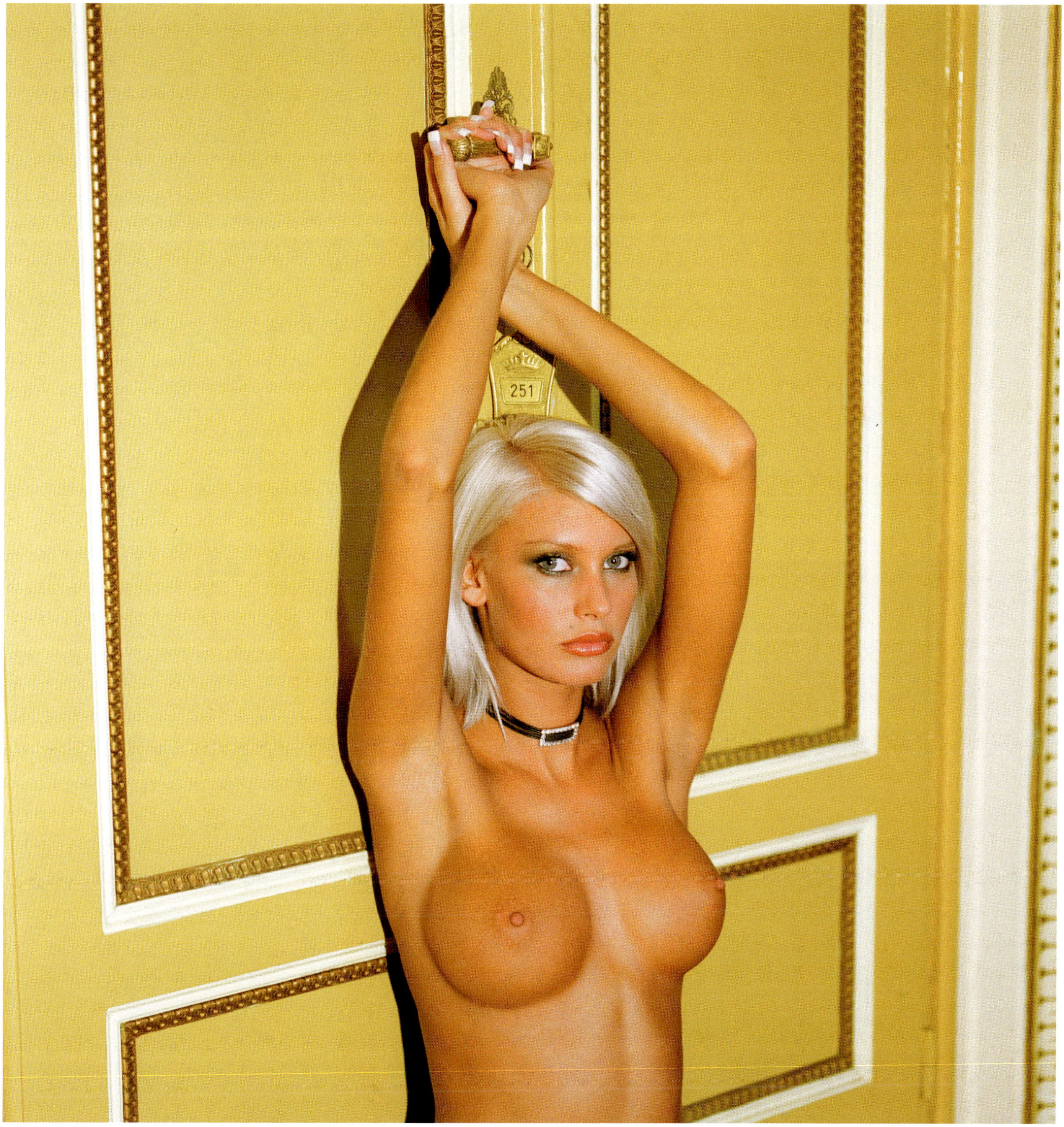

Untitled, 1997
(left)

Tereza from Below, 1997
(opposite)

Marc Atkins

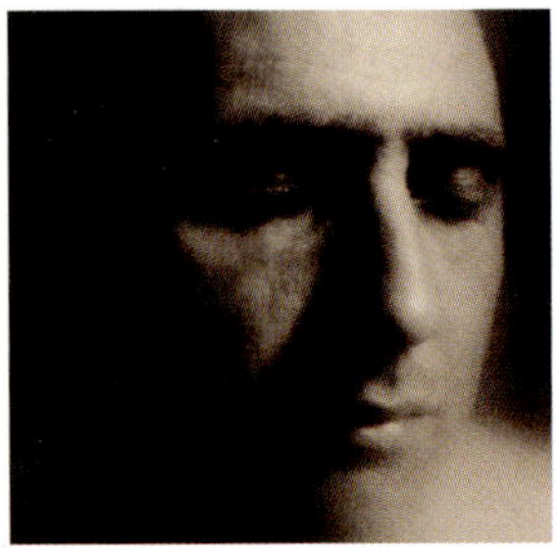

The striking, statuesque, multilayered images of English-born Marc Atkins reveal a past that is based not only in photography but in other art forms as well. With his postgraduate work in video, film, and performance at the Jan Van Eyck Akademie in the Netherlands, as well as his undergraduate degree in sculpture at England's Cheltenham School of Art and Technology, it's easy to understand why many of his photographs display a vast range of styles, influences, and appearances.

"I love working with materials—their textures, weights, the marks you can make on them, in them, with them," says the 41-year-old Atkins about his varying techniques. "I've always seen the photograph as an object—a piece of paper with chemically induced marks on it, the marks being the signifiers of scenarios. The photograph to me is one good way to present an object that conveys concrete and abstract concepts within a single medium.

"I also just love messing about in the darkroom, with chemicals, different papers, lights, lenses, and general mark-making things. I don't like being limited to one technique or process. If an image looks better one way than another, why compromise that for the sake of having a unified look across all of one's images?"

For Atkins, a love of photography came quite early—at the age of four to be exact—when he received his first camera as a gift from his grandparents. Shortly thereafter he discovered his brother's book on the world of art, which led him toward his interest in representations of the nude. "I would sit for hours looking through that book," says Atkins. "I guess as a young boy the nudes attracted me for obvious reasons, but I became fascinated by all the pictures. I would draw copies of them, trying to understand the way the shadows worked and the twists and turns of the figures. Some of them were impossible, like in William Blake or Botticelli. And those early impressions have stayed with me. So then, later, as a young man and as an art student, I had the opportunity to work at making my own images, in paintings, drawings, sculptures. I would do full-body, nude life casts of the models, as well as modeling them in clay—and, of course, [I did] photography."

Atkins prefers to use nonprofessional models and friends because they don't have a "realized image of themselves photographically, or preconceived notions of how they should look." He also seeks out women with a confident, strong, and assured manner and attitude because of the importance he places on revealing personality in his images. "I believe there is as much personality in a part of a person's body as there is in their face. If there is no evidence of the personality of the subject, then the figure is just a naked body," says Atkins. "I want to feel I know something about the subject, as well as something about the artist."

An Atkins image cannot be pigeonholed. He slips effortlessly between color and black-and-white, between classical and technological, and subjects washed in milky blues and muted reds. Some prints are constructed in layers, like peeled wallpaper revealing hidden surfaces. Others appear like characters from a Kafka short story: they are lost in thought and deep, shifting shadows, creating an enigma and a sense of the unknown. His mix of cameras is part of his chameleon-like character. "Cameras are tools for making shadows on light-sensitive materials, so I'll use anything that comes to hand," he says. "I have reconstituted throwaway cameras, two Nikon FM2s, a Pentax 6x7, an East German Pentacon 6x6, an M3 Leica, various Polaroids, a 1936 twin-lens Rolleiflex, and various 'snappy' cameras. For a shoot I tend to load them all. I never use an assistant, unless it is for a commercial shoot. It is useful, and enjoyable, handling different cameras anyway, it makes for subtle changes in the way one is viewing one's subject—certainly the way one is depicting them."

Atkins's photographs have appeared in several books, including his first publication, *The Teratologists* (Panoptika, 1998), and 2002's *Thirteen* (The Do Not Press). His work has also been exhibited around the UK, Poland, the Czech Republic, and his current home, France.

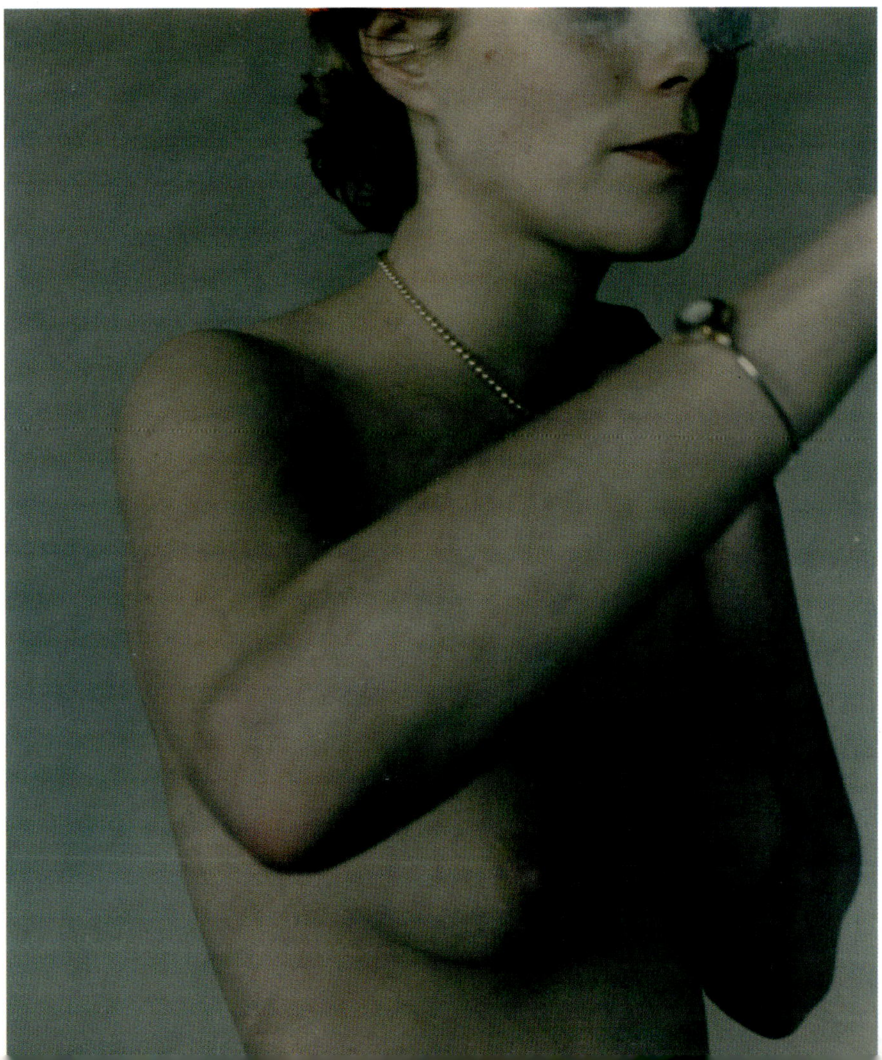

Del 358, 2004 *(right)*
"Del and I had a particular working method, in that she would not hold a pose. She walked and sat about, and we would talk, and I just kept photographing her. I was especially pleased with this image when I turned the light on in the darkroom (I work completely in the dark when producing color prints). I liked, and continue to like, the soft tones, the color, and the subtle textures of the print, as well as the mien of the figure."

Emma Video 577, 2003 *(right)*
"Sometimes I will make a few minutes of video of the models, then later take stills from it by photographing the monitor screen. I like the texture, color, and distortion the video and monitor give to the image. Here, Emma's shape and the light down the side of her body I find exquisite—she was just beginning a turn away from the camera while walking around. Another reason I take to using this process is that one can "still" the image at a crucial moment during action. It's like being able to pause time first before taking the photo."

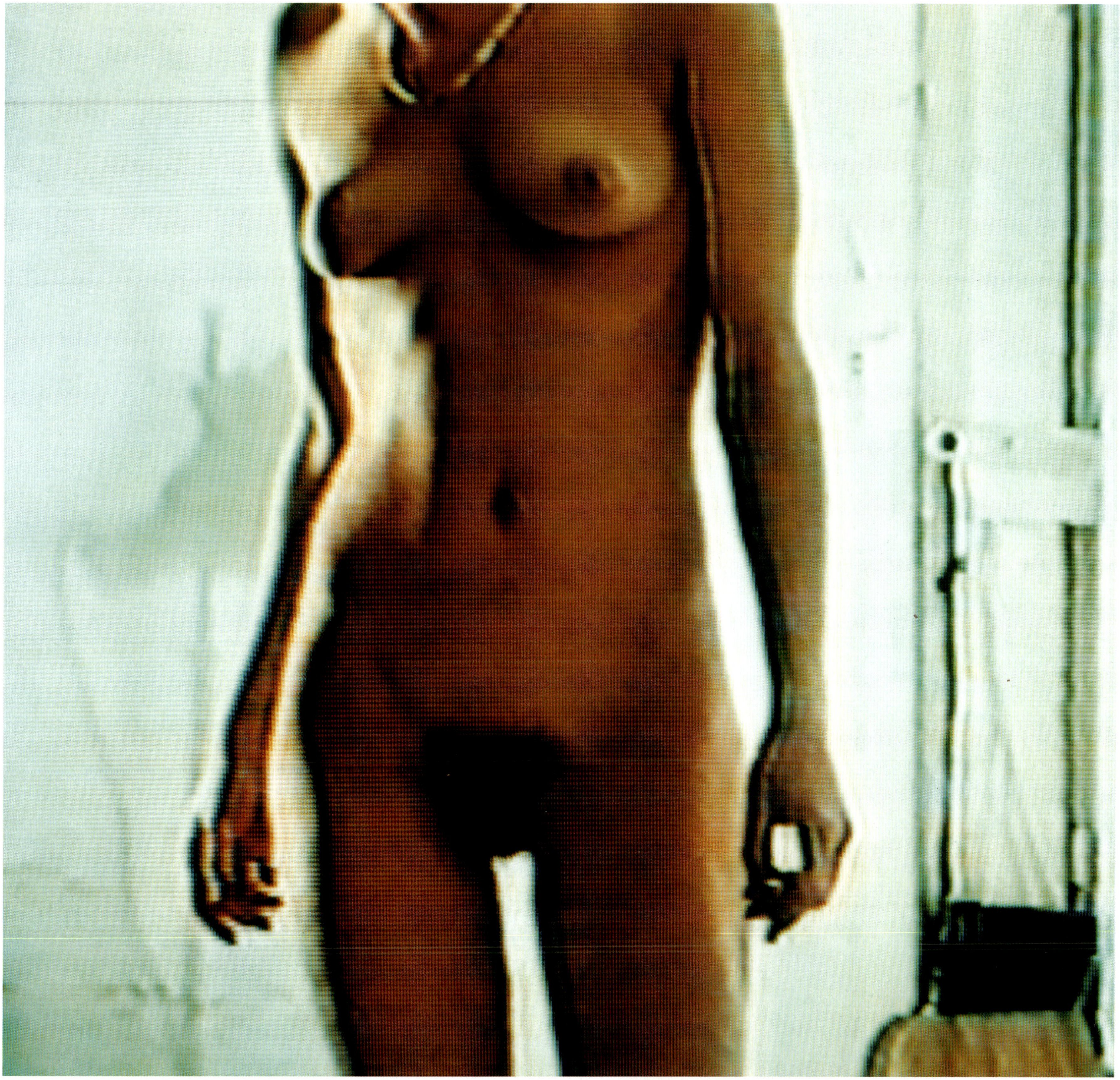

Marc Atkins

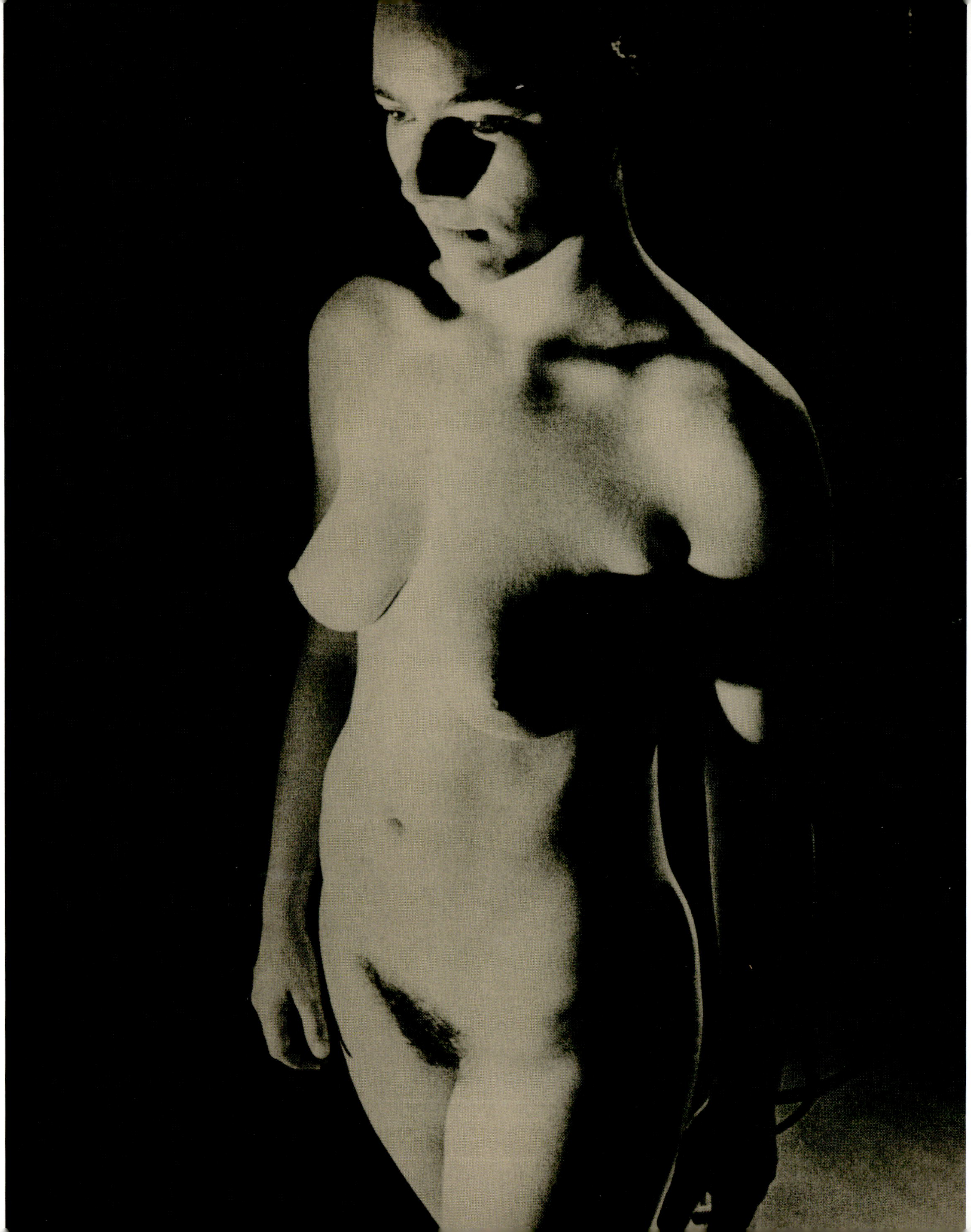

Sarah 62, 1992
"A beautifully statuesque woman, Sarah was an ex-dancer. It was wonderful photographing her. Slowly or vigorously she would move around the studio, then stop and hold a position, like a photograph, stilling a moment. I really enjoy this image, again because of the sculptural form, but also the chiaroscuro lighting [artistic distribution of darkness and light], which works well with the graininess of the lith process."

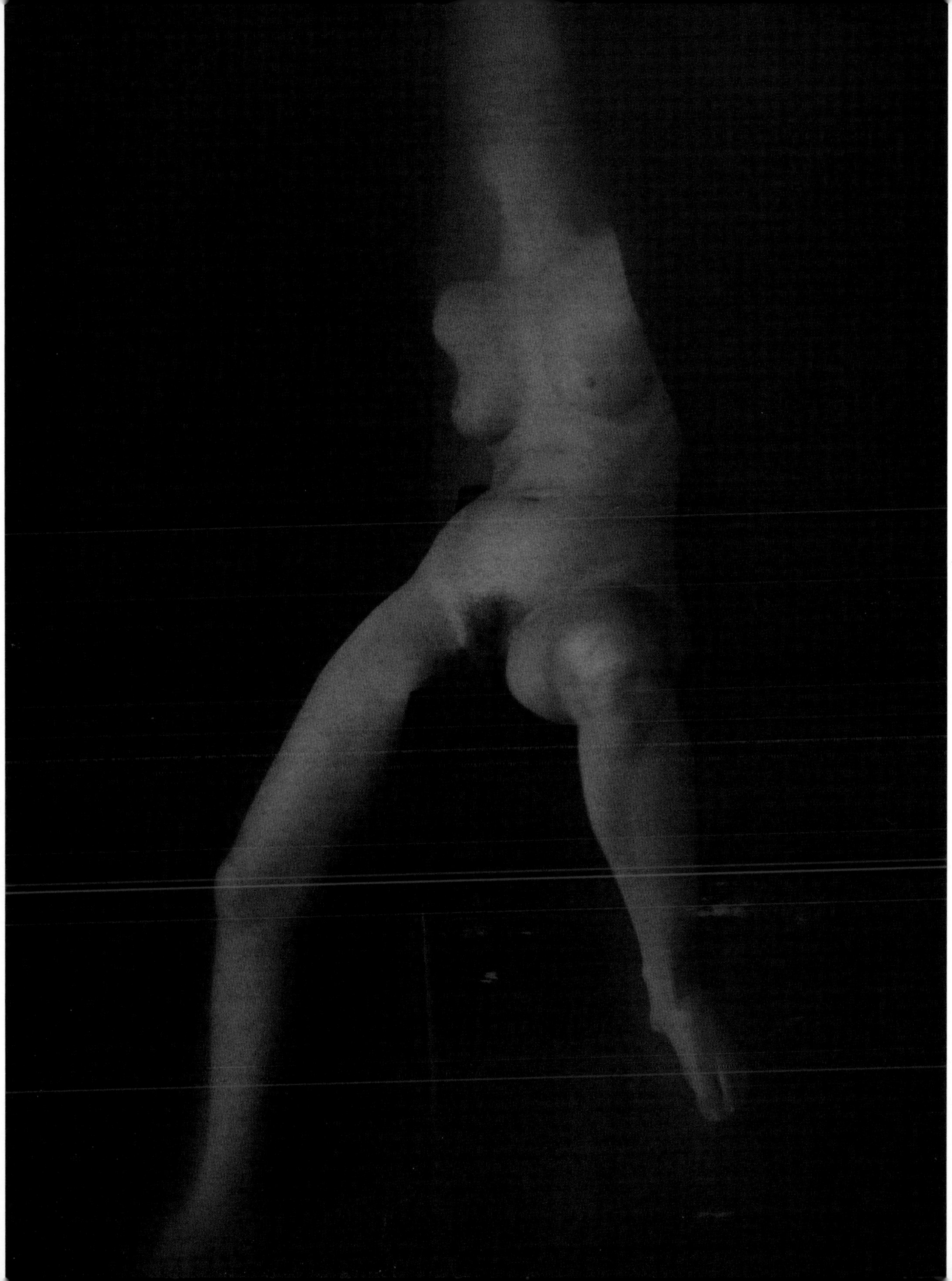

Tasha 342, 1993
"This image I took over ten years ago, but only printed it about three years ago. I have many, many images that still remain to be printed. Sometimes there just isn't the time to print up all the images one likes in the immediate period after taking the photos; sometimes one has to be in the right mood for certain images, or one has to find the process that fits the image. This image is a mixture of all three. I often find it is good to delay printing an image anyway, since one can see it more clearly in isolation, more objectively, independent of the circumstance in which the picture was taken—that is, without the near memory of the photo session encumbering one's judgment of the image."

Marc Baptiste

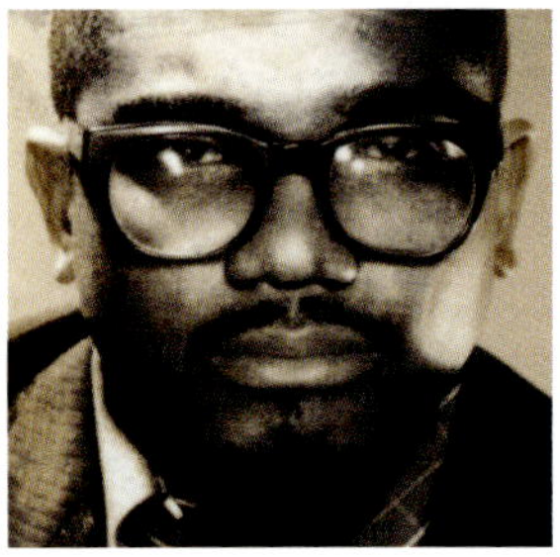

Perhaps the most difficult aspect of photographing a naked person is making them feel comfortable. Gaining the subject's confidence and trust is the most vital element in the photographer's ability to capture that person in a natural, genuine, and convincing way. Marc Baptiste not only knows how to do this, he is a master at it. He knows how to achieve something intimate—indeed, that is the title of his second book.

Baptiste, one of the most renowned fashion and portrait photographers in the world today (he has shot for *Vanity Fair*, *Allure*, *Vibe*, *Essence*, *Esquire*, *Rolling Stone*, *Cosmopolitan*, *Entertainment Weekly*, and German *Vogue*, among others) has published two of the most successful nudes books of the past five years—*Beautiful* (Universe Publishing, 2001), and *Intimate* (Universe Publishing, 2003).

Baptiste was born in 1963 in Haiti. After moving to the United States, he attended the New York Technical College and began documenting the environment around him. Inspired by Helmut Newton, Guy Bourdin, and Erwin Blumenfeld, Baptiste's initial venture into the realm of nude photography began in the same way that many photographers initiate themselves into that world. "I started by photographing my first girlfriend," he says. "Ever since, I have enjoyed shooting female nudes because the female form is so interesting. I love it."

Beautiful was a distinctive and intriguing book that focused exclusively on women from ethnic minorities, capturing both people who are used to appearing in front of the camera (actresses Rosario Dawson and Vanessa L. Williams, singer N'Dambi, and model Beverly Johnson), and women from the more "everyday" world.

"Creating these images of multi-ethnic women is social progress," says Bethann Hardison, a model, designer, writer, and fashion-show producer, as well as a member of the New York African Film Festival board of directors, in the book's introduction. "Society's standard of beauty is merely a media-driven idea. There is no interest on the media's part to explore beauty of other cultures. I have decided that the media's perspective is not prejudice or racist. It is purely ignorant. But this book is a wonderful step in the right direction."

What also makes the book distinctive is the quotes from many of its subjects. Each woman discusses how she feels about her body, how that view has changed over the years, and what their emotions are toward being exposed in front of Baptiste's lens. Actress Stacy Dash, for example, had this to say about her photo: "I found the idea of posing nude so terrifying that I knew I had to do it because the most beautiful women in the world—regardless of their physicality—are those who feel genuinely comfortable in their own skin." Non-model Isabel Celeste Dawson, who describes herself simply as a "mother," also appears in the book. Her quote—"I'm not ashamed of my body because I've earned every mark it bears"—is a perfect illustration of how *Beautiful* also highlights women with body types that do not fit society's view of an "attractive" figure.

"I try to keep my work more honest and more sexy as opposed to more shocking," says Baptiste. "A successful nude photograph relies on many things—sincerity, the right expression, the body language, and the composition. It is also important that my subjects are confident."

Baptiste's second book, *Intimate*, continued his journey into the confidential. Yet this time he expanded his subjects, inviting women of every race to pose for him. The images echo the warm, hush-hush style of *Beautiful*, but whereas the first book showcased a number of studio sessions, *Intimate* features Baptiste climbing inside the personal spaces of his subjects. Private bedrooms and clandestine rooms are filled with skin and looks of seduction. Couples are also prominent, with a number of sexual trysts being recorded on film.

Baptiste is currently putting in time on his third book, *Innocent*, which is due to be published at the end of 2005.

"Marc Baptiste takes some of the most fashionable pictures around—often without a scrap of fashion in them. And he gets away with it!" says nerve.com photography editor Whitney Lawson. "In this way, he is a kind of heir to Helmut Newton. Like Helmut, he is ultra un-PC in his approach to the female nude, and his pictures are brimming with old-school sexuality—talk about a male gaze. But unlike Newton, Baptiste is more of an observer than a director. He uses what he has learned from fashion and brings it to his own personal theme of intimacy, aloneness. The pictures are quietly stunning, and they absolutely ooze style. They prove a classic Newtonian law: that nudity is the most avant-garde outfit of all."

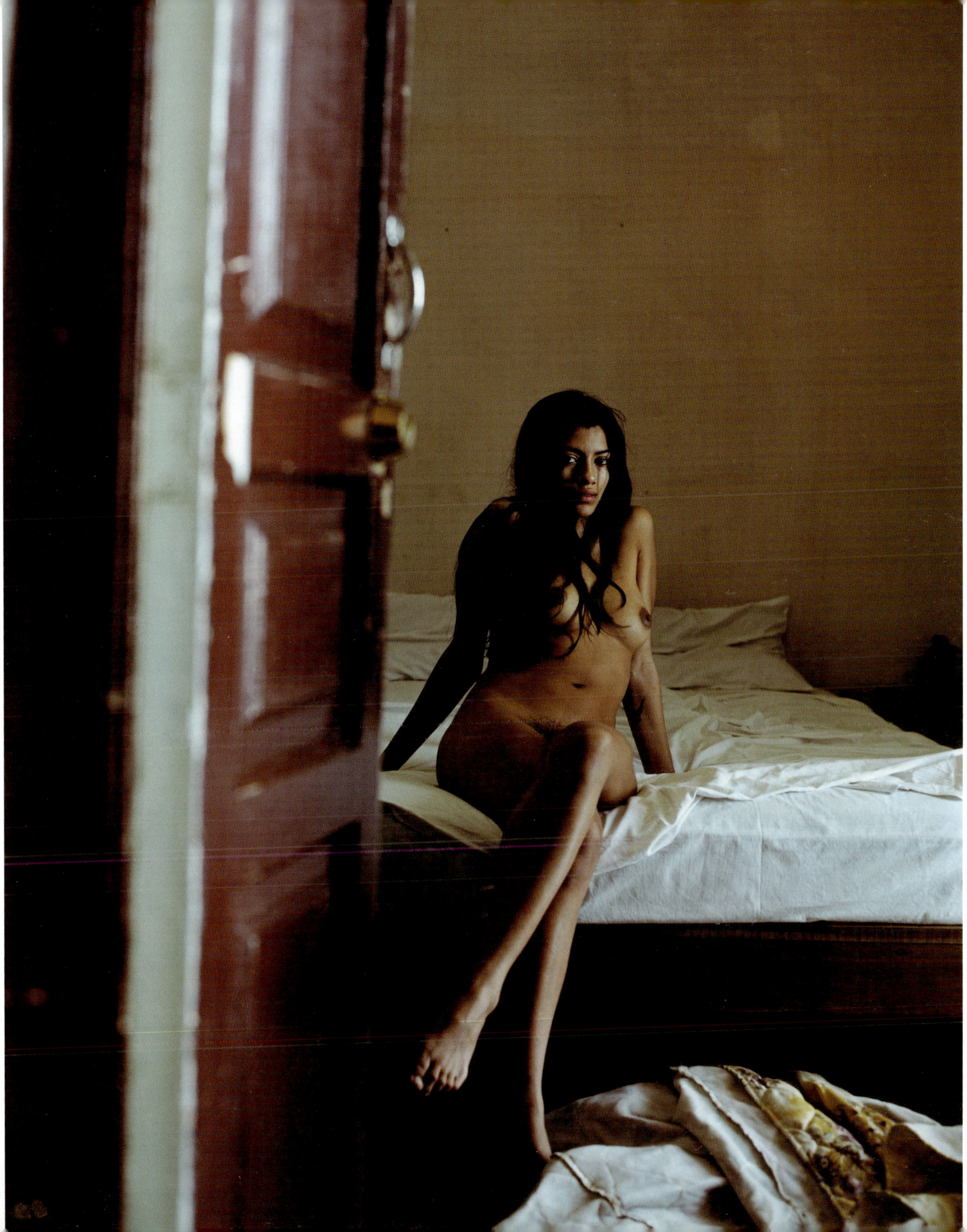

Vanessa, 2005
"I like to let my subjects be themselves, and I'm always honest with them—that is how I get them to trust me. I'm not aggressive at all. Plus, they know I'm married and madly in love with my wife."

N'Dambi Smoking, 2001 *(right)*

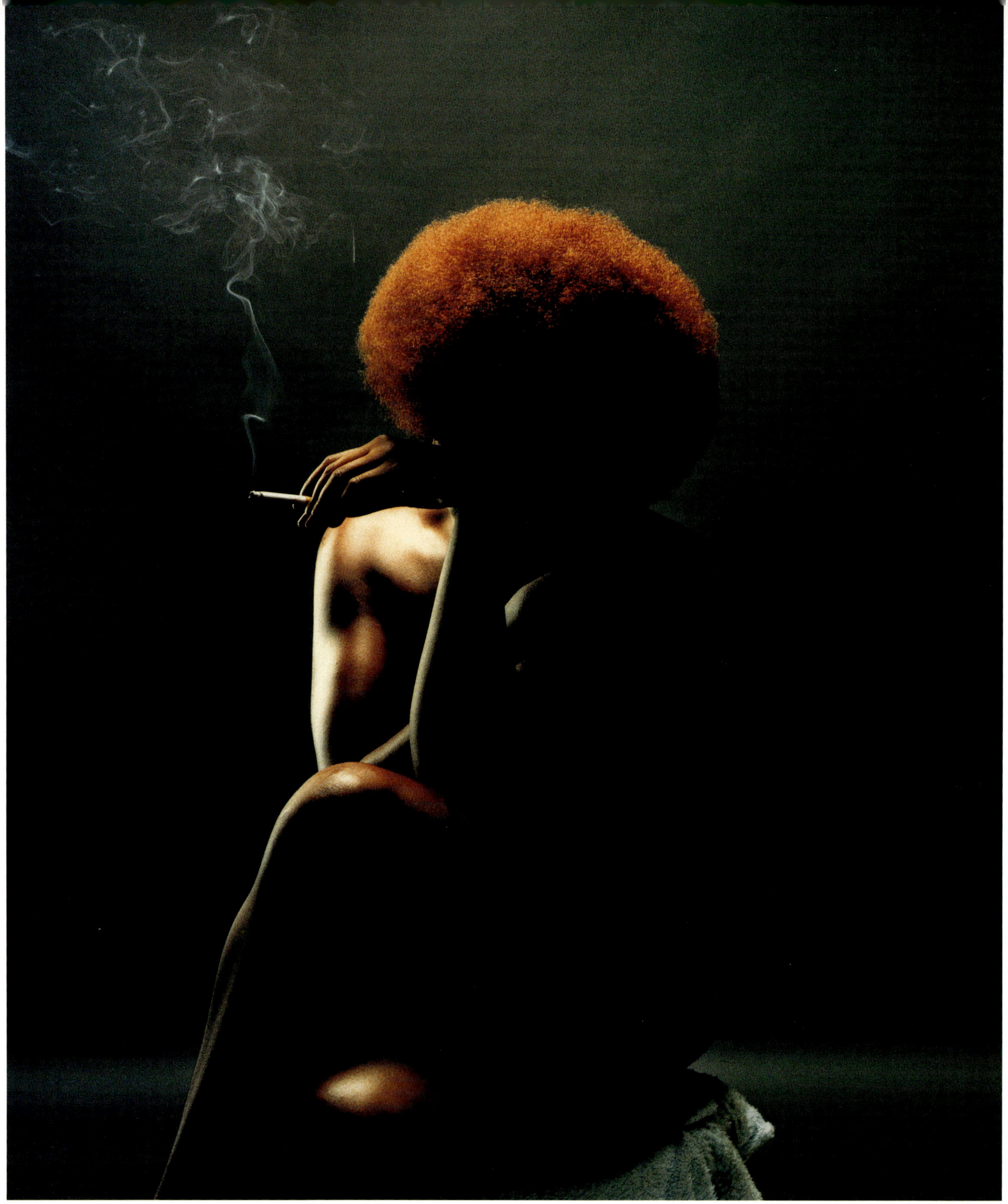

Melida, 2003 *(opposite)*
"Every day we grow and learn—it's an evolution. I'm using more natural light with the nudes because it complements the curves of the body, which is how I started. It's like coming full circle."

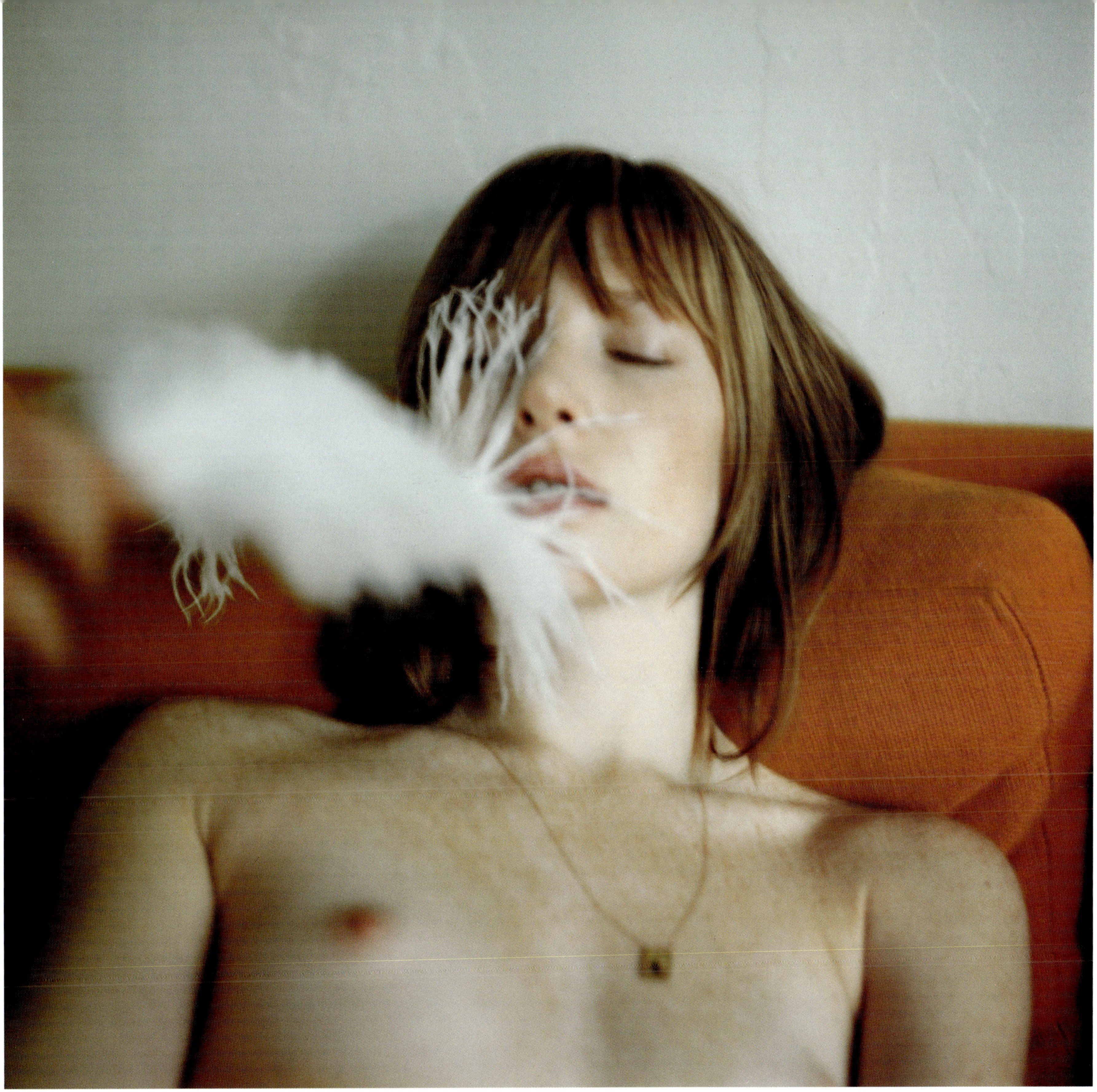

Marc Baptiste

Andreas H. Bitesnich

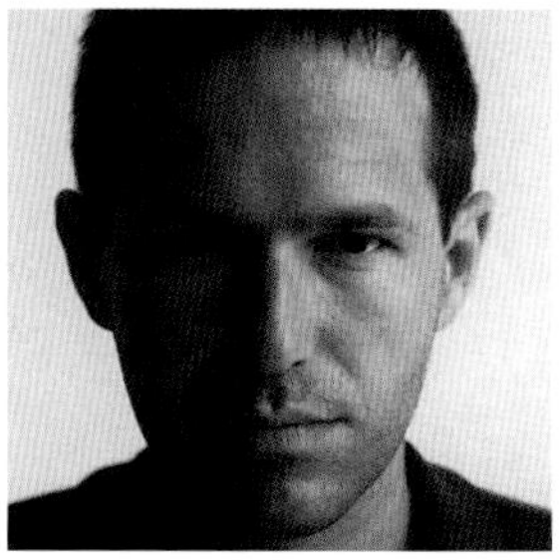

"I always think a picture that creates a reaction is a good picture, whether the reaction is positive or negative," says Austrian photographer Andreas H. Bitesnich.

Fortunately for him, reactions to his photographs have been overwhelmingly positive. Whether created for art or advertisements, for editorial assignments or calendars, a Bitesnich nude stands at the intersection of anatomy and geometry—sleek, beautiful bodies in carefully choreographed poses that at their tightest resemble elegant human knots, and at their loosest a search for a Platonic ideal.

Born in Vienna in 1964, Andreas Bitesnich spent a decade as a home-electronics salesman before discovering his latent passion and talent for photography. "I discovered photography very late. I was 25," he says. "I fell in love with the camera overnight and just went for it."

The life-changing experience that opened his eyes to the camera's potential was a simple matter of looking at the photographs of a friend who was working as a photographer's assistant. "I asked him to show me his work and I was just so overwhelmed. I thought, 'If he can do it, I can do it.'"

Initially, Bitesnich thought he wanted to become a fashion photographer—Irving Penn topped his list of favorite photographers—but he soon realized that Austria has little in the way of a fashion industry to shoot. It was three years later, in the mid-1990s, that he photographed his first nude and found that he had both a flair and a feel for the human form.

"I started doing graphic, formal, sculptural nudes," he recalls. "I spent two, three, four years getting that look together. Now the positions are more loose." By "graphic," Bitesnich does not mean "explicit"; rather, he means something closer to "diagrammatic." The nudes that brought him international acclaim were startling and stylized images of couples so elaborately entwined that they almost became living glyphs, Gordian knots of flesh to be studied and solved. As symbolic as those early compositions appear, Bitesnich insists they have no meaning for him beyond their curves and surfaces. He works intuitively, without a preconceived notion of what a photograph should mean, or be.

That said, the cover photograph of his first book, *Nudes* (teNeues, 1998), is one of the few exceptions, being an image that came to him in a dream—a male-female, yin-yang circle that resembles a human pinwheel. Most of the poses in his work, however, are worked out in front of the lens. "I don't think about the reaction a picture will have," he explains. "I only think about shape and form—and the moment they come together I take the picture. There is no formula. Most of the time the models come to me and ask me to take their pictures. Fortunately, my commercial clients want exactly what I'm doing anyway. Only I know what I can do with a particular model."

Given the thousands of photographers who have taken millions of nude photographs over the years, Bitesnich believes viewers still find the unclothed human body endlessly fascinating and new. "I think we are all curious in general, so we love to look," he says. "It's still something taboo—in the States more [than elsewhere]. It's a combination of the curiosity of the viewer and the human body being captured within the frame."

By 1995, Bitesnich had enough images to begin thinking about a book, but he spent another three years preparing *Nudes*, which went on to win the 1998 Kodak Photography Book Award. "Nudes opened a lot of doors for me. That book is still working for me," Bitesnich says. "I recently asked a creative director if he had seen my books and he said, 'Your books are in every good advertising agency library.' That made me feel proud."

Woman (teNeues, 2001) consists mainly of previously unpublished female nudes taken while shooting assignments for magazines such as German *Playboy* and Italian *Max*. "For me, the main thing is that the women in the book were aware of what they were doing," says Bitesnich. "They use the photographs for themselves, and they use the viewer. They present themselves in the way they want to be seen, and that makes them untouchable and strong."

Most of Bitesnich's nudes use the models' names as titles, suggesting the personal nature of the relationship between artist and model. "Every human being is different. I respect my models a lot," says Bitesnich. "They feel this, and that is why they are comfortable."

Nudes and *Woman* were both shot in black and white, but in his most recent book, *On Form* (teNeues, 2003), Bitesnich presents the color photography that has occupied him exclusively for the past four years. Color has a way of softening and warming bodies that black and white renders stark and cool and, as though in response to this gentling of the medium, Bitesnich's most recent work is less taut and tense than his early nudes. "At first I used really sculptural poses and only one light," he explains. "Now the lighting is more sophisticated, and the positions are more loose, more casual."

Bitesnich did all his own printing for *Nudes*, but he scanned half his negatives for *Woman* and scanned almost everything for *On Form*. While he has tried to stay up to date with new digital technologies, like many master photographers, he is less interested in technique than he is in results.

"I use 35mm 4x6 and 6x7 cameras, but I don't think that way. In the new book I even used a tourist camera. It's not the camera; it's what you make of it."

In 2004, 40,000 viewers got a chance to see first-hand what Bitesnich makes of the human body in a major exhibition at the Kunsthaus, Vienna. But by the time the masses saw the show, Bitesnich had moved on. "I'm always inspired," he says. "I don't even put my own pictures on the wall. I only want to move forward."

Yvonne & Tom, Vienna 1994, No. 66 *(opposite)*
All Bitesnich is after in his nudes, he says, is a sense of visual equilibrium. "The main thing in a picture is a certain balance within the frame," he says. "I look through the viewfinder and the lens for a moment of a certain proportion. As soon as I feel it, I press the button."

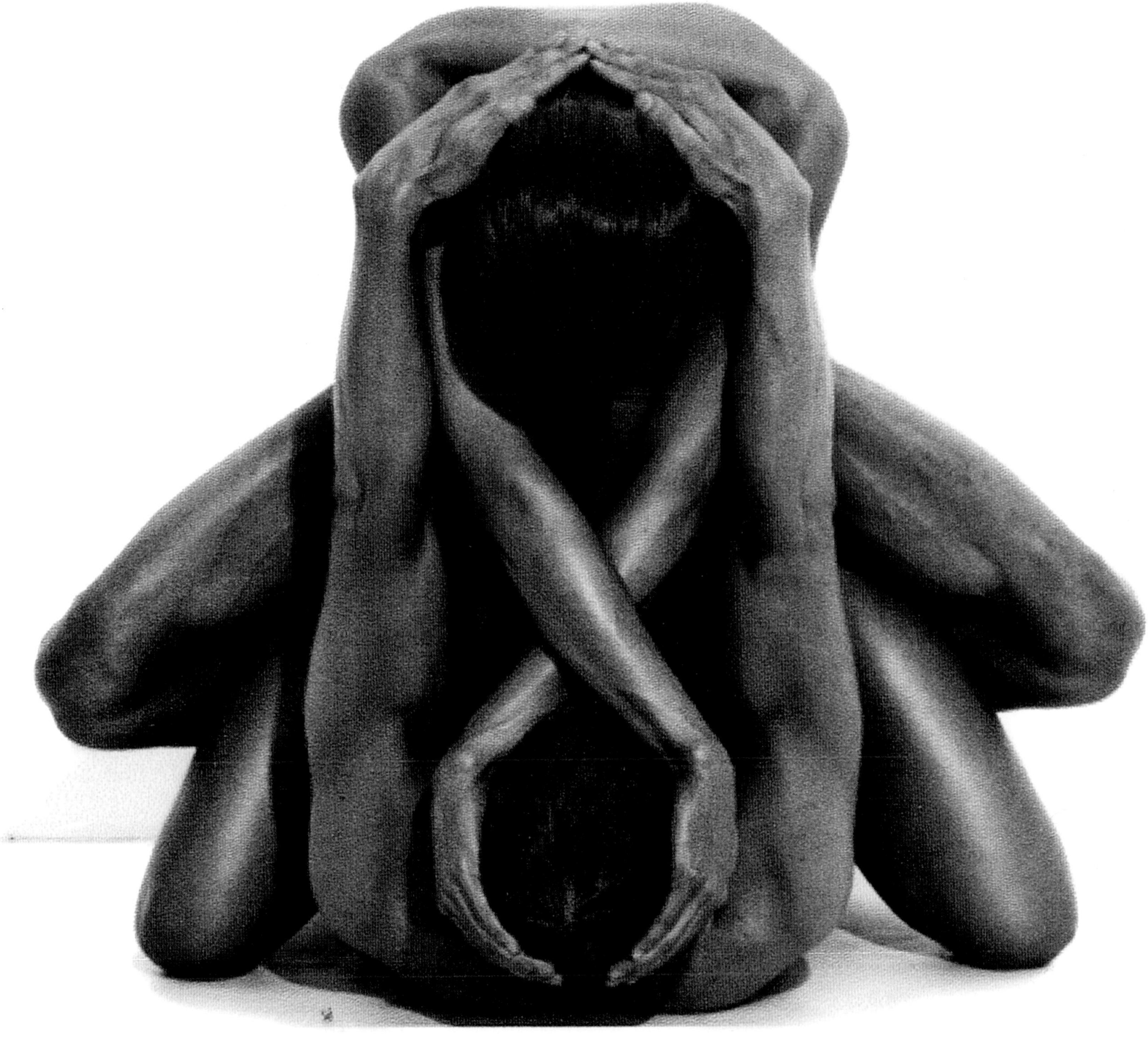

Andreas H. Bitesnich

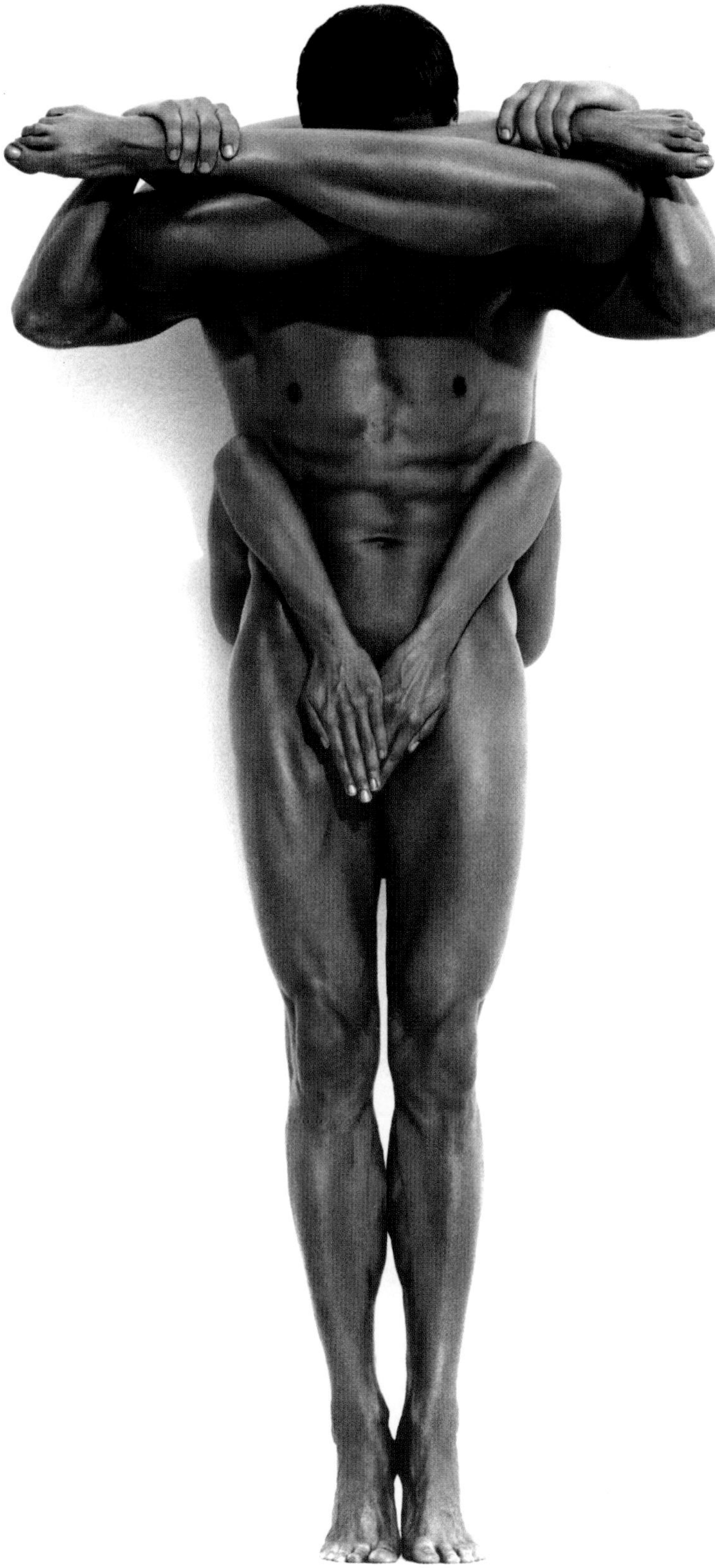

Yvonne & Tom, Vienna 1994,
No. 67

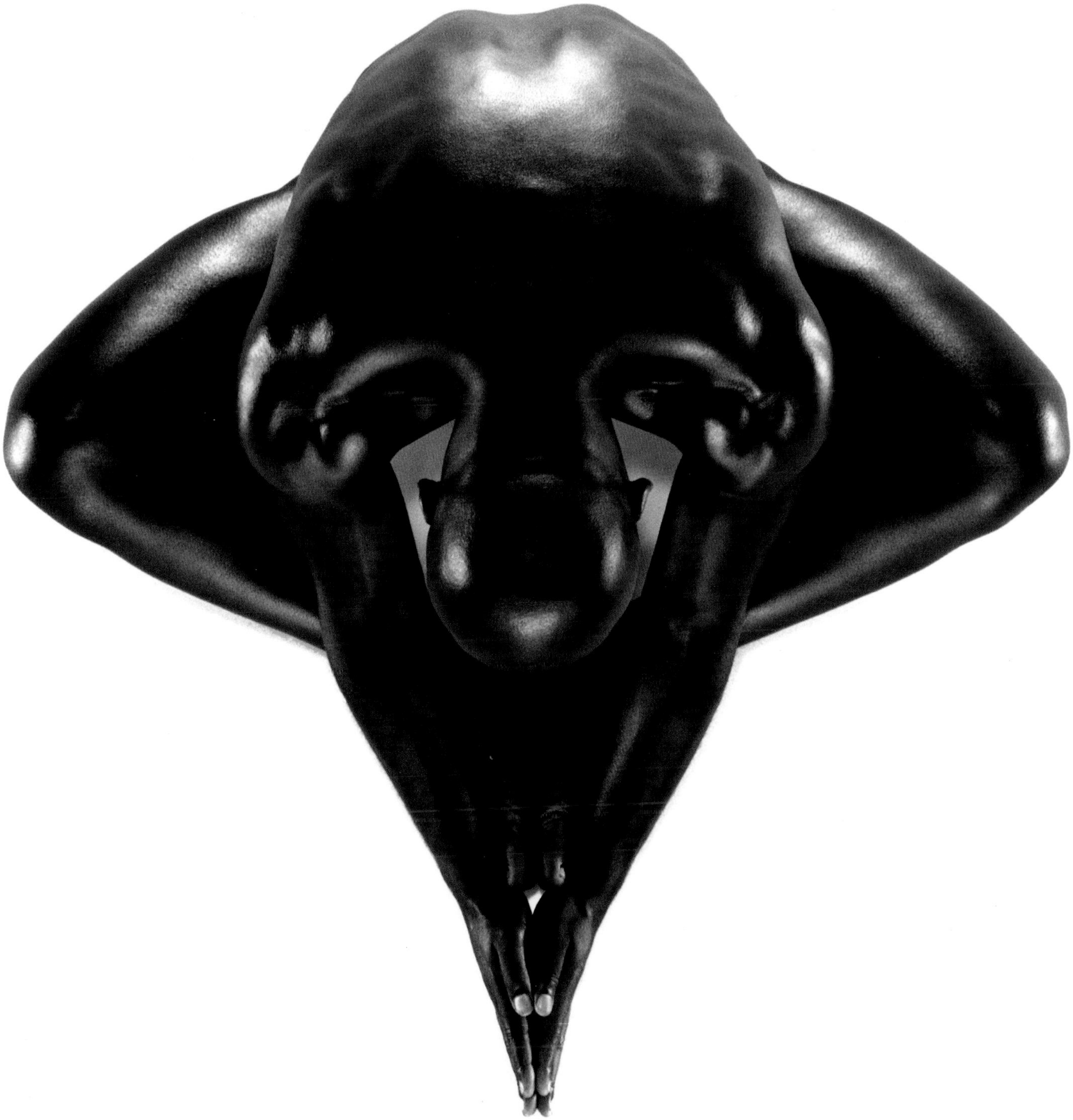

Roy, Vienna 1995, No. 1

Ingrid, Milan 2001, No. 2
(right)
"The human form is there, but balance and weight in the photograph is what I'm looking for. For me, it's about balance and proportion."

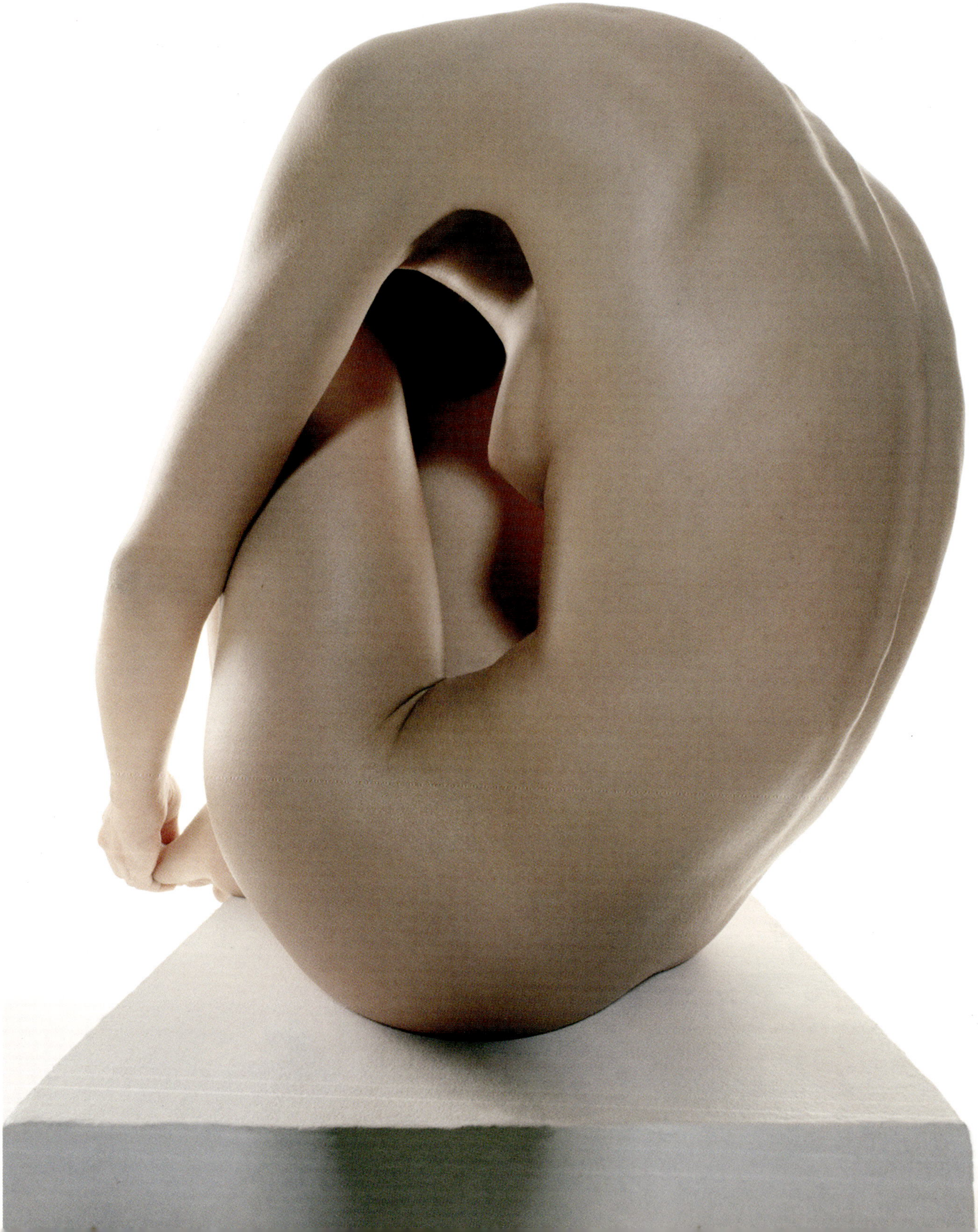

Jennipher, Vienna 2003
(opposite)

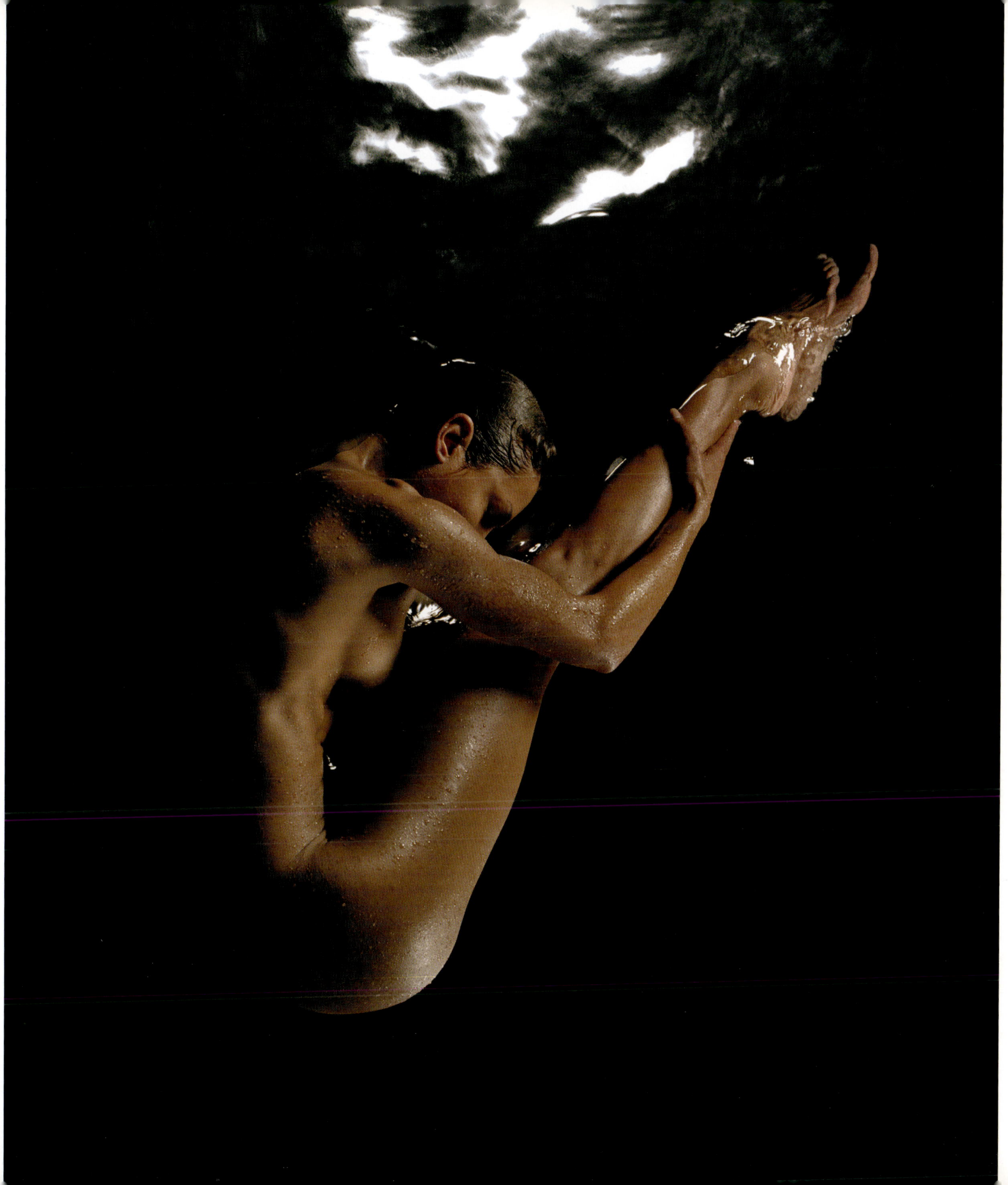

Sylvie Blum

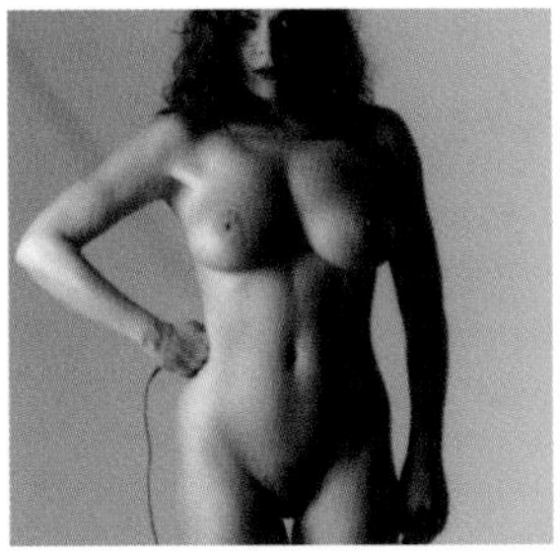

Sylvie Blum knows both sides of the camera. Having modeled for some of the greatest photographers of the past few decades, including Lucien Clergue, Jan Saudek, and Helmut Newton, Blum has experienced all parts of the process of creating a superior image. Being married to one of the world's best-known photographers of the nude, the late Günter Blum, has been another advantage.

Today, Blum is more often behind the camera than in front of it. She currently has her own studio in Mannheim, Germany, and has produced a prolific amount of erotic imagery in a very short space of time. In the past five years alone she has published four books with Edition Braus: *Venus Selbst* (2000); *Hotel Orient* (2002); *Nudes* (2002); and *M* (2004).

"There is nothing else like photography—it is my obsession," says Blum, who uses both film and digital cameras, including a Hasselblad 500cm and a Nikon D1X. "I like to tell a story from my mind. To stop one moment for longer than just a second. You can walk through pictures for many years, but only if the picture is good enough."

Born in 1967 in Austria, Blum moved to Germany in 1974 and started modeling at the age of 16. In 1986 she met Günter Blum and became his favorite model. Soon after, she became his wife. When Blum died in 1997, Sylvie stopped posing and started shooting—taking up the torch from her late husband.

Her images have a style that recalls the late Newton: they are daring, erotic, and adventurous. Many of her models, whether they are women or men, are tall and powerful, boldly exhibiting their bodies for the camera. They stare at the viewer with a self-assured intensity that allures, while at the same time challenging us to turn away.

"I've been hunting for beautiful minds in perfect bodies," says Blum, who was inspired by the German portrait photographer Hugo Erfurth. "The nude person is the purest and most interesting subject to shoot. Skin reflects the light in so many different facets, and, for sure, the nude is the most classical subject for creating a picture without any expiration date. The human body is the most exciting thing."

Her 2002 black-and-white book, *Nudes*, featured images she shot around the various landscapes and environments of Hollywood, Miami, Berlin, and the island of Majorca, off the coast of Spain.

Hotel Orient focused on an infamous hotel in Vienna that rents its rooms by the hour, catering to men and women looking for a place to hold discreet sexual trysts. Even the last Austrian

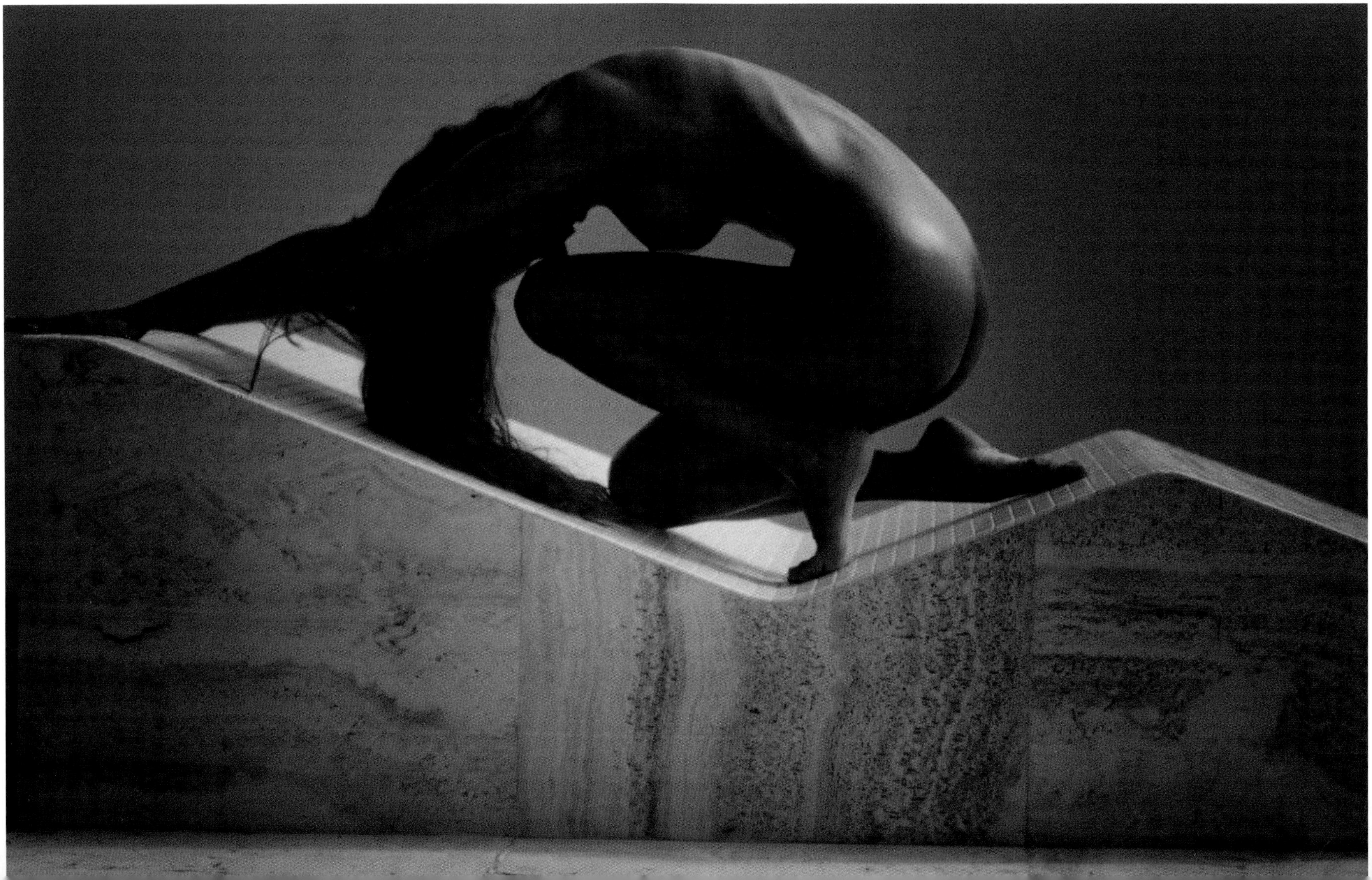

emperor was rumored to have been a guest at the establishment. Blum's images, a mix of washed-out colors and classic black and whites, illustrate the history of the hotel through imagined characters and constructed encounters. Models roam in and out of abundantly decorated rooms, while couples inhabit every public and private space of the building, including unmade beds, Victorian-style couches, old wooden staircases, and open window ledges. "It is exciting to shoot pictures as a female photographer in an establishment like that," says Blum. "To touch a world made for men."

Her latest book, *M*, is her first venture into publishing an all-male book. "I have really enjoyed showing the male nude body with a woman's eyes and a female view of the erotic male," she says. "There is a big difference between men and women. You expect different expressions, and you have to find out what triggers the best expression at the moment of the shot. Every person is different, and every shoot is new and exciting. If the atmosphere is easy and everything fits together, then you have a successful photograph."

The Palm, 2001
"A beautiful location always inspires me. This picture was taken on the island of Majorca. To get a perfect harmony between nature and the human body, I set my focus on my view of my environment. My work is mostly about watching my surroundings and being sensitive to every little thing that comes through me. The connection between nature and humans is one of the initial forms of human existence."

Rock I, 2001 *(left)*

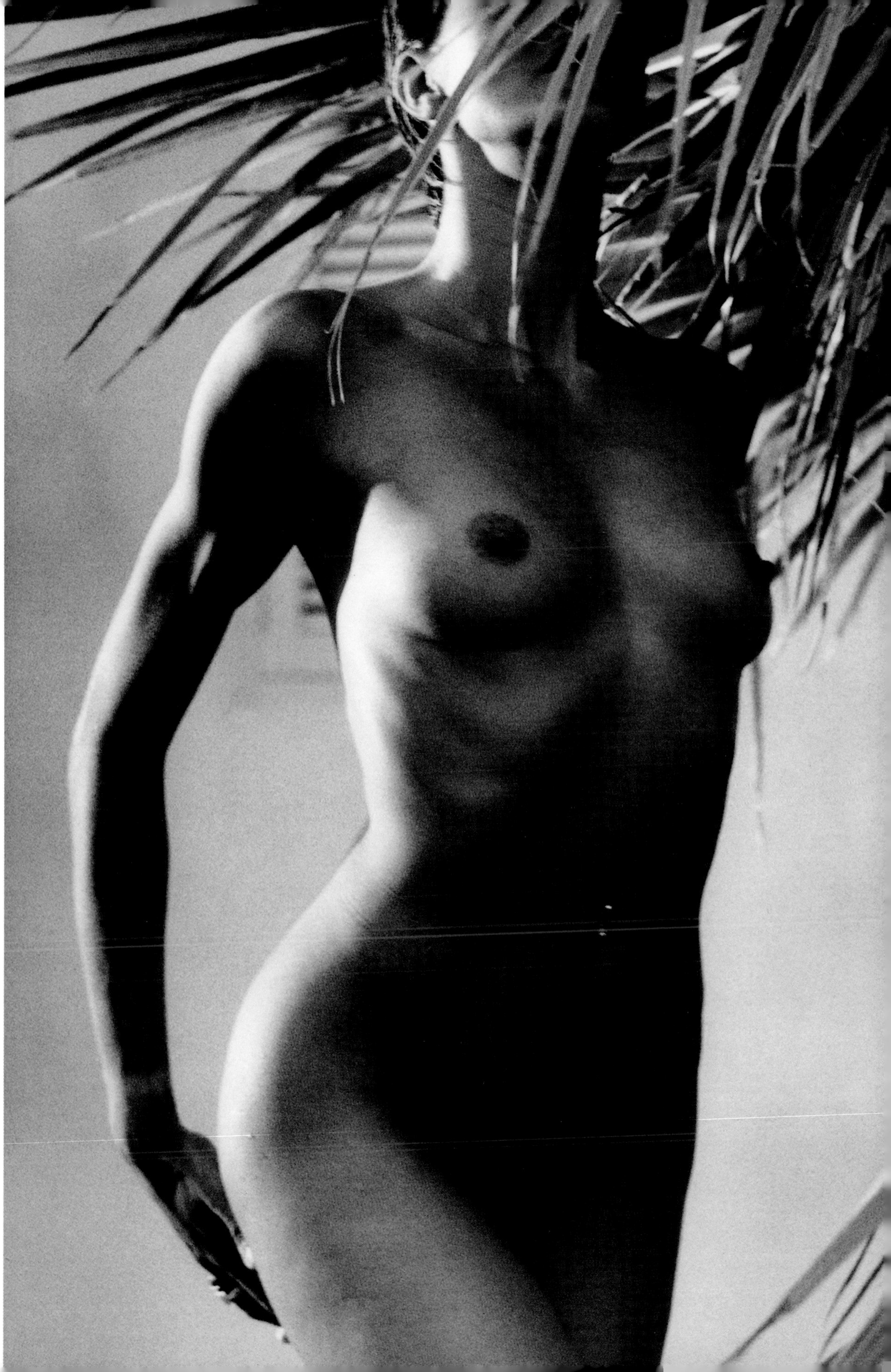

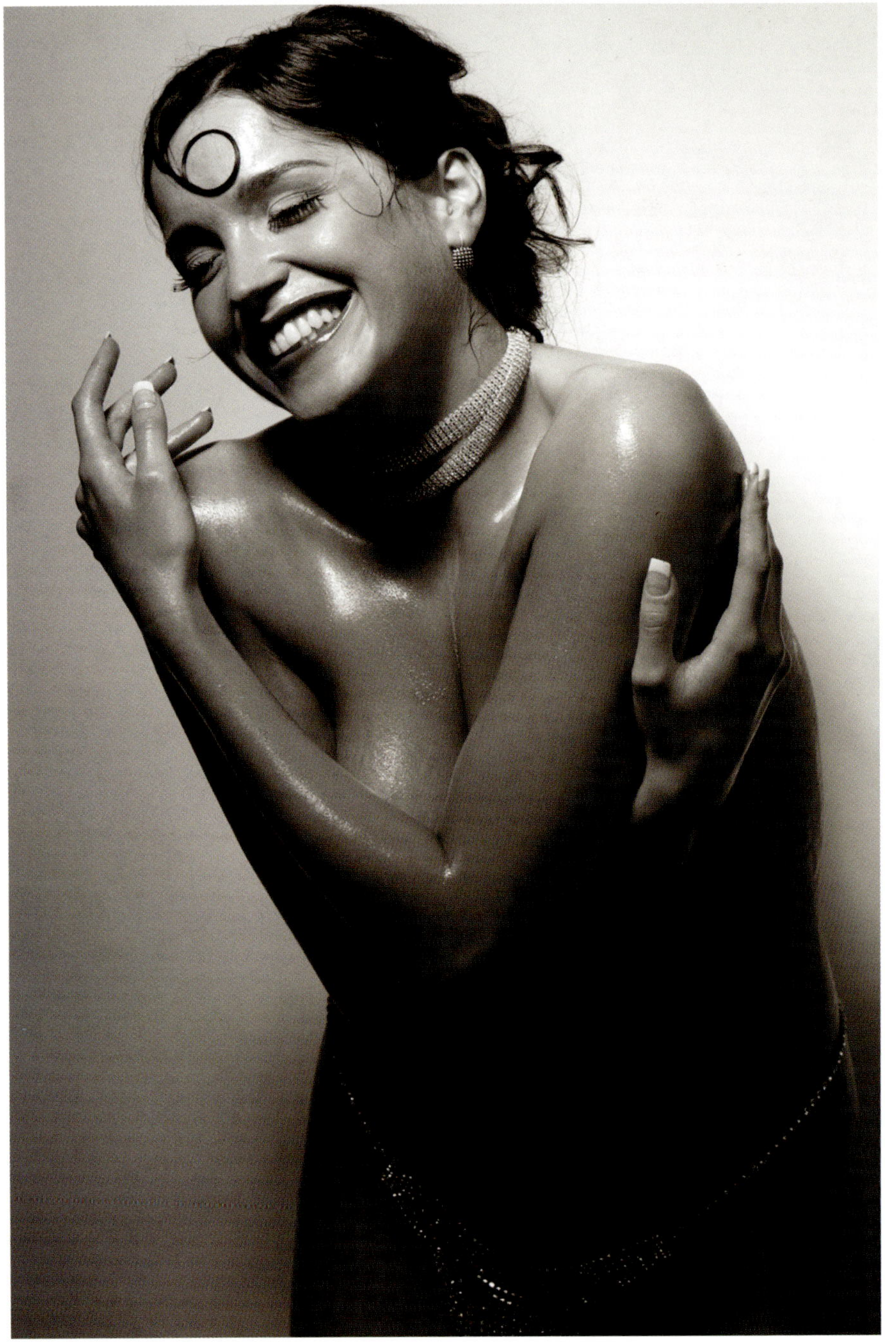

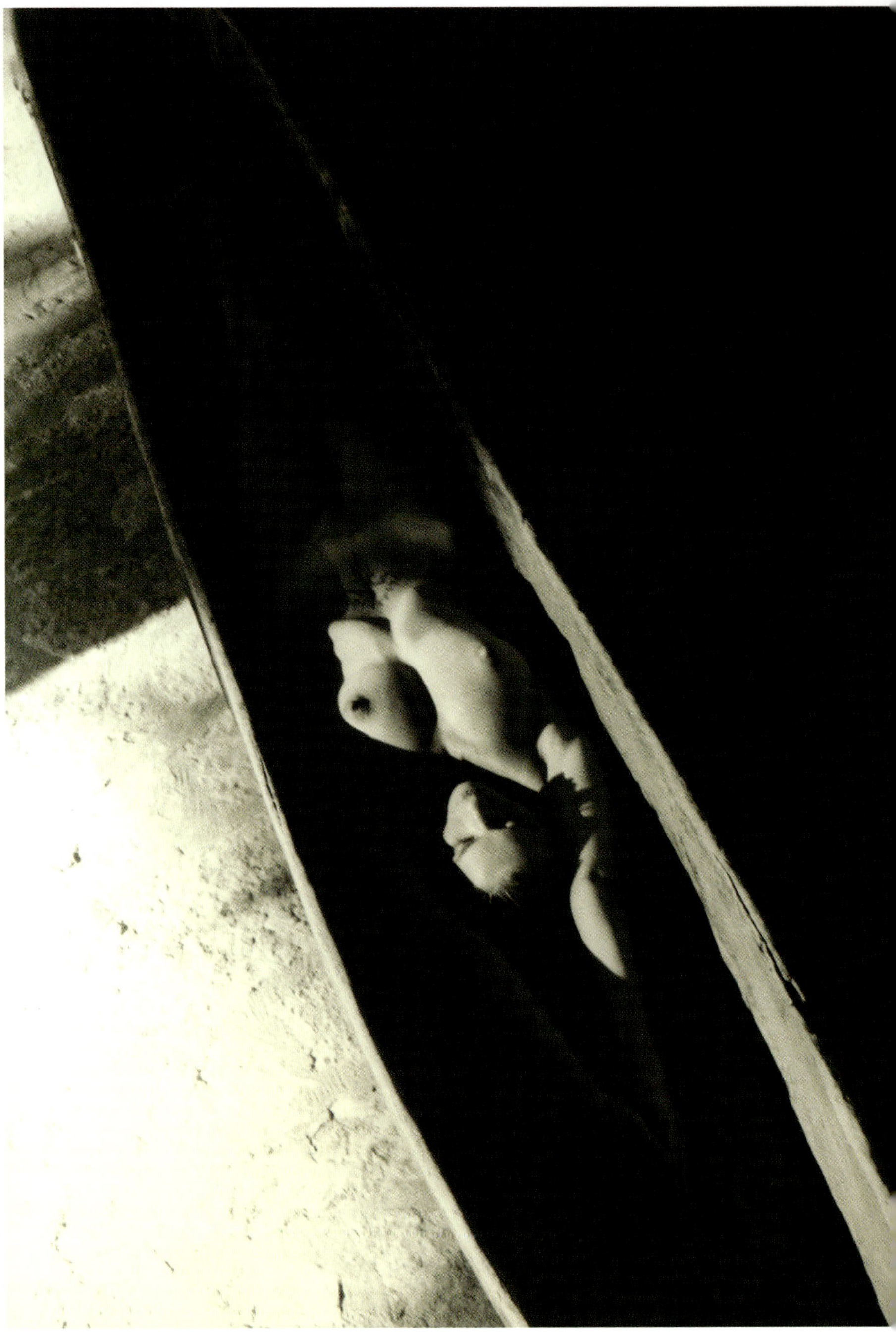

Studio, 2004
"My focus lies on the self-confidence and timeless elegance combined with the modern style of today's women. I wanted to let them be pinup girls for a moment, and I was impressed that they picked up that feeling very quickly. The aura of my models always stays at the center of my attention, and I try to display their personalities through my pictures."

Styx, 2001
"I took these pictures of a model named Natalie in Spain. She used to be one of my favorite muses. During the sessions we always developed a tight atmosphere between us.

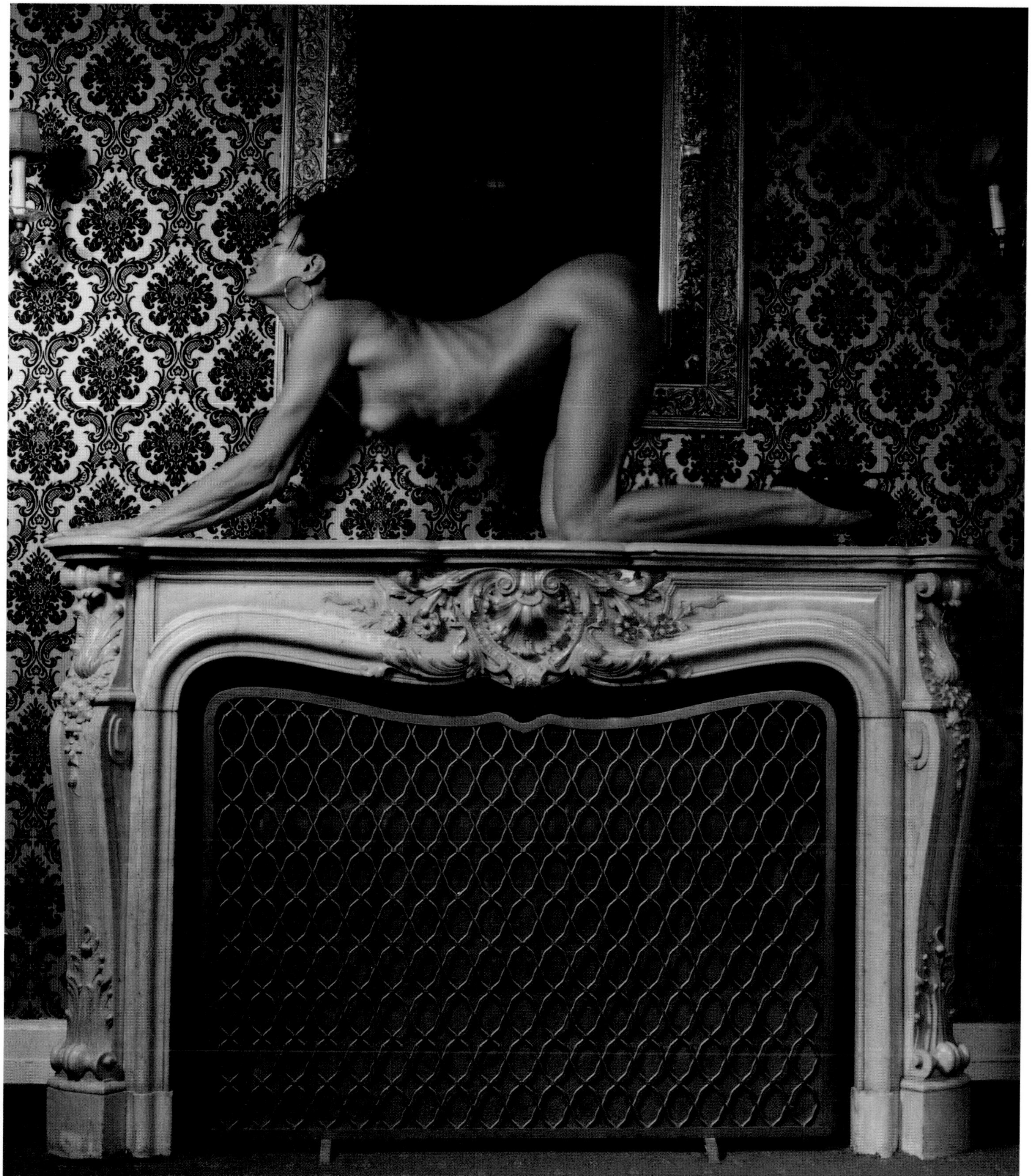

Kaisersuite, Hotel Orient,
Vienna, 2001

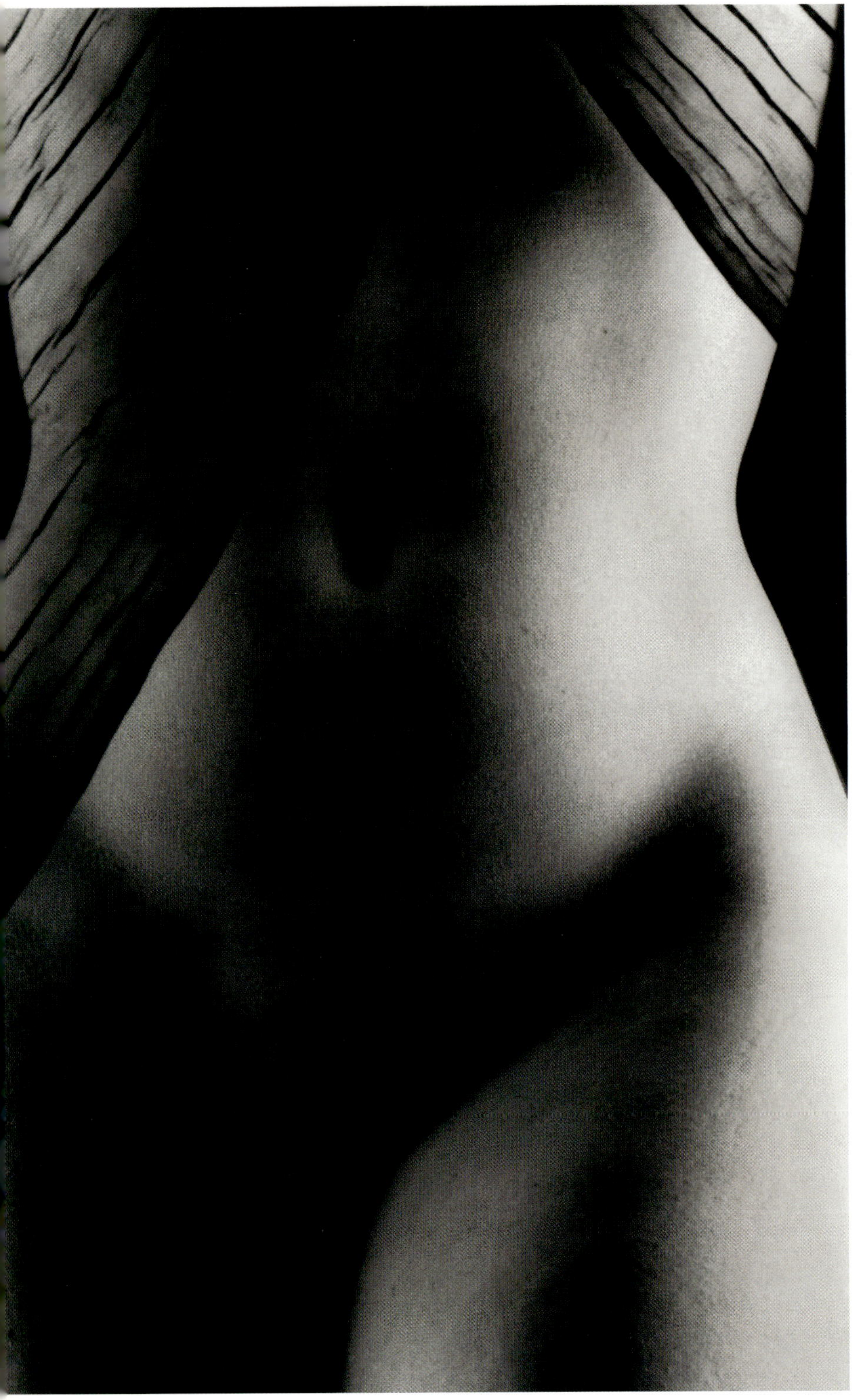

Torso, 1998

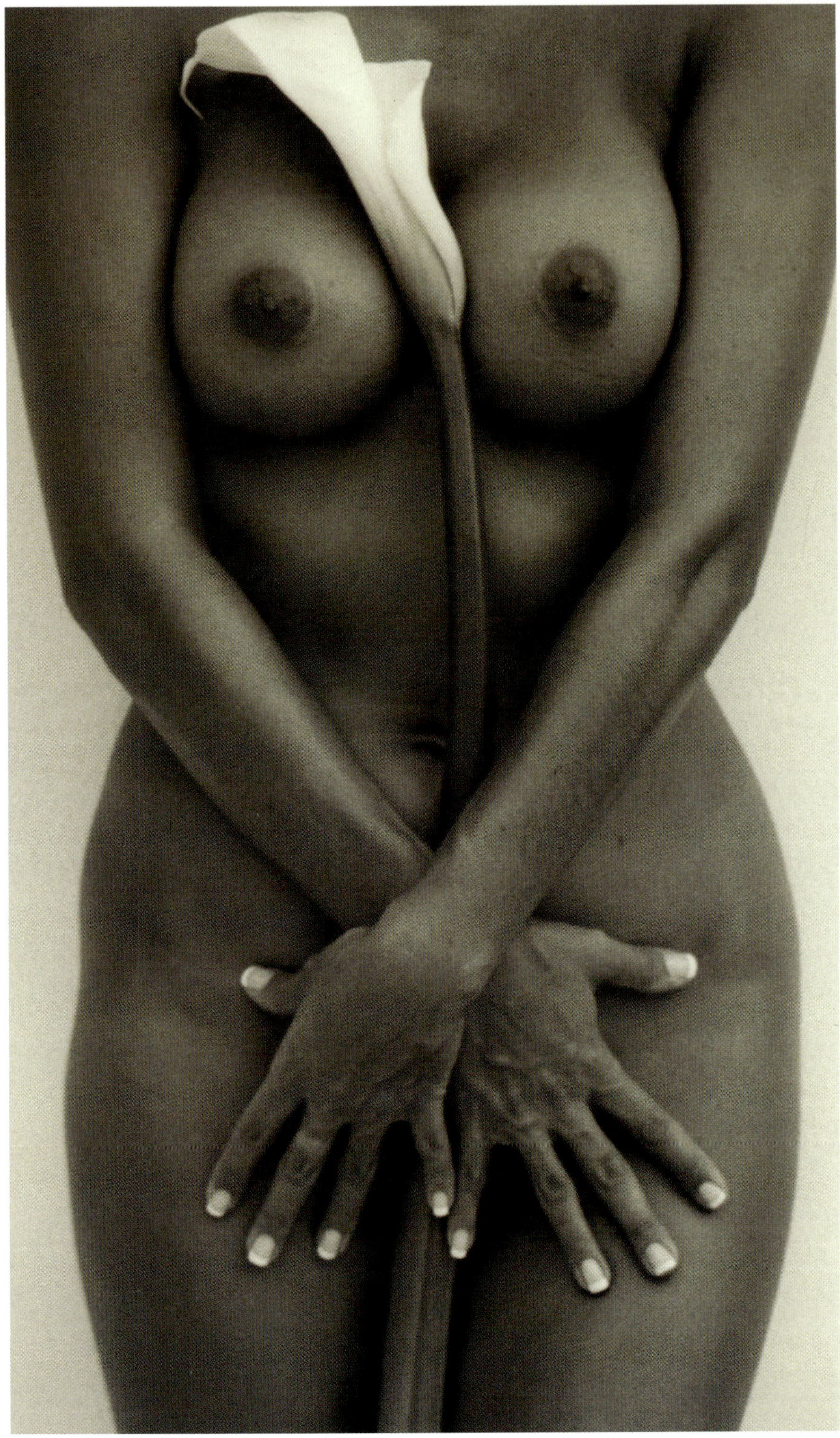

Callas, 2001

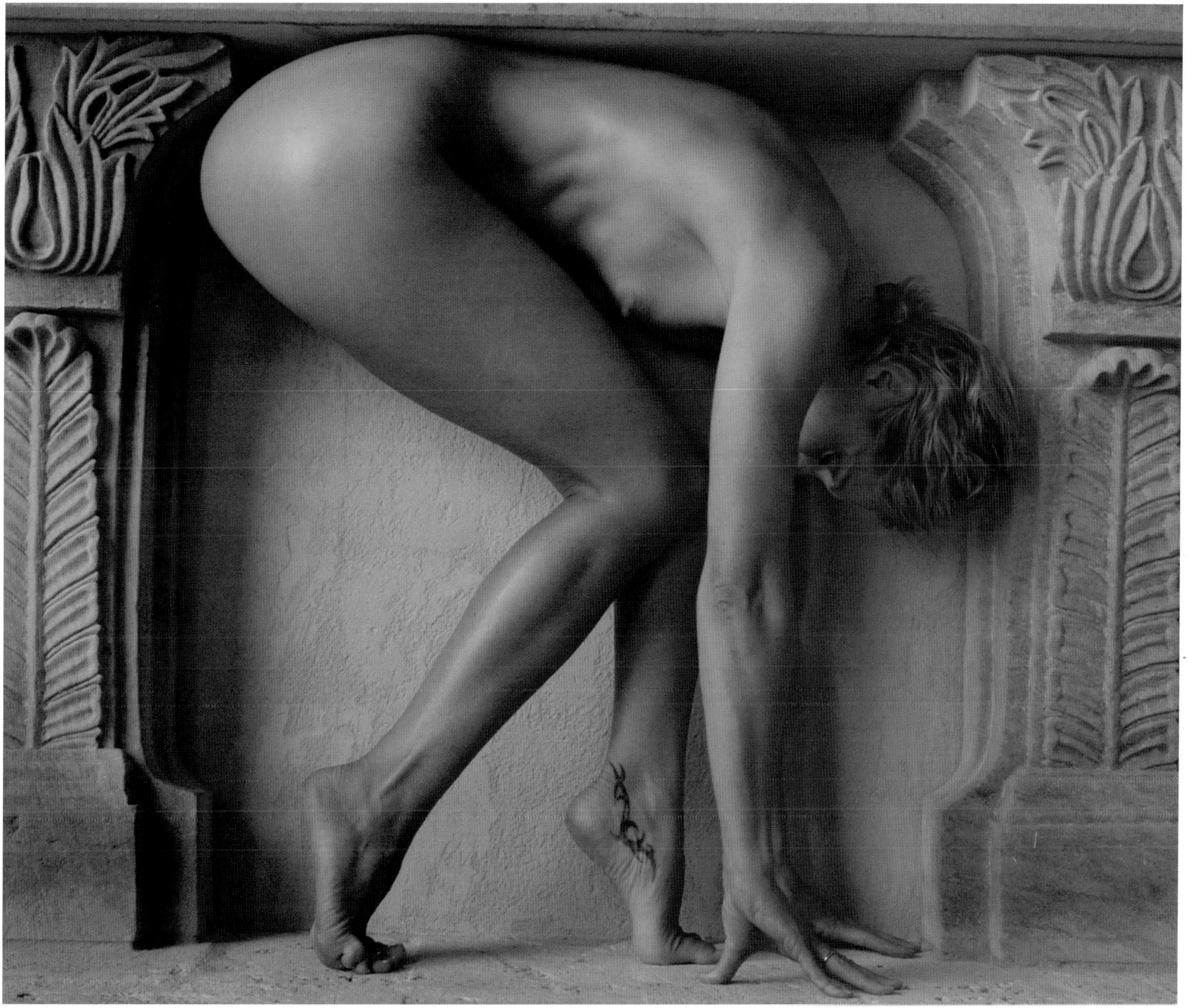

Natalie, 2004
"She has the talent to create a very relaxed situation on the set, and it is an outstanding feeling to work with her. In the long time we worked with each other, I got to know every inch of her body and have a sense for every single move that she had."

Barbara Bordnick

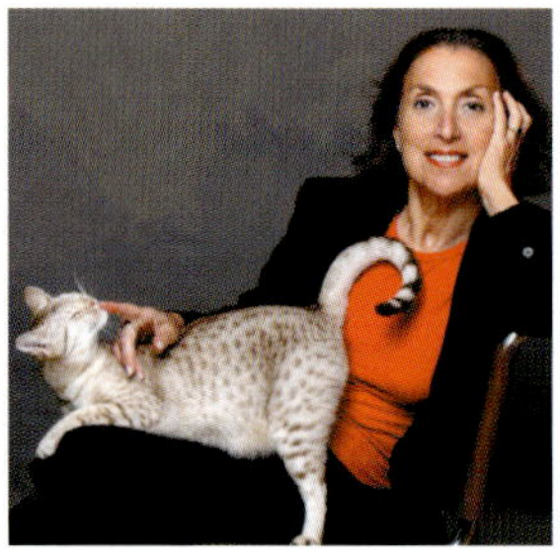

Barbara Bordnick has been one the premier practitioners of nude photography since the 1980s, as well as one of the world's foremost fashion photographers. As if this wasn't impressive enough, she has also received international plaudits for her gorgeous color photographs of flowers after the publication of *Searchings: Secret Landscapes of Flowers* (Welcome Books) in 2003. If Bordnick's fashion work is noted for her romantic sensibility, then it is no surprise that her floral images and her nudes share a similar sense of romance.

"I treat my subjects like lovers," she has said, "giving caring attention to the people I photograph."

Bordnick's approach to the nude is to embrace the human body with her camera. In black and white and in color, she focuses both on the way light touches the figure and the way figures touch one another. "Photographing flowers is exactly the same as photographing nudes," she says. "It's about this incredibly sensuous landscape. It's as though, when I'm photographing it, I'm feeling it, I'm touching it."

Barbara Bordnick was born Barbara Goldman in the Bronx, New York, the daughter of Ukrainian immigrants. Her early childhood playgrounds were the Bronx Zoo and the Bronx Botanical Garden. At the age of 11, however, her family moved to Far Rockaway on Long Island, where Barbara began to dream of escaping to a more romantic life. "I wanted to be a fashion designer because it seemed that fashion designers all went to Paris."

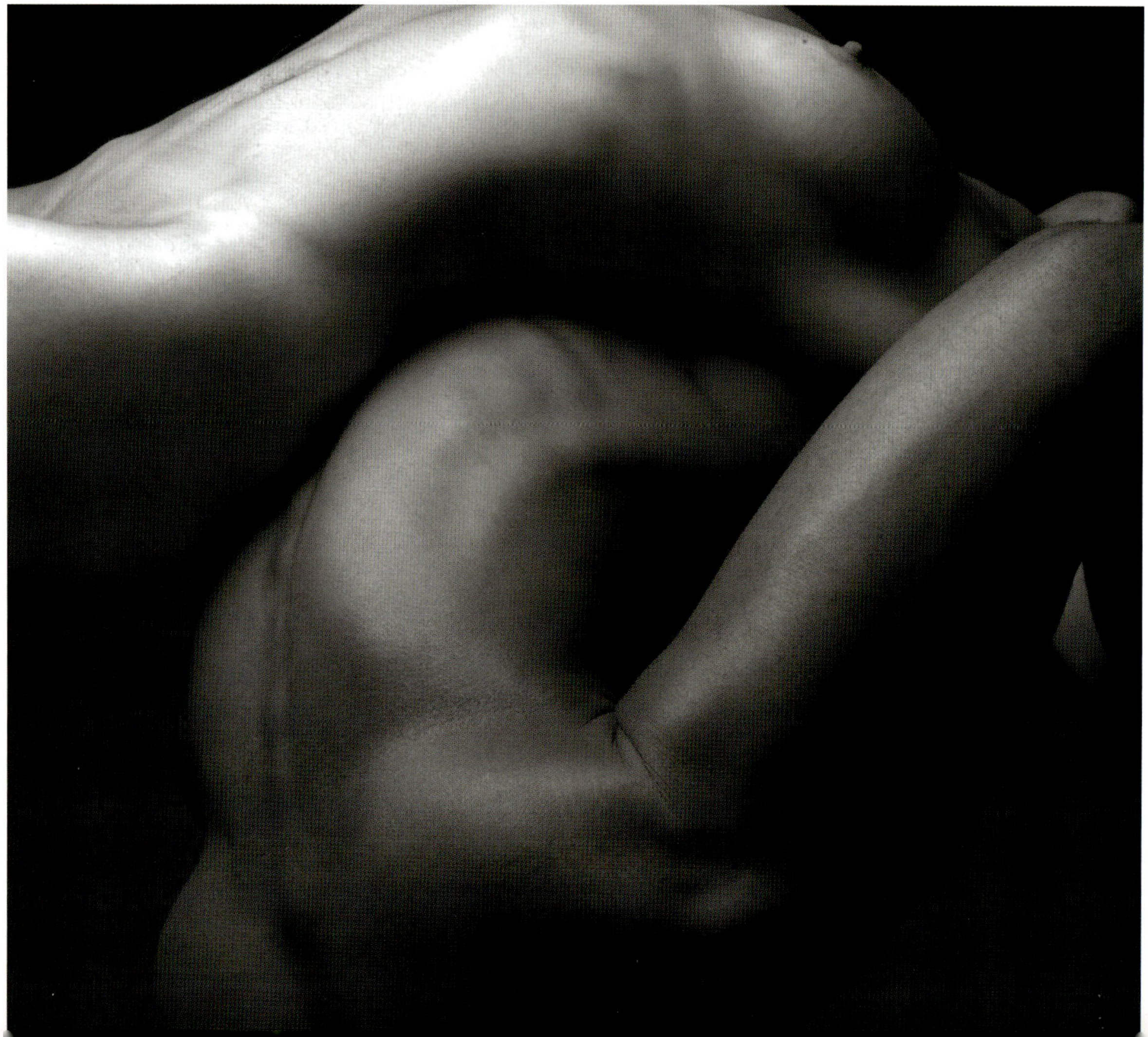

As soon as she entered Pratt Institute in Brooklyn (on a full scholarship), however, Bordnick discovered that she didn't like fashion design at all, so she took most of her electives [chosen courses] in the fine arts. She also took a single course in photography, the only formal training she ever received.

After receiving her BFA, Bordnick and her new industrial-designer husband headed for Europe in the free-spirited 1960s. But when her husband landed a job in Copenhagen, Bordnick discovered she was not cut out to be a stay-at-home wife. In search of work, she took a portfolio of eight art-school photographs illustrating poetry to Danish publications. When she was offered $9 apiece for them, Bordnick's new direction was clear. "I'm going to be a photographer. It's so easy," she announced to her husband. "Of course," she now reflects, "it was anything but easy!"

From Copenhagen, Bordnick moved to Paris, her childhood dream destination, where she made a connection with Marion Capron, editor at the French edition of *Harper's Bazaar*, who introduced her to all the fashion photographers in Paris. "I decided I wanted to be a fashion photographer," recalls Bordnick. "But I didn't *just* want to be a fashion photographer—I wanted to be a fashion photographer for *Harper's Bazaar*."

Although she never succeeded in getting published in *Harper's Bazaar* in Paris, Bordnick had better luck when she returned to New York. Unable to find work as a photographer's assistant, she set up her own studio and started calling *Harper's Bazaar* until the magazine finally called her back.

"I started with small pictures at the back of the book, but gave them the same attention I would give to a feature, so I was quickly given pages."

In what might be described as a serendipitous career, Bordnick admits that chance has played a large part in her evolution as a photographer. "I'm very technically unsophisticated," she says. "The best things I've ever done are things I'd never done before, but I was asked to do them by people who had more confidence in me than I did."

Today, Bordnick normally shoots black and white with a Deardorf 8x10 camera and a 19-inch lens, and she shoots digital with a Leaf back on a Hasselblad, but her first nudes were shot in 1982 with a Polaroid 8x10. She had been commissioned to photograph a calendar of "Great Women in Jazz" with a large-format Polaroid camera and was eager to try it out on something other than portraits.

Fashion led to portraiture, portraits led to nudes, and nudes led to flowers. In fact, Bordnick began her *Searchings* series when a model failed to appear at a nude shoot. Undeterred, she photographed the floral props instead. "As I did them," she recalls, "they felt like nudes."

And "felt" is the operative word when it comes to a Barbara Bordnick nude. Not only do they have a gentle, feminine touch, but the images are also often brought to life by the subject's hands. In fact, several Bordnick "nudes" are entirely of hands.

"I'm obsessed with hands," she admits. "People express themselves most successfully and most emphatically through their eyes and through their hands. I'm also a very tactile person."

And it is this sense of touch that most distinguishes Barbara Bordnick as a photographer of the nude. As she is fond of saying, "I photograph nudes in a way I'd like to be touched."

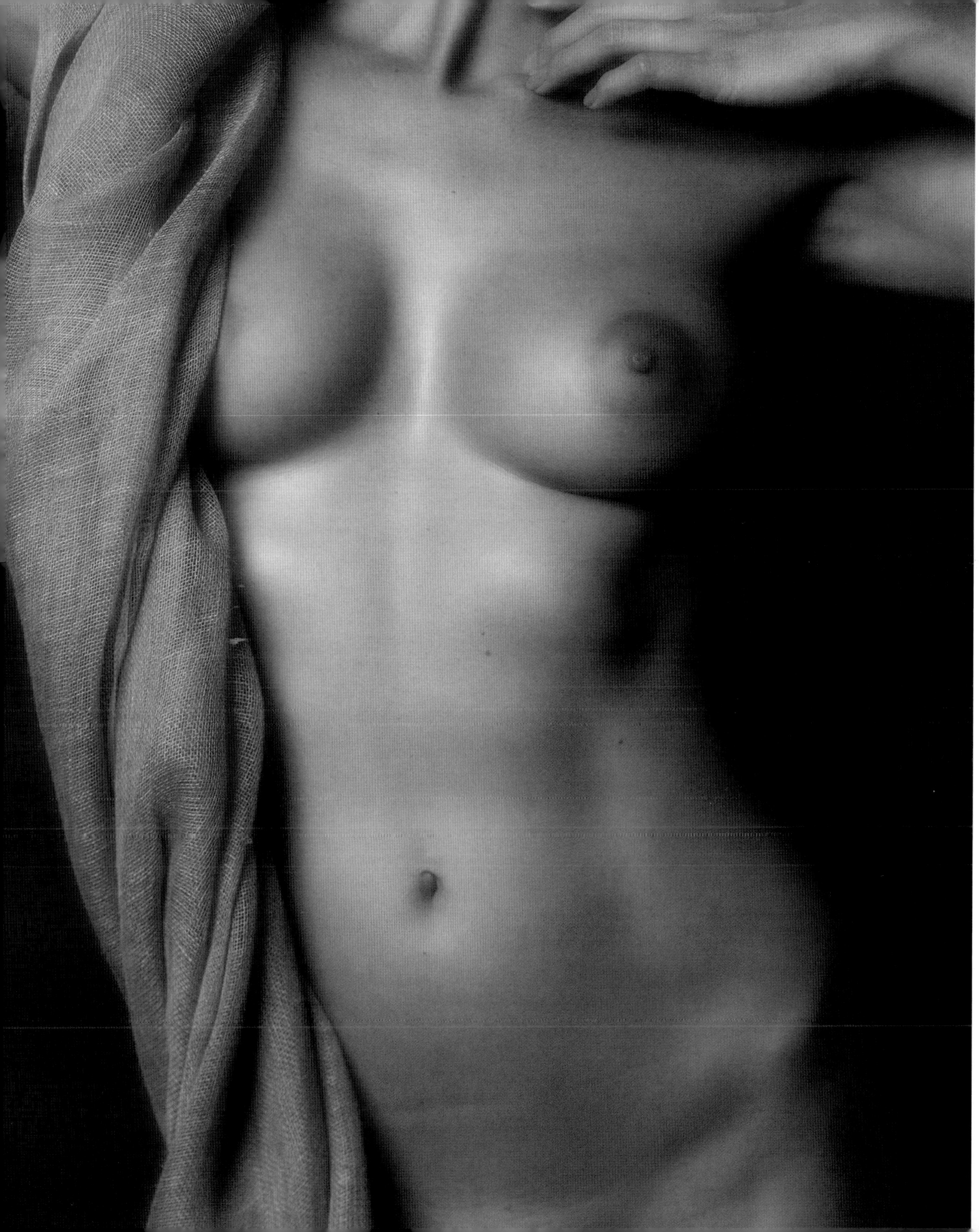

Untitled, 1996 *(opposite)*

Untitled, 1982 *(left)*
"That was from a personal series of nudes while I was doing the 8x10 project. I was working with a lot of fabric at the time, because I was doing a campaign for Dayton's. Why it's so meaningful to me is that it was a very creative time in my life. I wanted to explore the 8x10 camera with nudes, and this was a combination of the best things I was doing at the time."

Untitled, 1996 *(page 36)*

Untitled, 1996 *(page 37)*
"These were dancers from the Alvin Ailey dance company. I've always been fascinated by dancers. I've always made dance a very important part of my life and my creative work. While other people do more with movement than I do, there is a kind of very sensuous movement that has always attracted me to dance. It's the lyricism of the body. They incorporate both a sense of design and sensuality. It's a very graphic sense of the tactile quality of touching. The dancers were standing just like that, waiting for me to set up. The only thing I did was take her right hand and place it right there. It's exactly where I would want to put my hand."

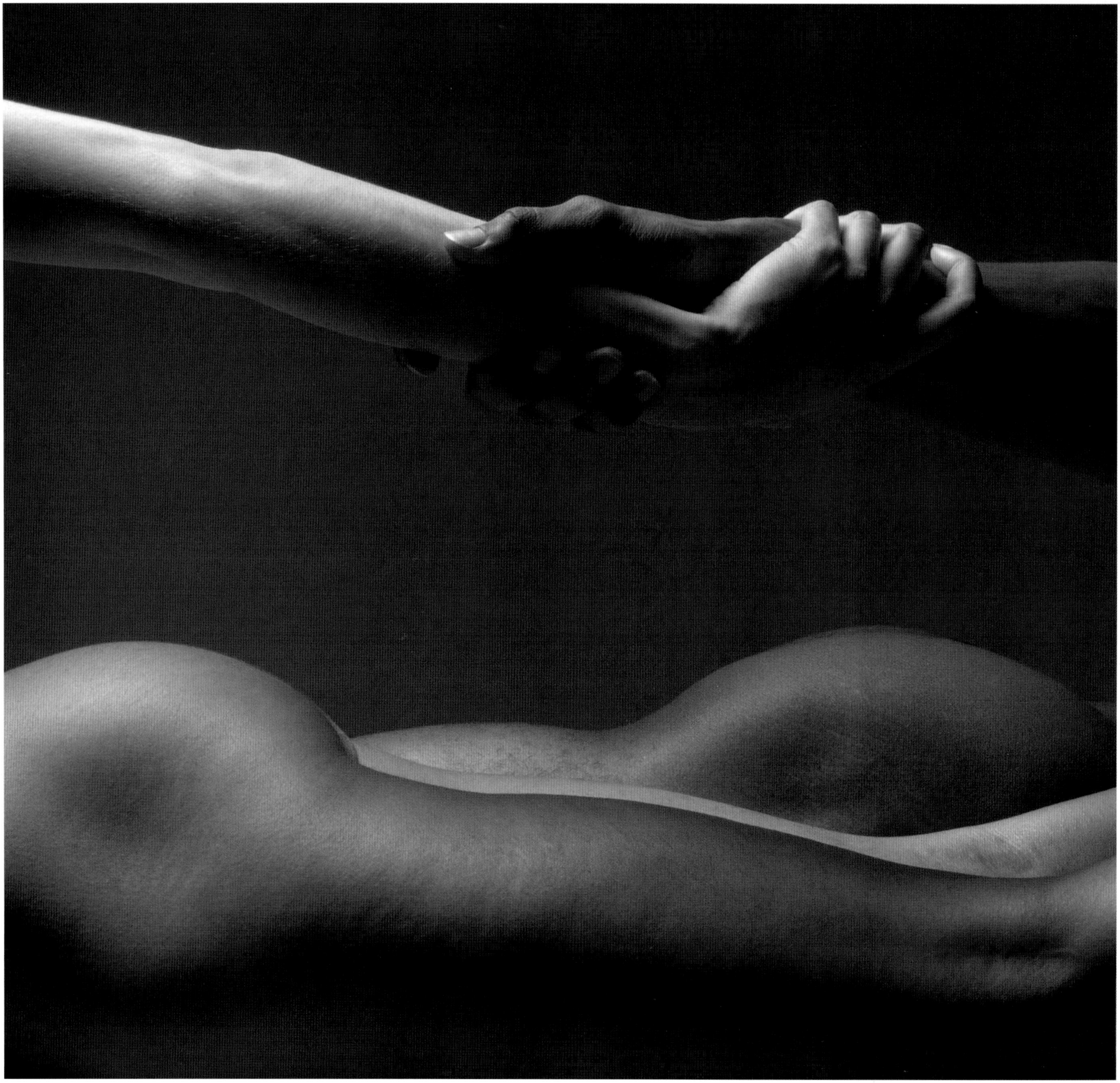

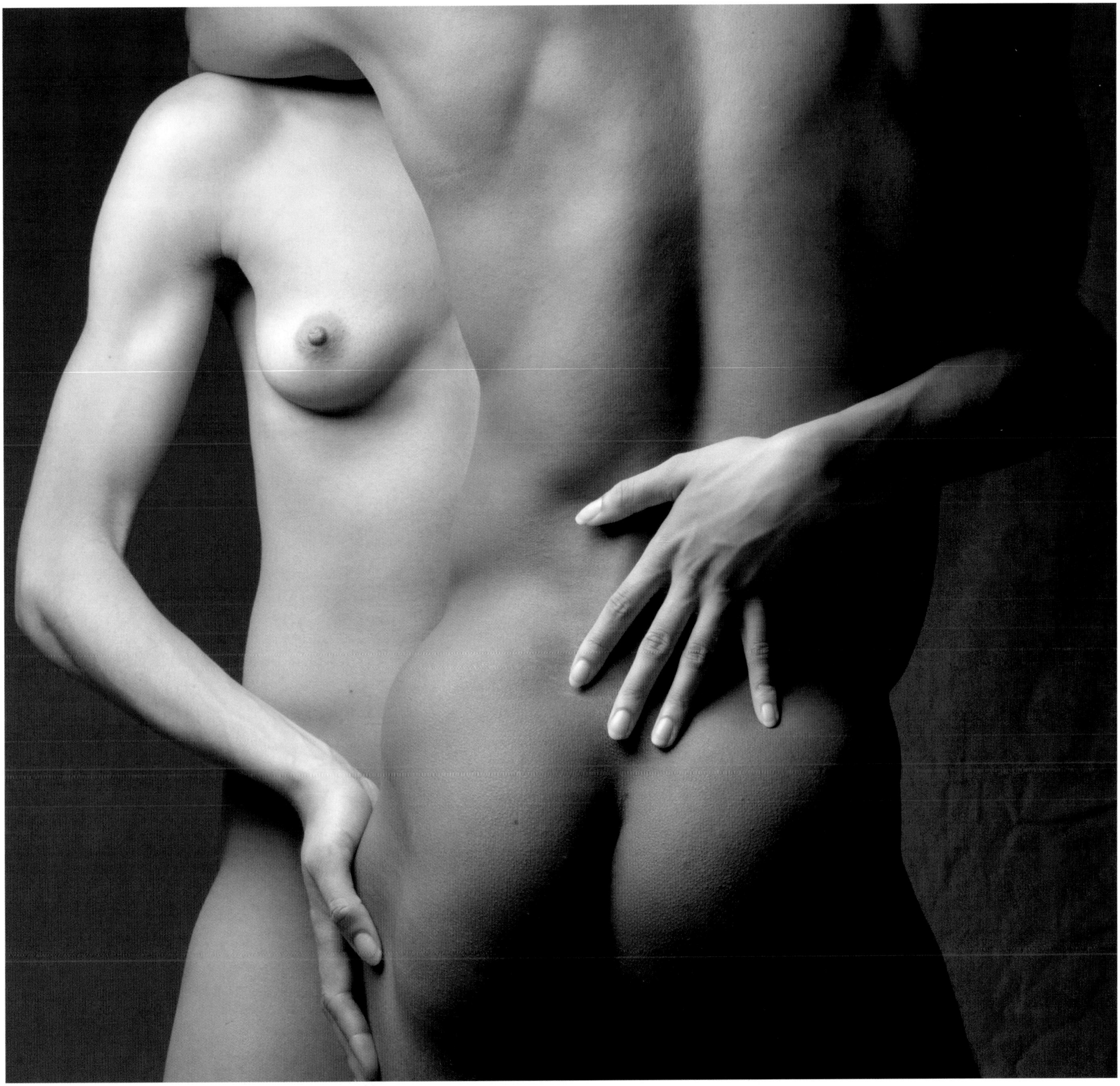

Barbara Bordnick

Guy Bourdin

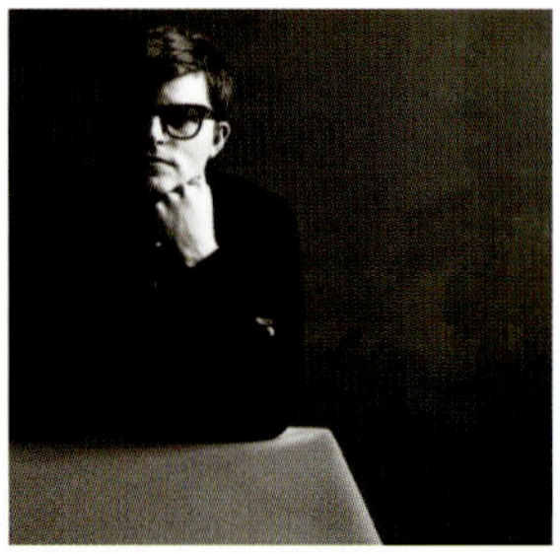

There is no easy way to describe the images of Guy Bourdin. They are, by turns, peculiar, grotesque, beautiful, decadent, obscene, unique, rude, incomprehensible, morose, and unimaginable. These phrases piece together parts of the artist and his creations, but they do not bring you any closer to solving the complicated and bizarre puzzle that was Guy Bourdin. Even today, more than 14 years after his death, Bourdin's influence remains substantial in a world where visual media devour everything in their path in the search for new ideas. His work still inspires hundreds of photographers in the advertising, fashion, editorial, and fine-art markets.

Bourdin was born in Paris in 1928. He was sent off to boarding school then, later, to the home of his grandmother. After meeting Lucien Henry, an art dealer, at the age of 18, he decided to become an artist and spent six months drawing and painting in Henry's house in Provence. In 1948 he entered the French air force where he acquired his first training with a camera, working as an aerial photographer while stationed in Dakar, Senegal.

In 1950, following his return from the military and after various odd jobs, Bourdin ventured into the gallery world by exhibiting his paintings and drawings at the Rue de la Bourgogne Galerie in Paris. Two years later, his photographs were hanging in a show at Galerie 29 in Paris, the catalog of which included an introduction by Bourdin's friend, Man Ray. After other exhibitions of both photography and drawings, Bourdin began a long career in the world that he would influence the most—fashion—with a series of images depicting hats published in the 1955 February issue of French *Vogue*. While he continued to paint for a number of years—even having exhibitions in New York, Paris, and elsewhere—Bourdin was now focusing on the camera, and its ability to transfer his theatrical imagination into the real world.

After entering his images into the Photokina art fair in Cologne in 1966, Bourdin soon received his first editorial assignments from *Harper's Bazaar* and *Photo*. In 1967 he shot his first photographs for Charles Jourdan shoes, and it was this relationship, along with his relationship with *Vogue*, that produced some of Bourdin's most tremendous imagery. It also established him as a photographer who could successfully cross between fine art, editorial, and advertising.

Today, the twisted glamor of Guy Bourdin fills our eyes with glitz and danger. His off-center ideas and high-concept designs have become part of the cultural mainstream, surviving a blitz of homages and inadequate dilutions of his work. Variations on his eccentric visions adorn billboards, magazine pages, music videos, and television commercials.

Bourdin's images were unlike anything before them. They were snippets from some preposterous movie of his imagination. Faces were cropped out or layered in swaths of makeup; lifeless bodies were draped over furniture and floors like melted Dalí clocks; and spilled blood was a frequent prop. He positioned models in scenes that ranged from the absurdly morbid to the ridiculous and comical. More than anything, though, his work was fresh and instantly memorable.

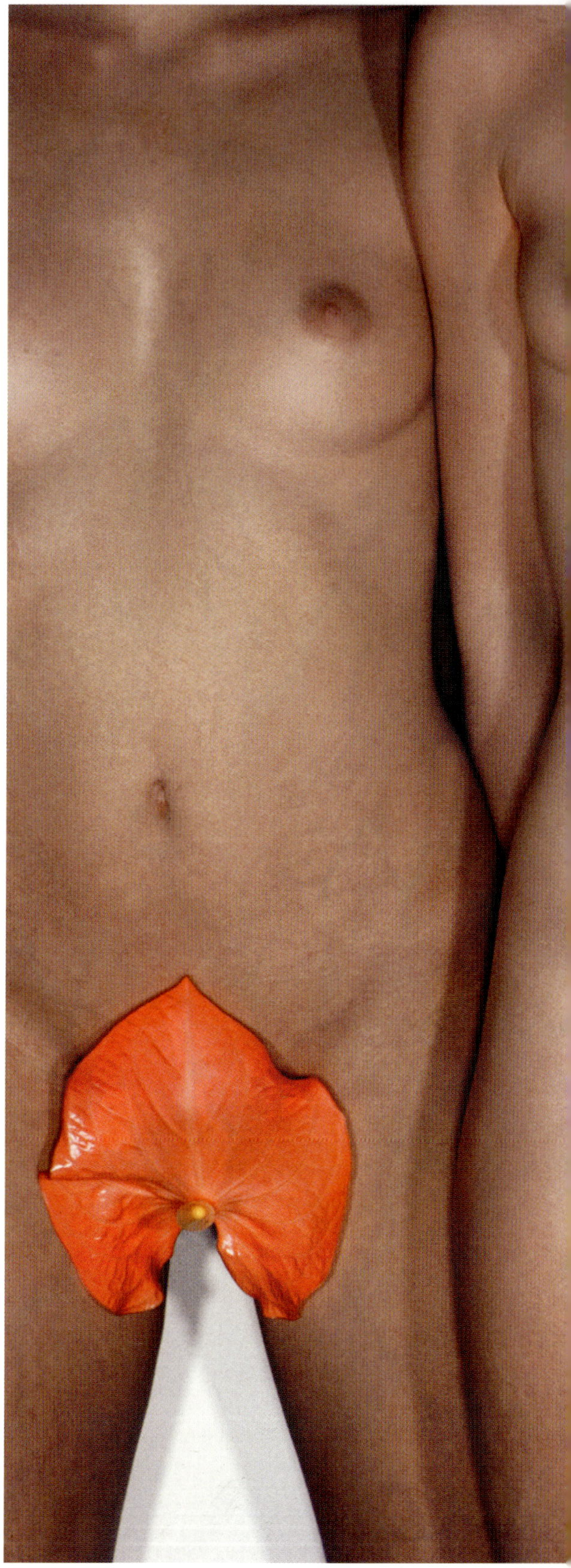

French *Vogue*, December 1976
(opposite)
Bourdin's infamous photograph taken for a French *Vogue* swimsuit spread. Also published in *Exhibit A*, a publication that was edited by Bourdin's son, Samuel.

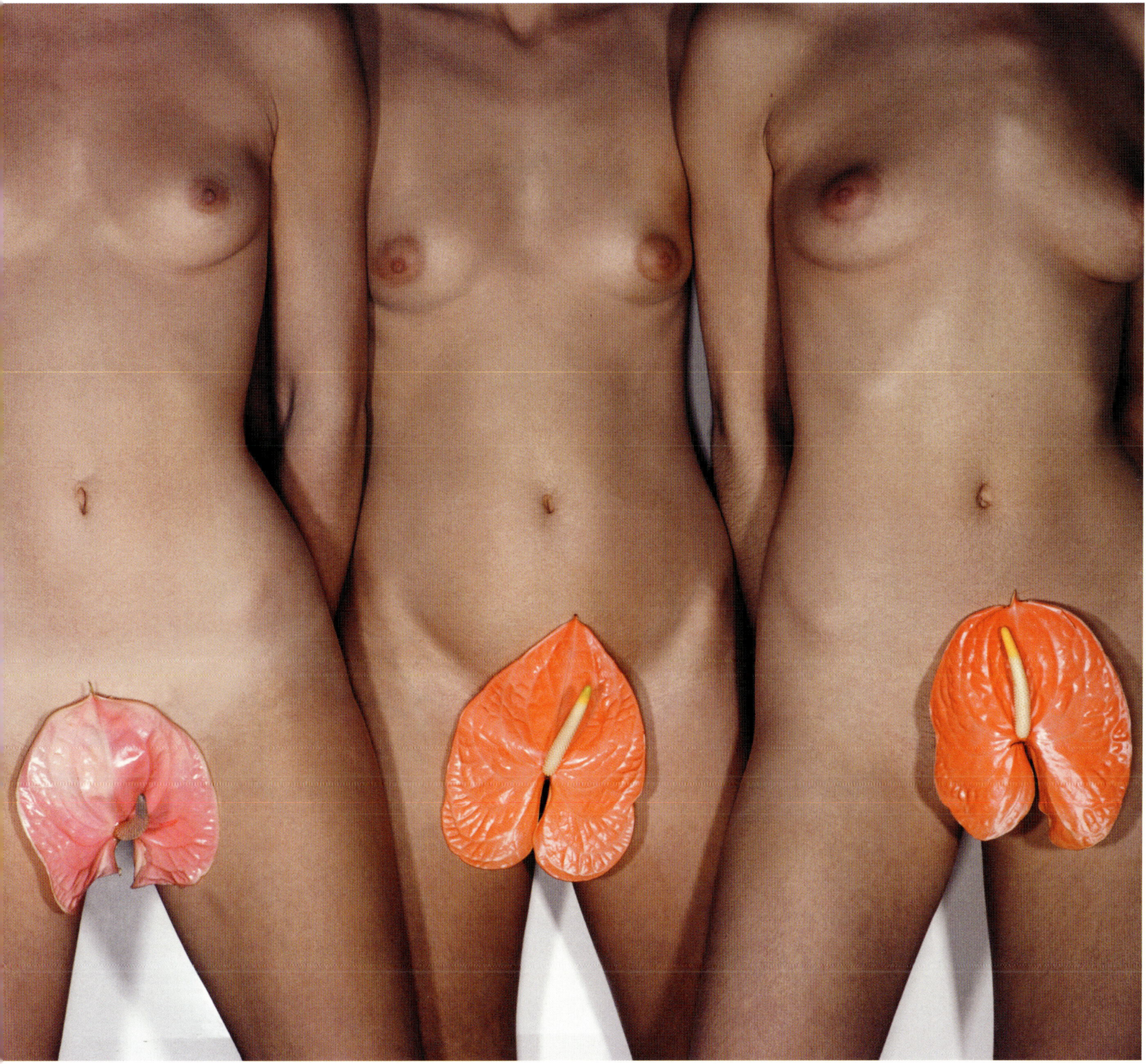

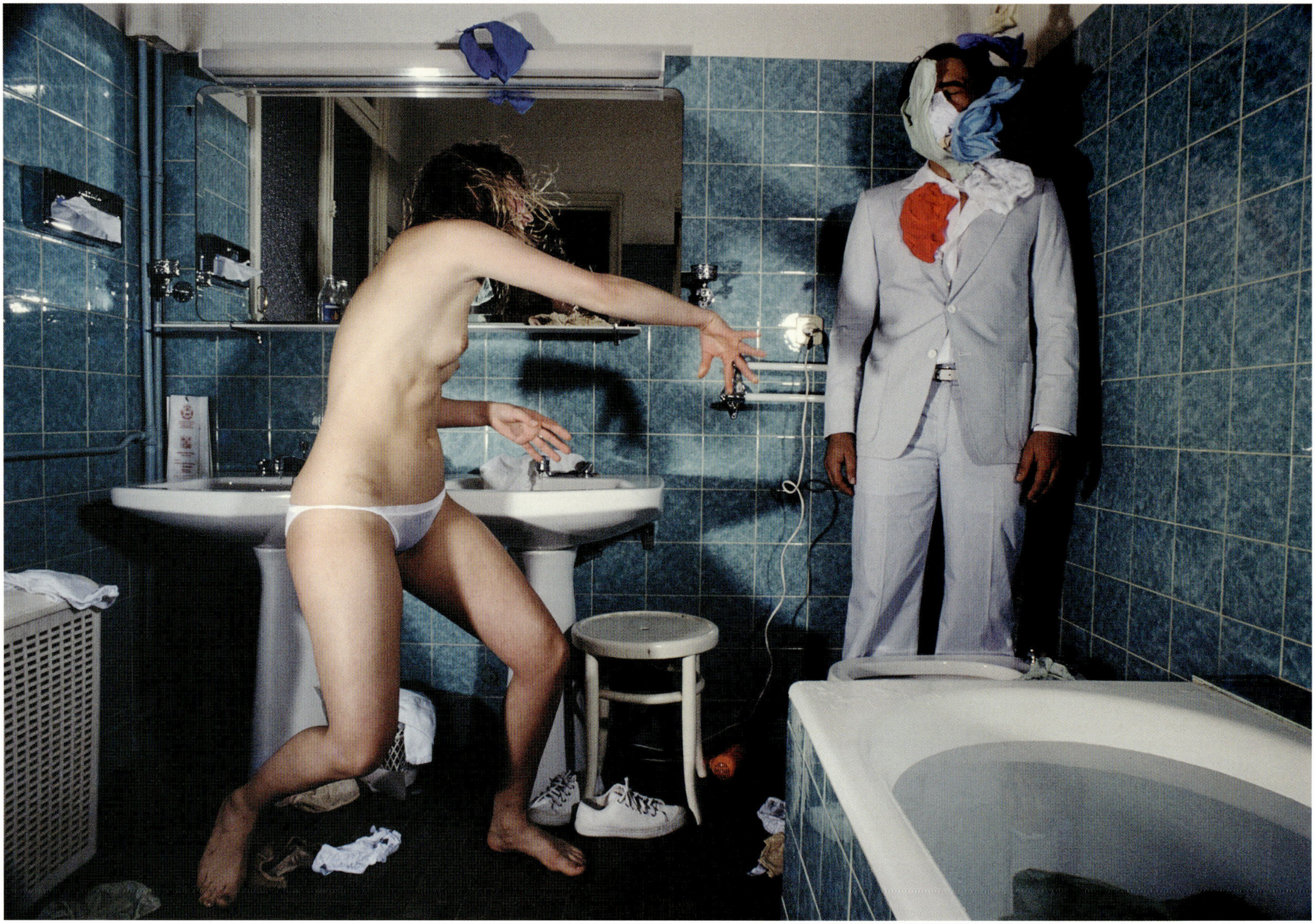

Vogue Hommes, June/July 1977
This image, which appeared in French *Vogue* advertising lingerie for Valisere and a suit for Façonnable, perfectly reflects Bourdin's offbeat vision and unique method of exhibiting clothing. Also published in *Exhibit A*.

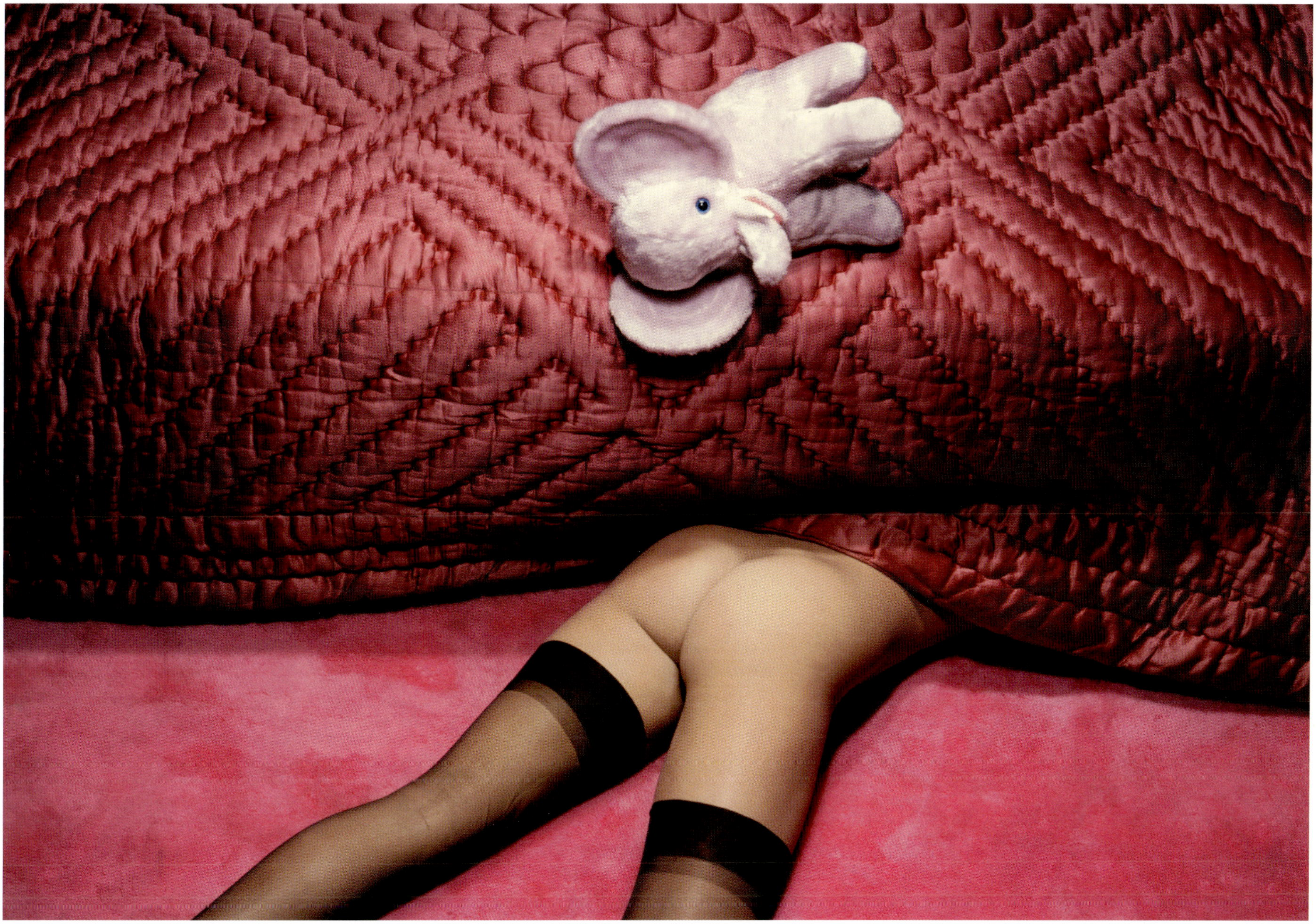

Pentax Calendar, 1980
This photograph, which also appeared in Bourdin's posthumous book *Exhibit A* (Bulfinch Press, 2001), was taken for the Pentax camera company.

Bob Carlos Clarke

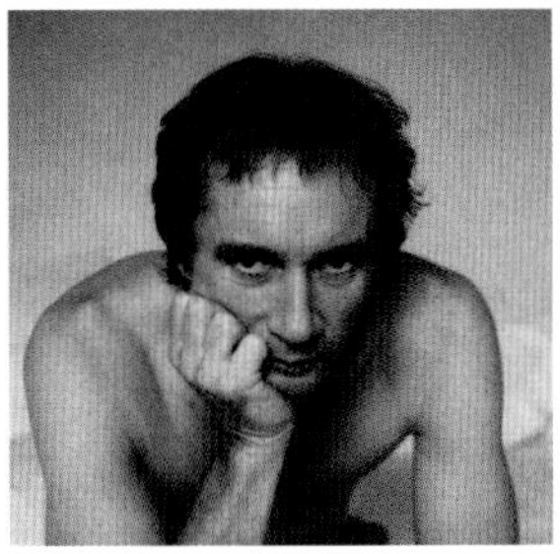

If Bob Carlos Clarke were not a photographer, he might well have been a revolutionary in some tumultuous, unstable country, decked out in fatigues, chomping on a chewed-off cigar, and firing a gun into the open sky. Fortunately for us, his weapon of choice is the camera, and with that and his passionate opinions, he has conducted his rebellion.

Known for the satire in his images as well as the shock value, Clarke relishes his ability to poke fun and provoke his audience, "especially now that the media has degenerated into a sex- and celebrity-obsessed farce," he says.

Born in southern Ireland in 1950, Clarke moved to England in 1964 and studied at the West Sussex College of Art, The London College of Printing, and finally The Royal College of Art, where he received an MA. Always candid, Clarke admits that he entered nude photography for one reason alone: sex. After some time in journalism and advertising, Clarke, on the advice of a friend, tried to attract the interest of a girl in his college by using photography. Not only did he find his first wife, but also a new career.

In the 1970s and 1980s, Clarke began making his mark in the erotic-photography world. He followed his first book, an illustrated version of Anaïs Nin's *Delta of Venus* (Gallery Books, 1980), with a concentration of fetish images in *Obsession* (Quartet Books, 1981) and *The Dark Summer* (Quartet Books, 1985). It was during these years that his signature image—women in skin-tight rubber garments—would become prominent.

At the same time, Clarke was also shooting advertising work that had the same edge as his personal imagery—a difficult trick to pull off. This trend, which included a campaign for Agfa, as well as later shoots for Levi's, Volkswagen, Pirelli, and Smirnoff, continues to this day. Recent campaigns for Wallis and Urban Stone clothing have helped keep Clarke's name in the spotlight.

These commercial images, which mimicked a previous Clarke series of black-and-white images of early morning promiscuity in nightclubs, featured a threesome of nonprofessional models engaging in sexual activity in a clublike atmosphere. The results were, by normal advertising standards, scandalous. In fact, the Urban Stone images were dubbed the "rudest" and "most explicit" ads ever seen by some critics. Needless to say, Clarke was delighted. "A successful nude is one that doubles the heart rate," says Clarke, who has shot for dozens of magazines, including *Maxim*, *Tatler*, and *Loaded*. "An image that doesn't rattle somebody is worthless. I want to supercharge sexuality beyond what is actually achievable. I want to connect with Man's animal instincts."

Clarke took some time off from his erotic imagery in the 1990s and produced a book on the renowned chef Marco Pierre White called *White Heat* (Trafalgar Square, 1999). He also gave lectures for film specialist Ilford, and designed a series of calendars for UK utility company PowerGen.

It was not long before Clarke was back in the field that made him famous, however. His latest book, *Shooting Sex: The Definitive Guide to Undressing Beautiful Strangers* (Georg Olms Verlag, 2002), is a "how-to" manual on photographing the nude in the provocative Clarke style. His 2004 UK exhibition, *Love Dolls Never Die*, was his first in 12 years. It was also the first show in which he used digital technology to create the prints.

Clarke cites influences as varied as Brassai, Weegee, Helmut Newton, and Leni Riefenstahl. In terms of his own working methods, he mainly uses a Pentax 6x7 and a Fuji 6x9, and he gains his subject's confidence by "staying in their eye line, fully dressed." He admits that he chooses them with one emotion in mind: lust. That, along with the fact that he clearly loves women, comes through stridently in his photographs.

There is nothing boring about Bob Carlos Clarke's nudes. They are carnal, bold, sexual, and frank. They emphasize and use every technique, prop, and look that has ever been used to turn on a male. Even when they have a classic style, his nudes still retain something adventurous. He pushes back the boundaries and then passes the new boundaries again without blinking.

"Do it for pleasure," says Clarke, when asked for his advice on breaking into nude photography. "Do it to get laid. But get a real job."

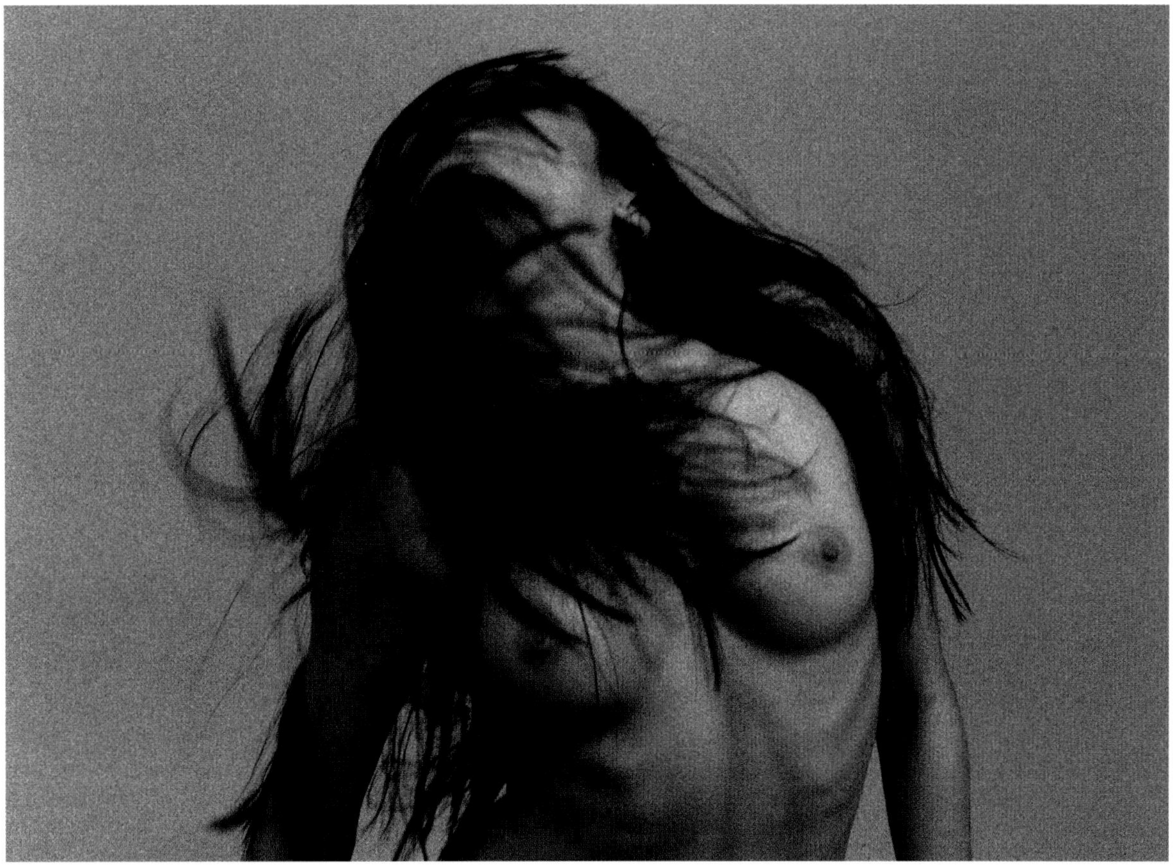

Lainee Dancing, 2002
"She was the first Asian girl I ever photographed and she was very seductive."

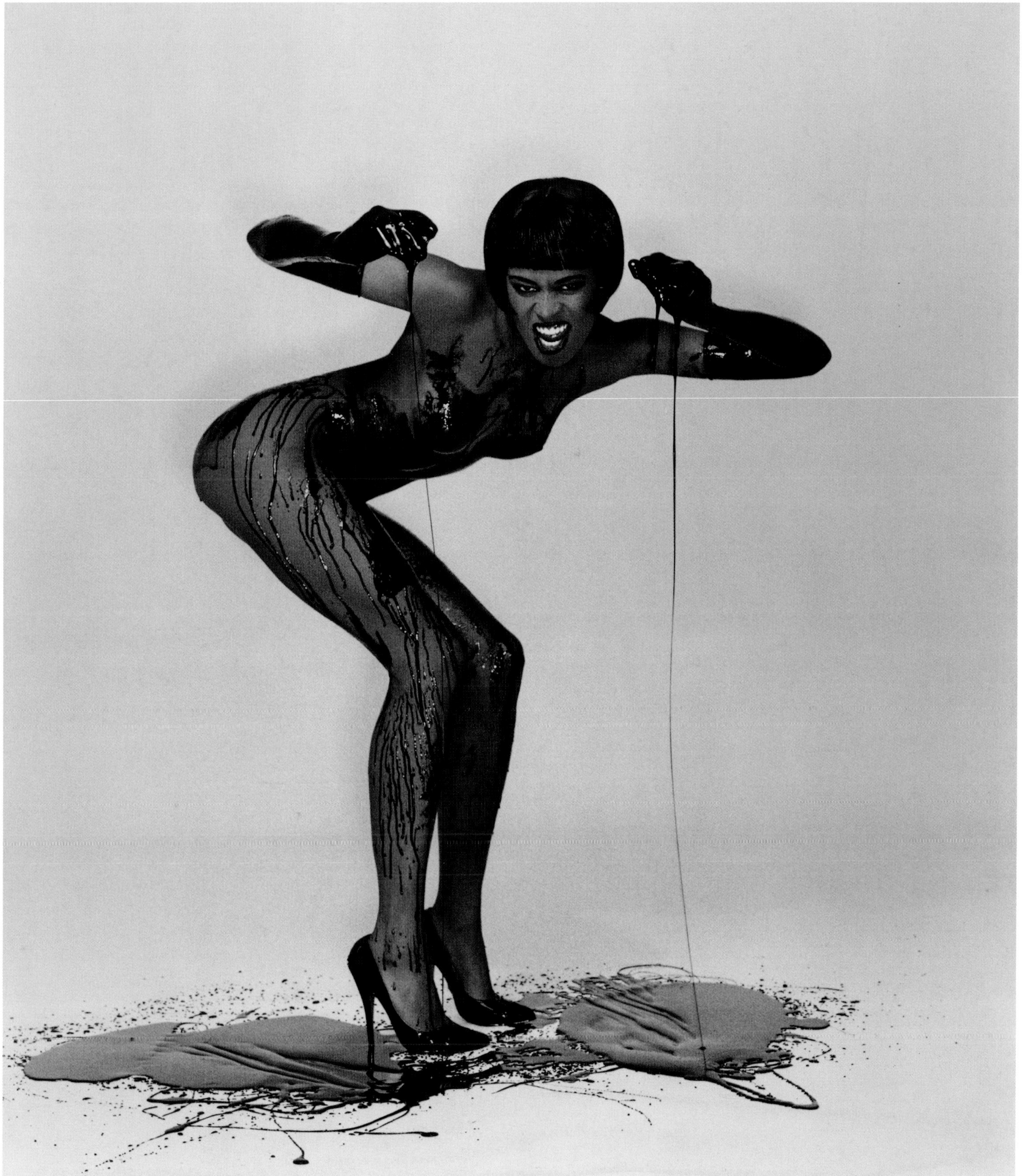

Sticky Fingers, 1999
"I like this one 'cause I love sweet things."

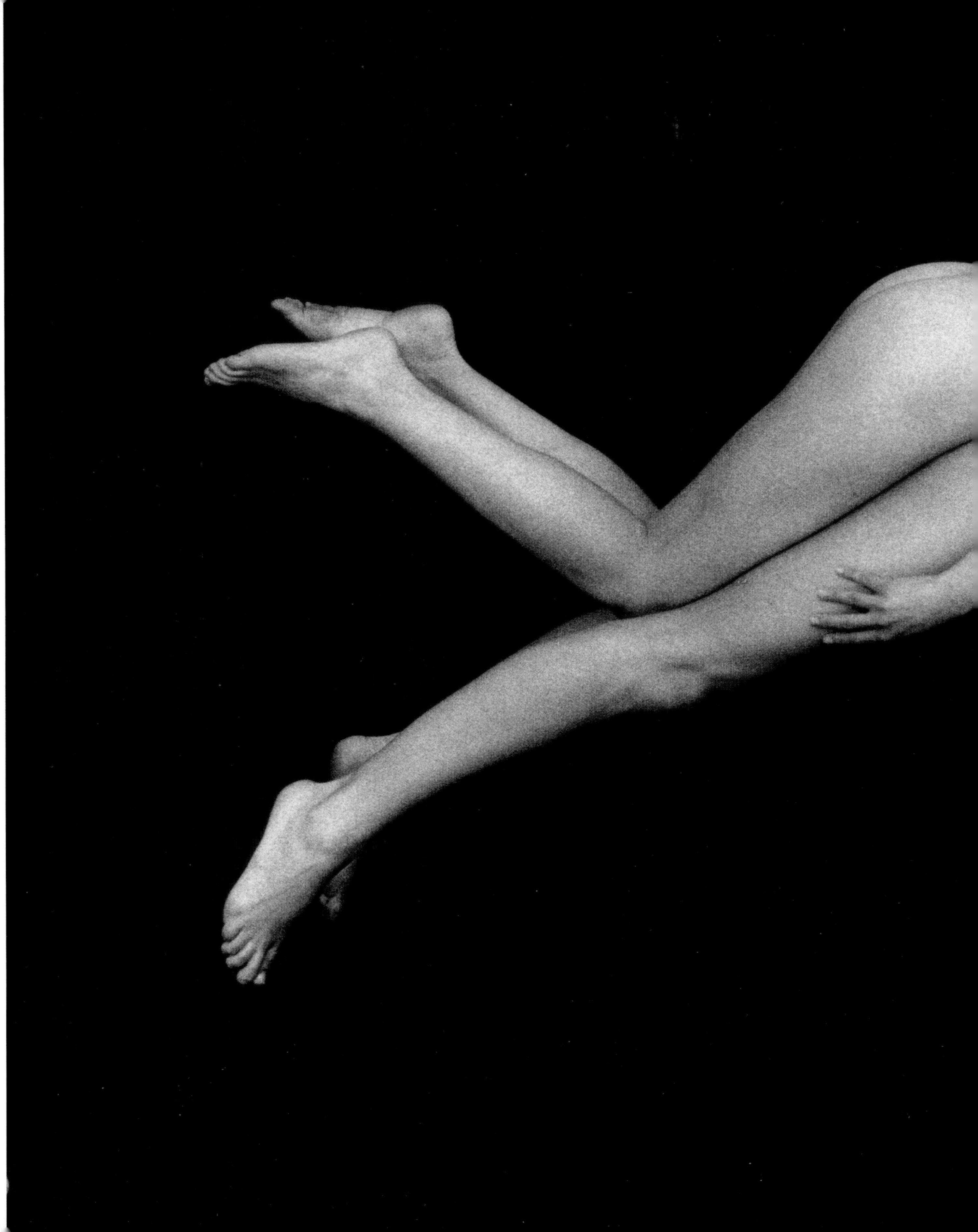

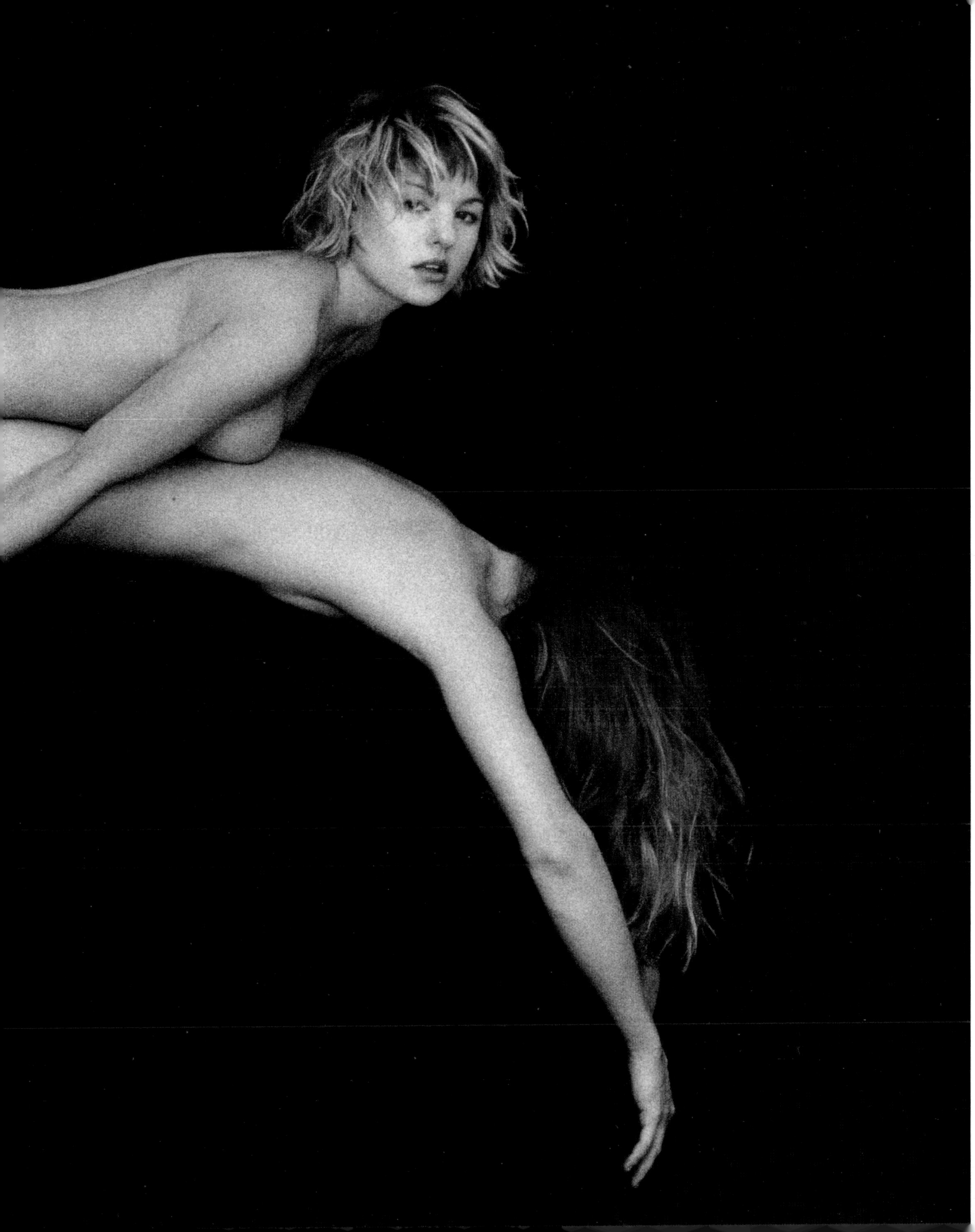

Nightflight, 2000
"I like two girls on top of each other naked."

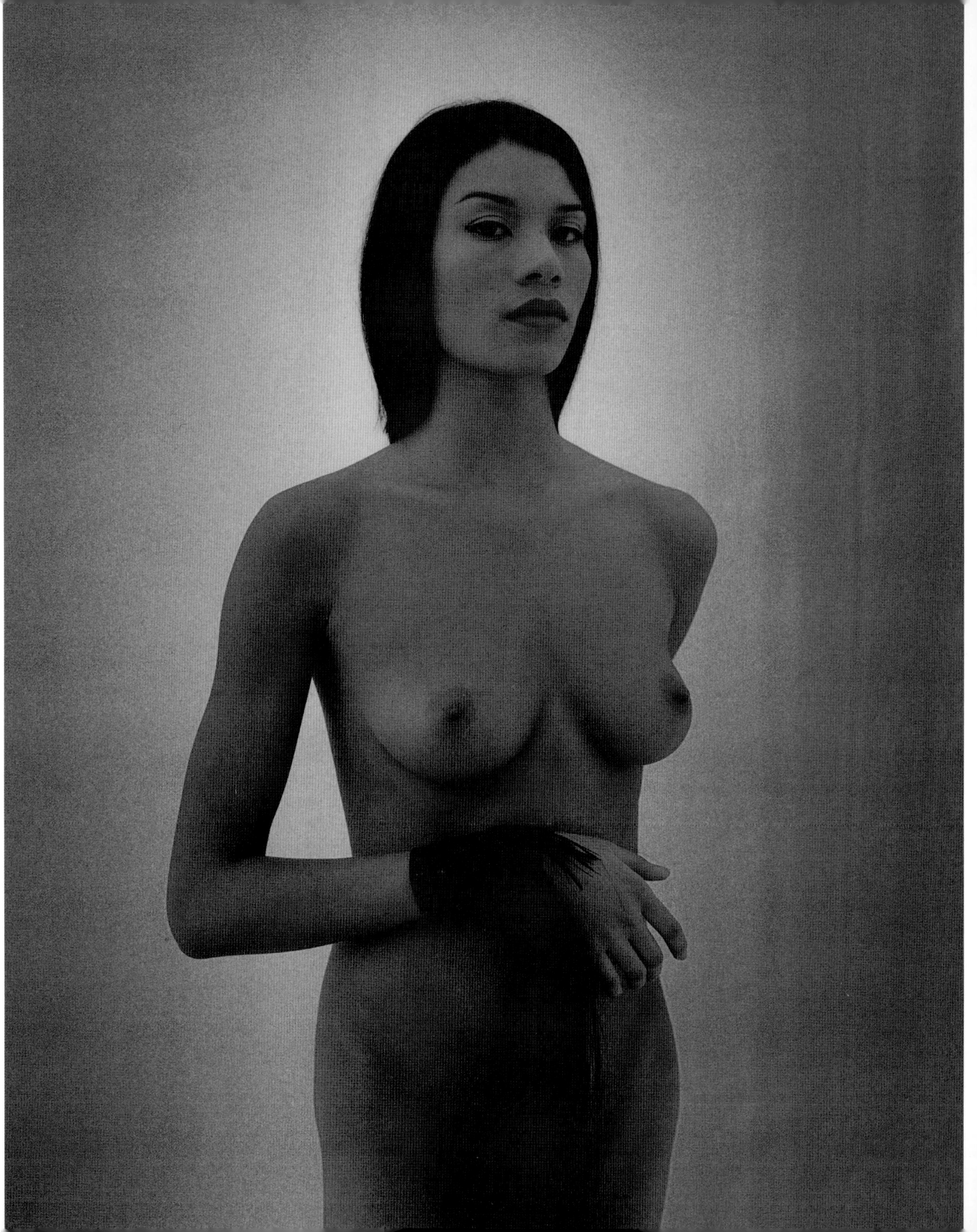

Mimi, 2002
"She was a nightclub dancer. I love her because she hates clothes."

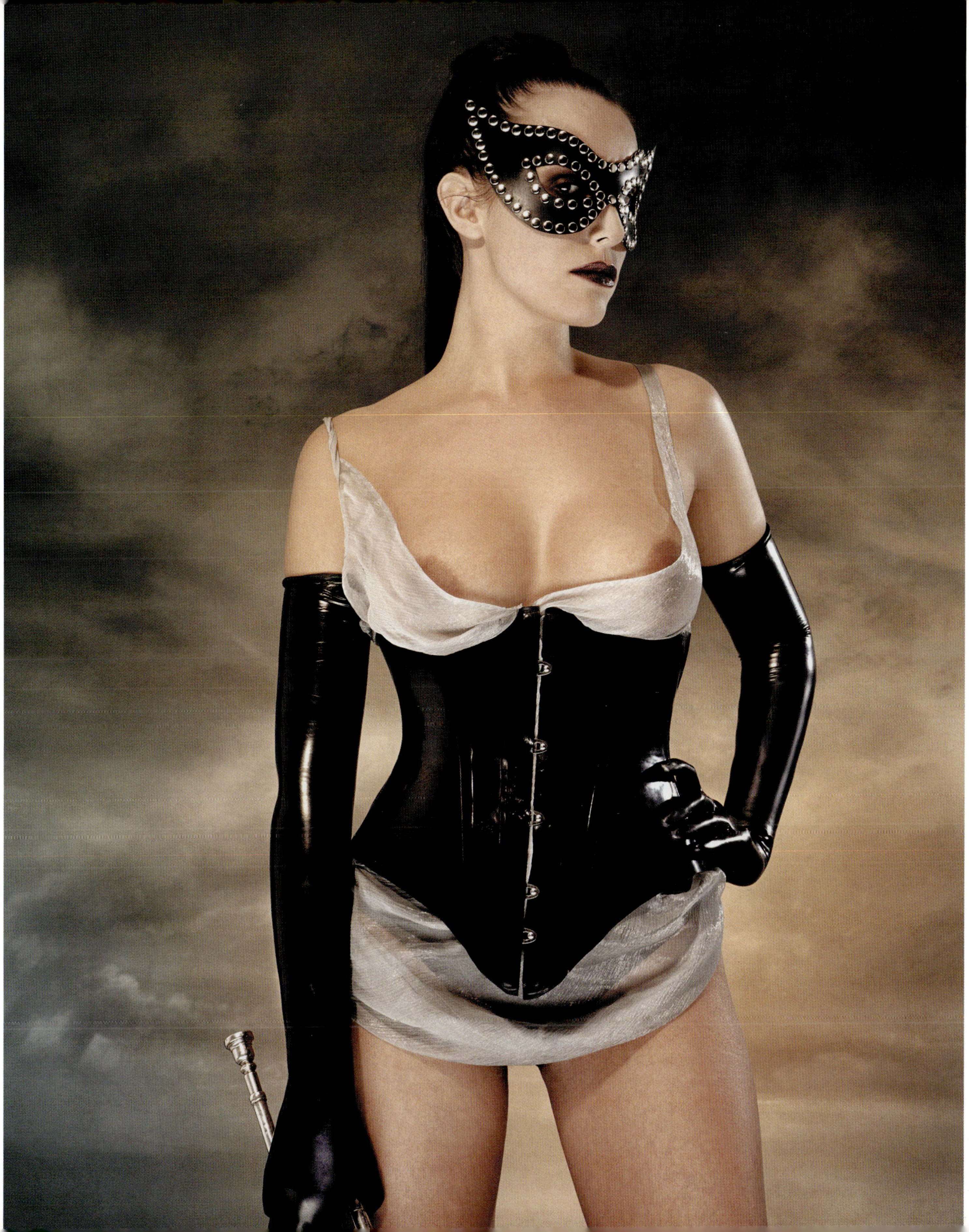

Femme Fatales Threaten
Family Values, 2004

Regina DeLuise

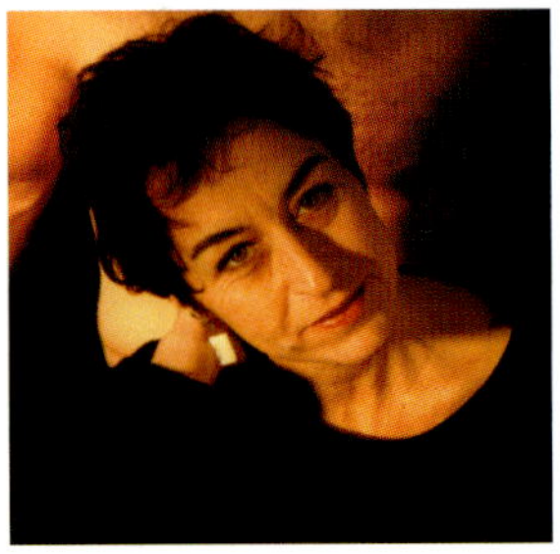

It is easy to classify the nude images of Regina DeLuise as simple and traditional renderings of the human body. However, looking beyond the classical feel of the understated, black-and-white imagery that the photographer has created, there is vivacity and warmth, along with a latent feeling of pure eroticism filling each of her frames that is neither easily accomplished, nor often discovered.

Born in Brooklyn, New York, in 1959, DeLuise began making photographs in high school after spending most of her time in drawing classes. Her motivation at the time turned out to be a photographer whose style and soul lives on in her images today.

"When I first started making pictures, Edward Weston was a real inspiration," she says. "The sensual nature of the images was captivating. My brother gave me Weston's *Daybooks* for Christmas in 1978. I remember poring over those pages, both for the love of the image, and also as a look into the life of an artist. Weston seemed so exotic to me. To think about what dedication and commitment to one's work could bring, to collect one's life and experience in images and make that experience so palpable to others was truly thrilling."

DeLuise studied fine arts at the State University of New York at Purchase, and after graduating in 1981, she experienced an event that rarely happens to any photographer, let alone a young graduate. "After I left Purchase, I worked at the Daniel Wolf Gallery in New York," she explains. "I learned that The Museum of Modern Art reviewed portfolios each week. Just drop off your work on Wednesday and pick it up the next day. I decided to bring in the work that had been my senior show at Purchase. Susan Kismaric called me back to her office that Thursday and said that John Szarkowski wanted to buy two images for the collection. What better first break could you imagine?"

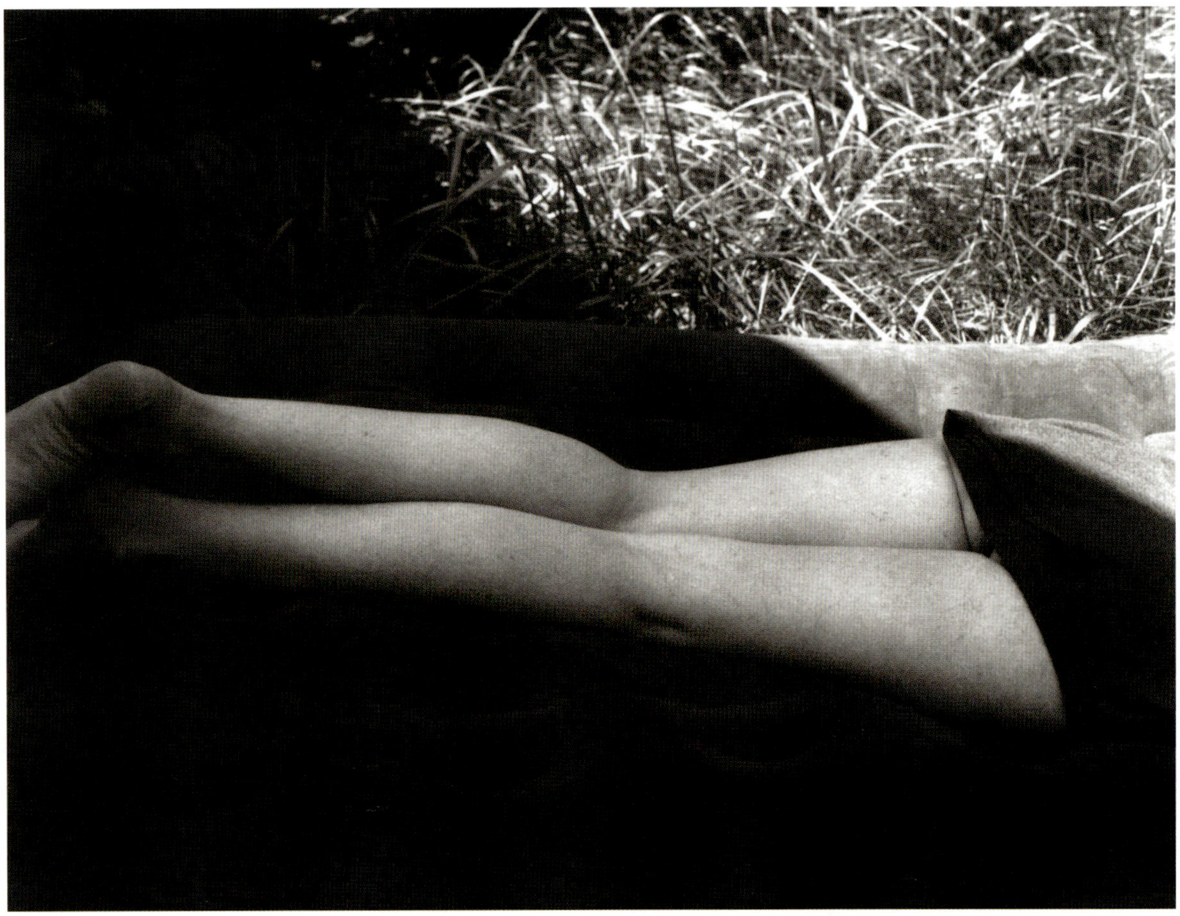

Indeed, and that was merely a sign of things to come for DeLuise. She received an MA from the Rosary College Graduate School of Fine Arts in Florence, Italy, in 1984. It was there that she concentrated on portraits, nudes, and landscapes, establishing her subtle, intimate approach to photographing the world around her. DeLuise's early nudes were lovely studies of form and tone. *Marble Nude*, an image that displays an intensely pale, female torso stretched horizontally across a black sofa, was an indication of the photographer's attraction to a time-honored, flowing, graceful style.

"I do come out of a very classical tradition of photography, light being at the heart of all the images," says DeLuise. "It's a challenge for me to work in an area that is so classical and try to make the pictures relevant, beautiful, sensual, and real. The idealized and overly romanticized nude doesn't interest me. Imprints of clothing on flesh, gestures of limbs, the person, and not just the body in life, are interesting to me.

"I don't think of the nudes as different than any other images I make," continues DeLuise. "They relate to portraiture to me. And the portraits relate to my idea of landscape. My work naturally gravitated toward the landscape during my graduate studies in Italy. Initially, I made some very uninteresting pictures. I didn't know how to get at the vast beauty that was all around me. One of my teachers, a painter, Itza Petrozzani, came into my studio to look at my work. Among my images—portraits, nudes, and poor attempts at landscapes—was a picture of two trees. She said, 'Dante said all you need to make a landscape are two trees.'" Seems so simple. What I heard in that was that relationship is everything. My connectedness to place was so important. That was my way in. I stopped looking at the Tuscan hillsides and looked in the corners of the villa where I was studying. I looked closely at the places I loved to be, places I knew, and the work became much more interesting. I began thinking of the pictures as portraits. I tried to capture the essence or soul of the land. That's what I was after. So you see, it's all connected."

Besides her skills in rendering the quintessence and fundamental nature of a subject, the power in DeLuise's images also lie in her phenomenal mastering of the palladium printing process. Using an 8x10 camera, along with the 19th-century method that she learned from her teacher Jed Devine during her years in college, her photographs take on a radiance that breathes life into her subjects. "My initial attraction was simply the beauty of the image, the softness and relationship of tone, what the surface looked like, what the emulsion could render in terms of range," says DeLuise, whose images have been exhibited in 15 solo shows and more than 20 group shows around the world. "There was a way that I missed using 'artist materials' when I began to do photography—the brushes, beautiful paper ... these kinds of things. With palladium you can bring that element back in. You are responsible for making a lot more than just the negative. You're mixing your emulsion and coating your choice of paper —not working in the dark, since the emulsion is only sensitive to ultraviolet light. All of these things contribute to making the process more satisfying for me."

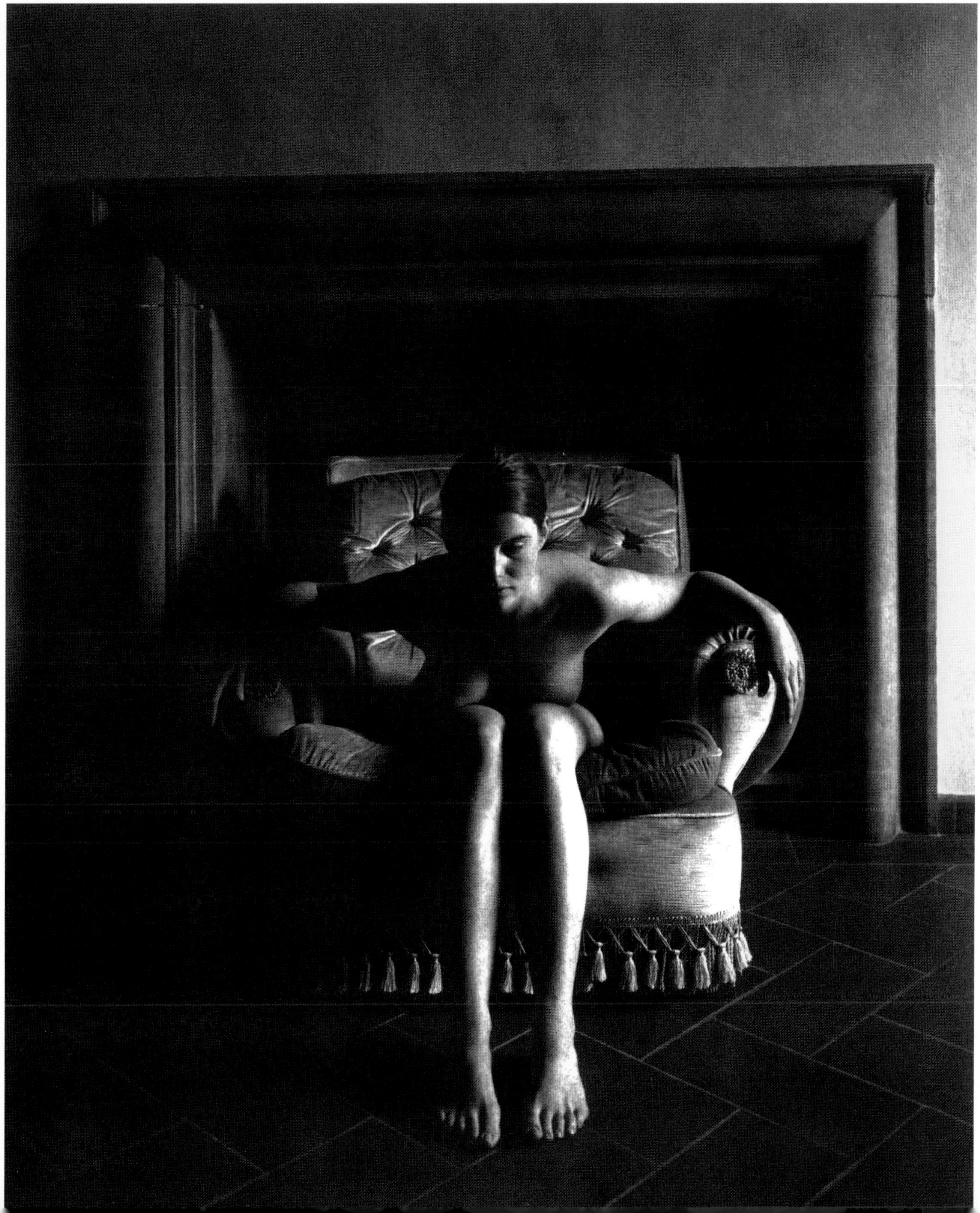

Legs on Air Mattress, Fairfax, California, 2000 *(opposite)*
"My dear friend Stephanie is the subject of many of my nudes and portraits, from the first images I made with a camera 25 years ago, to the present. There is a real collaborative quality to these images for me. She has the patience and understanding to allow me to dance around her with the 8x10 camera, willing to work with me until I have what I need. She has been my most generous model. These pictures were made around her home in California. There is a way I need to take the romantic element out of the image of the nude. I want the body in its real life. The air mattress was an object that caught my eye, the sense of mass, as the body might have, but so artificial. The delicacy of the line of the legs and the turn of the feet floating on top of this strange and unnatural form was oddly beautiful to me."

Nude in Chair, Cortona, Italy 2001 *(left)*
"This picture was taken in an Italian palazzo were I lived during the winter of 2001. It was a grand place, high-beamed ceilings, stone and marble everywhere—just magnificent. The mantle seemed like a stage to me. I would watch the light shift and change, falling beautifully on this enormous velvet chair. I was fortunate enough to have the perfect model eventually grace the stage."

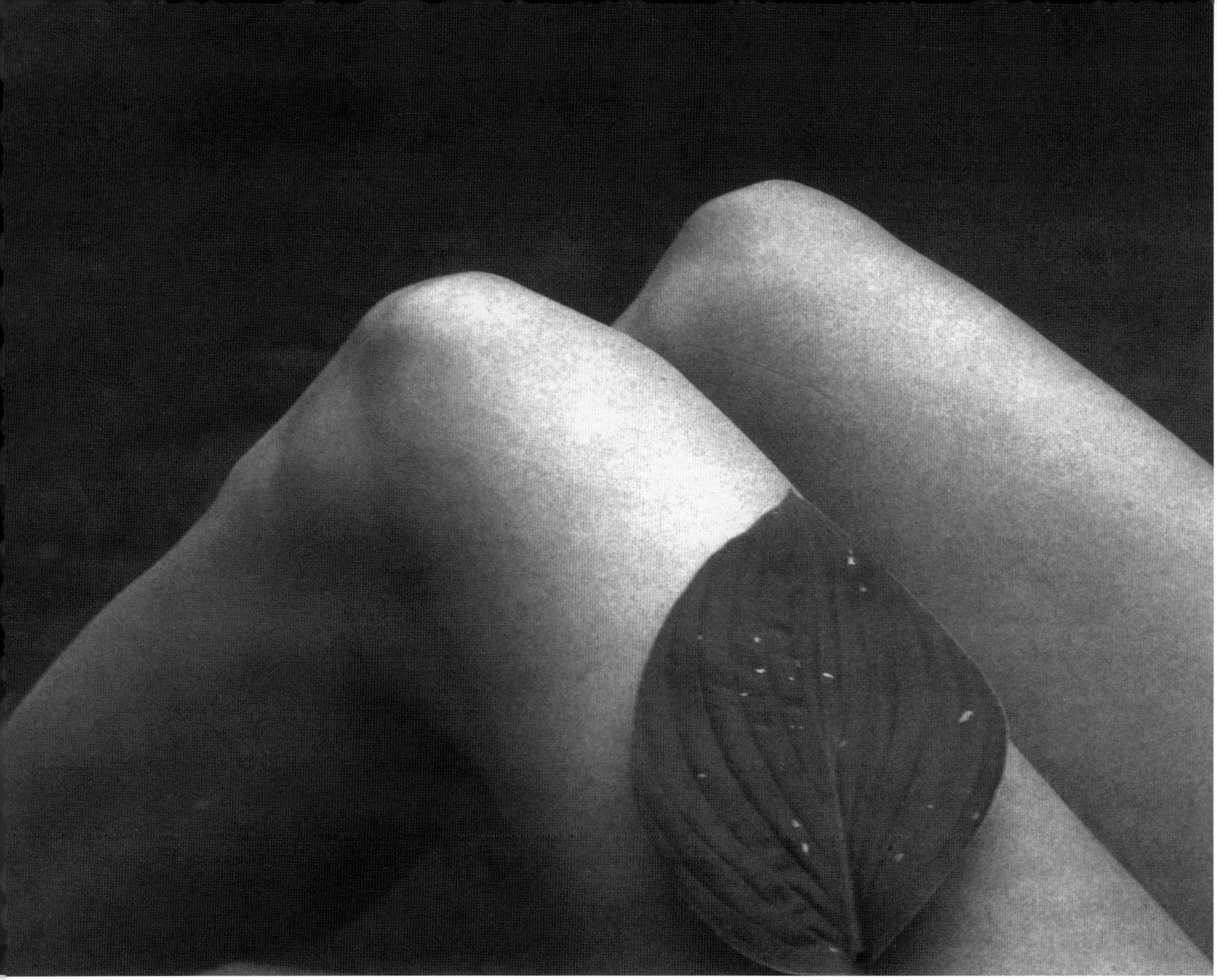

Martha's Knees, Dorset, Vermont, 1997 *(above)*
"*Martha's Knees* is so much a reflection of the place it was made. I had been living with this gentle landscape for a number of years. The worn, rolling mountains are certainly evident here. Something as simple as this leaf aligning with the line of the leg is a detail one has time to see in a place like this."

Currently living in the Washington, D.C., area and working as a professor of photography at the Maryland Institute College of Art in Baltimore, Maryland, DeLuise's recent images have centered on Cortona, Italy, where she has produced still lifes and nudes. She has been drawn to photographing in Italy her whole life (in addition to studying in Italy, she used a Guggenheim Fellowship in 1993 to explore Europe, as well as Nepal and India), and her photographs have focused on the mystery and intrigue found while photographing subjects at night.

"I've become more interested in the figure in context—a broader view," says DeLuise. "I hope that the subtle shifts in my work reflect the changes in myself, a greater maturity artistically, and an understanding of the emotional and psychological complexities of our lives."

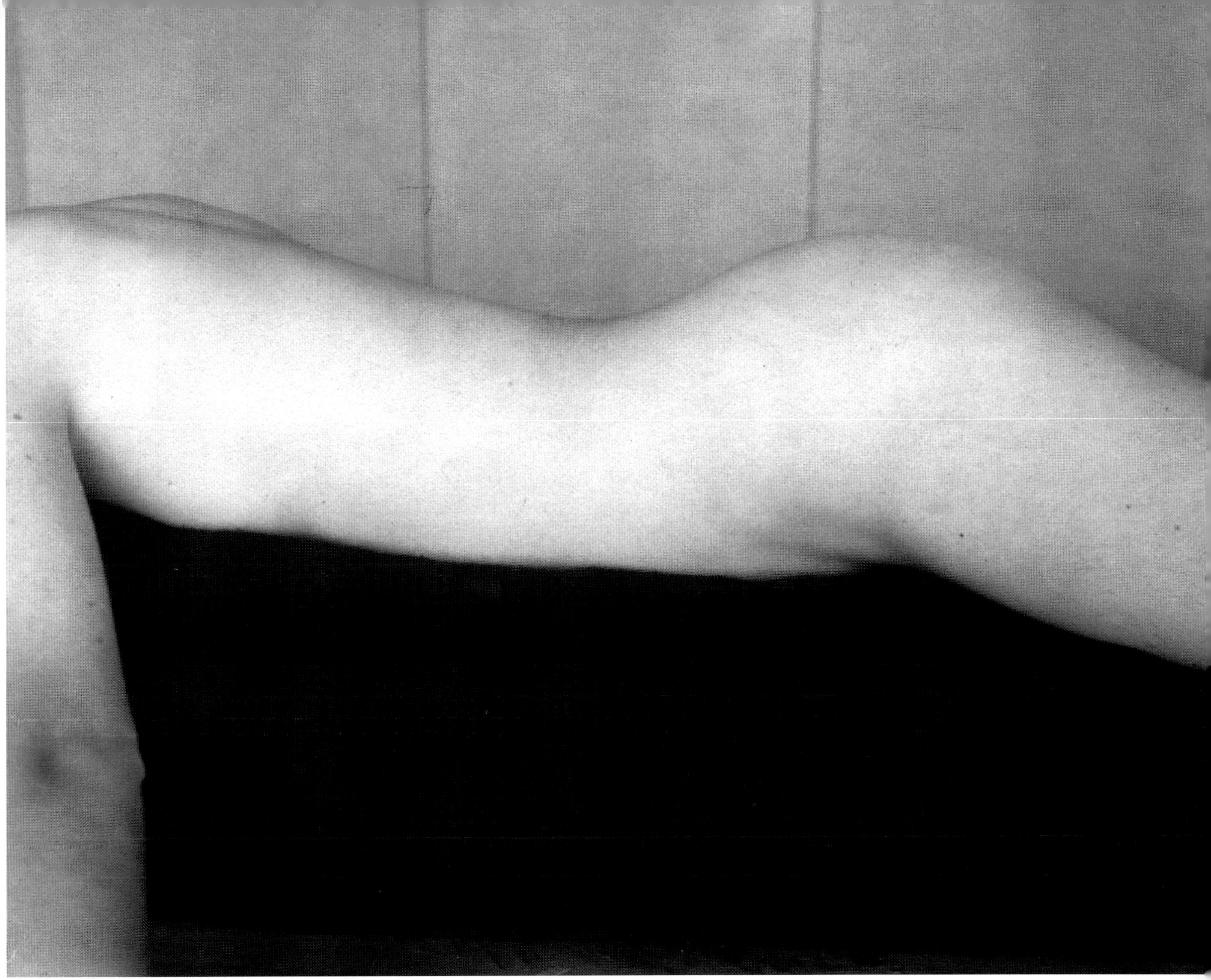

Marble Nude, Florence, Italy, 1984 *(above)*
"The subjects in my photographs are people I'm close to in my life. There is a sympathetic relationship here —a collaboration, really. My dear friend Stephanie has been in my pictures since I've been making pictures. She, like all my subjects, allows me great access. They are all flexible and very patient. Being photographed with an 8x10 view camera is very different to being photographed with a handheld camera. It takes time. Because of my relationship with these people, the element of trust is implicit. If the image is successful, I think it is informed greatly by this very feeling."

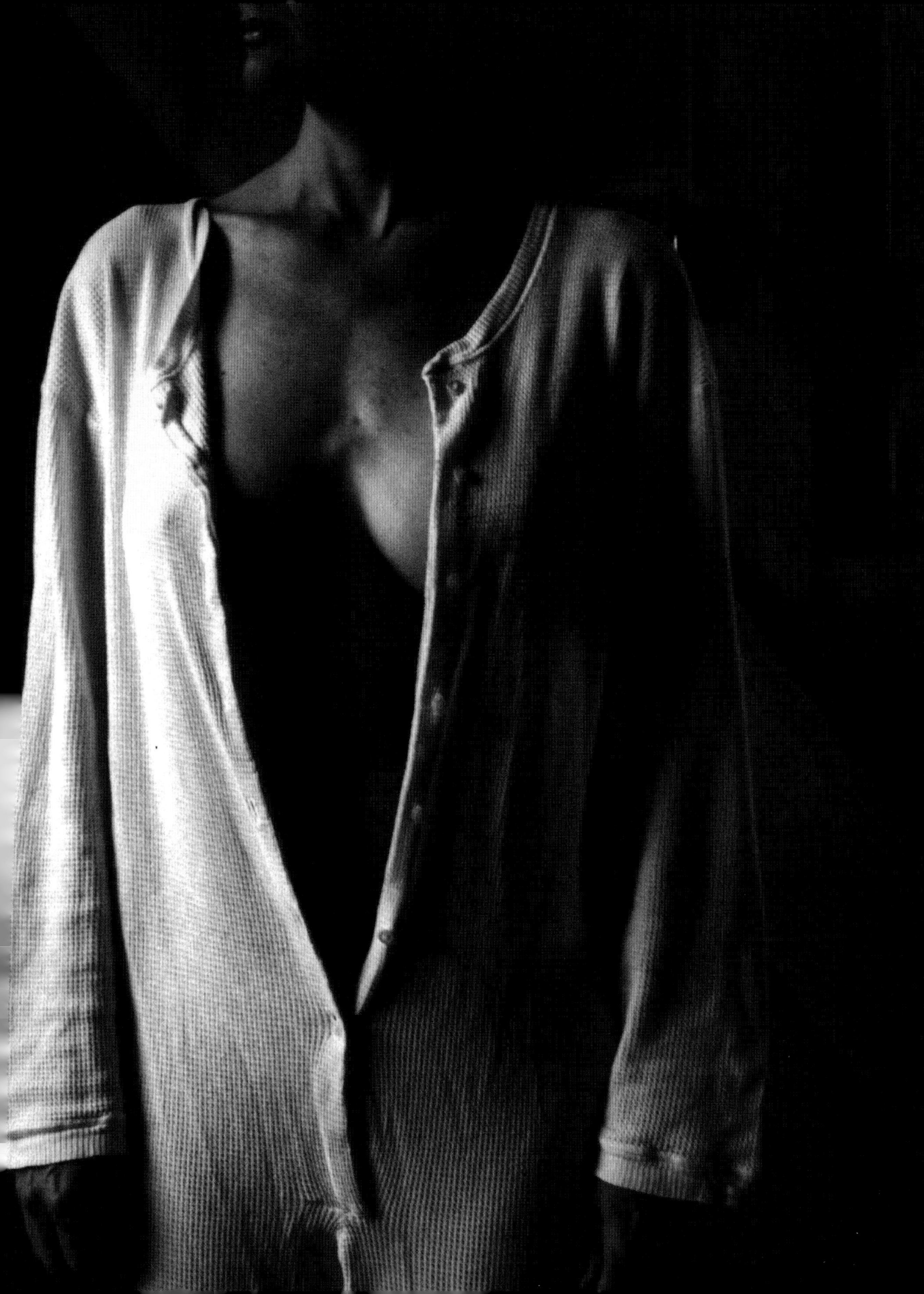

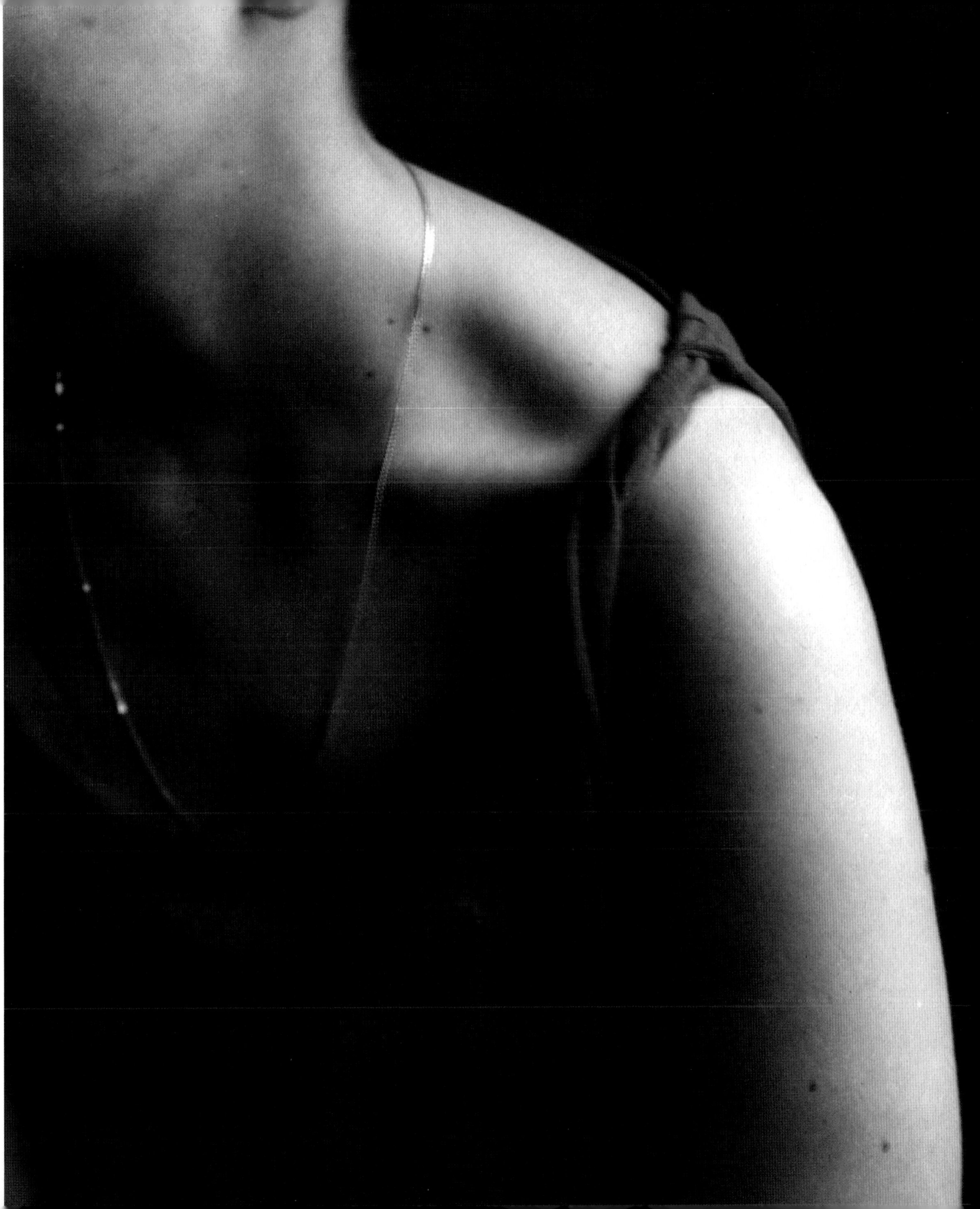

Nude in Long Johns, Fairfax, California, 2000 *(left)*
"Her body in the long johns is so strong, has such a presence. I wanted to take some of the details of the body away, to create this 'V' of a body with the most unglamorous clothing possible. The clothing is plain, the location banal, yet the body remains powerful, almost heroic."

Shoulder, Purchase, New York, 1981 *(right)*
"This image was acquired by the Museum of Modern Art just after I left Purchase. Actually, it was part of my senior show as an undergraduate —a series meant to break away from traditional portraiture. To me, it's strength is in its simplicity, grace of line, and form."

Yuri Dojc

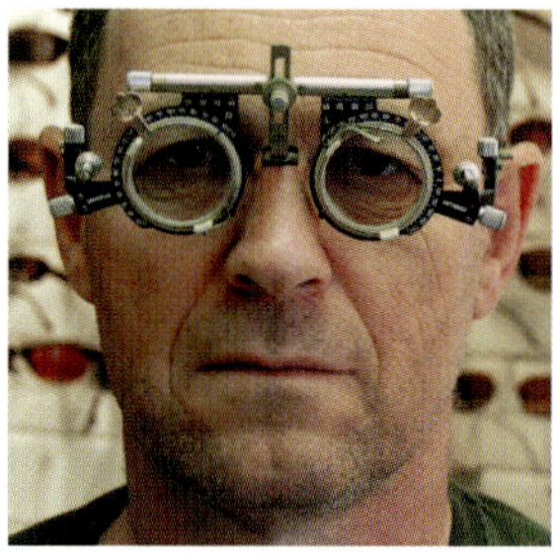

Yuri Dojc has come a long way. In the summer of 1968, while staying in London as a student, his homeland of Czechoslovakia was invaded by Russia. Not able to return home, he remained in London until the following year, when he decided to travel to Toronto, Canada, seeking "dreams of freedom and opportunity." Landing halfway across the world, with exactly six dollars to his name, Dojc had no idea in what direction his life was headed. He tried his hand at being a waiter, a driver, a draftsman, and a laundry deliveryman. None of them stuck. It was then that he discovered photography.

"I happened into photography during a conversation with a roommate of mine about the future," says Dojc. "My plan was to go back to Europe, and he suggested I study photography, something I didn't know squat about. While loitering in the hallways of Ryerson Arts College I came upon a faculty member, and we got to talking about photography, and I was admitted into the school without a portfolio or even my own camera."

Dojc clearly made the most of his education. Freelancing since the early 1970s, he delved into the advertising field, working for clients ranging from ING Direct to Bell and the Bank of Montreal. He went on to win dozens of national and international awards over the next three decades. His photograph *Fish Kiss*, chosen by Kodak for a national campaign, has been copied and imitated so extensively that Dojc has won several lawsuits defending it. His images have appeared in magazines across the world and have become part of several public collections, including the Canadian Museum of Contemporary Photography in Ottawa.

But aside from his commercial success, it is Dojc's nude and erotic work that has brought him the greatest acclaim. His black-and-white studies are widely recognizable, especially his image *Legs*, which was one of the biggest-selling posters of the 1980s. His 1993 book, *Marble Woman* (Firefly Books), was also highly acclaimed, and in 2003 the Italian magazine *L'Espresso* included Dojc in a series of monographs of the work of 17 well-known erotic photographers, including Robert Mapplethorpe, Man Ray, Ellen Von Unwerth, David LaChappelle, and Bill Brandt.

Dojc tends to combine a classic impression of the nude with a sense of humor. Many of Dojc's images are whimsical ventures that, as he puts it, are "equal parts mystery, serendipity, and happenstance." He also has a knack for finding the perfect prop for his models. Everything from tiny plastic dinosaurs and farm animals to musical instruments have adorned his photographs. "Each individual is different," says Dojc. "The perspective I capture through my lens is unique to my vantage and my vision."

An admirer of Guy Bourdin—"I could not wait to get hold of French *Vogue* to see what he'd come up with next"—Dojc brings his wife into the studio for a few minutes before a shoot and uses

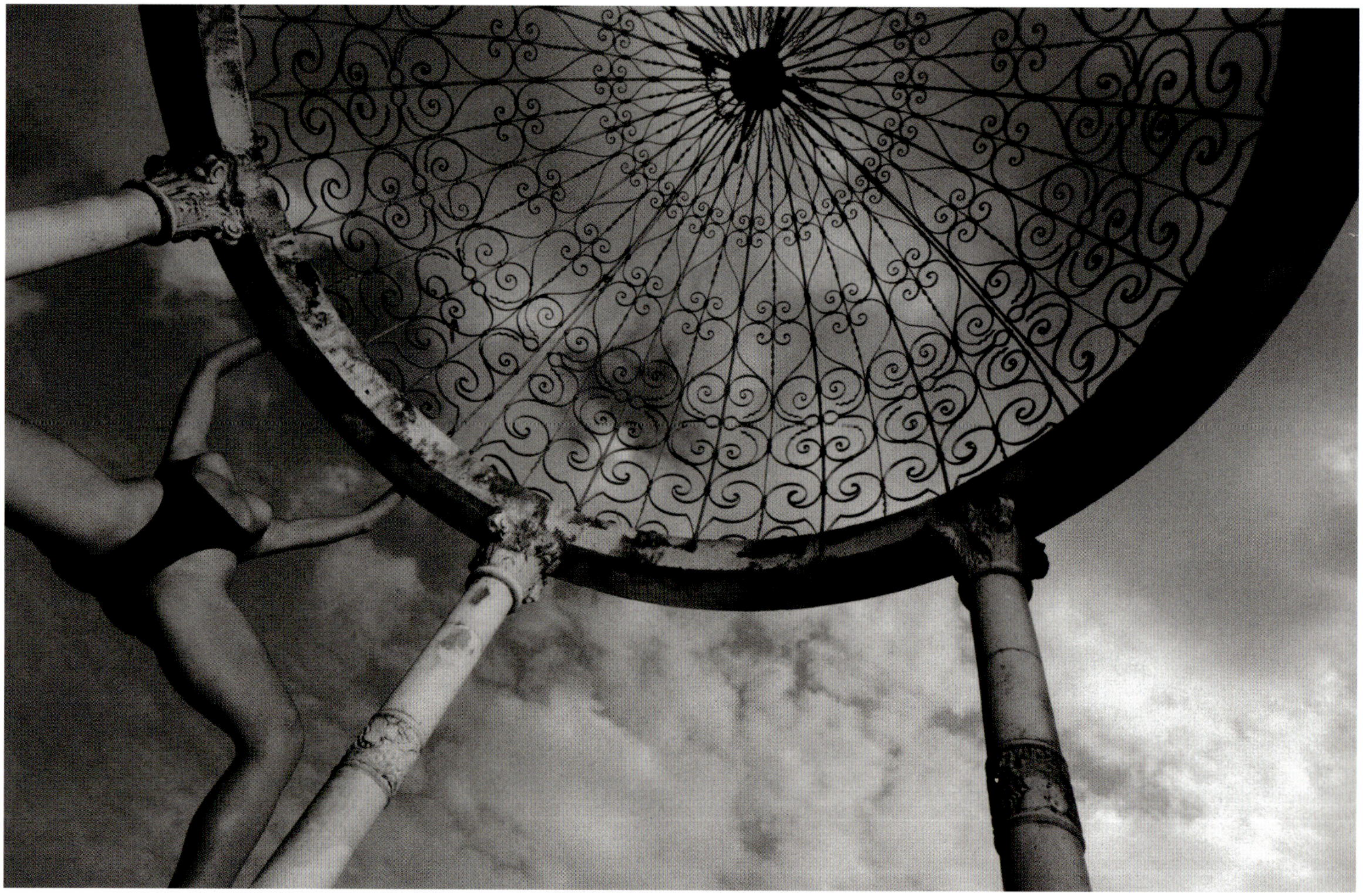

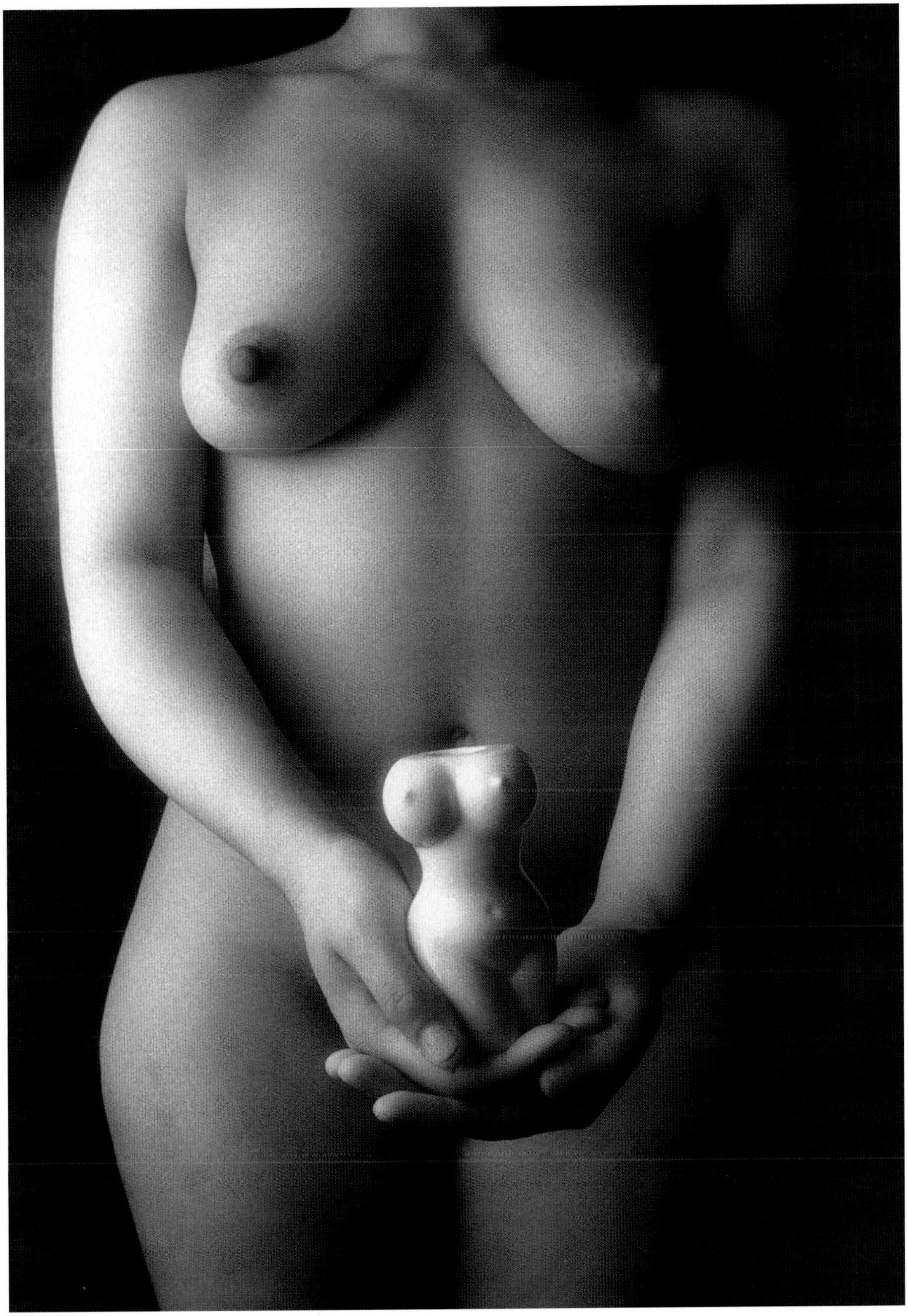

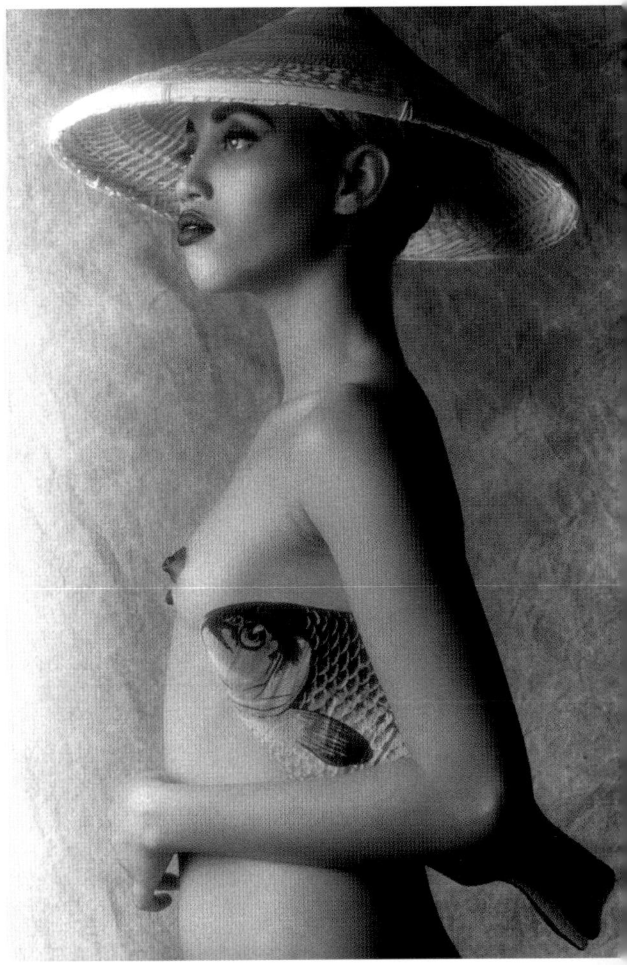

Spider Woman, 1985 *(opposite)*
"It is obvious why people are attracted to the world of nude photography, but it is the high-end nudes that are interesting to me. They are like a breath of fresh air in a world suffocated by porno."

Fisherman's Wife, 1988 *(above)*

Venus, 1989 *(left)*

Yuri Dojc

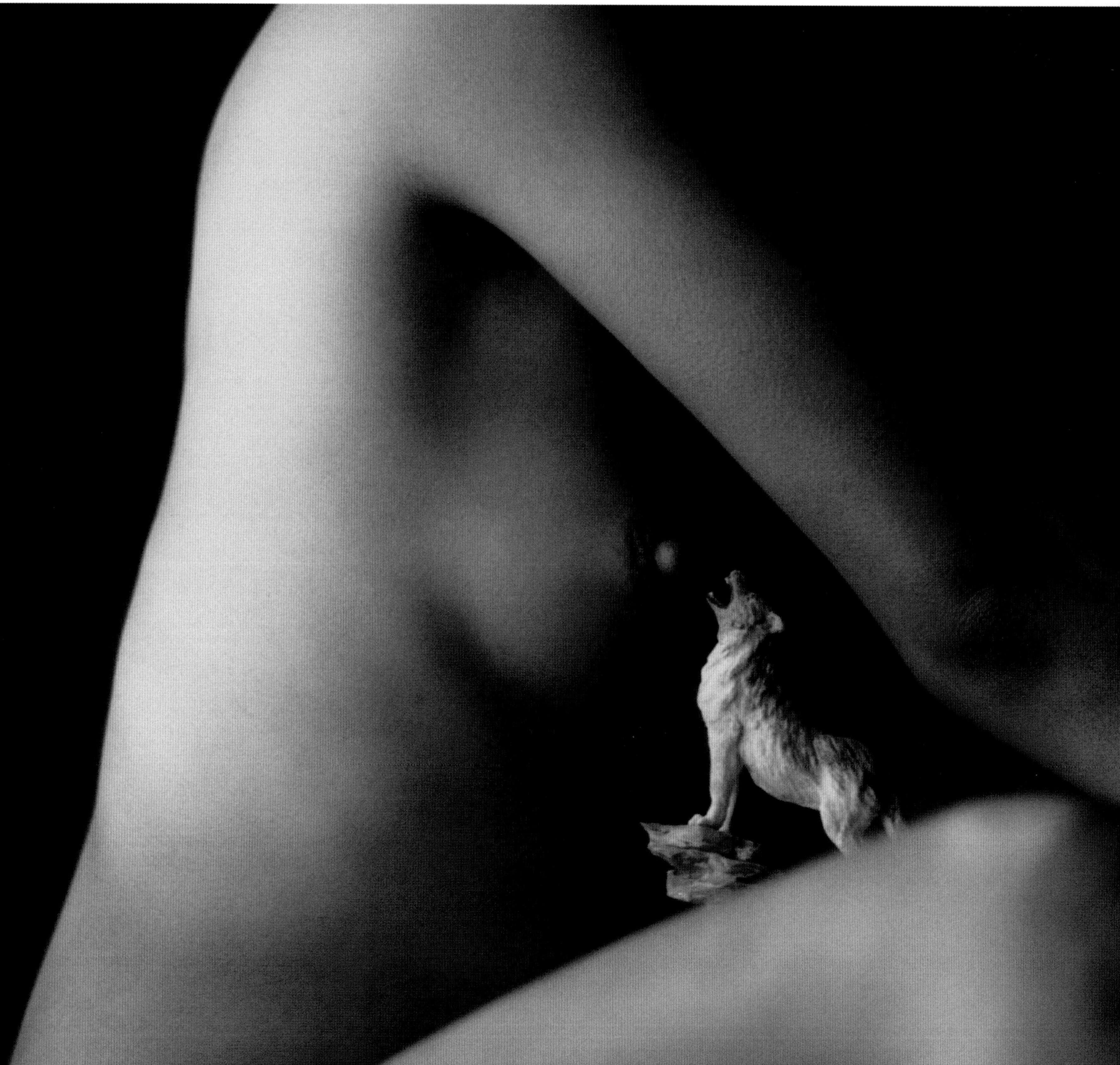

female assistants in order to make his subjects feel more comfortable. Using different types of SLR and 6x6 in the past, Dojc now prefers a high-end digital SLR, along with his favorite piece of equipment—natural light.

Today, Dojc has moved away from black-and-white, studio imagery into color work, producing some of the most compelling photographs of his career. His series, *Nude in House*, is an engaging, unique turn for Dojc. Placing models inside the home, Dojc uses familiar household items such as teapots, dishwashers, televisions, and kitchen sinks as props. *Nude in House* has added an original twist to his quest to provide, as he puts it, "shock, awe, and enlightenment" for viewers.

"Apart from being color versus strictly black and white, the setting of this series—the houses of models and friends—is a major departure from my nude studio studies of the past," says Dojc, who calls his new locations "a cozier yet creatively combustive" environment. "I had a strong attachment to the studio, and it was hard to leave, but in order to produce stronger work I had to make the change. It was a very freeing experience."

"Nude photography is so serious," says Whitney Lawson, photography editor at nerve.com, one of the most respected Web sites in the world dealing with nude photography. "Even worse than serious, it is often really respectful. I think it has to do with how many great photographic nudes there are—what a classic subject the female form is in art. Photographers know they are paying tribute to the greats when they make nude pictures.

"Yuri Dojc seems to be having none of it, possibly because his influences are more film and fashion—think David Lynch meets Guy Bourdin. His women are not timeless forms, rather they are retro (desperate?) housewives from hell, characters in a noir that takes place in the vivid light of day, captured just before, or just after, something has happened. The dishwasher fallen open on a dead-looking pair of legs makes one think of the house falling on the Wicked Witch of the East in *The Wizard of Oz*. Like Dorothy [in that film], you are left a little bit horrified. And then doubly horrified that you might find such a thing funny! I hope his work catches on with the next generation of young photographers. Yuri would make a great guru."

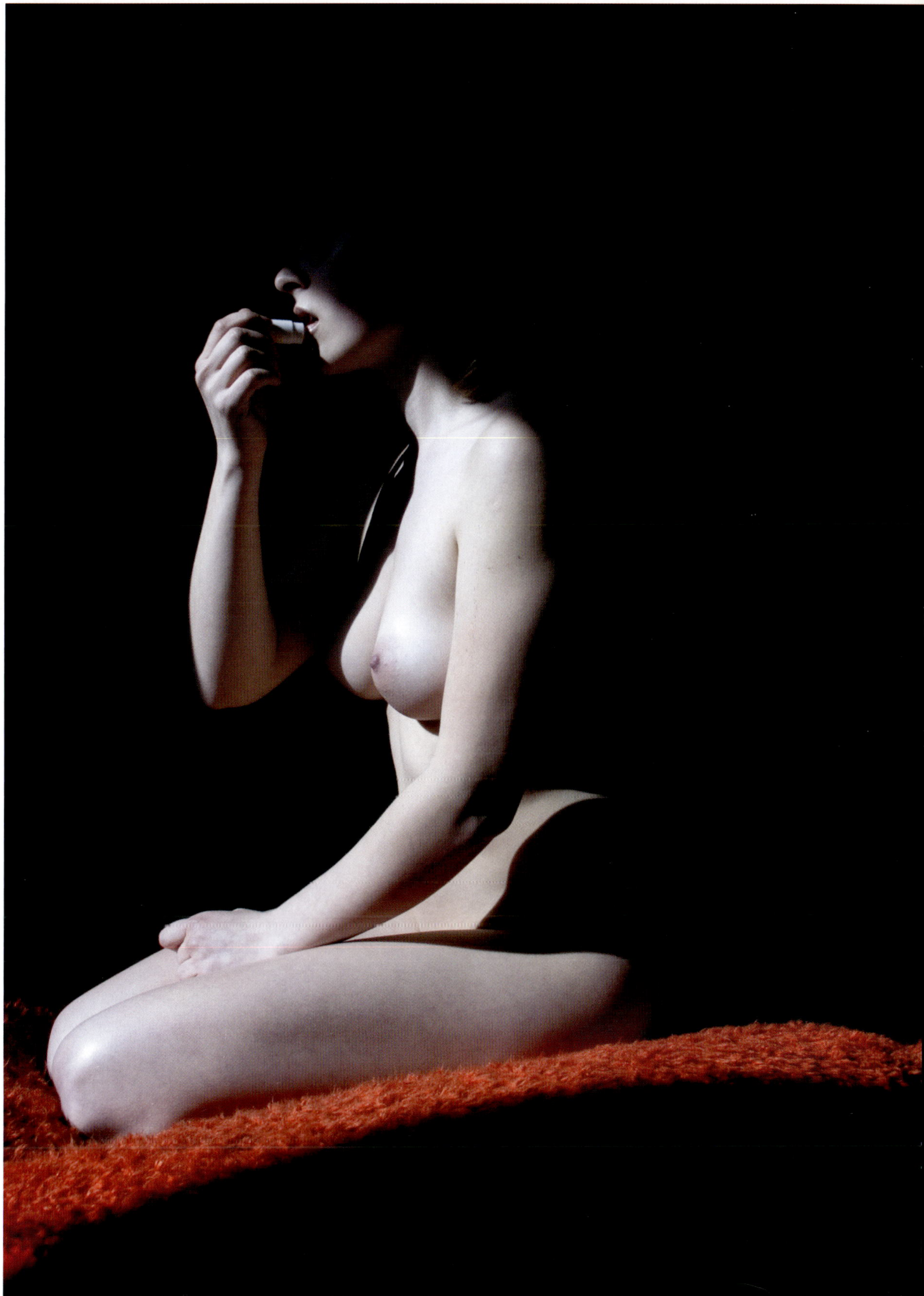

Howling Wolf, 1995 ***(left)***

Lipstick, 2003

Tea, 2004
"*Nude in House* is my newest venture into exploring the nude subject. It began when I got tired of shooting in the studio and found the real environment much more stimulating. It was a logical transition for me from my old work."

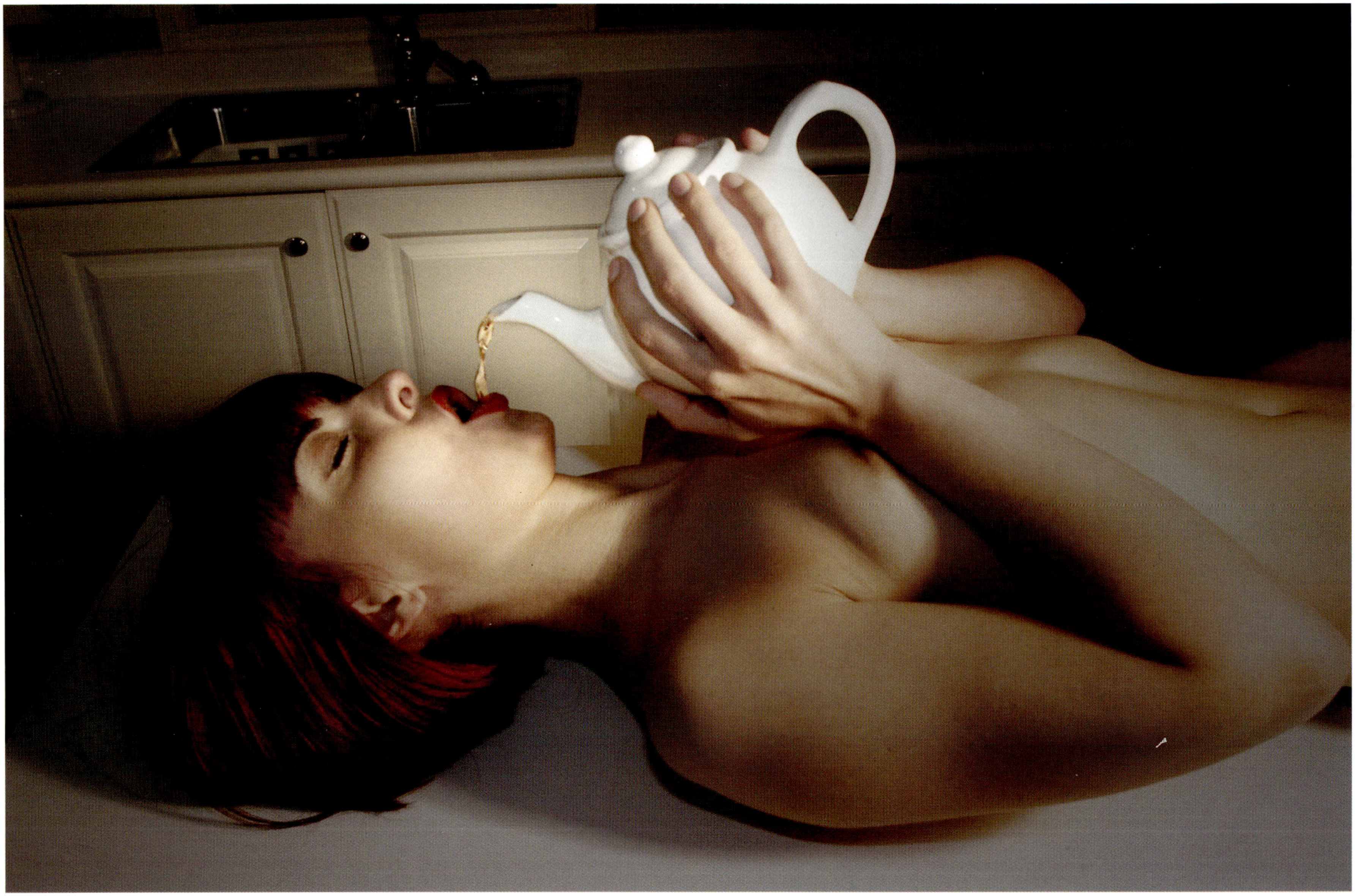

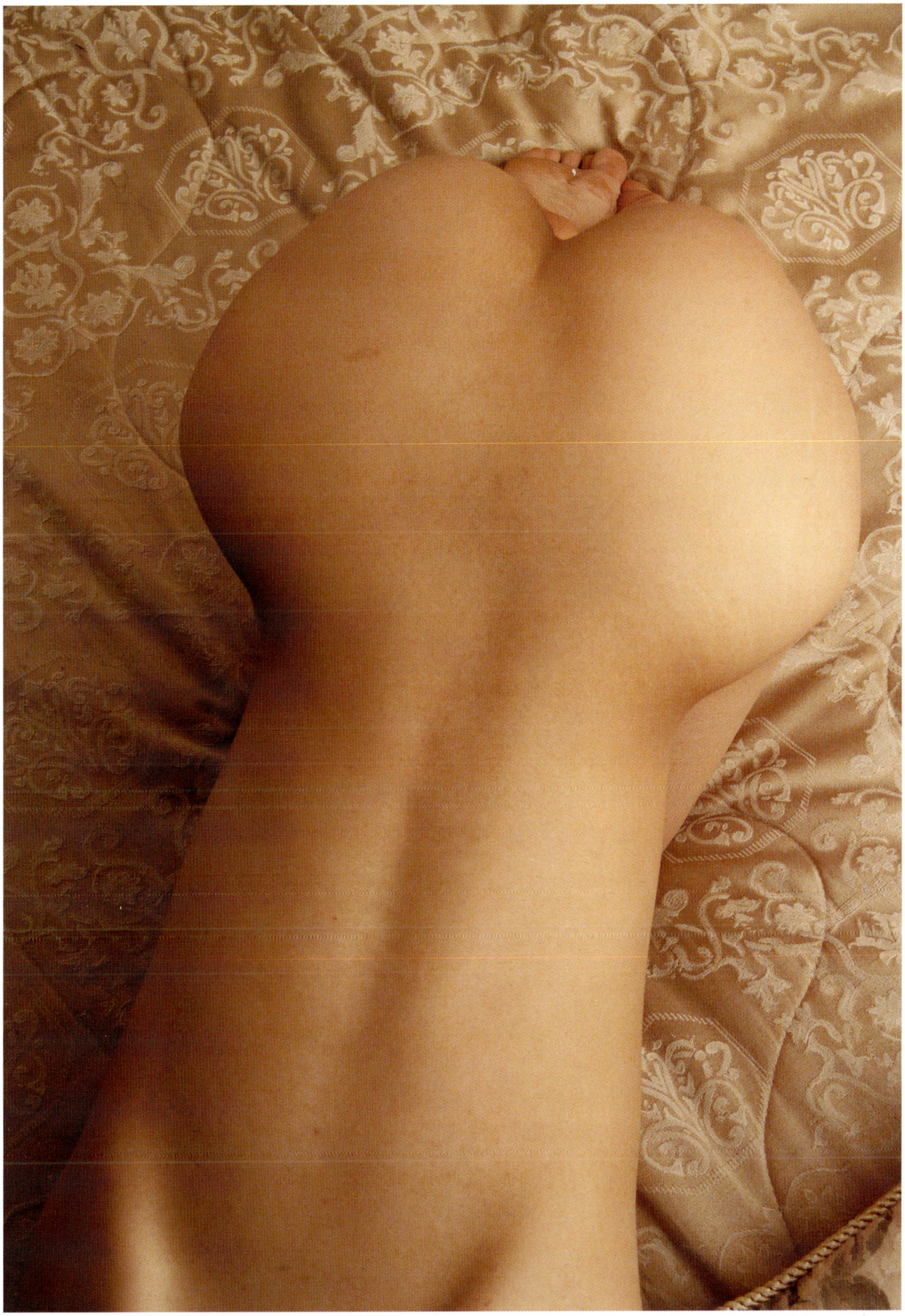

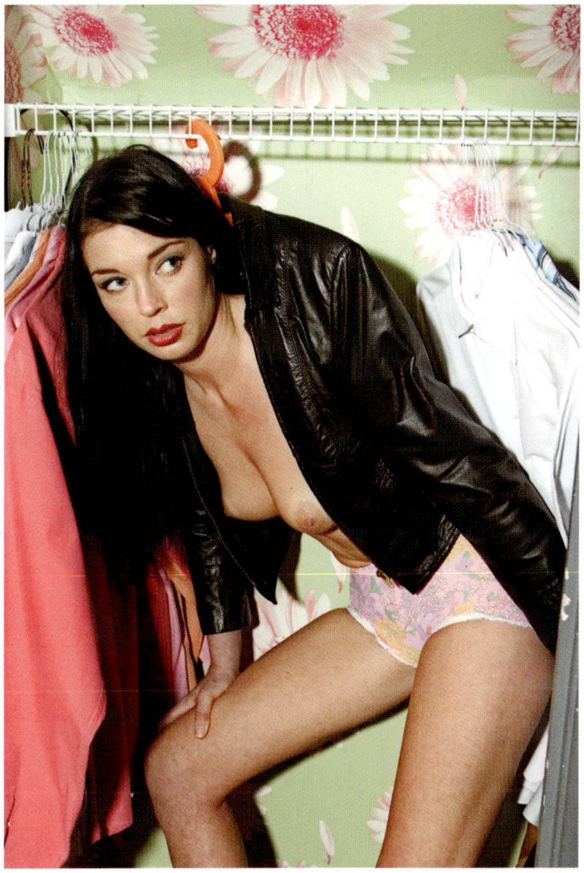

Body, 2002 *(left)*

Closet, 2002

Robert Farber

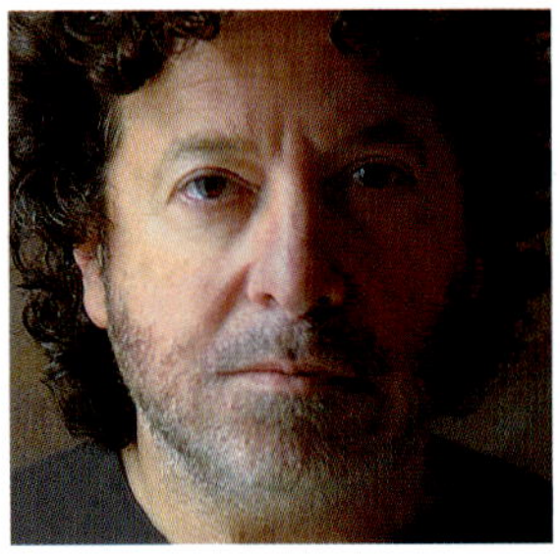

Through a steady stream of books, a pair of popular Web sites, and a busy schedule of workshop teaching, New York-based photographer Robert Farber has quietly had a profound impact on the field of nude photography during the past 30 years. Where others have pushed the envelope of erotic art, exploring the sensational and the taboo, Farber has been a force for restraint, championing a discrete aesthetic of painterly good taste. He is a master of the romantic mood.

"Mood is just capturing a feeling the way I see it," Farber explains. "I see light in a dramatic way. I'm after a certain mood, a romance, sensitivity, and a sense of wanting to be there. When I shoot a nude, unless it's a portrait or a beauty shot, I keep the face turned away. I think that keeps it from being an invasion of privacy and creates a certain mystique about it. I like to shoot a nude as if I'm not there."

Classic Farber nudes (appropriately, also the title of one of his books) are portraits of female modesty, often depicting only a model's bare back, a woman turned away from the prying eye of the camera lens, or with her genitals lightly draped or shadowed. But what animates Farber is the same primal attraction that inspires most photographers of the nude. "There is nothing more beautiful than a beautiful woman," he says simply.

Farber was born in Newark, New Jersey, grew up in South Orange, and attended the University of Miami for two and a half years in the 1960s. Although he painted as a student, he did not major in art or photography. His family felt that a college education should have a more practical focus, such as medicine, law, or accounting. But it was as a student in Miami that Farber discovered his true calling—albeit in a less-than-romantic fashion.

"I was walking on the beach and I saw this woman knitting," Farber recalls. "She was wearing the smallest string bikini I had ever seen. There weren't many string bikinis in the 1960s, and she weighed about 400 pounds. I remember thinking, 'I wish I had a camera.'"

When Farber did purchase a camera and started photographing in earnest, his nudes possessed a painterly look from the very beginning. Indeed, there are Farber nudes that look as though Vermeer might have come back as a contemporary photographer, shooting women by window light just as he painted them in the 17th century.

Farber says, "I have always been influenced by the directional light of the Dutch- and Flemish-school painters, and also by the soft focus of some impressionist painters."

In the early 1970s, Farber began showing his nudes, still lifes, and landscapes at outdoor art shows around New York. In fact, in

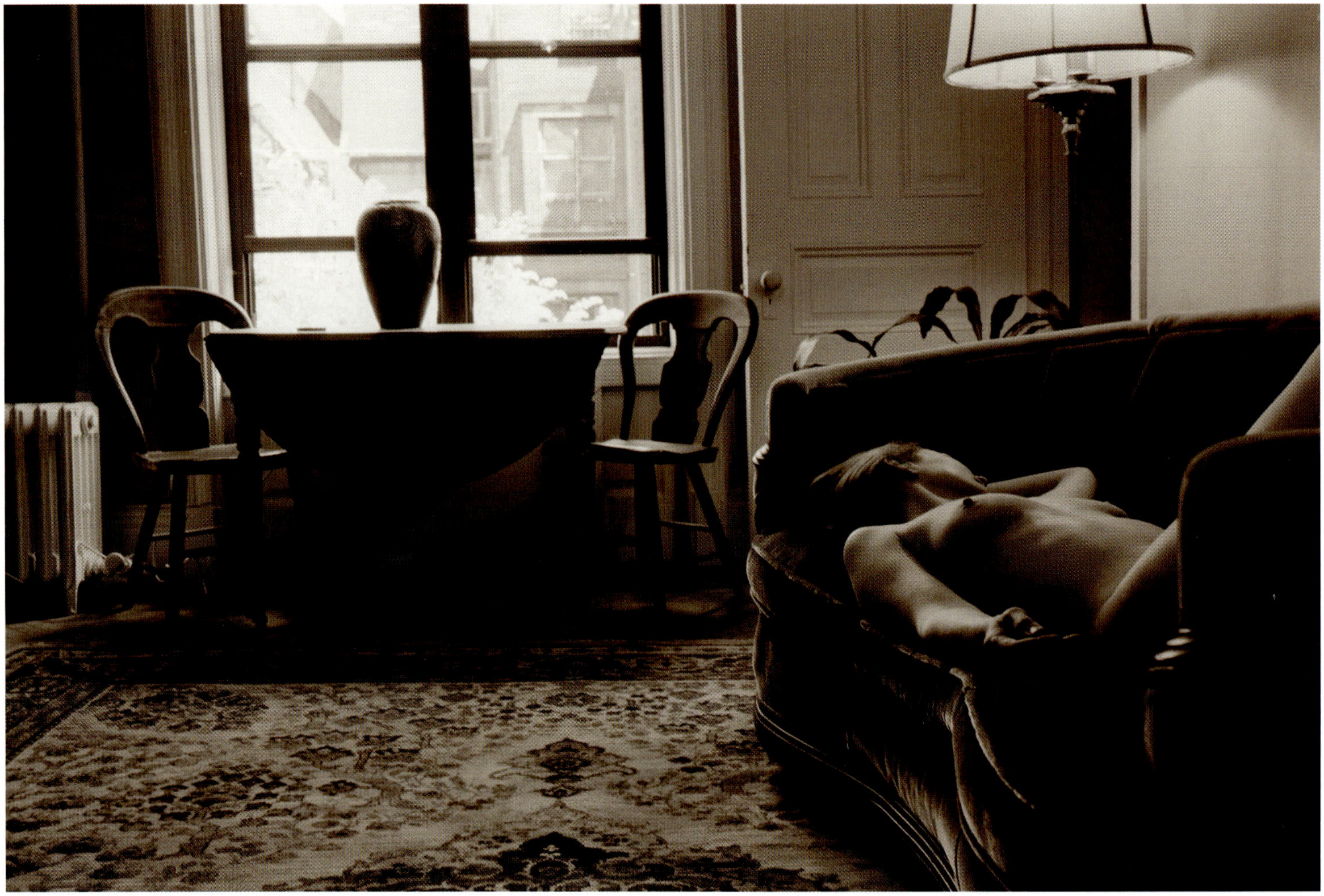

Quiet Room, 1991 *(right)*
"The model is lying on a couch with her face turned away, but the focal point is the mood of the room itself, which is created by a lot of natural light."

Two Women, 1975 *(opposite)*
"This is one of the originals in *Images of Woman*. I was shooting one model in the studio when another model came in, so I photographed them together. It's very grainy and has a nice feeling to it."

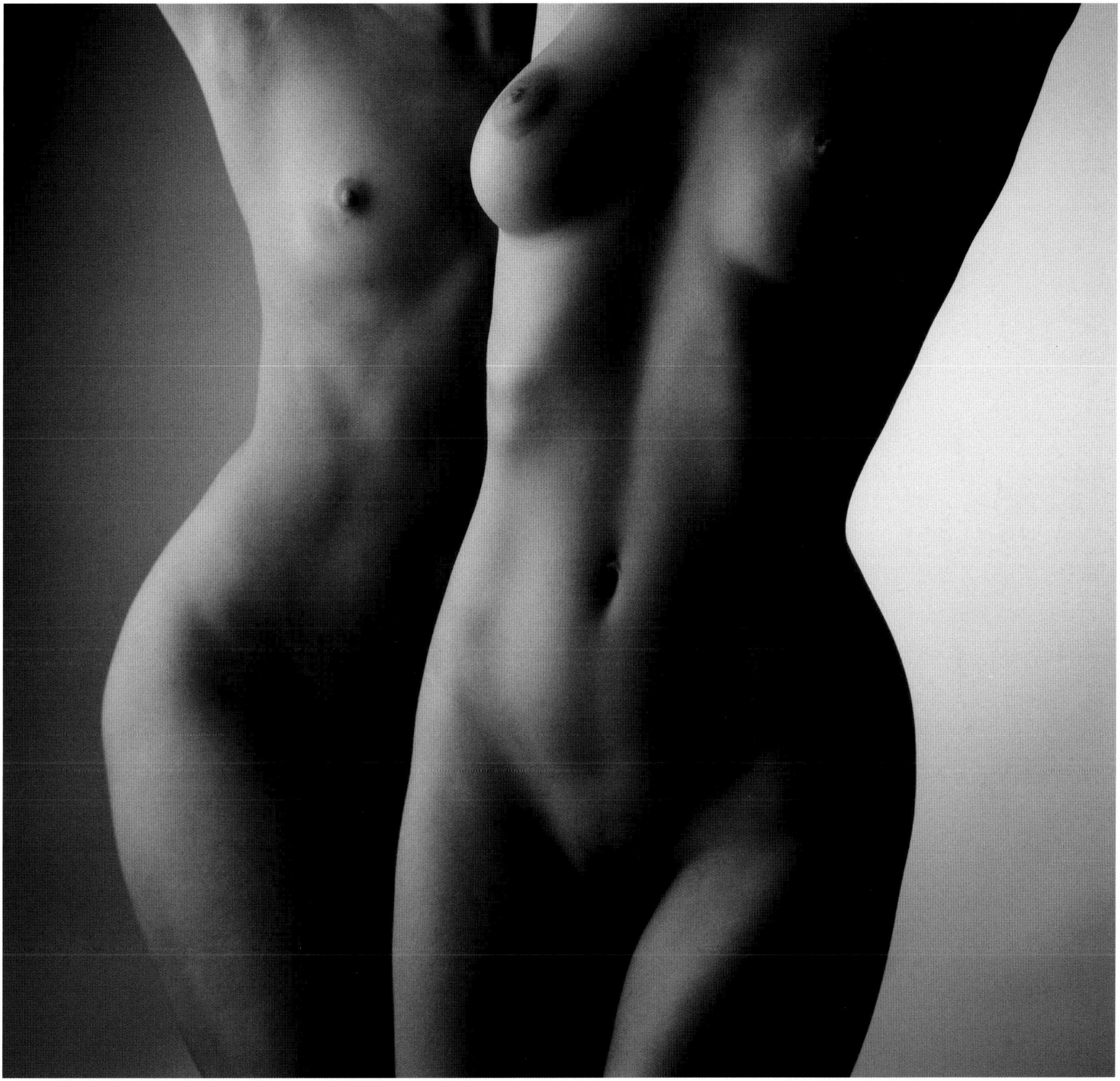

Robert Farber

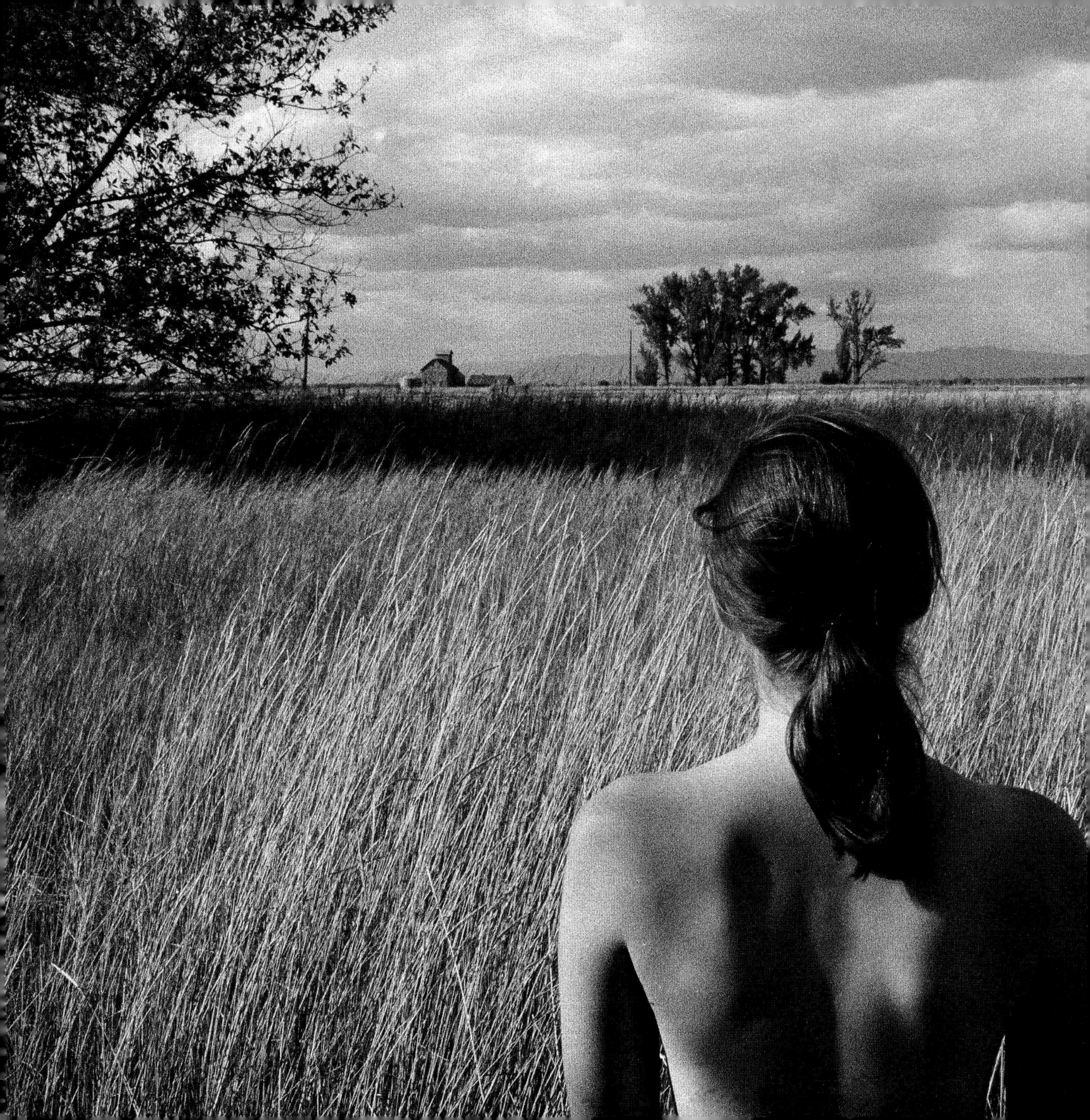

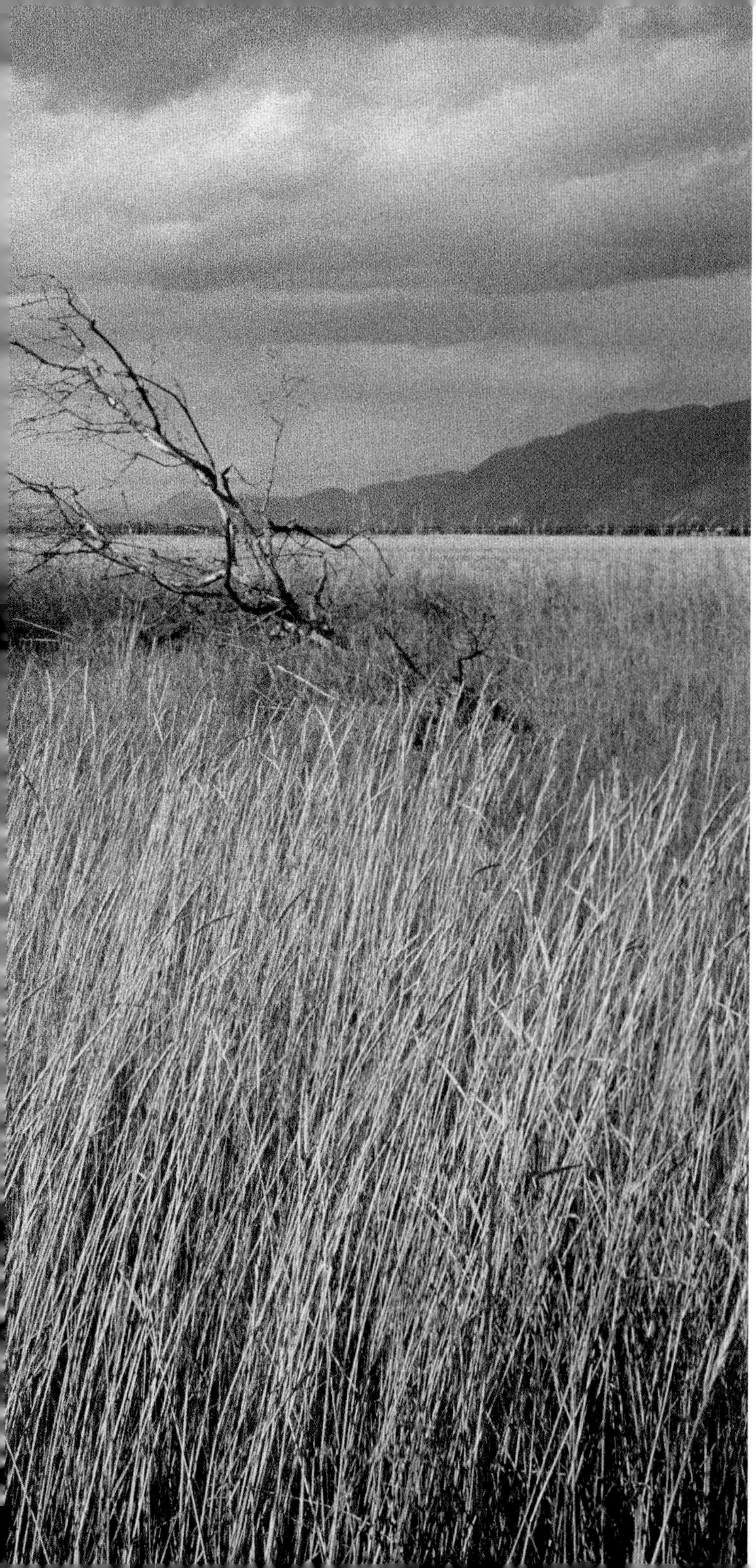

Seeing Montana, 1990
"In a way, this has an [American realist painter] Andrew Wyeth's *Christina's World* feel about it. I was traveling with a former girlfriend who happened to photograph well. In *American Mood* there is a photograph of an old barn in Montana. Then I swung back and took this photograph of the model in the field. It was two shots for the price of one."

one infamous incident, he was asked to remove his photographs from an outdoor exhibition in Greenwich Village when the show's director discovered they were not paintings.

The distinctively moody look of a Farber nude became well known in 1976 when he published *Images of Woman* (American Photographic). His first book was quickly followed by a series of successful books that both publicized his work and advanced his career. *Fashion Photography* (American Photographic, 1978), *Moods* (American Photographic, 1980), *The Fashion Photographer* (Watson-Guptill, 1981), and *Farber Nudes* (Columbus Books, 1983) brought Farber to the attention of Jacqueline Kennedy Onassis, who, in her late career as a book editor, suggested a book of nudes, still lifes, and landscapes taken at seaside resorts. *By the Sea* (Melrose Square) came out in 1987. When Jackie O's estate was auctioned off, her copy of *Farber Nudes* sold for $4,800.

Farber's more recent books include *Classic Farber Nudes: Twenty Years of Photography* (Amphoto Books, 1991), *Natural Beauty* (Merrell, 2001), a revised edition of *Natural Beauty* retitled *Natural Beauty, Farber Nudes* (Merrell, 2001), and *Robert Farber: American Mood* (Merrell, 2004).

In 1994, Farber was one of the first major photographers to establish his own Web site, Farber.com, as a gallery of his work. Farber.com is now linked to an even more ambitious educational Web site, Photoworkshop.com, where Farber maintains an Internet workshop, and promotes his own work and that of other contemporary photographers through the online magazine *double eXposure*. Photoworkshop.com has become Canon's official educational Web site, receiving 30,000 unique visitors a day from an expanding universe of 85,000 registered users and 2,500 paying members.

Despite the how-to nature of Photoworkshop.com, Farber insists he is not much of a techie. "When I'm shooting nudes, I'm not going to shoot like a commercial assignment. I like to work one-on-one with minimal equipment, just one body with a 28 to 125 zoom," he says. "I use a Canon EOS-1N for film, but lately I'm doing more and more digital. I wasn't shooting any digital at all until this past year, but now I'm almost exclusively digital."

Working with the Canon EOS 1DS Mark II and the Canon 20D, Farber says, has forced him to find digital ways to achieve the grainy, painterly effects he has always produced on film. "I've always tried to get a personality out of film. That's harder to do with digital because digital is so clean," he says. "You have to work it when you're shooting, because I'm not big on postproduction. What you shoot is what you get." Farber finds he can achieve that "Farber look" by underexposing, dragging the shutter, filtering, and blurring with motion.

Ironically, while Farber is justly famous for the discreet charm of his tasteful nudes, he does not consider himself primarily a photographer of the nude. "I've published 70 posters, and only 20 of them are nudes, but when I published *By the Sea*, people said, 'Oh, I didn't know you did that.' My work has always been more about landscape and still-life, but I wind up doing more nudes than anything else."

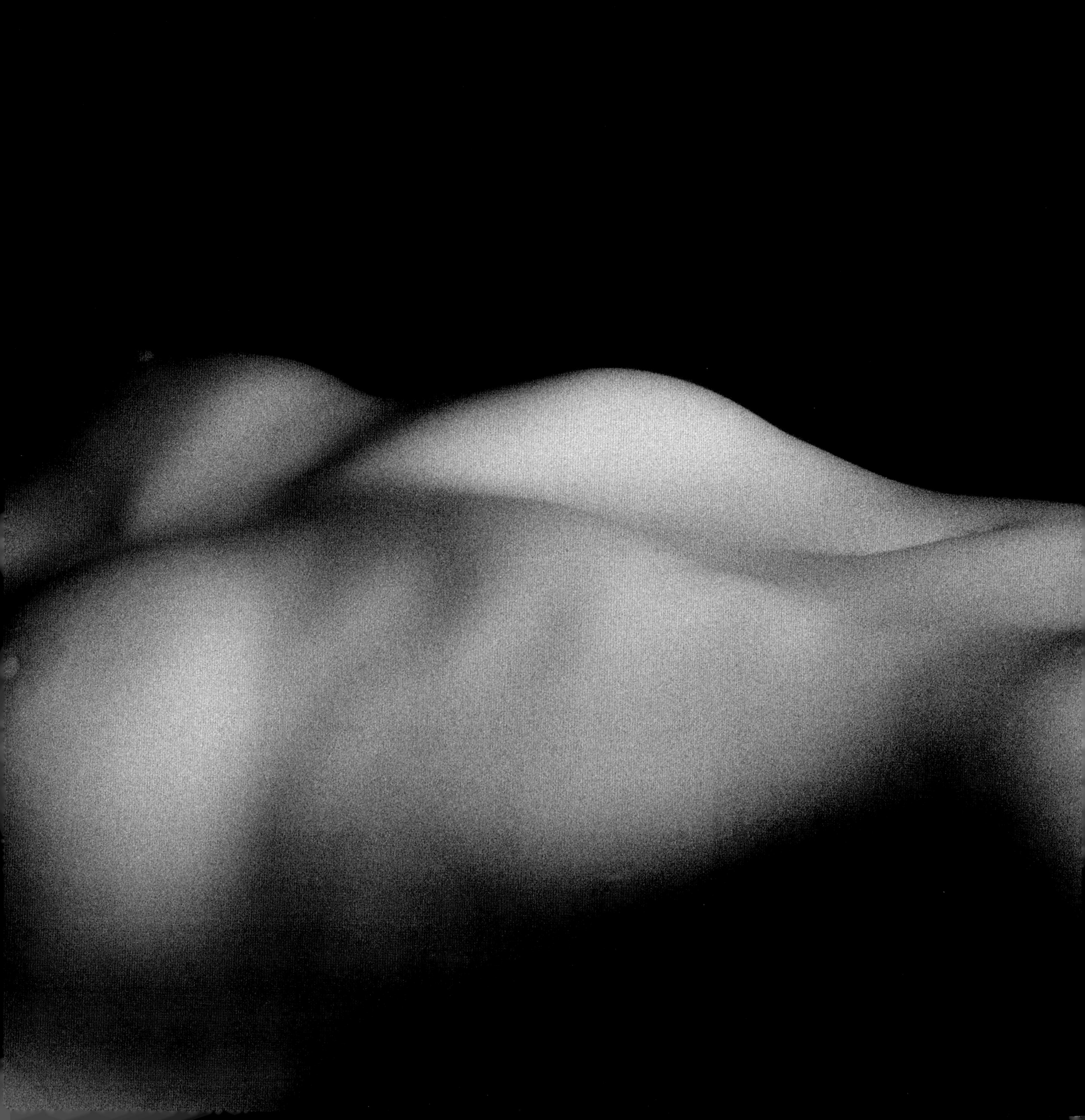

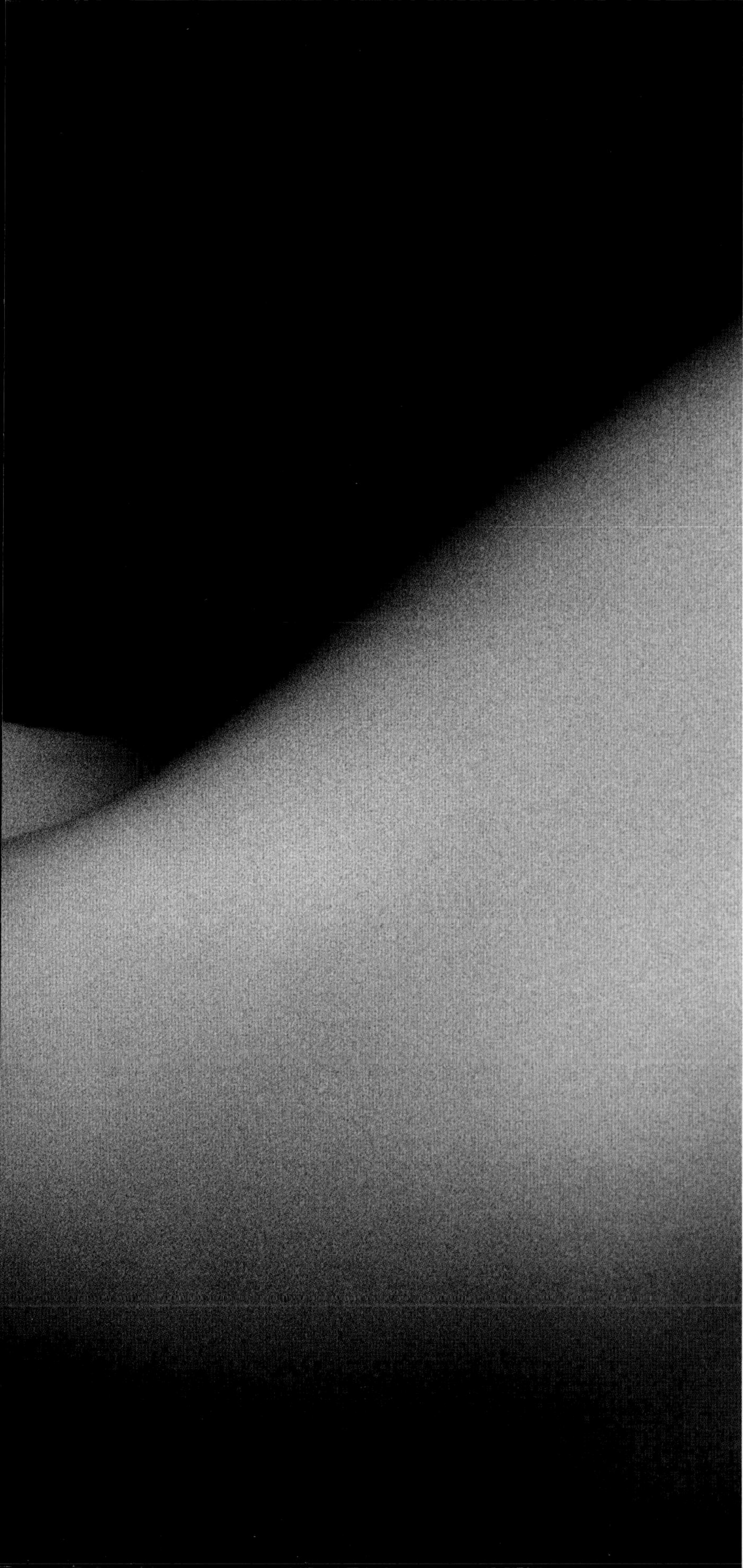

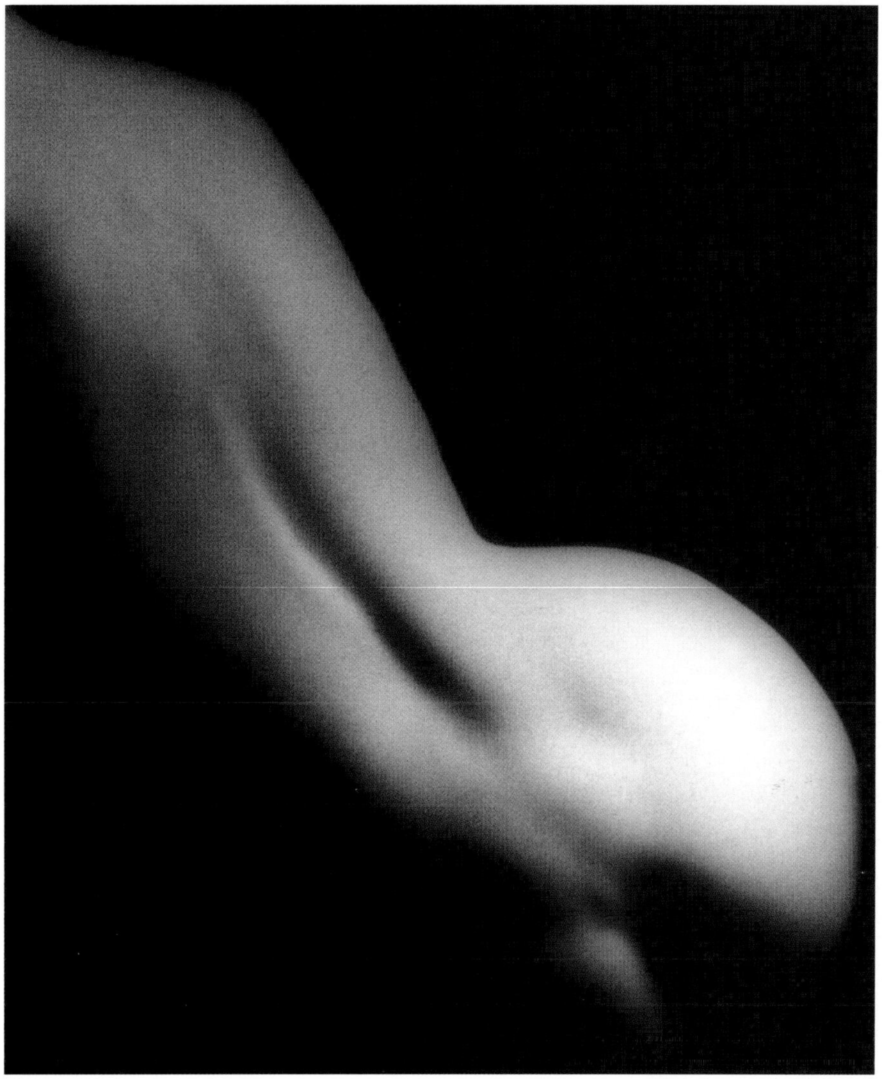

Torso, 1983 *(left)*
"With the stark black background and the clean line of the woman's torso, this photograph has a certain graphical quality to it. I like the clean line and the gradations of light into dark."

From the Back, 1994
"This is a woman with her legs out horizontal and her head down. The warm tones give it a subtle pastel feel. It has a feeling and mood I like."

Robert Farber

Greg Friedler

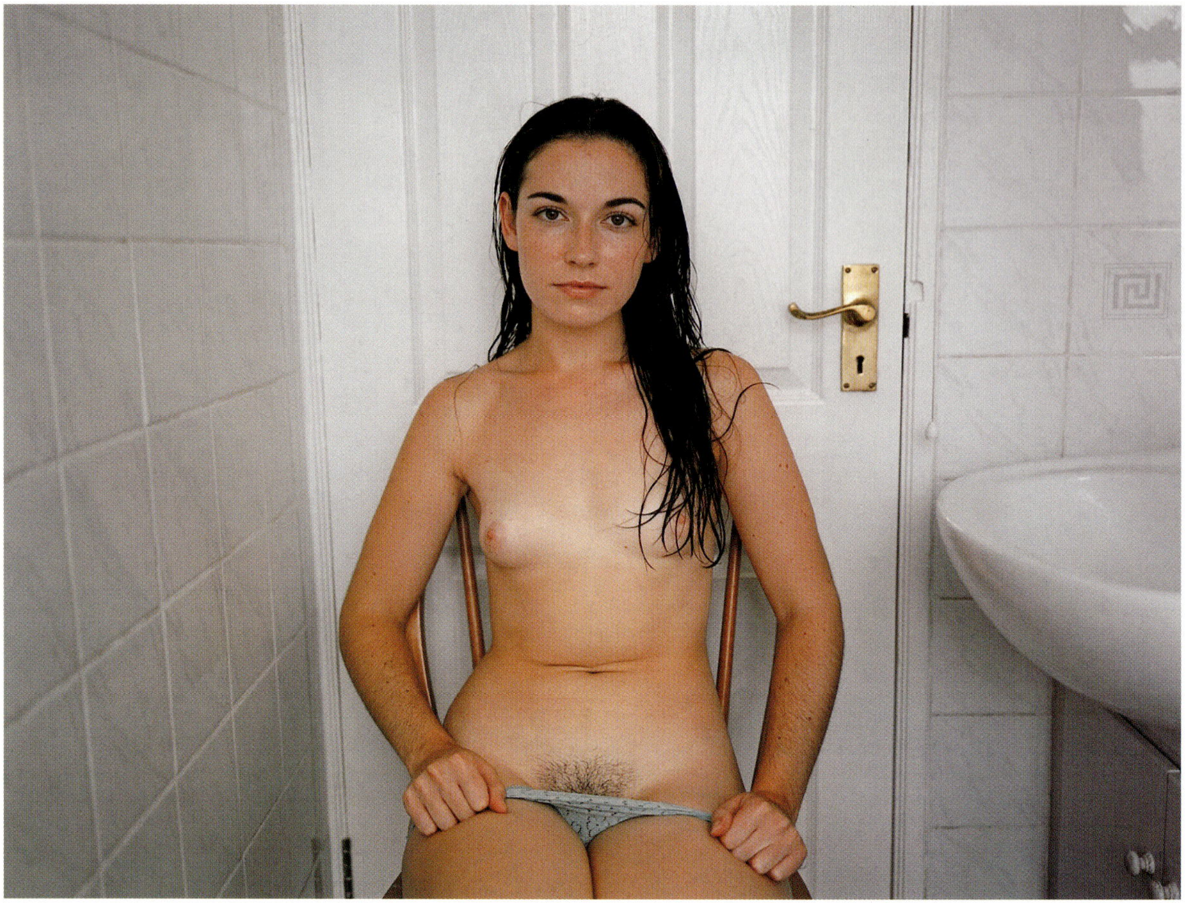

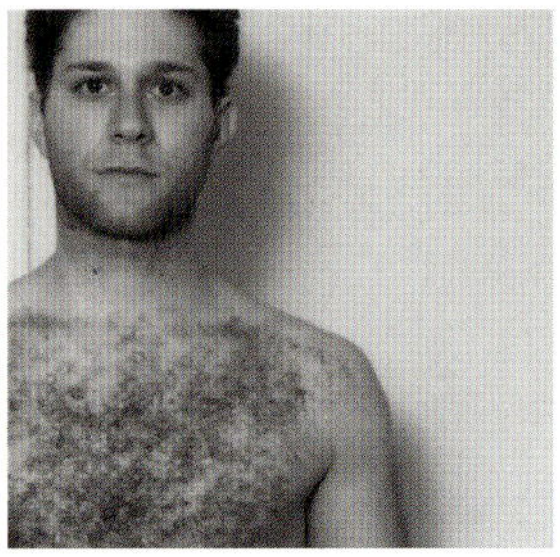

Pilar Number 11, 1999 *(below)* "This was shot at the model's Brooklyn apartment. I used my Mamiya 7 and strong natural light beaming in through a small window. I had been photographing her in the tub in and out of clothes for some time. I was shooting in color in one camera and black and white in another. I was taking a portrait of her when she made this gesture and yawned, and I captured it on film. I like the photo because we feel like we are seeing a private moment, almost like voyeurs. She is not looking at the camera as in my other portraits."

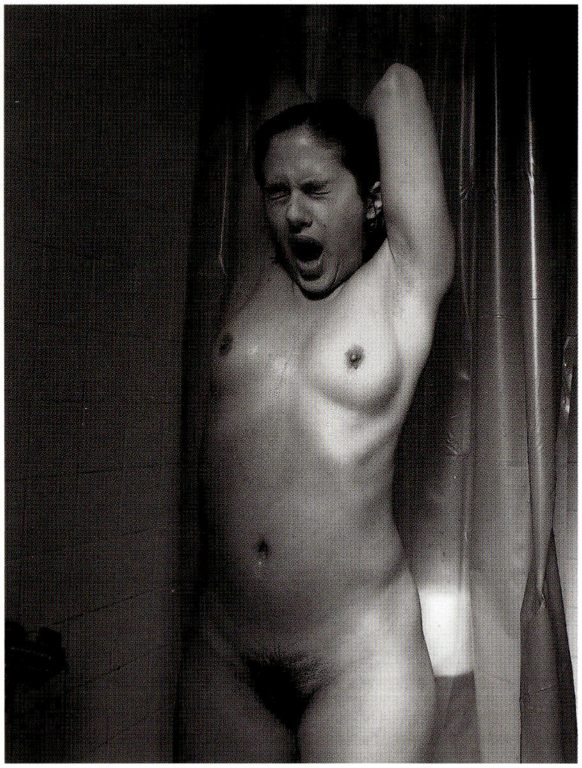

Greg Friedler's images offer a simple answer to the age-old question, "What would that person look like with no clothes on?" Using everyday people from all walks of life, chosen city by city, Friedler photographs his subjects first clothed and then naked in the same pose, then juxtaposes the two images. The results are revealing in every sense, and moving.

"I like nude photographs that reveal something about the person," he says. Friedler's elementary, side-by-side images have filled the pages of three W. W. Norton publications: *Naked New York* (1997), *Naked Los Angeles* (1998), and *Naked London* (2000). "Yet most nude photographs do not do this because the 'nude' does not represent the person but more of an ideal or our conventions of beauty."

Friedler was born in 1970 in New Orleans. He attended the University of Colorado and then received his MFA in photography from the School of Visual Arts in New York in 1996. The idea for his nude city project came about in 1995, after Friedler placed an ad in the *Village Voice* looking for models.

"I had about 20 people respond, and I initially interviewed them, wanting to know about their lives," says Friedler. "I first thought that I would shoot them naked in a studio, but then I thought a more natural setting would be better. At some point it occurred to me that I was interested in the whole person and not just the naked person. I wanted to include what they did for a living and their age, as a study of society seen both clothed and unclothed. I did New York because that is where I was living, and I then followed up with Los Angeles because it is the other really large American city. Also, because they are such polar opposites. I did London because I love that city, and because I was told that I would not be able to find enough people to photograph. When I finished I had photographed more people in London than I had in any other city. There was even a documentary made for television about the making of *Naked London*."

The images are striking and candid—a refreshing, unfettered look at the ordinary human, first dressed in their choice of clothing, then undressed, without the facade of fabric.

"I take very powerful nude portraits," says Friedler. "I like to have eye contact with the models because I am interested in the person, not just the body or 'the nude.' My photos have a certain raw sensuality to them. My photos look natural, because I don't glamorize my models, and I shoot them in an honest manner. They are formally beautiful photos with raw subject matter.

"I try to get beyond the subject's mask or veneer," continues Friedler. "Some of the photos are clinical, almost like medical photos. For me, I like nude photography because people are stripped of their clothes and we are allowed to see this raw, pure, organic being. We get to go beyond the person's public persona and see a more vulnerable person."

Friedler's latest book, *Mattress* (Goliath Books, 2002), does not feature the diptych approach, but still showcases his candid, forthright technique. The photographs exhibit women of all ages and backgrounds lying on an exposed mattress with a floral print.

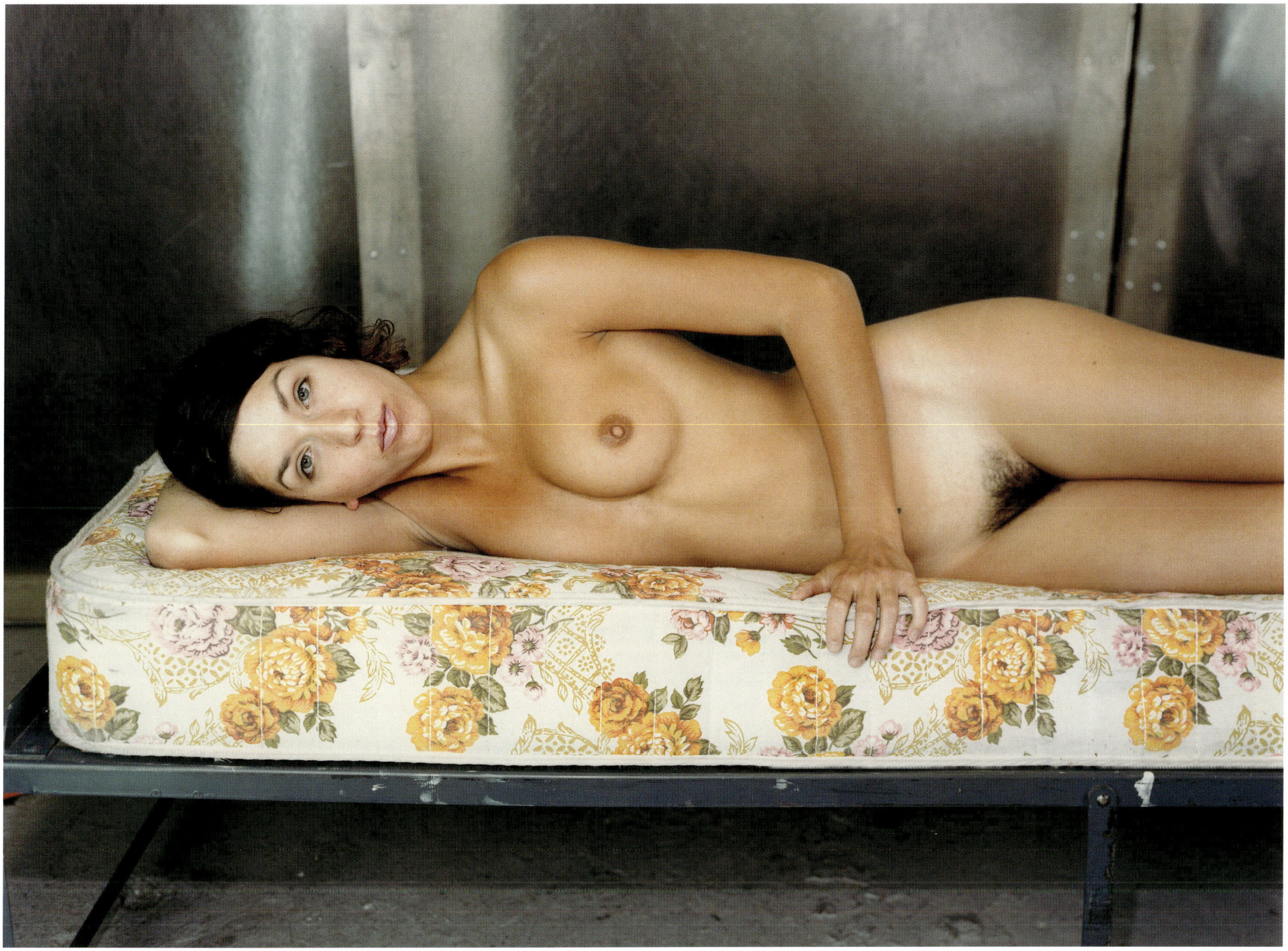

Naked London, Woman with Blue Panties, 1999 *(opposite top)*
"This woman was one of my models for *Naked London*. This was shot in my London apartment. I used my Mamiya 7 and natural light. I like that she tempts the viewer by pulling down her panties enough to see her pubic hair. Because of this gesture, and because of her innocent look, I think this portrait is quite erotic and sensual, much more so than most photos anyway."

Mattress, Number 4, 1998
"This photo was taken in my old New York studio. I shot it with my 4x5 Linhof. I used a bunch of strobes for a rather even-lit look. I originally got the idea for shooting women on the mattress because of a striking Lucian Freud painting. A friend of mine was moving out of his apartment and I helped him out. One of the things that was going out to the trash was a great flowered mattress. The model was referred to me by another photographer. She was great to work with because she had an open energy and I really connected with her."

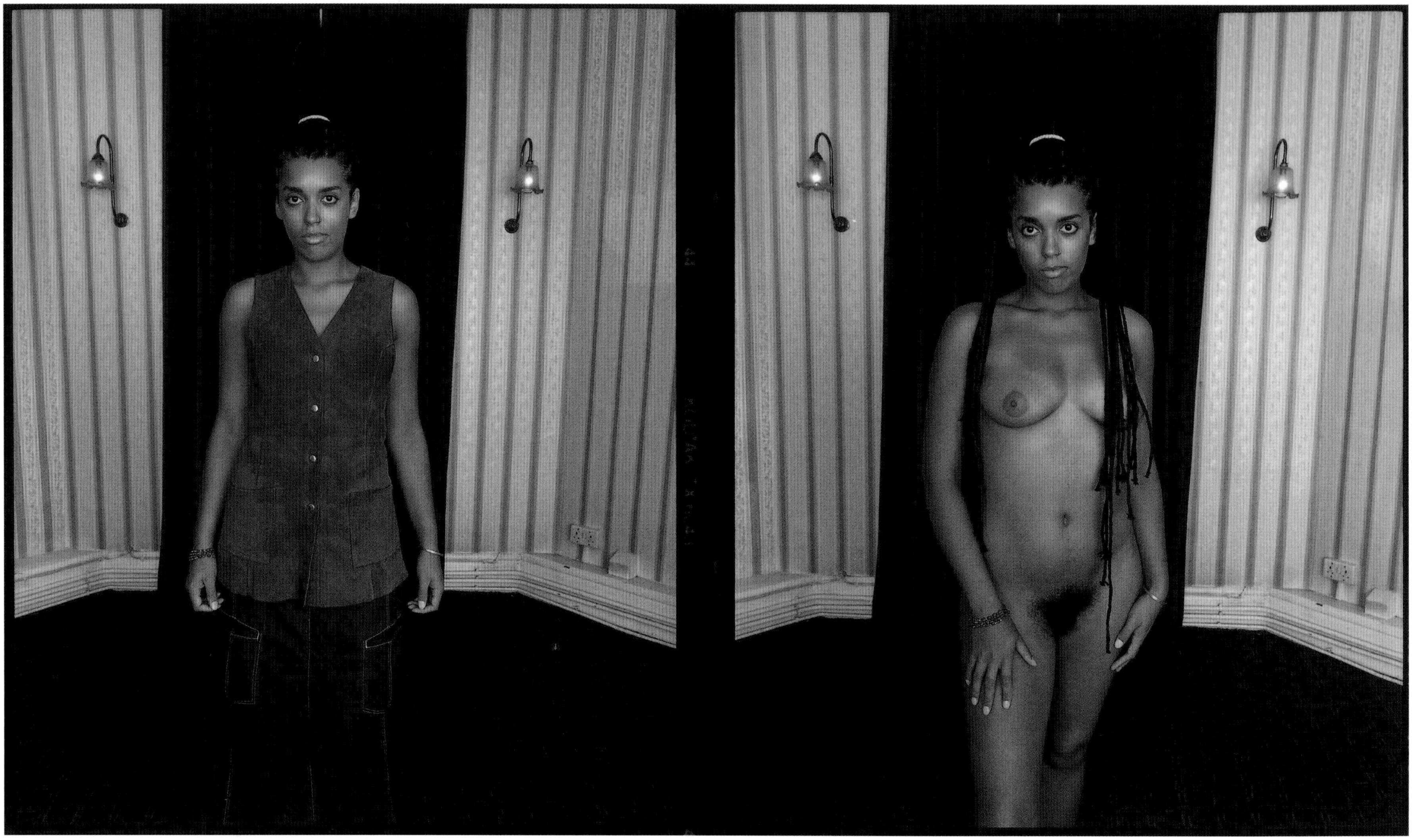

Naked London, Unemployed/Student, 1999
"This was shot for *Naked London*. This photo was made with my Mamiya 7 and a bunch of strobes bounced into white panels for lighting."

As in the images in his nude city series, Friedler did not style his models: they presented themselves as they wanted to be seen, and Friedler simply opened and closed the shutter.

"I love the work of Lucian Freud for the way that he renders the flesh. He has one painting with a nude on an exposed mattress—this was the inspiration behind my book. I remember seeing his show at the Metropolitan Museum of New York, and the paintings were nearly 30ft [9m] long. I was totally blown away. I like that he has a minimalist vision and does not let his paintings become too busy. I also love the way he paints, making people look like real people even if they are beautiful, or rich, or royalty."

Friedler entered the field of nude photography after he started shooting portraiture. "As my eye developed, clothes and other artifices began to go," says Friedler. Discovering his subjects through recommendations, newspaper ads, and even by finding them on the street, he looks for a range of qualities—anything from a simple, attractive face to someone who has an unconventional beauty or an androgynous look. He shoots his models with a Mamiya 7, a Linhof 4x5, and occasionally a Leica, mainly using natural light with the occasional strobe, which he diffuses in a way to make it appear natural.

Currently living in New Orleans, Friedler has had work published in numerous magazines and newspapers, including the *Washington Post*, *GQ*, *The Los Angeles Times Magazine*, *Village Voice*, *Stern*, *The Times* in London, *New York Observer*, and *Allure*. He hopes to one day continue his city series. "If I had the money to do another *Naked* book I would love to shoot *Naked Las Vegas*, *Naked Tokyo*, or *Naked Berlin*."

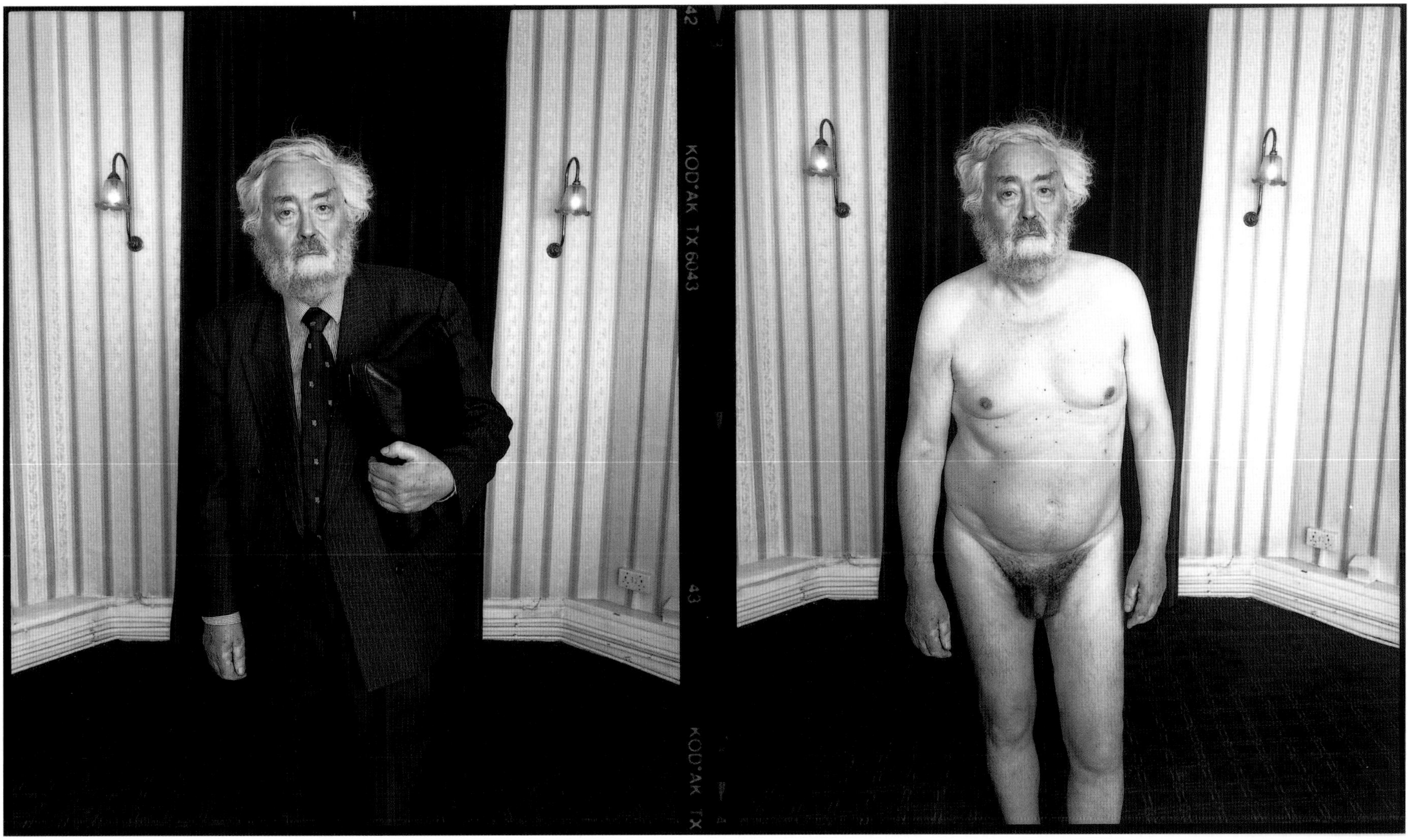

Naked London, Accountant, 1999 *(above)*
"The room I chose to shoot in was a tiny room above a pub. This was handy because if any of the participants were nervous they would arrive a bit early and have a drink or two before coming upstairs to have their portrait made. I shot this with my Mamiya 7 and a bunch of strobes bounced into white panels for lighting. I love this man because he represented the typical older, more conservative British professional—at least in his clothes. He was great because he said that he had never done anything like this before, and felt like he had to do something a little crazy. He did not want to be remembered as a boring accountant. He was so enthusiastic about my project that he persuaded his daughter to have her photo taken on the following weekend. It was fabulous that he responded to my ad because he was exactly the type of person the critics claimed that I would never get in England. These people claimed that a project like *Naked New York* was not possible to do in Britain because the British were too reserved. Well, this man, as well as all the other great people in the book, proved the critics wrong."

Naked Los Angeles, Number 15, 1998 *(right)*
"This was taken in Venice, California, on my set for *Naked Los Angeles*. It was shot with my Linhof 4x5 and a mix of ambient light and strobes. I like this photo because the model is so attractive, making it one of the more 'erotic' photos from the *Naked* series. I put down that she was a 'performer,' but what she really did was pose nude with a webcam for some porn company."

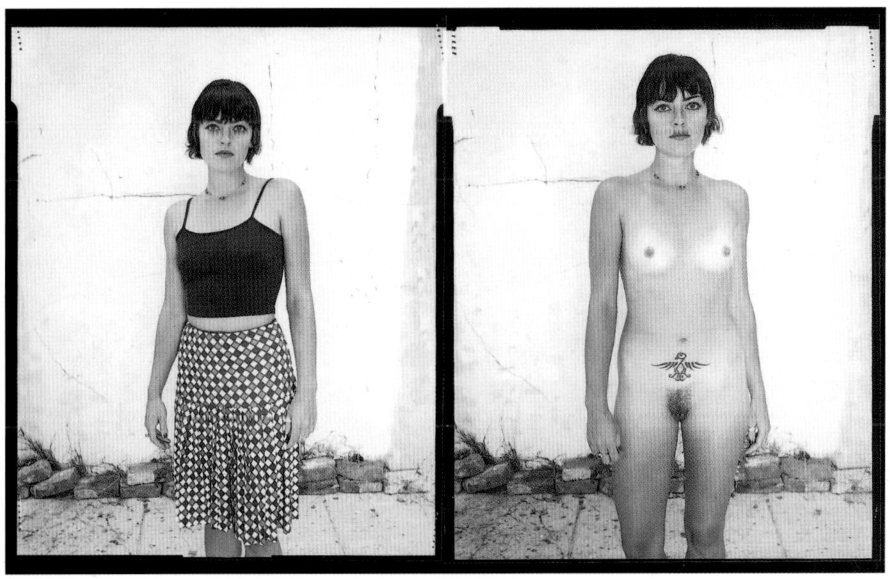

Ralph Gibson

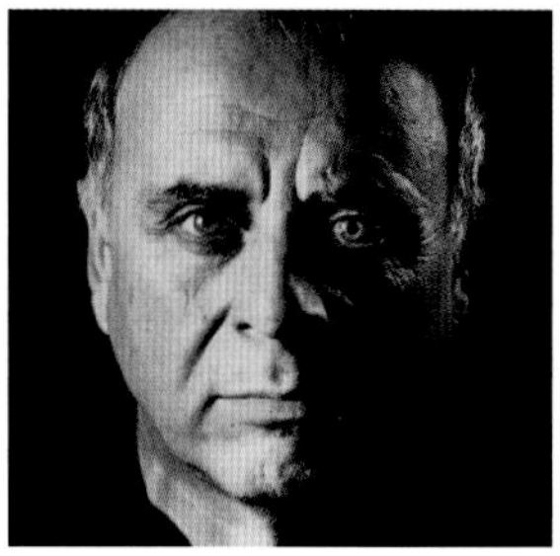

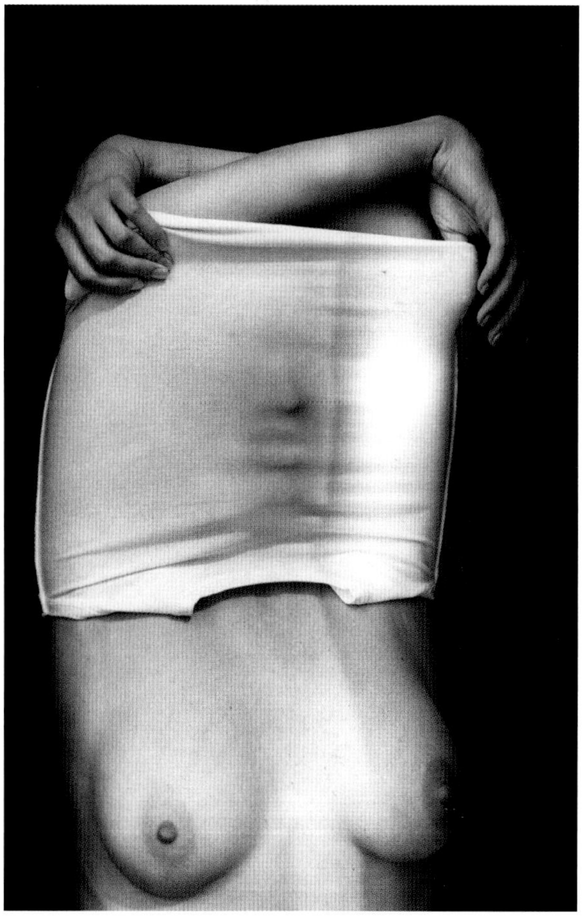

One might expect a photographer who assisted both Dorothea Lange and Robert Frank to take a documentary approach to the human figure, but Ralph Gibson is very much his own man. More poet than reporter, Gibson is an artist who uses the female nude as metaphor rather than a matter of fact.

The typical Gibson nude is an elegant set of curved forms carved out of the darkness with light. If he is not in search of the feminine ideal, Gibson is at the very least after an essence, cutting, cropping, and tightly focusing, so that the part—the landscape of a bottom, the silhouette of a torso, the swirling cosmos of a navel—must stand for the whole.

"I photographed my first nude in 1961, and I would say I have used it as a leitmotiv in my personal work ever since," he says. "Frankly speaking, I am a formalist. I am interested in the formal properties of things."

Born in Los Angeles in 1939, Gibson learned the photographer's trade as a photographer's mate in the U.S. Navy from 1956 to 1960. In 1960–62, he studied at the San Francisco Art Institute and worked as a printing assistant to Dorothea Lange. His work from California in the early 1960s is solidly in the street-photographer mode, and after he moved to New York in 1966 he went to work for the laureate of street photographers, assisting Robert Frank in filming *Me and My Brother*.

Gibson credits his legendary mentors with impressing upon him the importance of doing his own work and not imitating theirs. "You really have to be unique," he says. "You have to come up with your own visual signature."

In 1970, Gibson founded Lustrum Press in New York, and proceeded to publish a series of landmark photography books, including Larry Clark's *Tulsa* and his own early books—*The Somnambulist* (1970), *Déjà Vu* (1973), and *Days at Sea* (1975).

"Years ago, when I was assisting Dorothea Lange, I showed her some of my photographs and she said, 'You have no point of departure in your work.' And she was right. I could have been photographing toothpaste. It was then that I started working on *The Somnambulist*, my first important work."

"At lot of times, when I approach a figure, I have something in mind," explains Gibson. "It could be vivid and specific, or vague and abstract. I don't just point the camera and click away. I always have a point of departure."

As his point of departure for *The Somnambulist*, Gibson took the concept of "a dream sequence in which all things are real." The surrealism emerged not from staged scenes, darkroom trickery, or the characteristic collage techniques of the 1960s, but out of the artful way he strung together disjointed, fragmentary images into an irrational narrative. Among the nudes included in *The Somnambulist* are a woman floating on her back in a pond, the long, slender legs of a woman rising to the black garden of her pudenda, and a male nude struggling to climb a sapling. A technical master who travels the world teaching photographic workshops, Gibson has four Apple computers in his New York studio, but he much prefers developing his own film to digital output. A confirmed Leica man, he typically carries two Leica Ms—one for black and white, and the other for color—with 35mm, 50mm, and 90mm lenses at the ready.

Although he is best known for his black-and-white work, Gibson says, "I do photograph in color as well. I recently decided I'm going to do a color nude book in the near future. I have a box full of them."

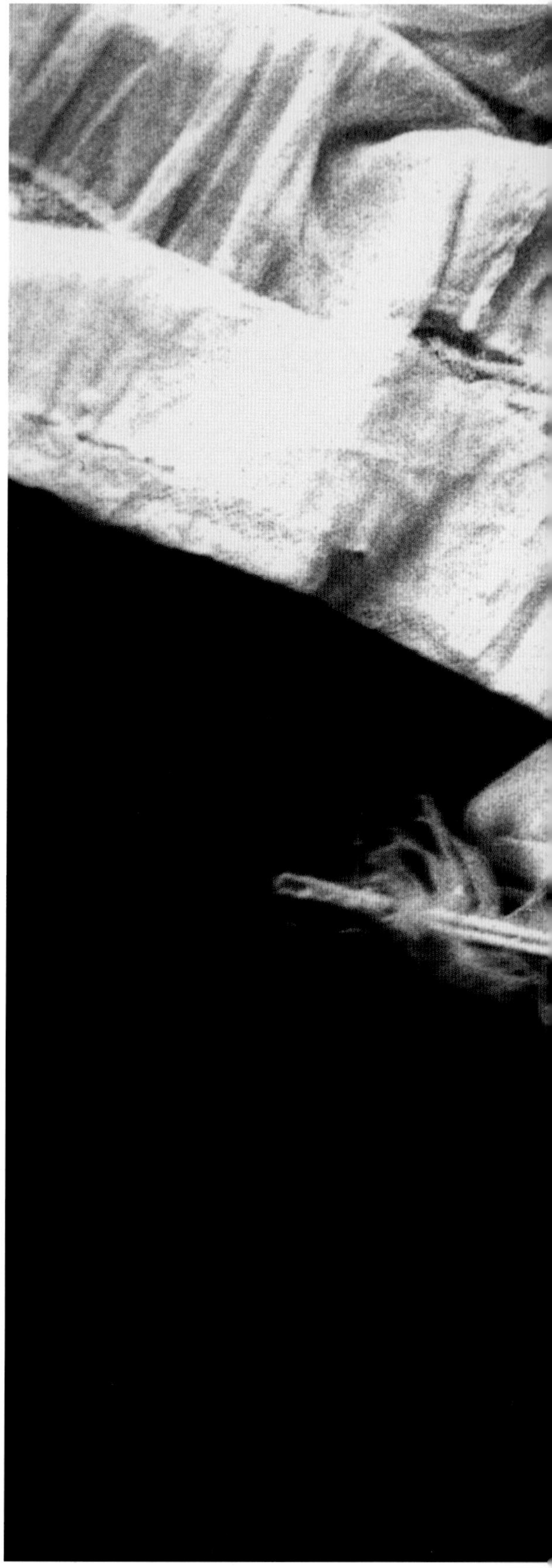

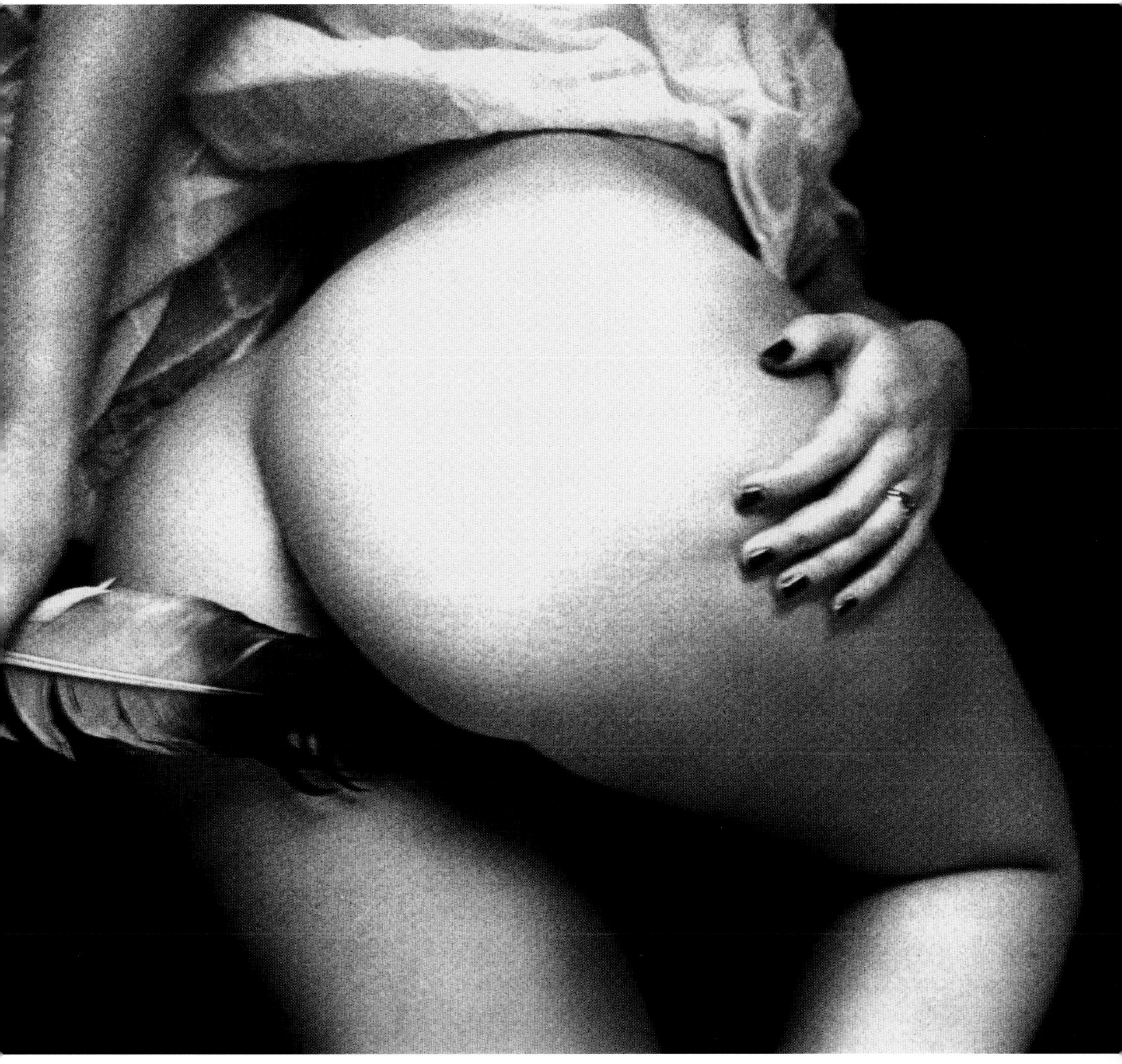

Ralph Gibson

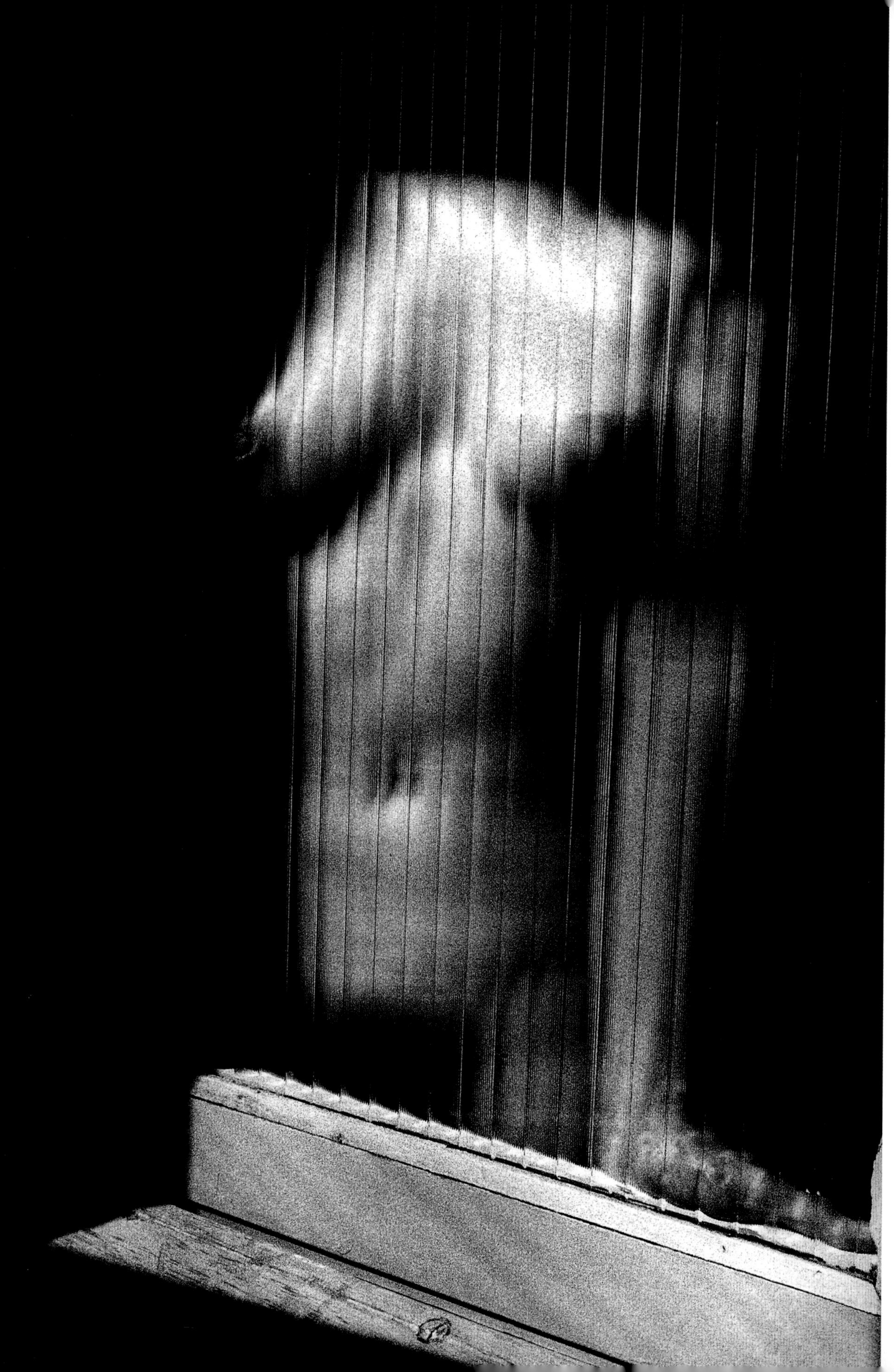

Most of Gibson's nudes are part of his ongoing *Infanta* series—an infanta being the daughter of a king who must marry a king in order to become a queen. "The psychological mirror of woman is always very intriguing," Gibson says of the *Infanta* photographs. "I like the way women look, and I like the way they think. I express my concerns and admiration for them in my nudes."

Gibson's nudes range from classical images of the architecture of a woman's body to blatantly erotic images of sexual acts, but his signature nudes most often involve a symbolic gesture: a woman tickling her vagina from behind with a feather; an odalisque examining her splayed fingers; a sunbather covering her eyes with a towel.

He approaches women as a mystery to be investigated, if not solved. Whether depicting the face of an unnamed woman, or the body of a faceless woman, his photographs become metaphors—what the poet T.S. Eliot called "objective correlatives"—specific details that invoke a world beyond the obvious and apparent.

Gibson is adept at finding these telling details in architecture and artifacts, as well as in anatomy. "If a photographer learns to photograph nudes and architecture, he can photograph anything in between," he says. "Every time I pose a photograph, it's for a different reason. What you're looking at is what I'm trying to do. I examine the questions and problems in my life through photography. I don't get answers, but I get more accurately defined versions of the questions."

Study of Lake Geneva, 2000
(page 70)

Nude with Feather, 1974
(page 71)
This is perhaps Gibson's most famous photograph. "I don't explain that photograph because it's too well known. I call it 'Leda.' I let the picture do for viewers what it will, and let the viewers draw their own conclusions."

Nude Through Ribbed Glass, 1989 *(left)*
"This is from a workshop in Madrid. It's a perfect example of a workshop producing an opportunity to make a strong photograph. Anybody can take the picture if you light it and pose it for them. I set it up and let them have a look."

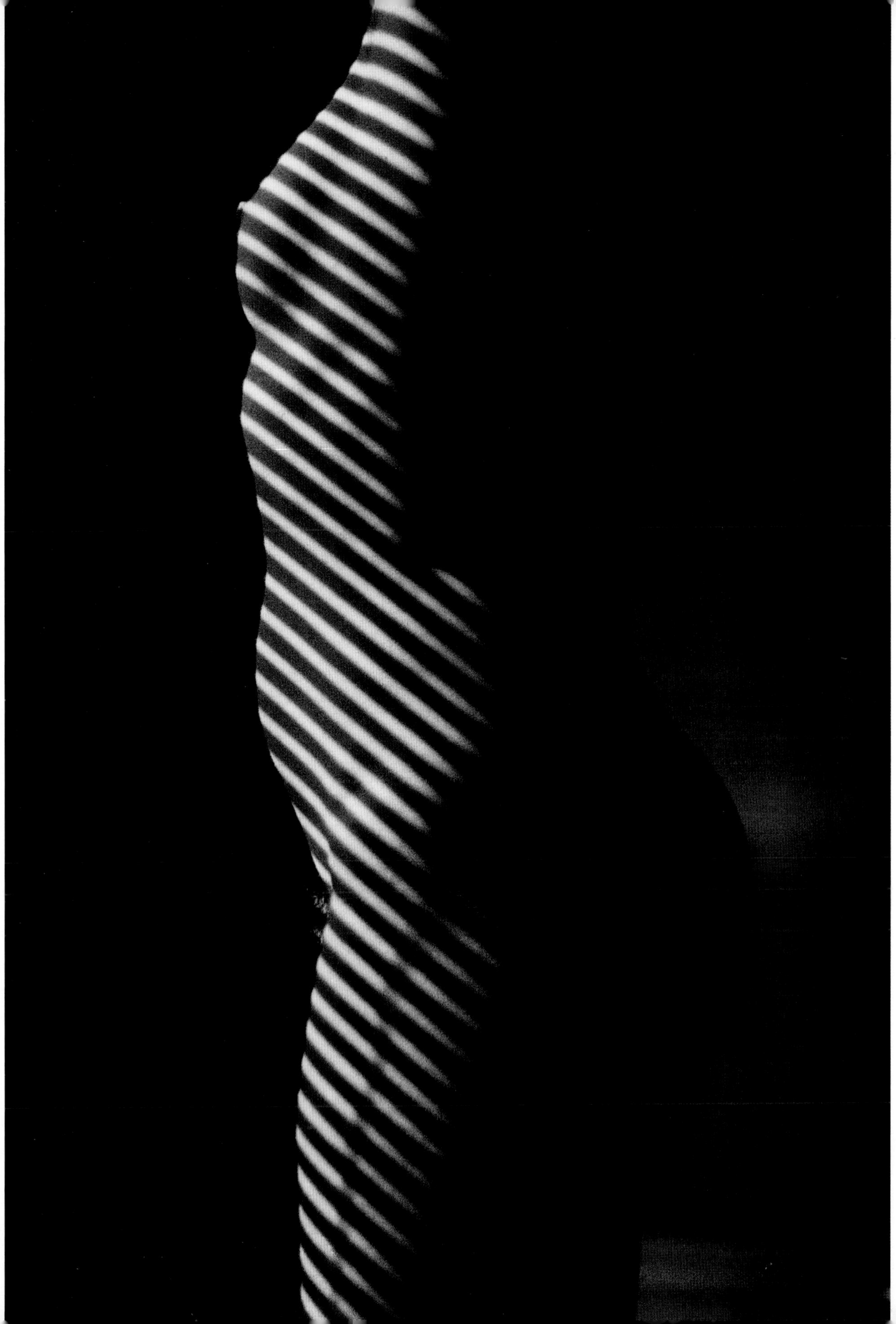

Striped Woman, 2003
"This is about the relationship of parts to parts, and the part to the whole. A set of proportions is what art is about. I shot it at a tennis camp in Florida."

Greg Gorman

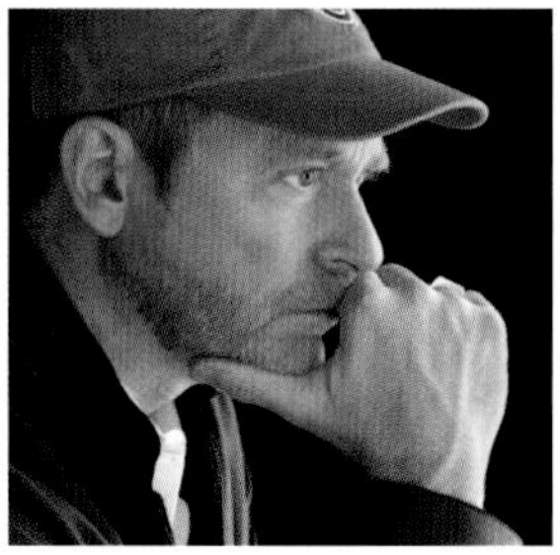

Jimi Hendrix changed Greg Gorman's life. As a student, Gorman attended one of the legendary guitarist's concerts with a photographer friend. He might easily have wound up in the family furniture business in Kansas City had he not accompanied his friend into the darkroom to process the Hendrix film. "When I saw the image come up in the tray I was hooked," recalls Gorman.

Gorman has been one of Hollywood's top photographers for many years. He makes his living shooting motion-picture ad campaigns, including those for *Tootsie*, *The Big Chill*, *Pearl Harbor*, and *Pirates of the Caribbean*, and he has been commissioned to shoot portraits of everyone from Bette Davis, Marlon Brando, and Sophia Loren, to Johnny Depp, Drew Barrymore, and Leonardo DiCaprio. But since the 1980s, Gorman has created an impressive portfolio of nudes.

Gorman has a preference for high-key, high-contrast, black-and-white images in which he sculpts shapes and details with light. Just as he might photograph actor Warren Beatty in man-in-the-moon profile, he is apt to suggest the lines of the human body by highlighting details rather than revealing the whole. His work is playful and seductive. His portrait work is firmly in the tradition of such great studio photographers as Horst P. Horst, George Platt Lynes, and George Hurrell, while his nudes are more influenced by Irving Penn, Richard Avedon, and Helmut Newton.

Born in Kansas City, Missouri, in 1949, Gorman felt compelled to study photojournalism at the University of Kansas from 1967 to 1969 after his darkroom epiphany. Thereafter he transferred to the University of Southern California, where he earned an MFA in cinematography in 1972. A self-described "control freak," he returned to still photography because he preferred the one-on-one dynamic to the collaborative nature of filmmaking.

During the 1970s, Gorman paid his dues doing layout and design work, and he began his career as a celebrity portrait photographer modestly, shooting headshots of aspiring actors and actresses for $35 a sitting. Slowly, as his work appeared in theater-arts magazines, he worked his way up to A-list celebrities. Big breaks came when he photographed rock star David Bowie and diva Bette Midler early in their respective careers.

Gorman's nude work began in the 1980s when, feeling the need to move beyond portraiture, he decided to "pull the camera back and take the clothes off." While he found that "it's much more difficult to do nudes," his formal concerns for "the interplay of shadow and highlight, shape and form" remained consistent across all of his work. Just as a sculptor finds the form locked in stone or wood, Gorman reveals images by chiseling them out of the darkness with sharp-edged light.

Gorman's nude photography is also distinguished by the fact that he creates male and female nudes with equal finesse. "I end up doing more male nudes," Gorman explains, "because the women come in and they've had so much cosmetic work done that they all start looking the same. I like the imperfection of the male nude. There's more of a dynamic range."

Gorman's early books—*Greg Gorman: Volume One* (CPC Publishing, 1990) and *Greg Gorman: Volume Two* (CPC Publishing, 1992)—featured both male and female nudes, but his most recent books—*As I See It* (powerHouse Books, 2000) and *Just Between Us* (Arena Editions, 2002)—have focused entirely on the male figure. *Just Between Us*, in fact, consists of some 250 images of one man, male model Greg Knudson.

Gorman's concentration on the male form also coincides roughly with his switch to digital photography from film. "In the last two years, I've primarily shot digital," he says. "Everything is captured in color and converted to black and white." Shooting with a Canon EOS 1DS Mark II, he says, "I'm getting the spontaneity of a 35mm camera with the quality of a medium-format capture. It's also freed me up creatively and shortened the shooting time by 70 percent. I get better quality, more flexibility, and it's put me back in the driver's seat in terms of my image-making."

Whether shooting male or female nudes, or working with film or digitally, however, Gorman says the secret of creating a successful nude photograph is never to reveal too much. Leave something to the imagination—a little mystery is powerfully seductive. "Nudes are so open to interpretation," he says. "Good nudes are not overly lit. The interplay of shadow and highlights should draw you into the picture and leave you wanting to know more."

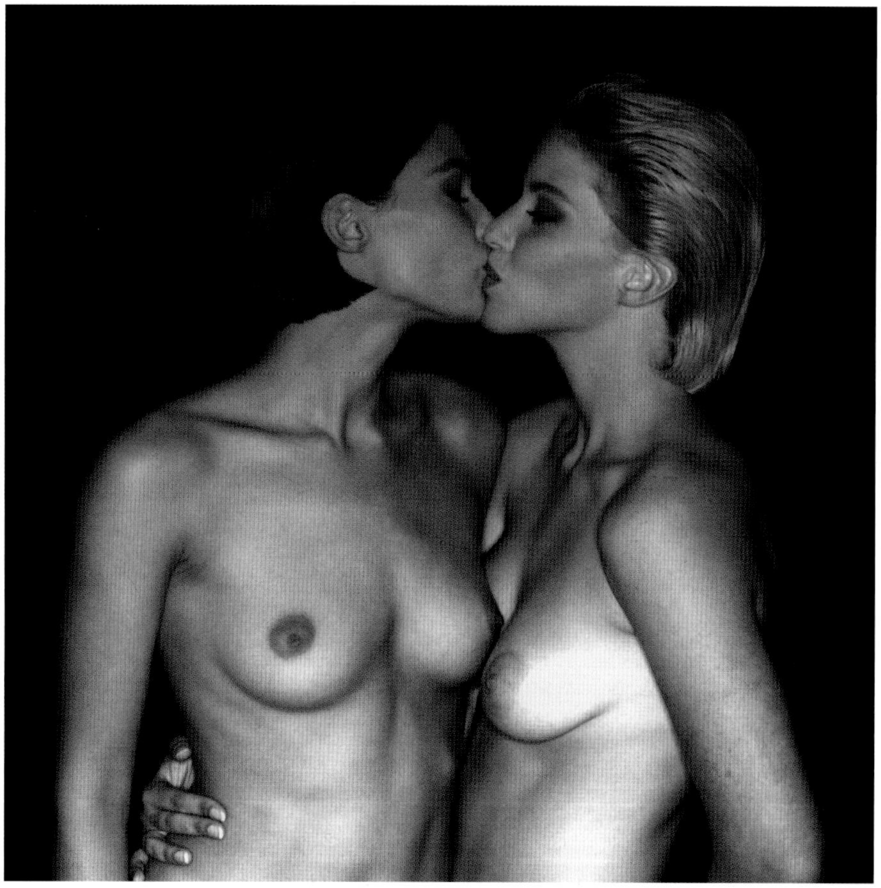

From the Mitzi and Kayce Martin series, Los Angeles, 1990
"This is my homage to Helmut Newton. They're dear friends of mine, and they're sisters. Two beautiful women caught in a moment of tension, kissing. It's lit boldly, high-key, adding a certain edge."

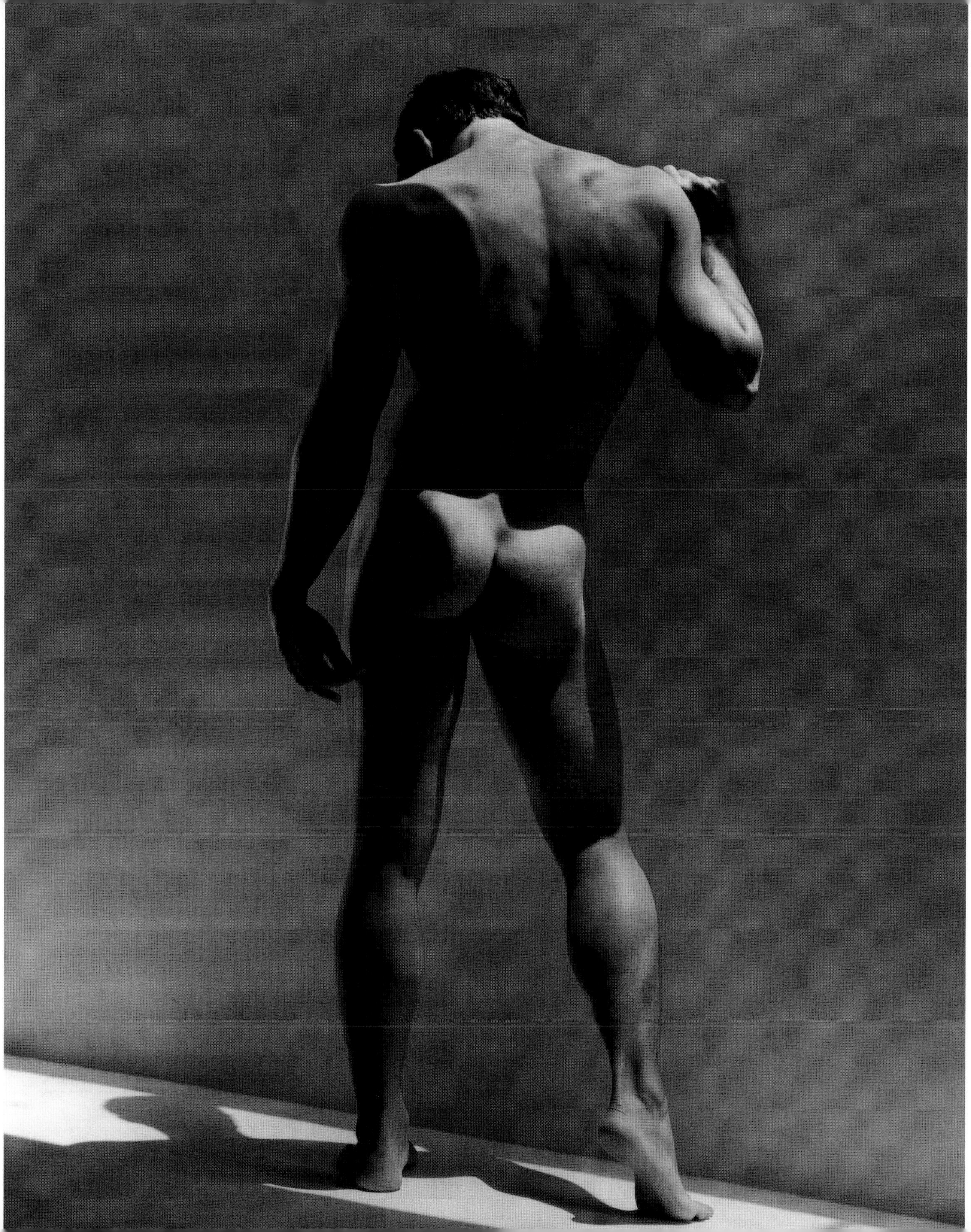

David Michelak,
Los Angeles, 1987
"Dave was a model who personified how I work. He has a very muscular build—strong and statuesque. He has this Romanesque quality, which is why I went for that pose. Dave has since become a very successful photographer in his own right."

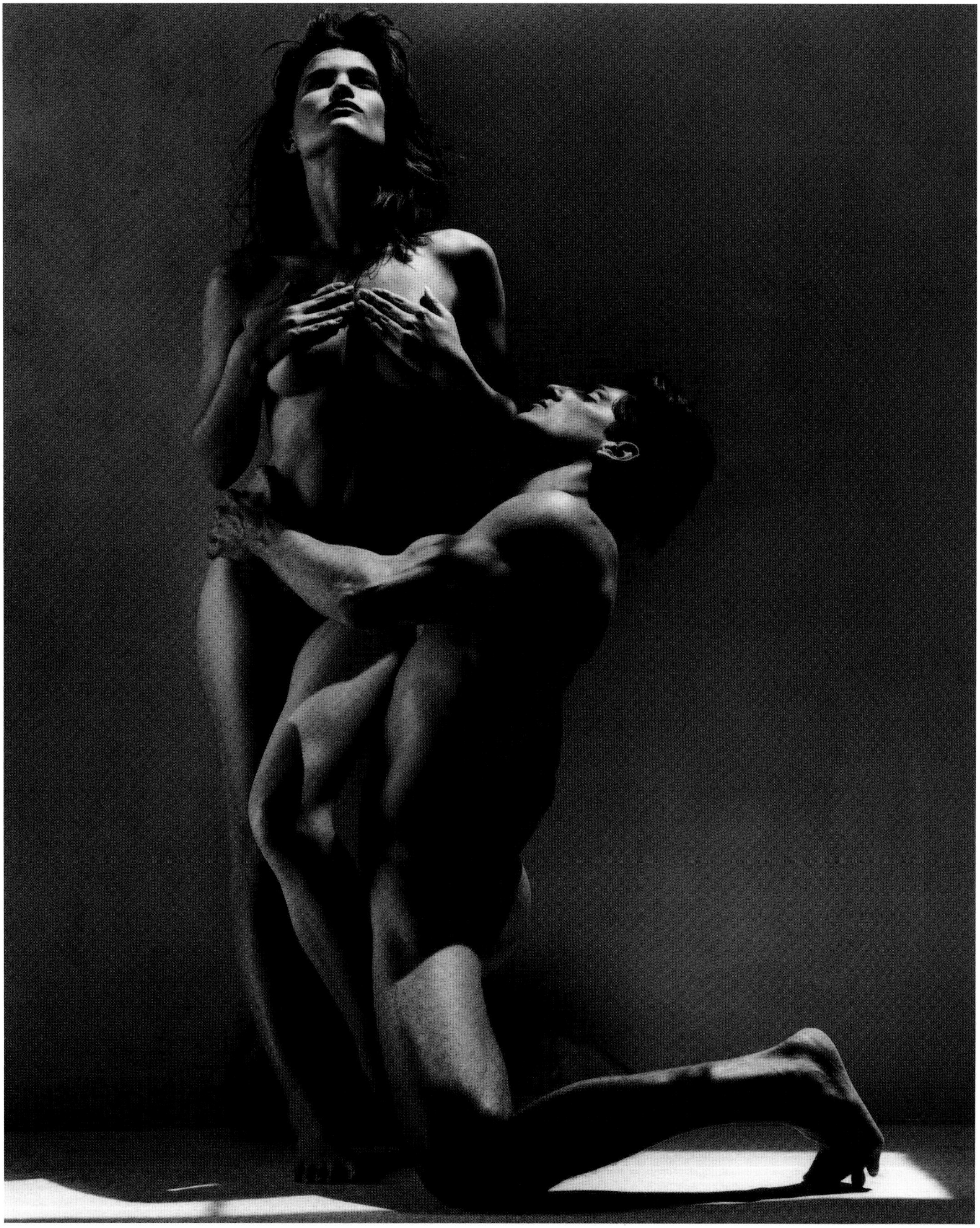

Tony and Rosetta series #3, Los Angeles, 1988
"Tony Ward will go down in history as being the most photographed male body. Herb Ritts shot him, Bruce Weber shot him, and I shot him. Tony for me represents the best of my male nudes. I got so many incredible shots the first time that I worked with him for the next 15, almost 20 years. At the time, Tony was dating Rosetta. She is now married to [actor] Balthazar Getty. I liked the interplay of the action between the two of them."

Mickey Hardt, Los Angeles, 1995
"Mickey Hardt is a model I photographed many times, starting at a young age. I find him strikingly handsome. He has a movie-star/rock-star look. He lives in Berlin and is married to an actress. I've photographed him six or eight times over 15 years, and it always takes on new meanings and new depths. There were copper rings in the studio, and this pose reminded me of DaVinci's [*Vetruvian Man*] anatomical drawings."

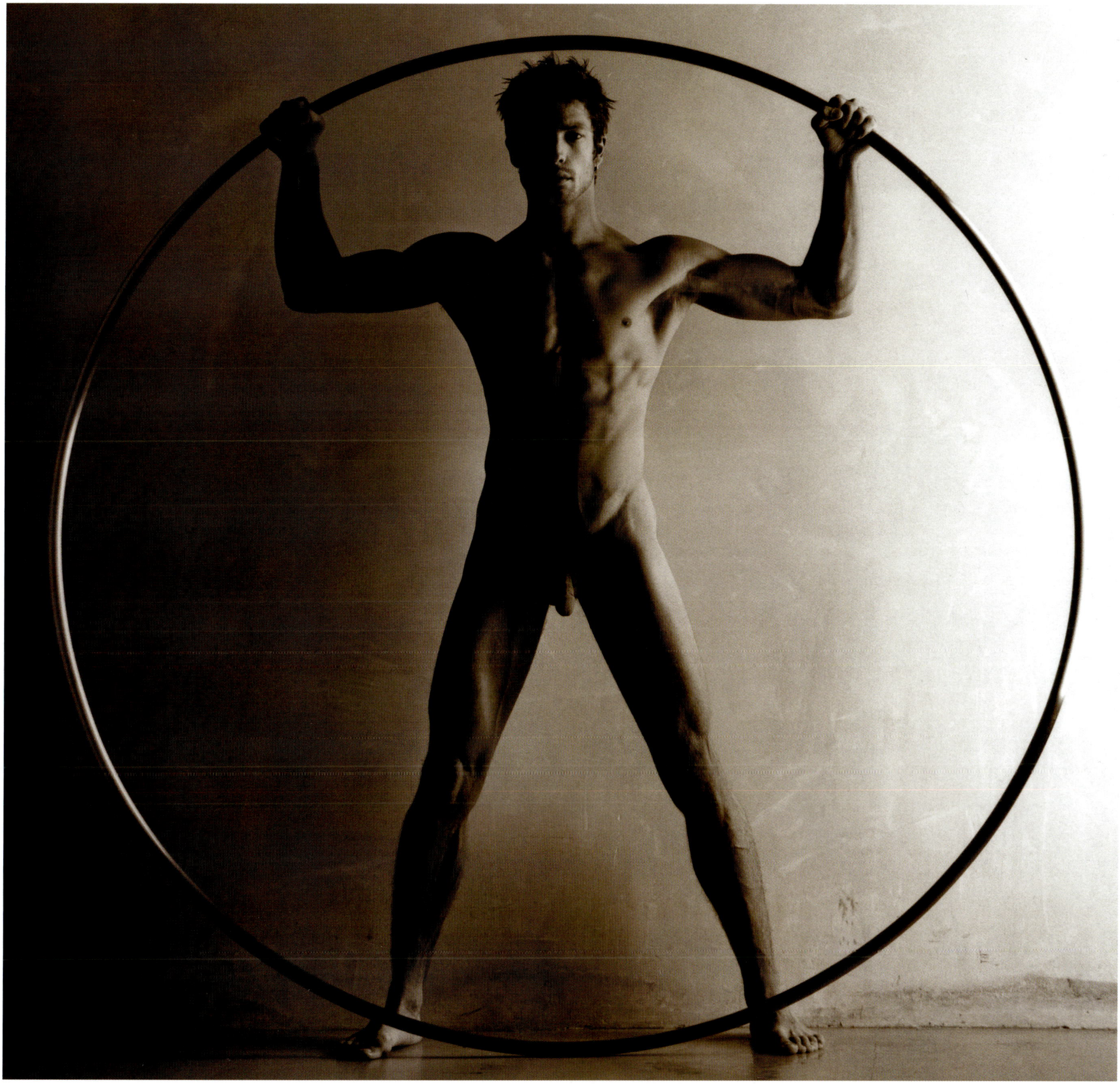

Greg Gorman

Peter Gorman

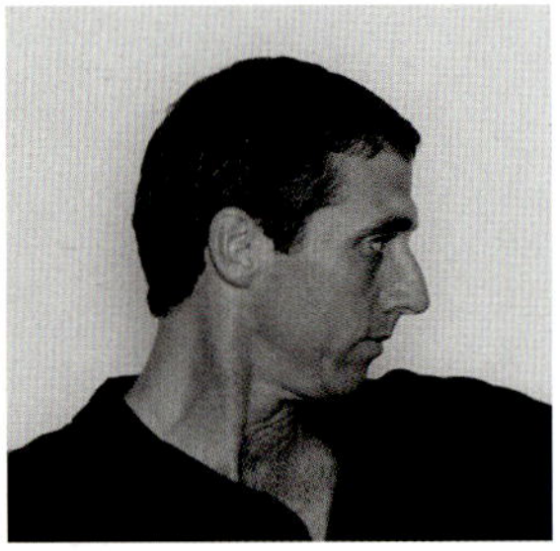

When you live within the confines of any major city, surrounded by the constant influx of strange faces and unknown lives, windows can, at times, be your only view into the personal spaces of people around you. There, among the looming, overwhelming presence of steel and concrete apartment complexes, they are portals offering brief glimpses into the worlds of others. Just as it was for James Stewart's character, clutching the telephoto lens of his camera in Hitchcock's *Rear Window*, voyeurism has a fascinating and dangerous allure.

Photographer Peter Gorman not only knows the power of the voyeur, but he takes it a step further. With his images of women within the walls of apartments and rooms (some his, mostly theirs), we are not simply peering through glass thresholds for a momentary glimpse; we are invited guests for an eternal instant.

"For me, what makes a naked woman exciting is seeing her in an environment," says the 43-year-old Gorman. "I would much rather see a nude standing next to a refrigerator than being posed against a seamless background."

Gorman's first book, *Naked In Apartment 7* (Goliath Books, 2001), brought him considerable recognition within the realm of erotic photography. Consisting entirely of edgy, black-and-white images filtered through the male gaze, each photograph within the 160 pages of the publication was created in Gorman's own New York City apartment. The women, most of them dancers who responded to flyers posted near their schools, are captured in nearly every corner and fissure of Gorman's place. And for subjects who do not make a living from being photographed, they exude an air of confidence and dominance that floods the tiny rooms. "I always meet with models before we set a date to shoot," explains Gorman. "This way, they can get a feel for me and see more of my work, and I can see them and get a sense of what they are comfortable with. Also, I always ask to see a model nude before I set a date to shoot. Besides wanting to see what they look like naked, I feel it is important for them to be nude in front of me for a couple minutes so that they can decide whether this is something they feel comfortable with or not. Better to find out in that first meeting that this is not for them than when we are in an actual shoot.

"The subjects also have to be someone that I find appealing in some way," he continues. "It could be the way they look, or the way they carry themselves, or the enthusiasm they have about posing nude. 'Looks' are not enough, and I have found over the years that I can't always tell who is going to come alive in front of the camera. I think that is one of the aspects of doing this that I find so exciting. Often the quiet, shy-seeming subject becomes a completely different person for the camera, and they even surprise themselves."

His second book, while continuing on the theme of depicting women in an apartment environment, leapt in a different direction. With *Naked Rooms* (Goliath Books, 2002), Gorman expanded his exploration of the living area. This time, he ventured out into the private spaces of his subjects. In bold colors rather than shades of gray, the images display women cradled inside their homes, surrounded by their everyday objects—everything from kitchen tables to exercise bikes appear in the photographs.

Early, from Stripped Naked, 2004 *(below)*

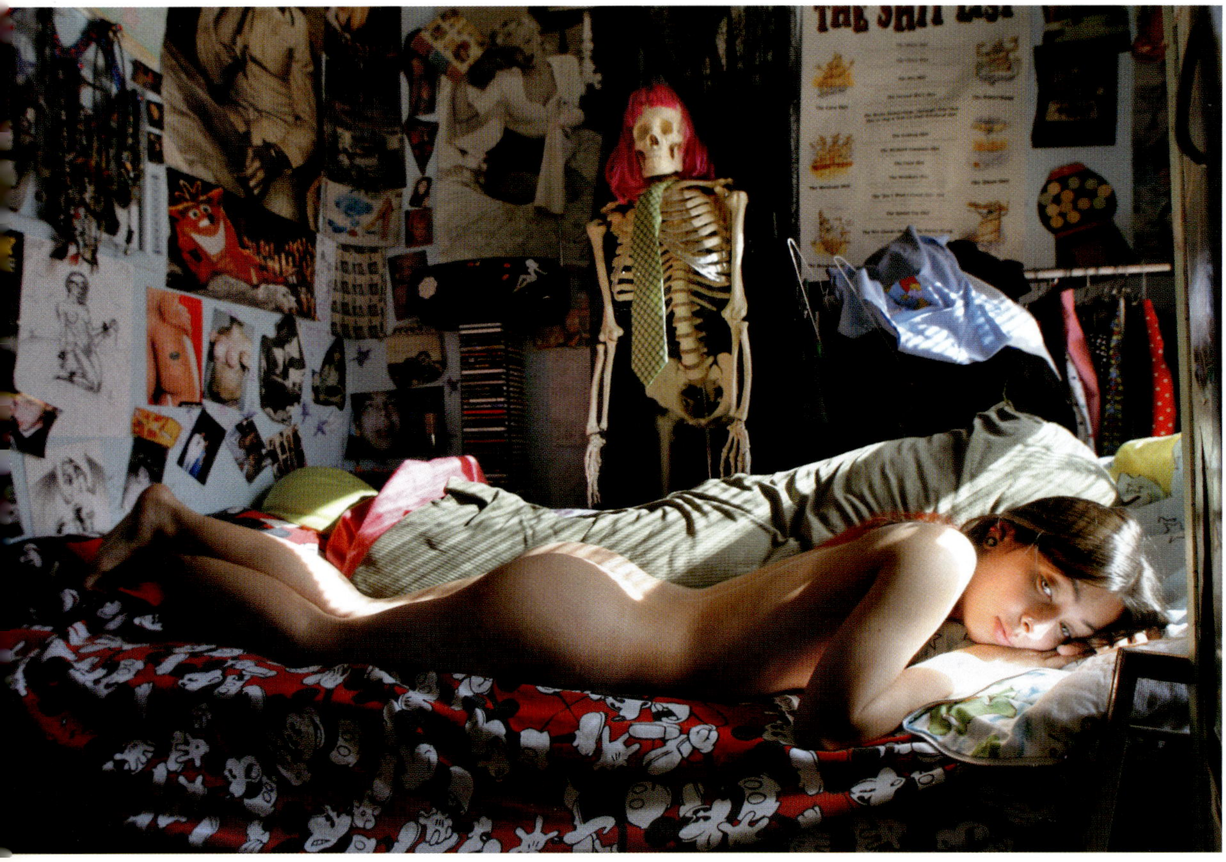

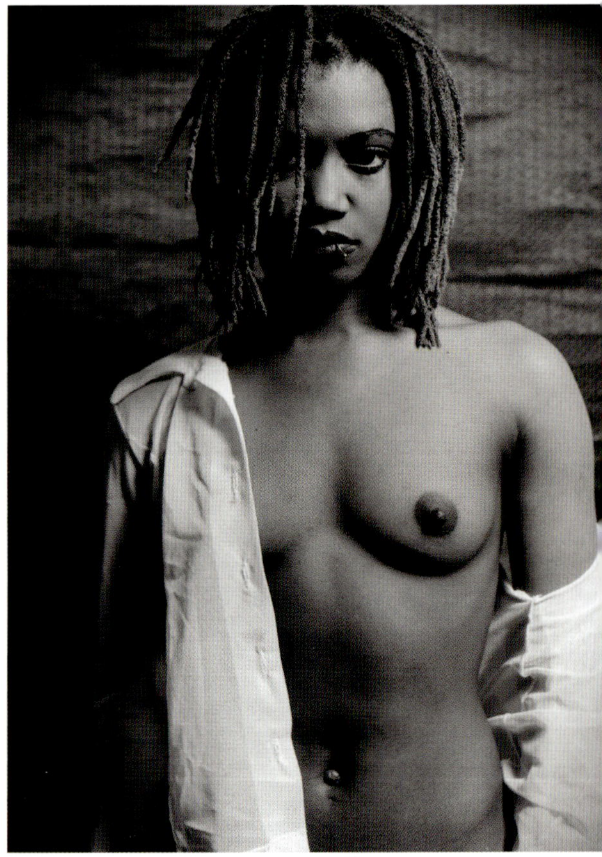

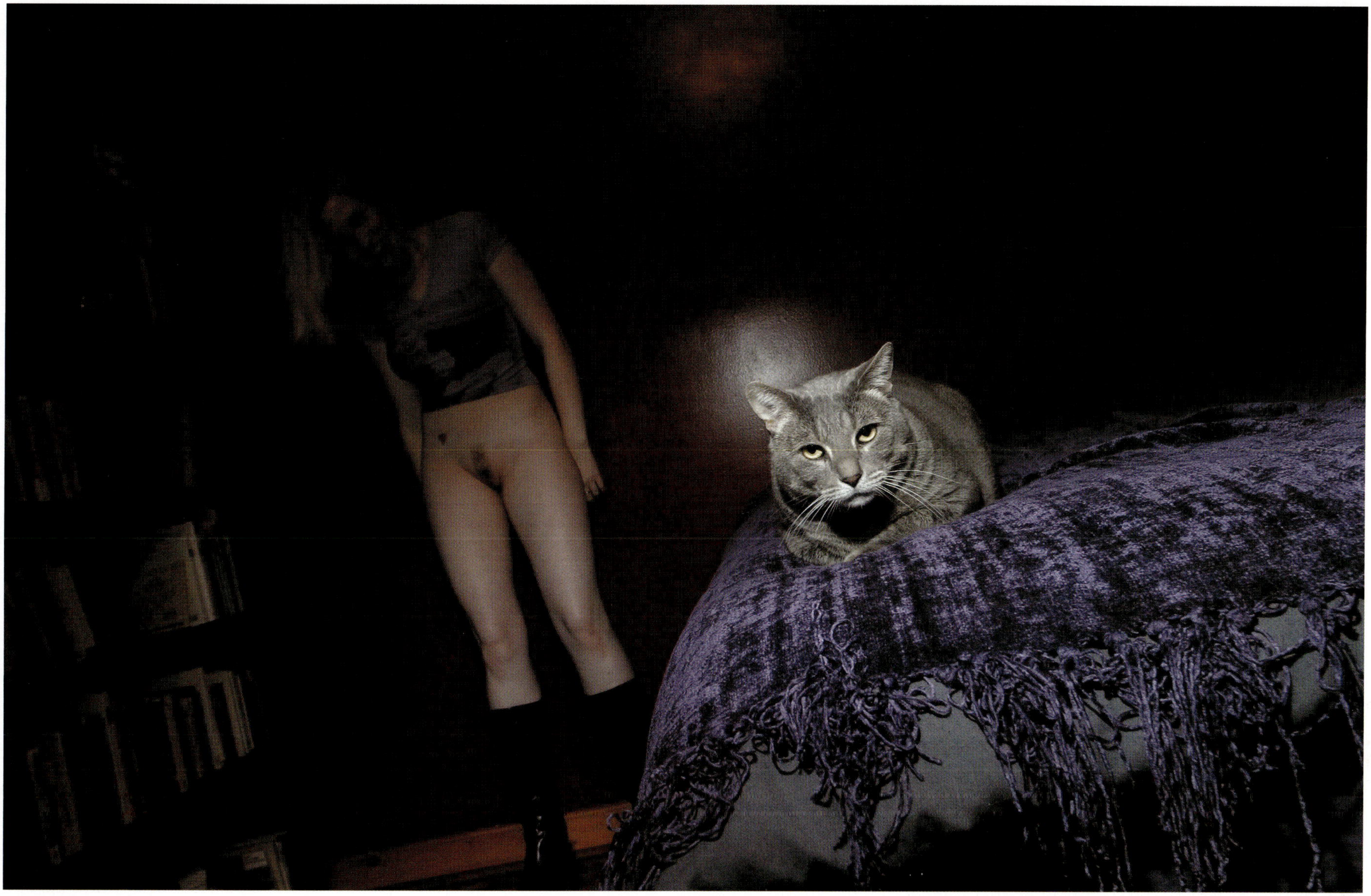

Naked Portrait No. 12, 1999 *(left)*
"For *Naked Rooms* and *Stripped Naked*, I shot the models where they live, and this grew out of being sick of shooting models in the same old setting, my apartment—I can only do so much with my place. This was made much easier by switching to digital and a handheld flash. My load was lightened, and that made the process of travel much easier. What I love about these series is that I am not only let into a women's nakedness, but I am also let into their world by seeing them in the rawness of their own lives."

Cat, 2003 *(above)*

"I want the photo to feel like I am peeking in on her life," says Gorman, whose latest book, *Stripped Naked* (Goliath Books, 2004), also features women in their own spaces. "I don't want her to clean up and straighten up. I want a real person, not a statue. I want to see her effects in the background, I want to see the mess of her apartment."

The photographs are filled with the self-assurance of the subjects. At ease in their world, Gorman didn't have to do much but follow the lead of the women before his lens. "I only direct to get things going, or if someone is a little stiff and needs a kickstart," says Gorman.

"What I really love is a model who just goes off on her own, while I follow her around, like a reporter, capturing what she is doing. I think that shows in my work. I try not to be too controlling. I found out early on that sometimes models would come up with ideas that I never would have thought of. I don't want to get so caught up in my own vision that I overlook the perfect shot that is right in front of me."

Besides the shift to color, Gorman also altered his equipment for his last two publications. This, however, was more out of need than preference. "The changes have been from film to digital, from setup strobes to one handheld flash, from planning a shoot to shooting from the hip," says Gorman.

"I used to shoot models in my apartment, and I could play around with light and ideas before they arrived, but now I shoot models where they live. I have no idea what their place is going to be like until I get there, so I have to be comfortable with being in the moment. I am always trying different directions."

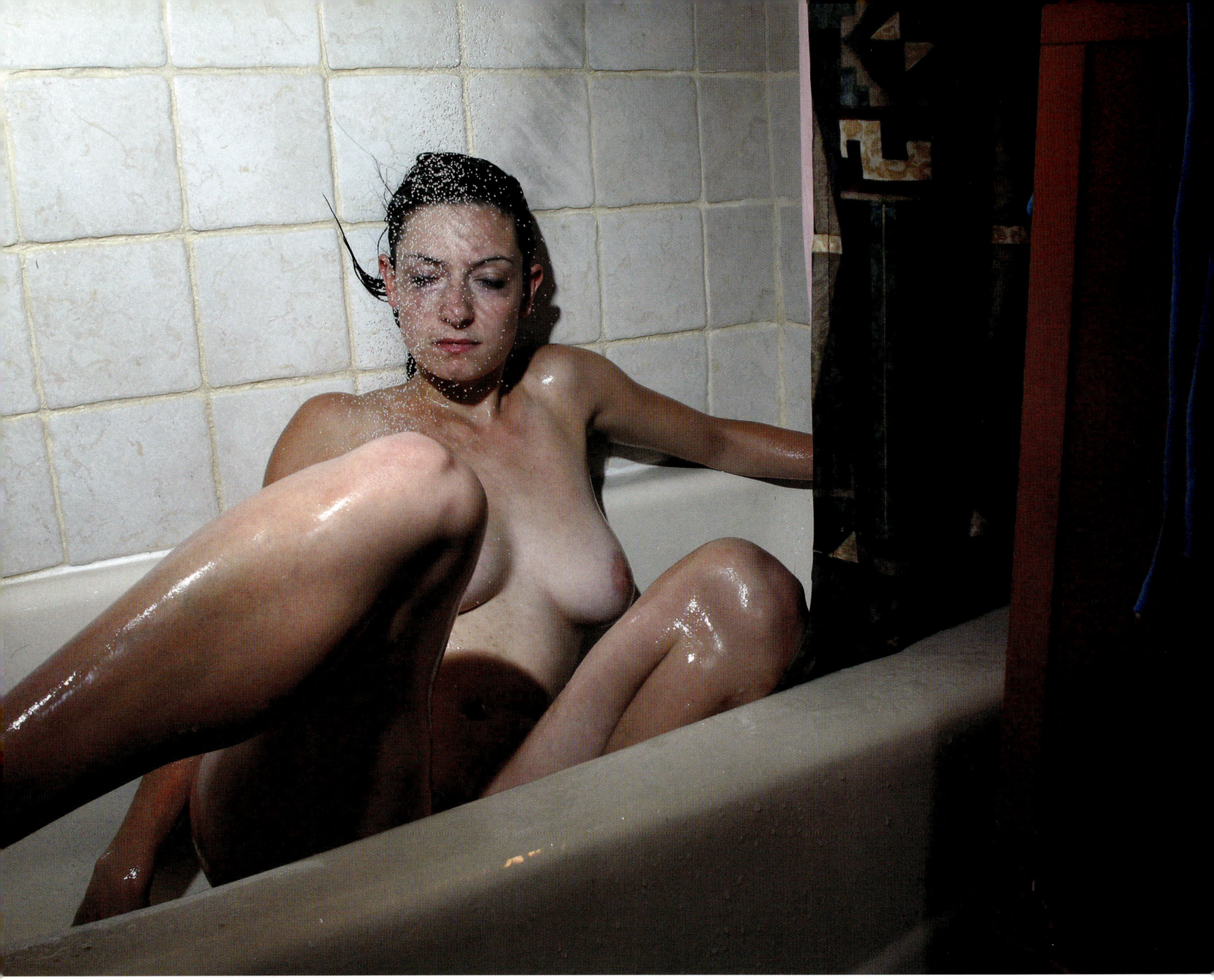

Splash, from Stripped Naked, 2002
"I only shoot digital now, and have for a number of years. Right now I am shooting with a Canon 20D—I had a 10D before, and a D60 before that—and a Canon Dedicated Flash fired by a wireless transmitter. When Canon comes out with a replacement for this camera I will be the first to buy it. I love technology and feel that each new generation of digital camera creates even better images than the one before it. My lenses are a Canon 17-40L and a Sigma 14mm. The centerpiece of all of this is my iMac G5. I travel light and prefer not to be bogged down with equipment."

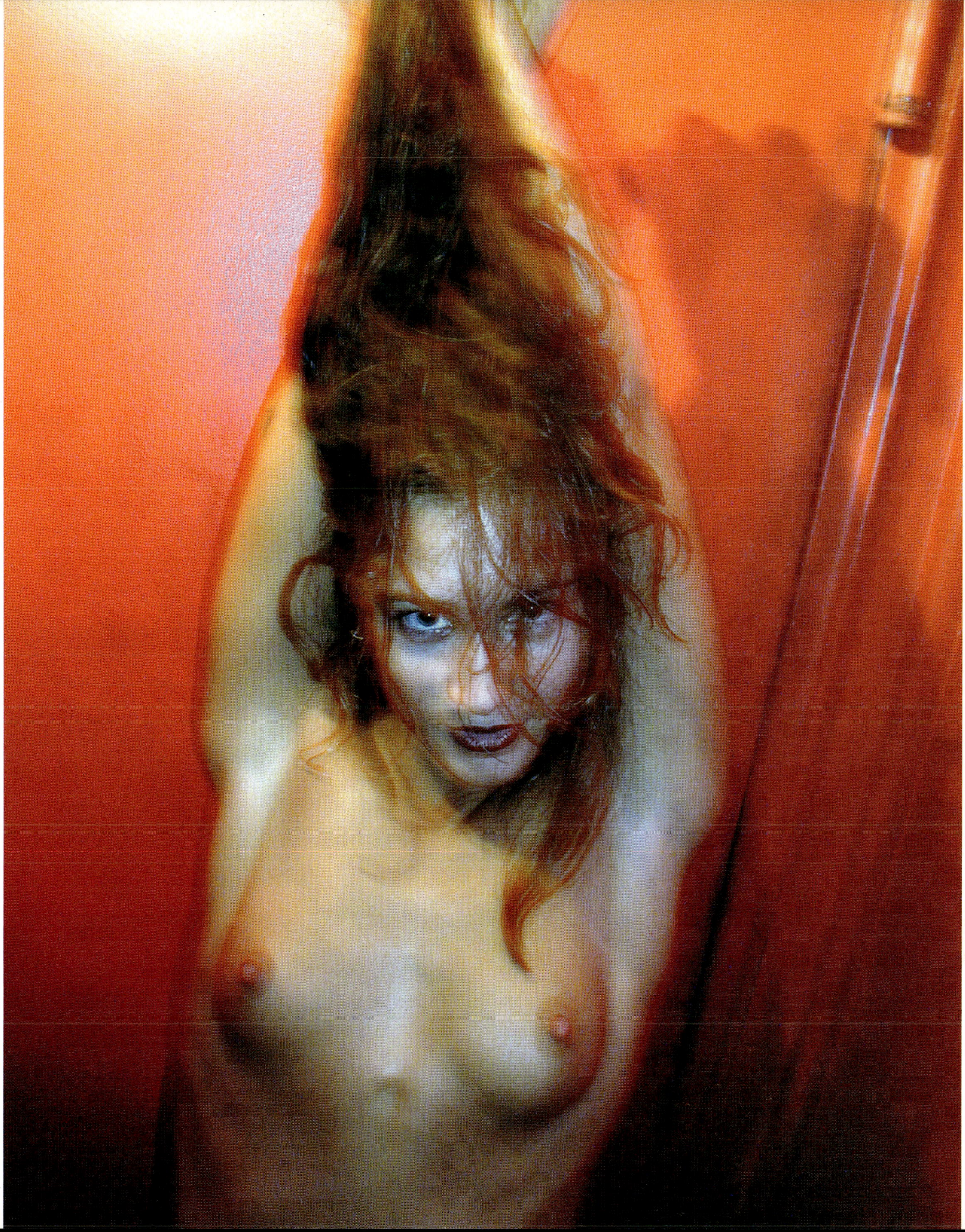

Hair, 2000

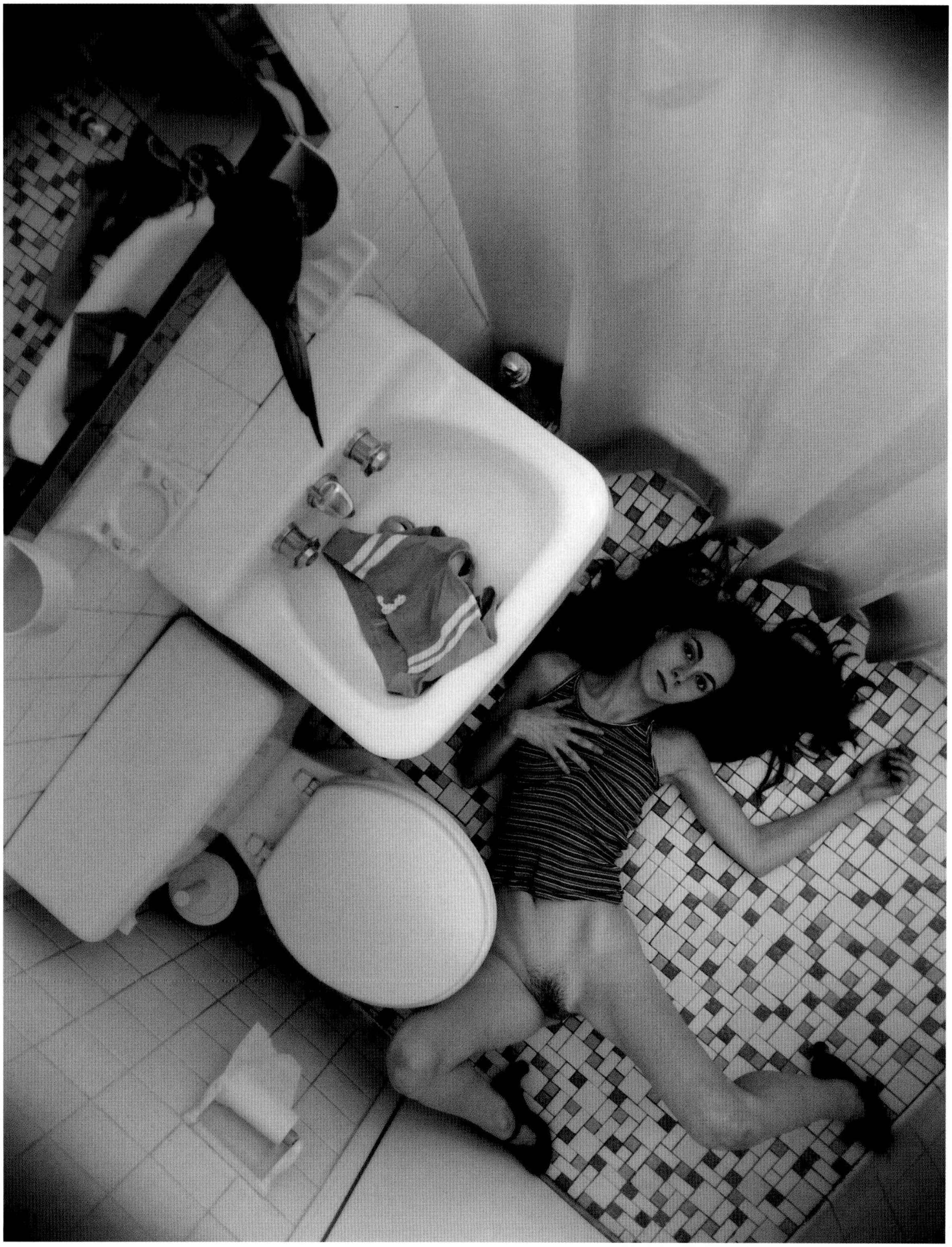

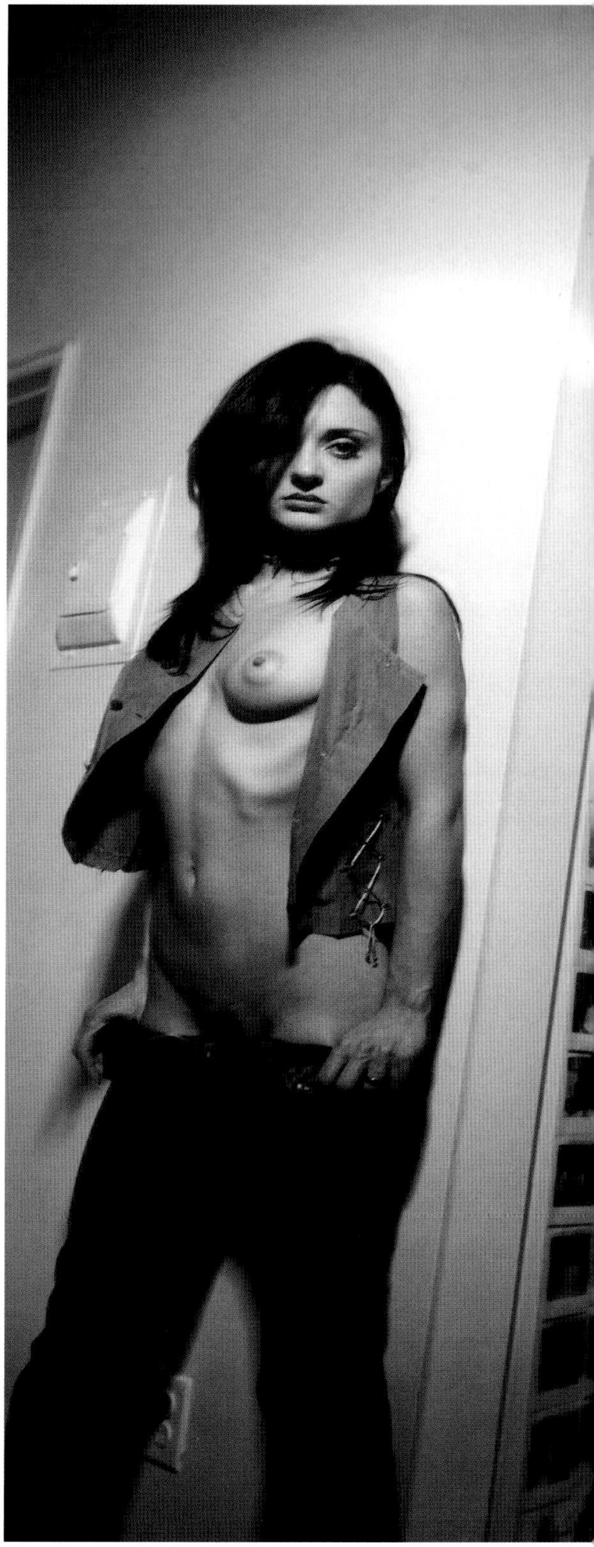

Melissa on My Bathroom Floor, from Naked in Apartment 7, 1999
"The images from *Naked in Apartment 7* were taken in my apartment—I live in apartment 7, and that series grew more out of convenience than anything else. I started to get a lot of models to work with, and I didn't know where to shoot them, so I thought why not just shoot them where all my stuff is, and use my place as the background? For that series I was using strobes and a medium-format camera, which is quite a load to carry around."

Help Me, 1999

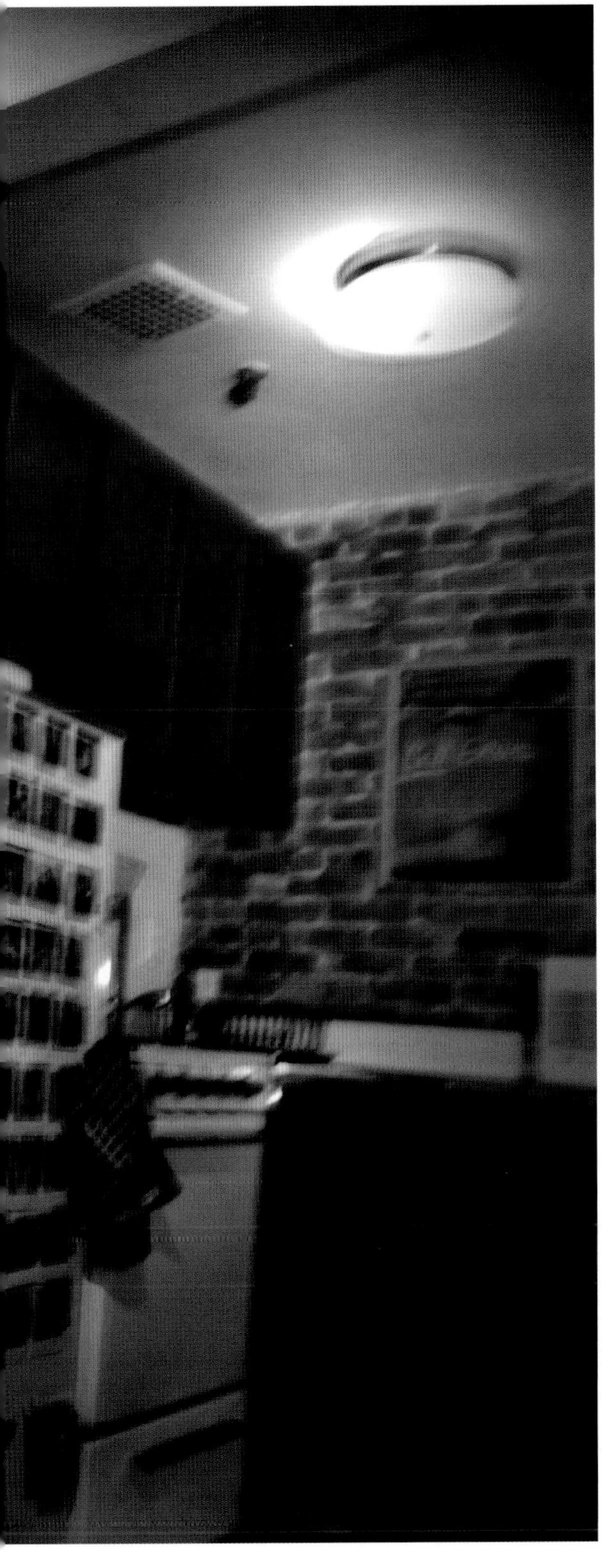

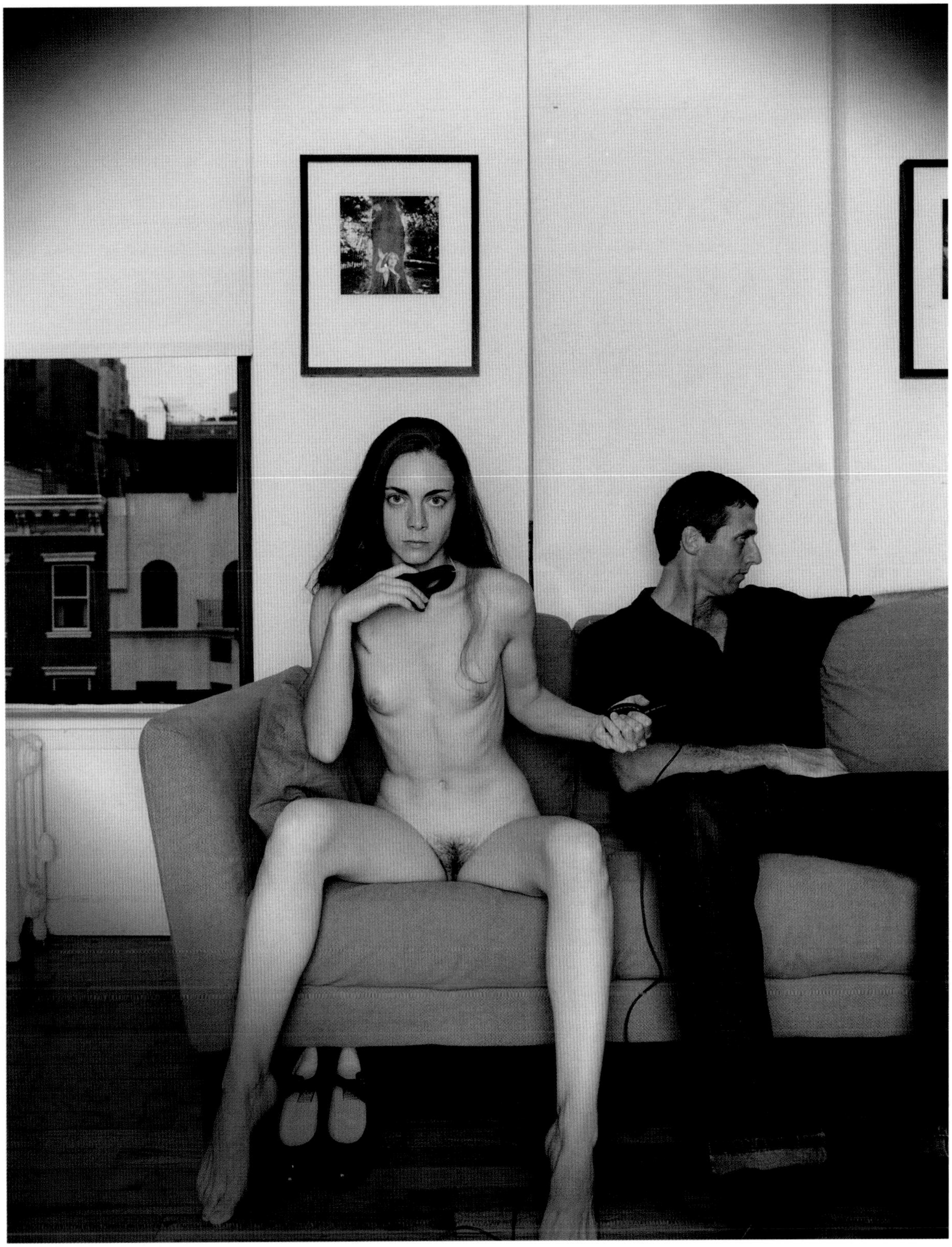

Peter and Model, 1999

Katy Grannan

Like a modern-day August Sander, photographer Katy Grannan has made a name for herself recording the average individual. Her subjects are the neighbors we never speak to, the waitresses hovering beside our table, or the nameless companions on our sidewalks and subways. They are the faces we see each day, everywhere, all around. Like the work of the famous German portraitist, Grannan's photographs of people in their homes and neighborhoods unearth and depict the unique qualities of the everyday soul, elevating them above the ordinary. However, instead of taking a straightforward, documentary approach, Grannan's images—many of which portray her subjects in the nude—are flooded with a sympathetic artistry that is not often found in Sander's work.

"I just love the kind of people that you pass every day. I find them to be more interesting subjects than any celebrities that I've photographed," says Grannan. "I love the spirit behind the people who let me photograph them. They are just as worthy of being photographed as the people we are used to seeing in magazines or films. Everybody has a story to tell, and even the most mundane details can be incredibly compelling."

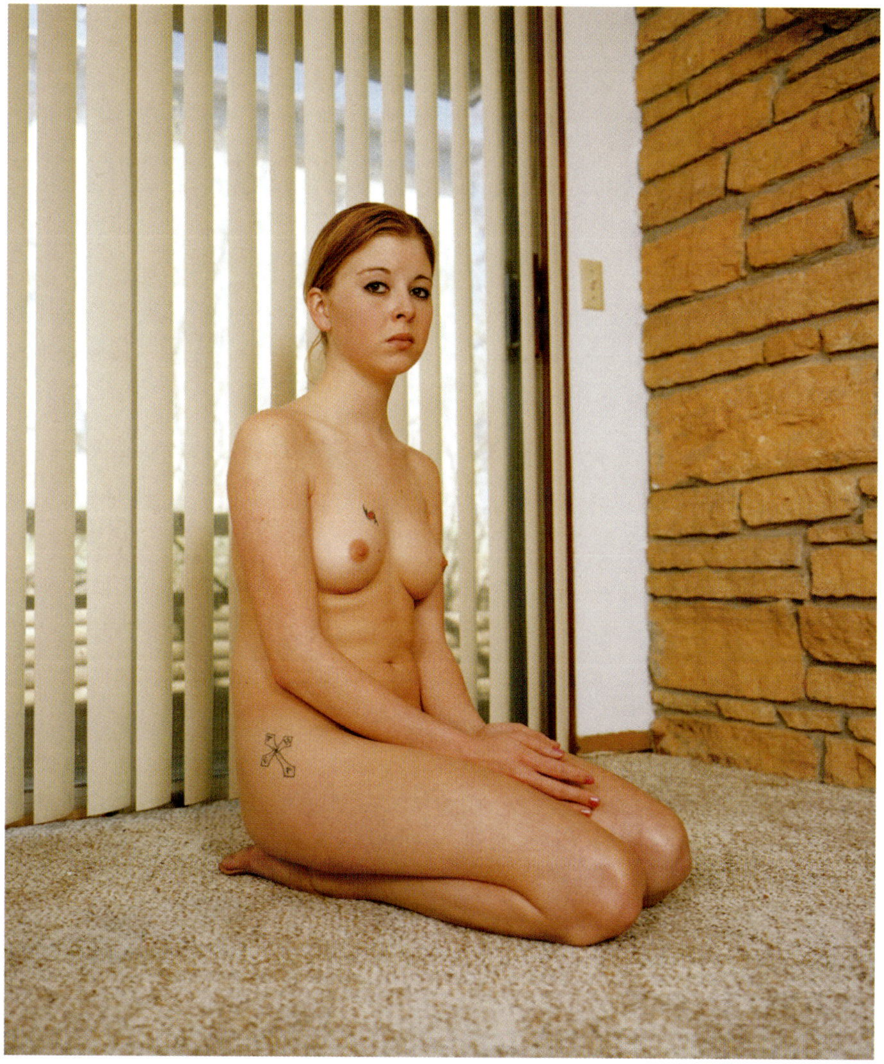

Middleton, WI, 2000
"*Dream America* was a continuation of the *Poughkeepsie Journal* series, but I was traveling around the United States making similar kinds of pictures. I just opened it up a bit more. It was also partly inspired by the questions 'What happens when I take this on the road?' and 'What happens when I go to the middle of the country, what will I find?'"

Born in 1969 in Arlington, Massachusetts, Grannan received her undergraduate degree from the University of Pennsylvania before going on to earn an MFA from Yale in 1999. Her first prominent series, titled *Poughkeepsie Journal*, featured images of subjects Grannan found through an ad she placed in a newspaper of the upstate New York town. She continued to use this method of finding people to photograph in her subsequent series *Dream America*, *Sugar Camp Road*, and *Morning Call*.

Grannan's images are of people surrounded by the textures of suburbia—backyards, wood paneling, thin carpets, scratched linoleum, and worn-out furniture besiege her subjects from every angle. Placing a spotlight on these details was a deliberate decision by Grannan. "With the homes it was intentional that I lit the location in the same way that I lit the people. It was all kind of wide-open, flat lighting, because I wanted the interiors to be equally important as the subjects because they relate to one another in a compelling way," says Grannan, who uses a 4x5 camera on her shoots. "And while I intentionally repeat certain things in the homes, it wasn't a judgment on my part. These are places I'm completely familiar with.

"With all of these interiors I felt like I was walking into a place that I knew. So I did purposely try to call out these repeated things because I thought that's probably one of the reasons someone would be motivated to be photographed and do something out of the ordinary like this. Because when you are shopping in the same stores and living in a place that's so similar to the one next door, you just don't want to get lost in this homogenous existence. I think that is part of the motivation why someone would want to be photographed and made to feel a little more important, interesting, or simply be seen and paid attention to. It could be very meaningful."

Many of her subjects are in the awkward margins of puberty and adulthood—and there is a strong atmosphere of despondency and gravity among her subjects. Eyes drift languidly toward distant objects or pierce the frame and the viewer with a solemnity, even a desperation, that haunts. In her *Dream America* series, for instance, a young girl from Middleton, Wisconsin, sits naked on a beige carpet, her tiny tattoos the only distraction from a stare that reveals a desire to be transported to another place, another time, or—perhaps—to another body.

"Katy's Grannan's work performs an uneasy balancing act between her subject's desires and the artist's vision of the sitter," says Sima Familant, associate director at the Greenberg Van Doren Gallery, Grannan's gallery in New York City. "Her portraits convey much about the subject's need for attention and become a collaborative meditation on identity, beauty, and fame."

Her two most recent series, *Sugar Camp Road*, and *Morning Call*, do stray from her usual boundaries. The former features Grannan venturing outdoors, where she explores the vacant lots and back roads that represent clandestine escapes from the confines of suburban rooms. In *Morning Call*, black-and-white film has replaced Grannan's usual color, and the indoor settings have greater vigor, with sunbursts featured in a handful of shots.

"Each series for me is a shift from the one before and influenced by the previous one," says Grannan. "I don't try to reinvent myself every time I make new work."

The gazes of the subjects in *Morning Call* are also slightly different, as faces and glances have an added confidence and magnetism, daring the viewer to look, and then look again. In the

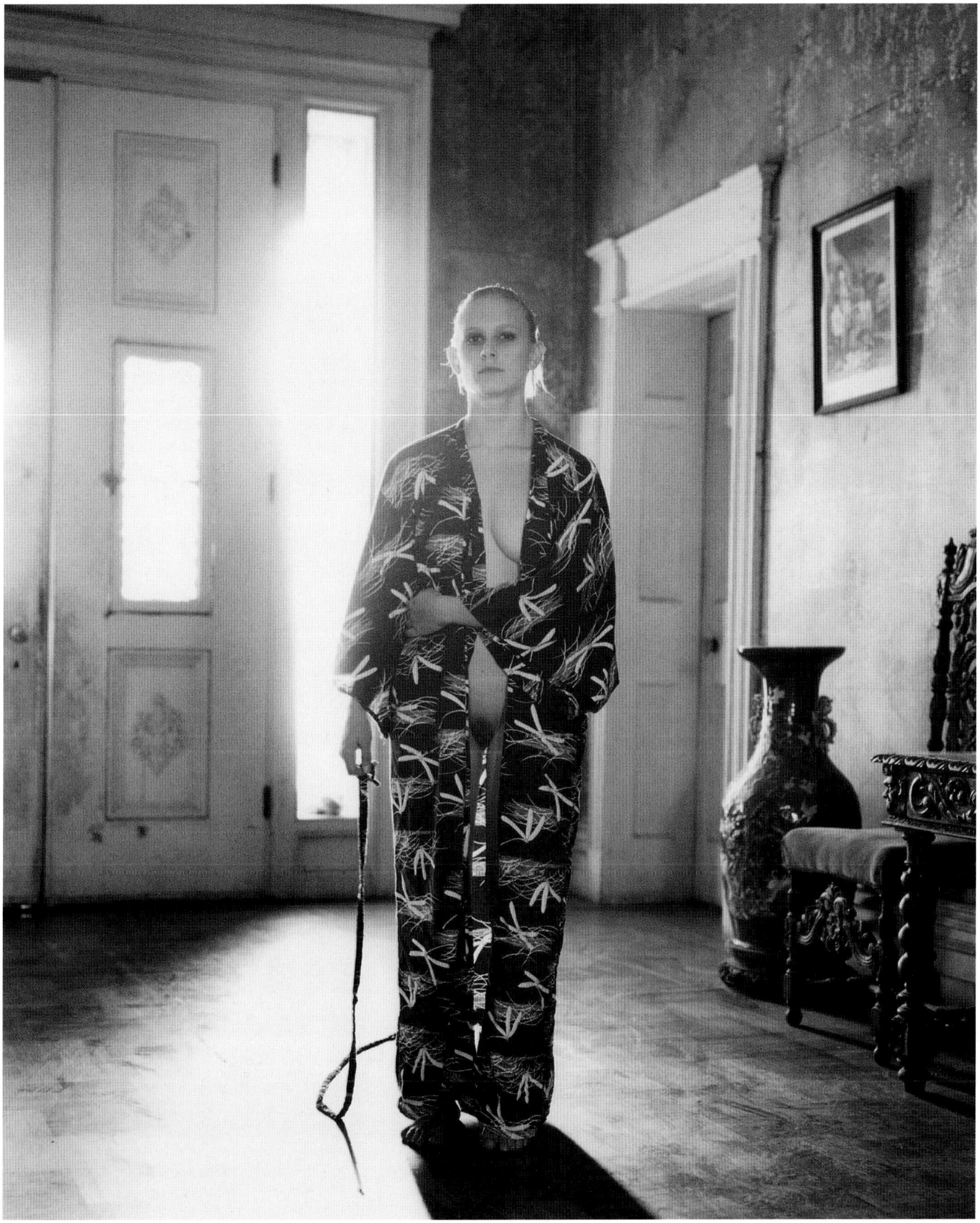

Alexis, Rokabe Farm,
Rhinebeck, New York, 2003

image titled *Alexis, Rokabe Farm, Rhinebeck, New York, 2003*, a woman stands alluringly in the middle of a hallway, the sun beaming through a nearby window. In one hand she casually holds the fabric belt to her robe—a patterned negligee pulled slightly open to reveal her body beneath.

"There's just so much to discover about somebody when you know nothing about him or her," explains Grannan. You tend to have these wonderful conversations—these very forthright conversations with people [you've met] for the first time. And it's really very exciting. I don't try to screen people for the way that they look. I want to see what happens. It's a roll of the dice to a certain extent. I love trying to figure out, during that moment, how to make a compelling photograph. And I think that for both of us there's not an attachment where I'm saying 'What if they don't like the pictures, will we still be good friends afterward? Will we both be a bit embarrassed later?' It's sort of this perfect afternoon together, and that's all we have."

Grannan's distinctive personal work has translated into a flourishing commercial career – with her images appearing in pages of *The New York Times Magazine*, *Fortune*, *Details*, *Vogue Hommes*, and *Toro* magazine. Here, too, her photographs feature expressions of sadness and world-weariness. Even fashion-spread models and celebrities like Billy Joel and Missy Elliott meld into this consistent mood. Her photographs have also been displayed in the Guggenheim Museum in Bilbao, Spain, the Los Angeles County Museum of Art, and the Whitney Museum in New York, where they were part of the 2004 Biennial. They are also included in the permanent collections of the Metropolitan Museum of Art in New York and the Guggenheim Museum, also in New York. Grannan's first monograph was published by Aperture in 2005.

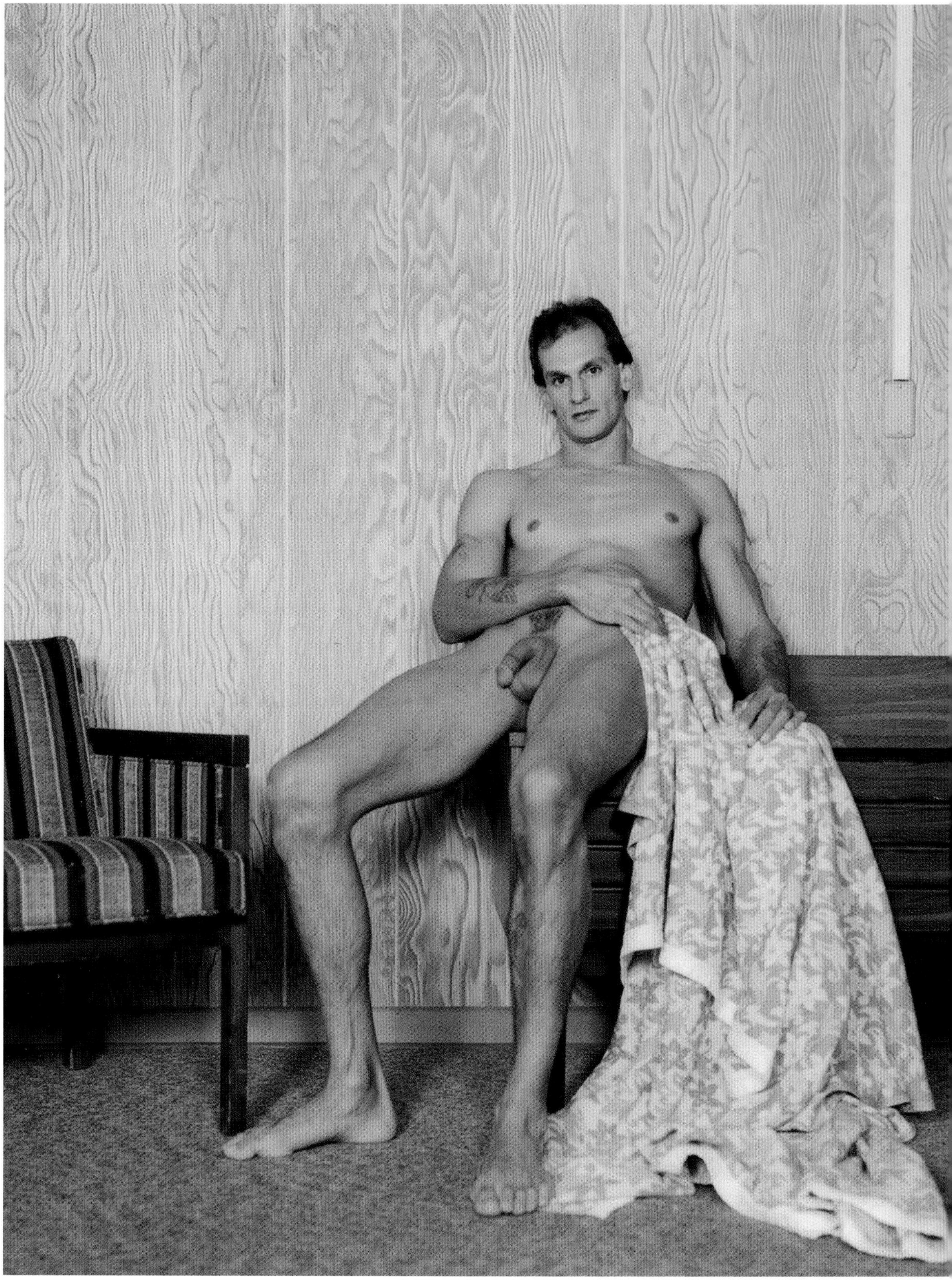

Mike, Hearthstone Motel, Upper Red Hook, New York, 2004
"This series was first inspired by Walker Evans's work around the town of Bethlehem and that area of Pennsylvania. As soon as you start driving around that area you realize that basically nothing has changed. The landscape is very much intact in the way that he described it in his pictures. The choice to use black and white was partly a nod to that era. And it was interesting to move inside of these homes—a lot of them being row homes. Using black and white made some of the more garish interiors almost sort of baroque and very beautiful."

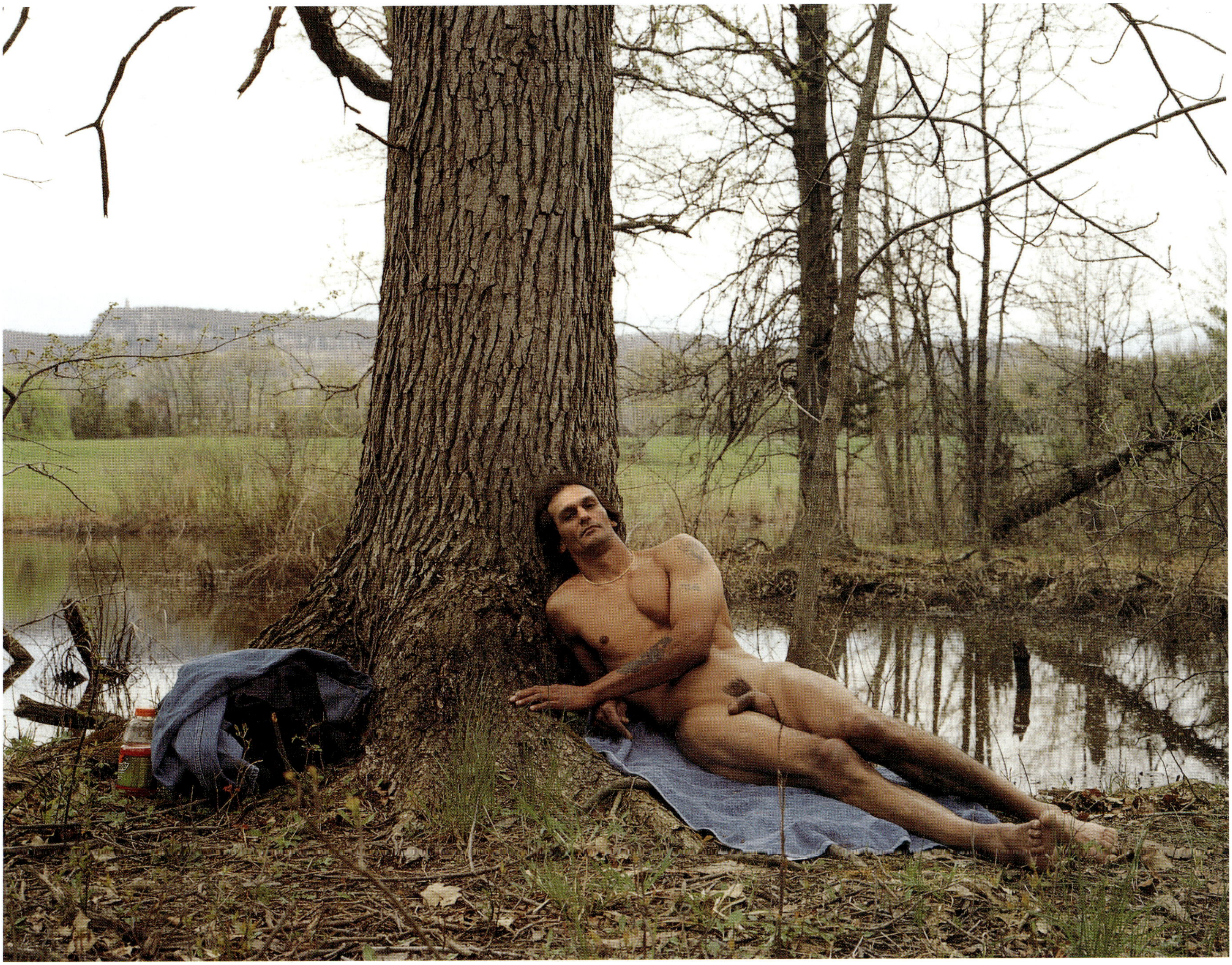

Mike, Private Property, New Paltz, NY, 2003

"This image was taken in an area in New Paltz that was private—we were actually trespassing. It was interesting because he is a construction worker with a very graceful body and all of these grim-reaper tattoos all over his body, and yet he's so perfectly groomed and obviously pays great attention to the way he presents himself. Plus he was also the only person who ever brought along a towel so that he wouldn't have to lie along the ground. Here's this macho man who doesn't want to get any dirt on his ass or bugs crawling on his body. I thought that was really interesting."

Mark Edward Harris

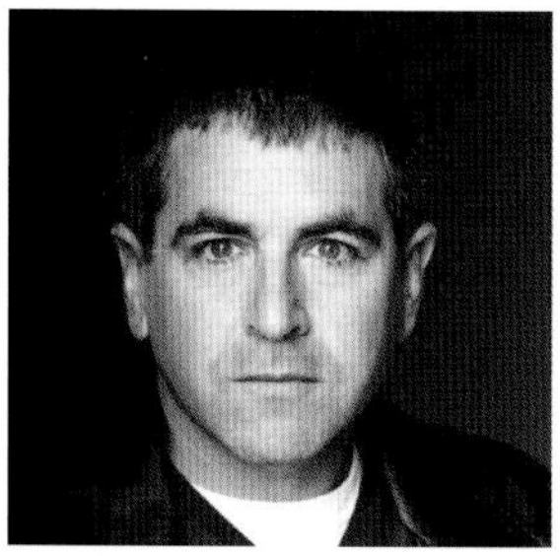

The refined, ethereal, black-and-white images that photographer Mark Edward Harris produced depicting the hot springs of Japan are worlds apart from the soft-focus, openly promiscuous photographs that occupy the glossy pages of *Playboy* magazine. But 47-year-old Harris is not only an expert on the healing pools of Japan; he is also a master of the type of nudes from which Hugh Hefner has profited since Marilyn Monroe graced the first *Playboy* cover in December 1953. He was even commissioned to search for potential playmates for Playboy's 50th-anniversary issue in 2004.

Harris was born in New York City, and then moved to San Francisco as a child. After earning a degree in history at the California State University, Northridge, he worked for a time arranging tours to Asia and the Pacific before undertaking a master's program in pictorial documentary history at the California State University, Los Angeles.

While living in Los Angeles, however, Harris found it easier to get work in the entertainment industry than as a historian with a camera. So, from 1983 to 1986, he worked as a photographer for *The Merv Griffin Show*, photographing celebrity guests on the set. When that job finished, Harris turned his attention to nude photography.

In 1987 he landed a position as a photo assistant at *Playboy* magazine, and his career and knowledge of photography took a dramatic leap. "That was a big break in terms of exposing me to all sorts of lighting equipment and lighting situations," he says. "*Playboy* is a great company to work with. We have great sets and the crews are fantastic. Stylists play an extremely important role on a *Playboy* shoot. A piece of clothing draped across the right place can make a hip or a stomach appear thinner.

"The most enjoyable shoots I've done for *Playboy* are the ones I've done on location. Going to Jamaica to do a reportage-style shoot on hedonism was a lot of fun—and it was a thrill to work with the band KISS as they performed to top-removing fans in concert."

But the jet-setting *Playboy* lifestyle, while fun, did not entirely fulfill Harris's artistic needs. "As Helmut Newton once told me—how's that for name-dropping?—'Any photographer who says he's not a voyeur is either stupid or a liar.' I think that among my many interests—history, travel, music—is a love of women. But my wife taught me a lesson years ago when we first started dating. She came over unannounced while I was shooting a former Playmate for my holiday greeting card and was very uncomfortable with the fact I was alone with this model. I tried to explain that I wasn't shooting the shot out of any prurient interest but simply as a piece of art. She asked: 'Then why don't you photograph a man?' That led to a bit of soul-searching and an epiphany of sorts. Other than assignments that are strictly commercial, we shoot what we are inspired by."

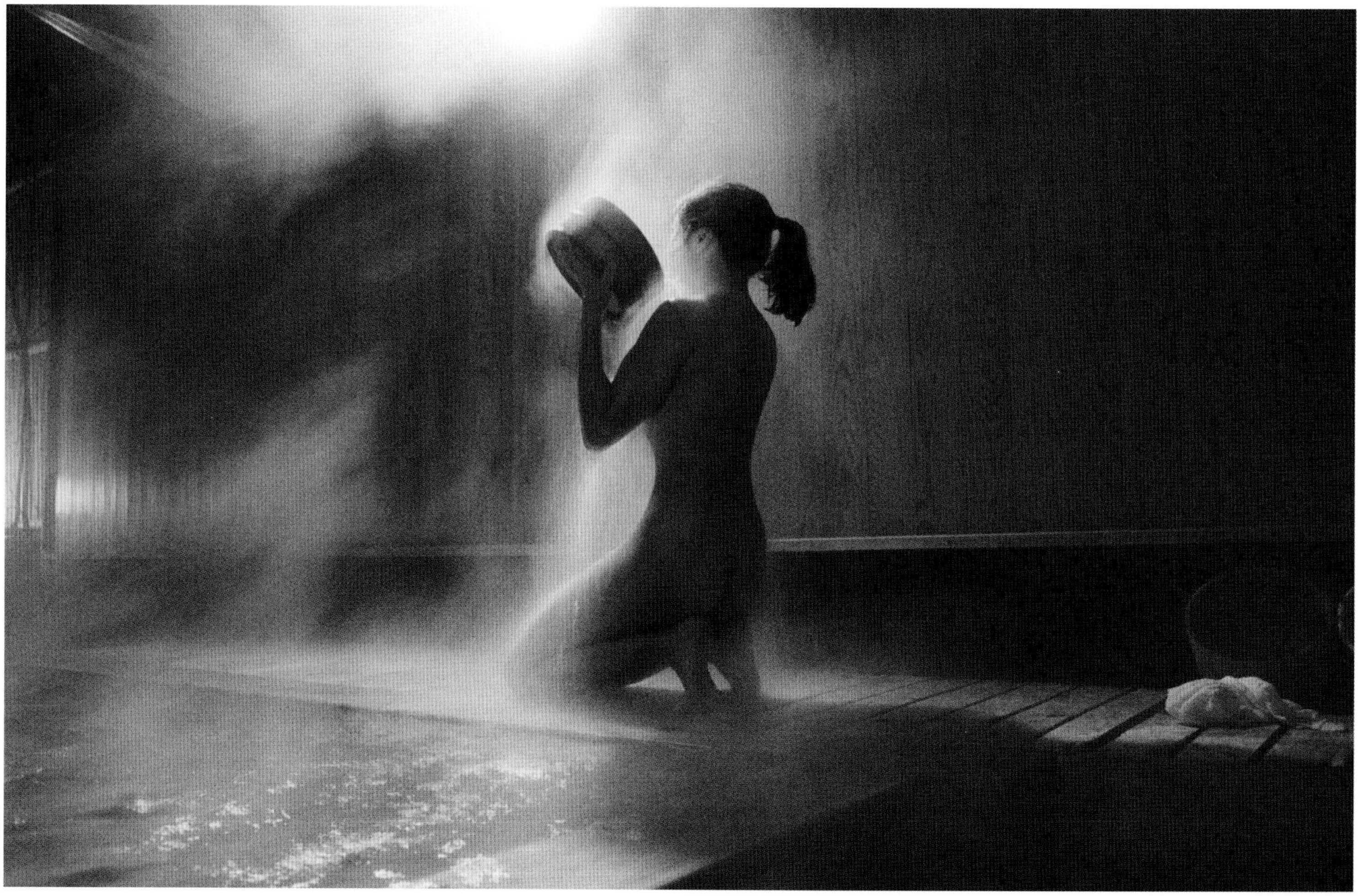

Yufuin Night, 2000
"The steam created from the hot spring water on a cold night—it was around 40°F—seems to add a timeless and perhaps surreal element to the photograph."

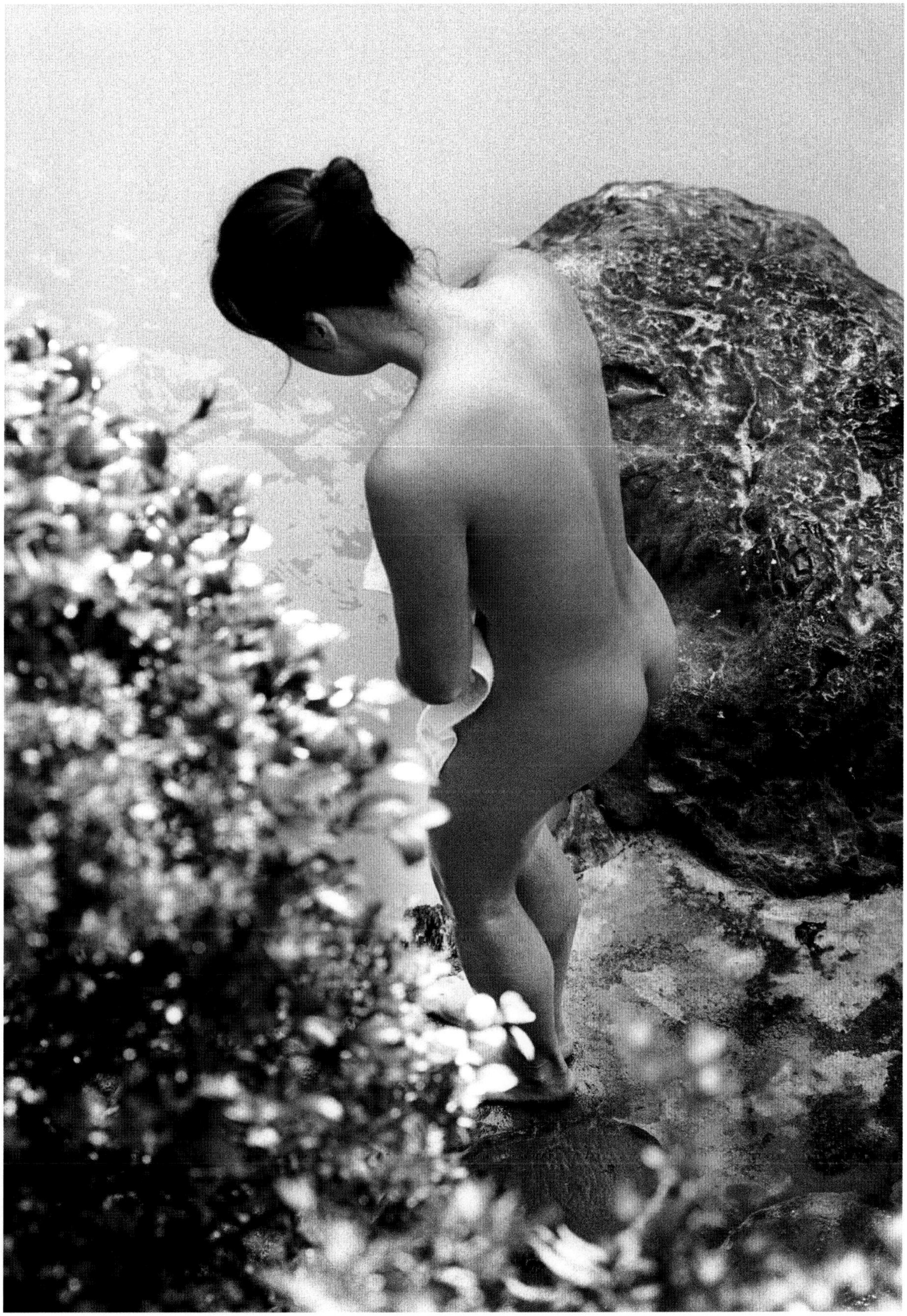

In the 1990s, Harris began work on a number of personal projects, and in 1998 he published *Faces of the Twentieth Century* (Abbeville Press), a collection of portraits by 20th-century photographers, including Mary Ellen Mark, Eve Arnold, Helmut Newton, and Alfred Eisenstaedt. In 1999, Harris, along with his Japanese wife, began a series of trips to Japan to document the thermal hot springs that the Japanese people use for relaxation and physical relief. His work culminated in the 2003 book, *The Way of the Japanese Bath* (Shashin Press). Joining the bathers in the water, Harris used a handheld Nikon FM2 and photographed only with available light. Shooting more than 200 rolls, he overcame the problem of lens fogging by heating his lens ahead of time with a hair drier—a tip he learned from a Japanese television cameraman.

The images in the book are intimate and lovely testimonials to the devotion Harris has to the subject. Bathers move through waterfalls, clouds of vapor, and milky-white baths of delicate liquid. Varying between the indoor pools and the intricate, exquisitely decorated outdoor springs, he is able to communicate the ritual perfectly, along with the transcendent coexistence of the bodies and these divine surroundings. "Too often we forget the importance of the environment we have our models in," says Harris. "We can use depth of field, light, color, tones, to bring the viewer through the frame. I often like to use a foreground to give the image dimension."

Beppu, 2002 *(left)*
"Beppu on the southern Japanese island of Kyushu is the most famous of all hot-spring towns and the setting for this photograph. It was here at the beginning of the 1990s that I discovered the magic of the Japanese bath."

Wakura, 2001 *(page 90)*
"The cascade bath at the Wakura Onsen can take the knots out of the stiffest of shoulders."

Hokkaido, 2001 *(page 91)*
"Steam in an uncontrolled environment—as opposed to on a set—is one of the most interesting and difficult elements to work with in photography. Among other things, the lens wants to fog up. I used a hair drier to heat the lens, which delayed the condensation obscuring any potential image."

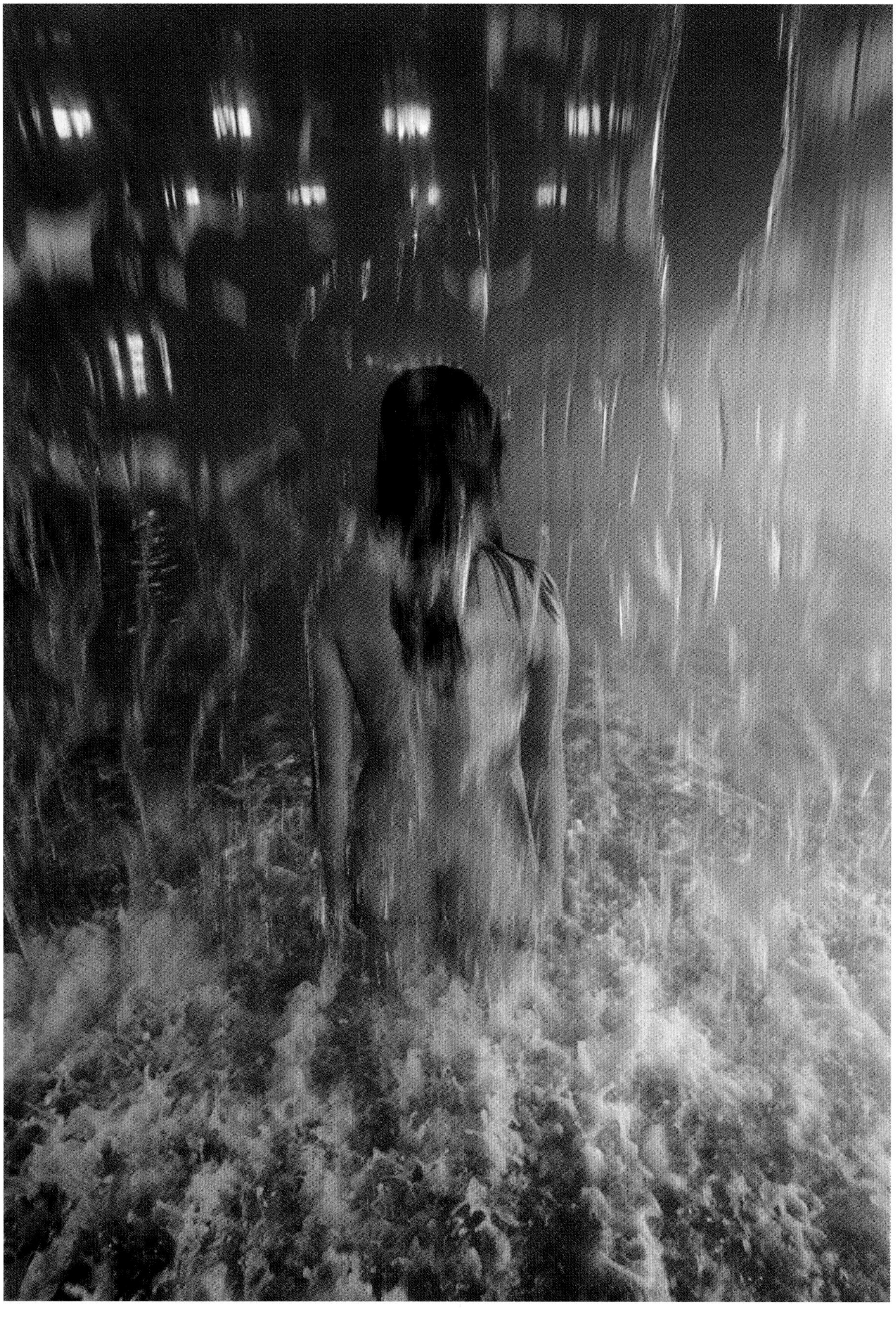

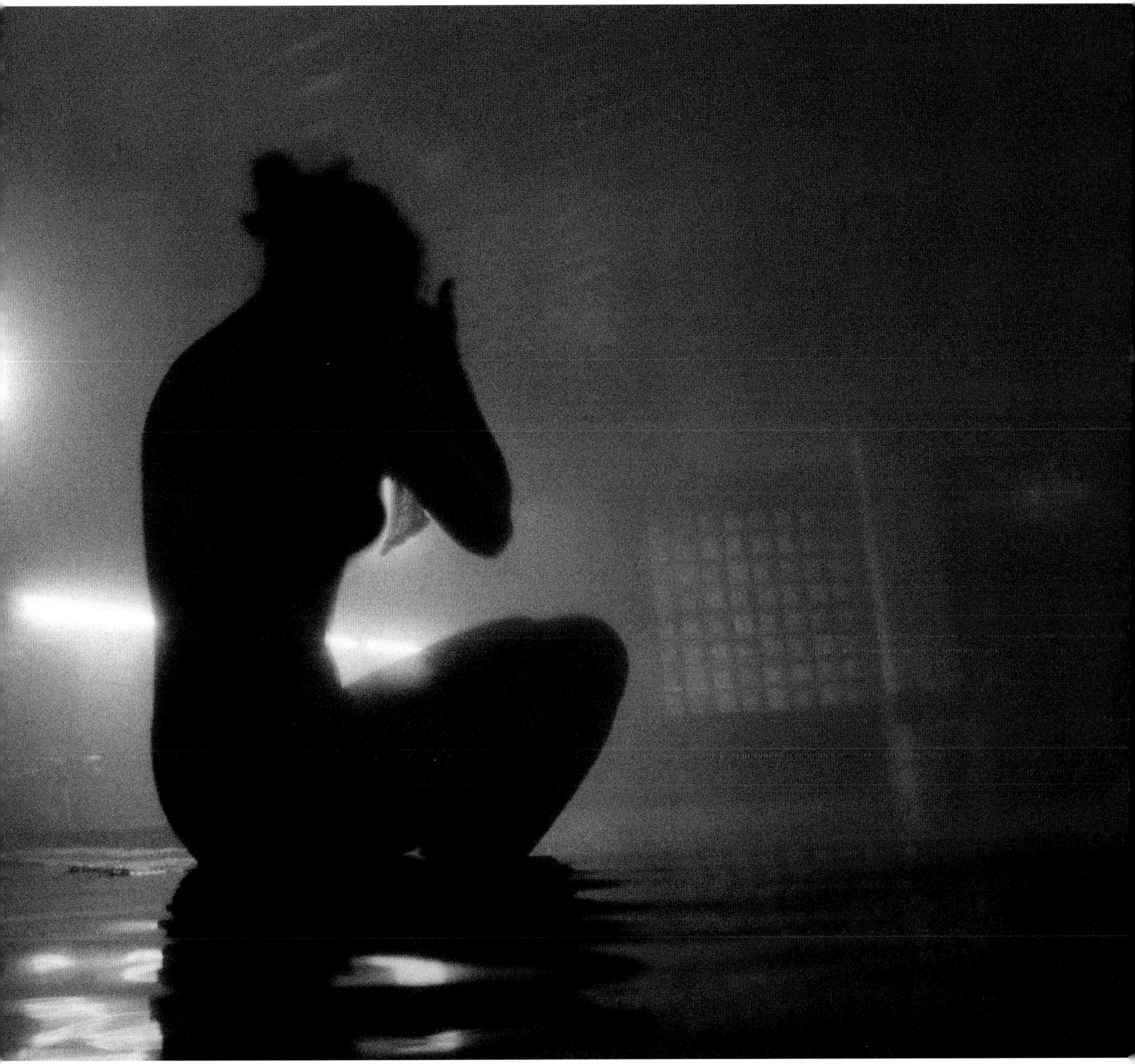

Mark Edward Harris

Sam Haskins

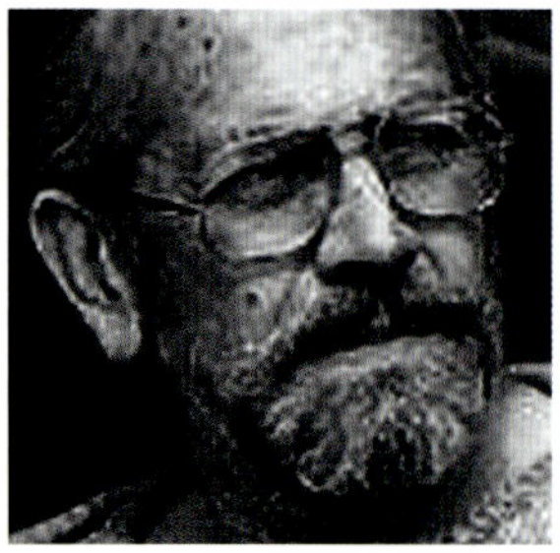

While the phrase often gets thrown around these days, Sam Haskins is indeed a visionary. His initial books and images, released during the turbulent 1960s and early 1970s, eschewed clichés and took a confident venture into the unknown, influencing generations of imitators.

Born in 1926 and raised in South Africa, Haskins studied graphic art at the Technical College in Johannesburg. In 1950 he traveled to London, where he studied photography in a small school that was the forerunner of the London College of Printing (now the London College of Communication).

"While studying in London I used to visit the library at the Victoria & Albert Museum to study the current magazines," he recalls. "*Graphis* magazine [the original, edited by Walter Herdeg] was one of the inspiring publications that I used to devour. In one issue they featured the photographs of Irving Penn, and I remember the profound impression they made on me. Those were invigorating times: the Festival of Britain was just one of the highlights of the postwar cultural renaissance; Carol Reed had just directed *The Third Man*; and ballet and opera flourished. This innocent from Africa was in heaven."

After returning to South Africa in 1952, Haskins and his new wife Alida built their own studio, and Haskins went on to become a highly successful advertising photographer and editorial illustrator. But he was not completely satisfied. "As much as I enjoyed my profession, a feeling of constraint crept in," he says. "Alida and I decided to develop an independent project in which I could enjoy full creative freedom."

That project turned into his first publication, *Five Girls* (The Bodley Head, 1962). The book, an inventive look at five young females in various states of undress, brought the nude form to life, rather than treating it like a museum figure. His work allowed both him and the genre to break free from a static, repetitive routine.

"Due to my years in art-school life classes, I am quite comfortable working with unclothed models, and I felt that the world could do with a book that celebrated the beauty of women with a fresh approach. My young models had an equally natural and intelligent attitude. The five young women were friends of our family. They came to my studio for experimental work whenever they had the time. This was an era when nudity was still something of an issue—when photographers pretended they were showing us classical statuary, not warm, breathing humans. I was fully aware that my book would not resemble anything else on the market at that time."

Years later, Philip Garner would paraphrase Haskins's first publication in *American Photo* with these laudatory words: "Haskins reinvented the nude, a genre previously dominated

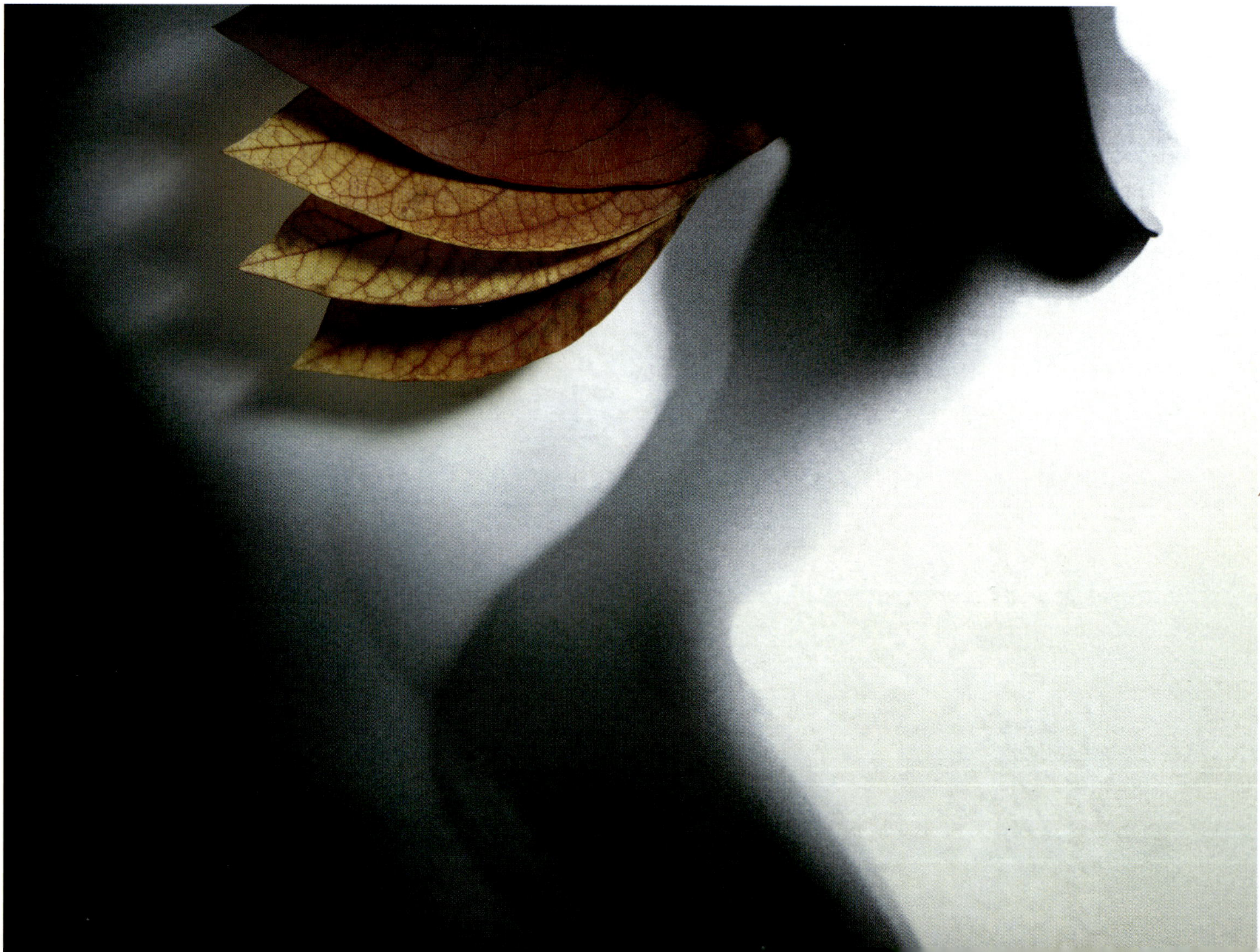

Blueberry Wings, 1978
"This is one of many montage images I made with the transparency sandwich technique well before the advent of Photoshop."

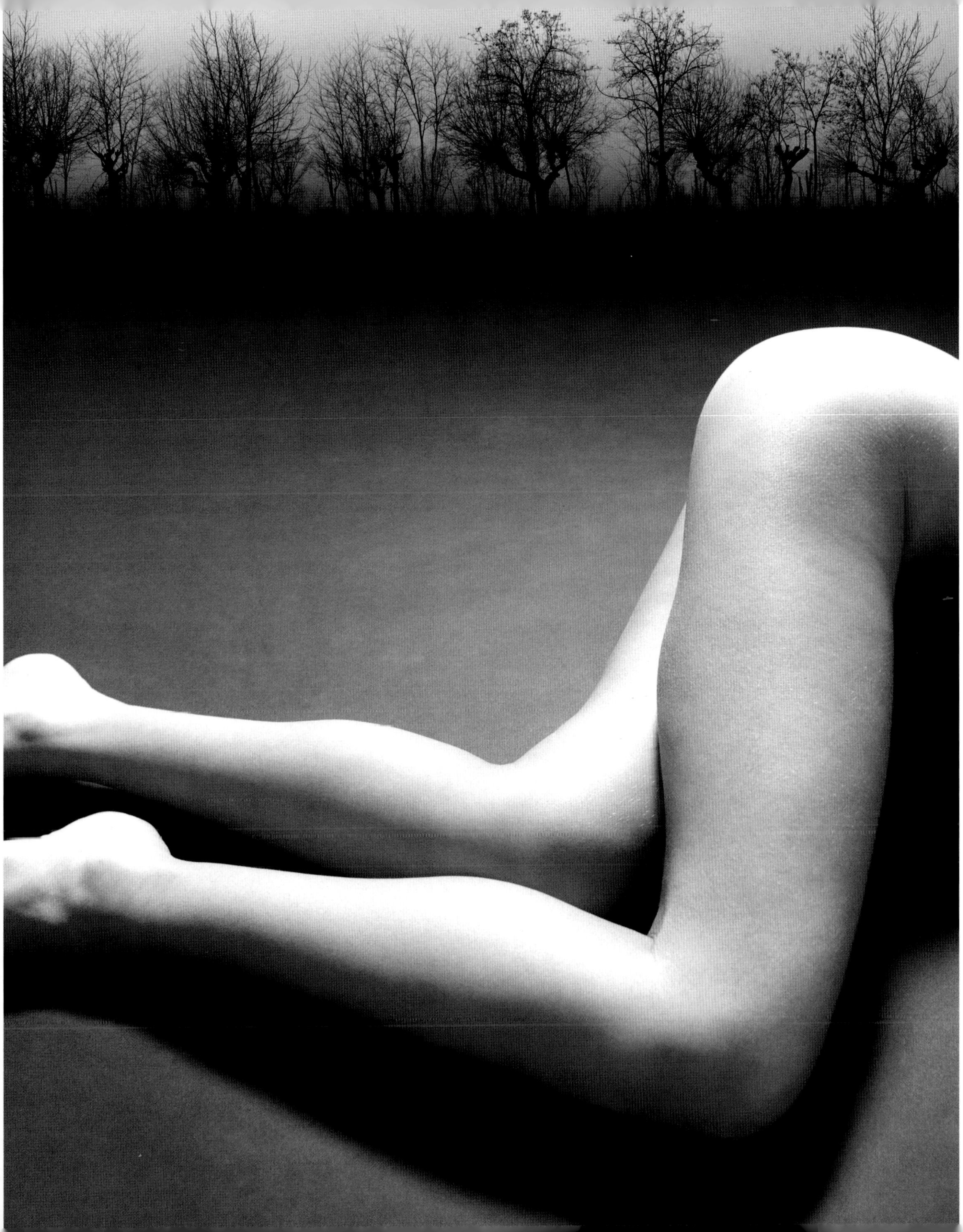

Trees + Legs, 1978 *(left)*
"Trees photographed in Tuscany, legs in London."

Cheating the Ace, Cowboy Kate, 1963 *(page 94)*
"The rich-black, stark-white, grainy image quality derives from my love of the juicy prints made with the stone lithographic process. At the time, I rigged a DIY point source light in my enlarger by substituting a 500-watt photoflood for the normal light source."

by traditions of academic formalism, tired clichés, and unconvincing artiness. He brought a cinematic approach, cleverly hinting at narrative, discreetly inviting his audience to engage with the girls as credible characters in his picture stories."

Five Girls was only the beginning. His next book, *Cowboy Kate & Other Stories* (The Bodley Head, 1964) won the Prix Nadar in 1964 and made Sam Haskins an instantly recognizable name in his field. Featuring a storyline straight from a bawdy Western, the book featured a long-legged, rebellious blonde and her exploits throughout the Old West. It was fun, cinematic, playfully erotic, and thoroughly unique. Quite simply, *Kate* was a revelation.

"I had taken a few experimental shots of a young woman—the one on the cover of the book—wearing something resembling a cowboy hat," says Haskins. "We were just having fun. When we looked at the contacts, the idea of creating a Western yarn emerged. The simple storyline was really a broth cooked up by Alida and me. By the time we were ready to go into production, the original model had left South Africa, so we had to complete the shoot with stand-ins, four in all.

"*Kate* was in every sense a book of its time, hence its resonance with the generation that rejected conventional values," continues Haskins. "Kate is a powerful woman portrayed with strong photography, the like of which had not been used in figure photography before."

Three other publications followed: *November Girl* (The Bodley Head, 1966); *Haskins Posters* (Haskins Press, 1972), winner of the Gold Medal of the New York Art Directors Club; and *Photo Graphics* (RotoVision, 1980). *November Girl* was the first book that featured Haskins's exploration of multiple-image techniques, a precursor to the modern world of digital manipulation.

"I did this in an effort to broaden the medium and facilitate the creation of narrative with images," says Haskins, who uses Tri-X film and Pentax cameras, particularly the 6x7 II. "I had so much fun with the concept 'one plus one can add up to more than two,' that the whole procedure became a bit of an obsession. [Later on,] after progressing to a larger proportion of color work, the montages took on a different hue. By superimposing transparencies it was possible to achieve a subtle melding of colors and tonal values that Photoshop and its Layers tool can only dream about.

"These days, I frequently combine images on the computer, and I love the process, but just as a digital audio generator could never, ever produce the exact sound of a Stradivarius, so it is with electronic image manipulation. Having said that, I relish the tonal palette made possible by digital image files printed on the new high-end ink-jet printers. The rich, juicy blacks we have grown to love in prints made by the stone lithography process are now possible with the click of a mouse."

Haskins is busy at work on a retrospective book as well as a "director's cut" of *Cowboy Kate*. He also continues to display his supreme talent for varied media, working on three new publications, *Apple & Eve*, *Remember Barcelona*, and *Heart of the Matter*, which combine photography with graphic design.

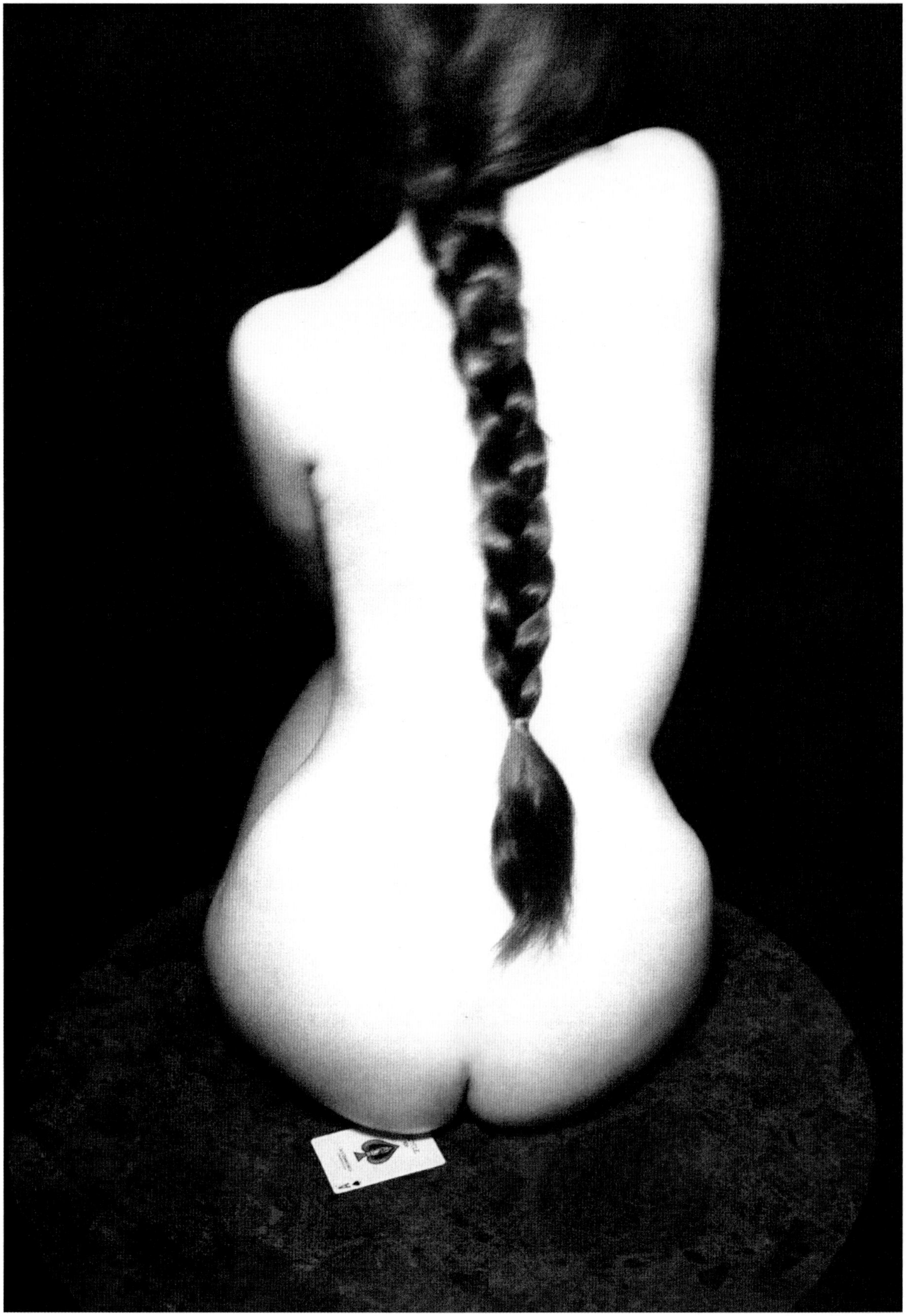

Cheating the Ace, 1963

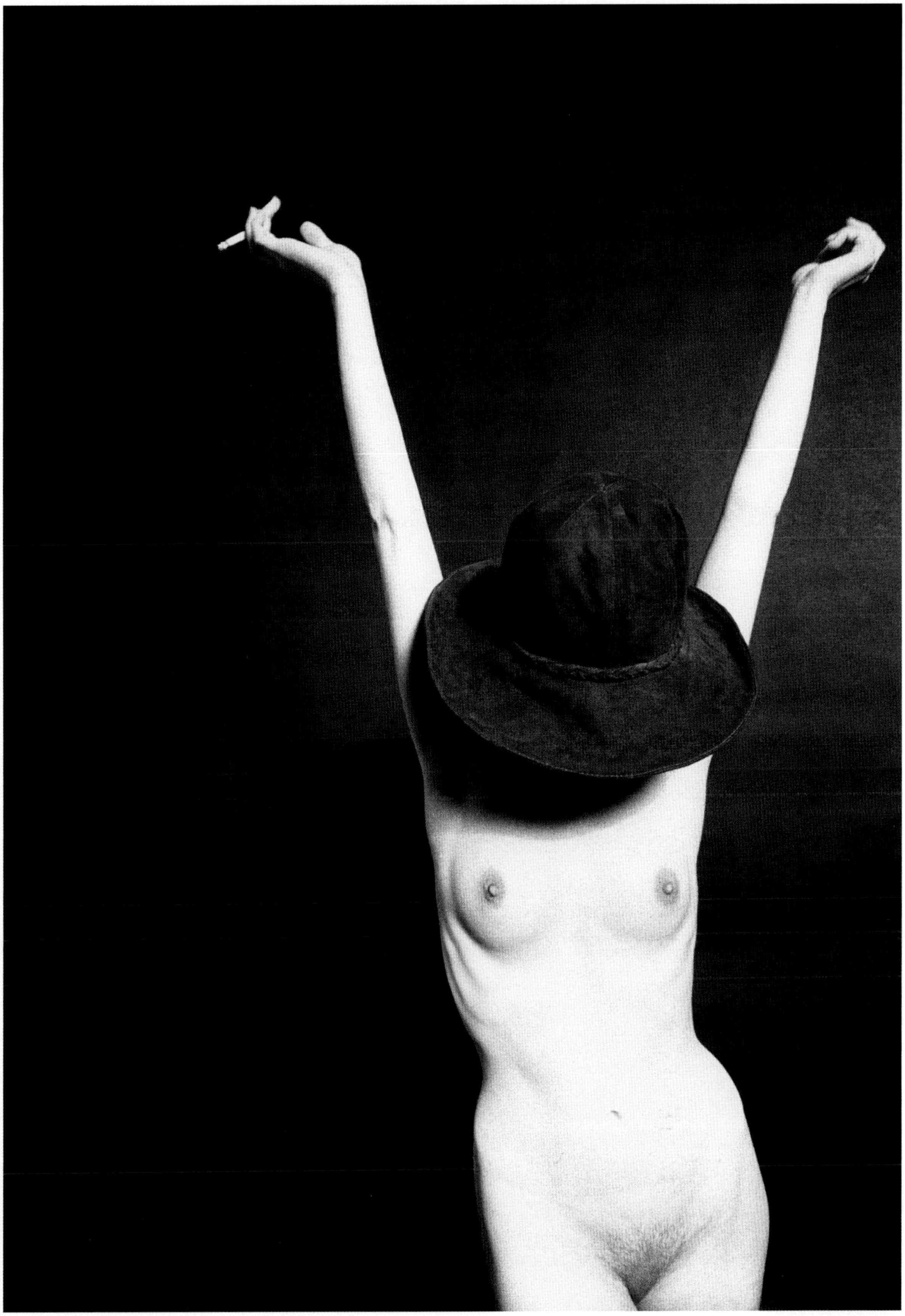

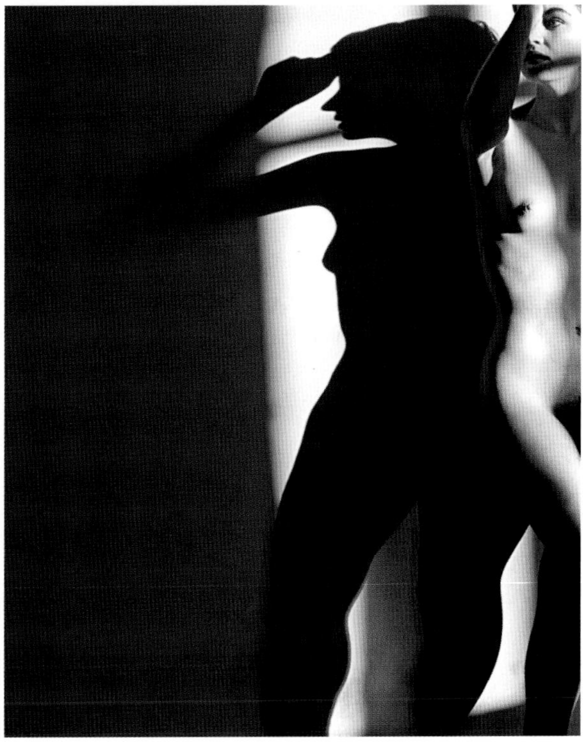

Shadow, 1959 *(above)*
"An unplanned grab shot with a clumsy 4x5 view camera. The sunlight on my studio wall was there for a few fleeting minutes before being obscured by a passing cloud."

Kate Stand-in, Cowboy Kate, 1963 *(left)*
"*Cowboy Kate* was in production over several months, and due to the migratory habits of models I was forced to use five different ladies for the role of Kate. This is one of the 'faceless' Kates."

Mobile, Five Girls, 1961
(page 96)
"Luck plays an important role when panning with the movement."

Run, Photo Graphics, 1979
(page 97)
"This is one of those deceptive photographs. The straightforward appearance belies the complex lighting involved. The model is running in front of a translucent screen placed in front of two sets of flashlights with a time delay between the two."

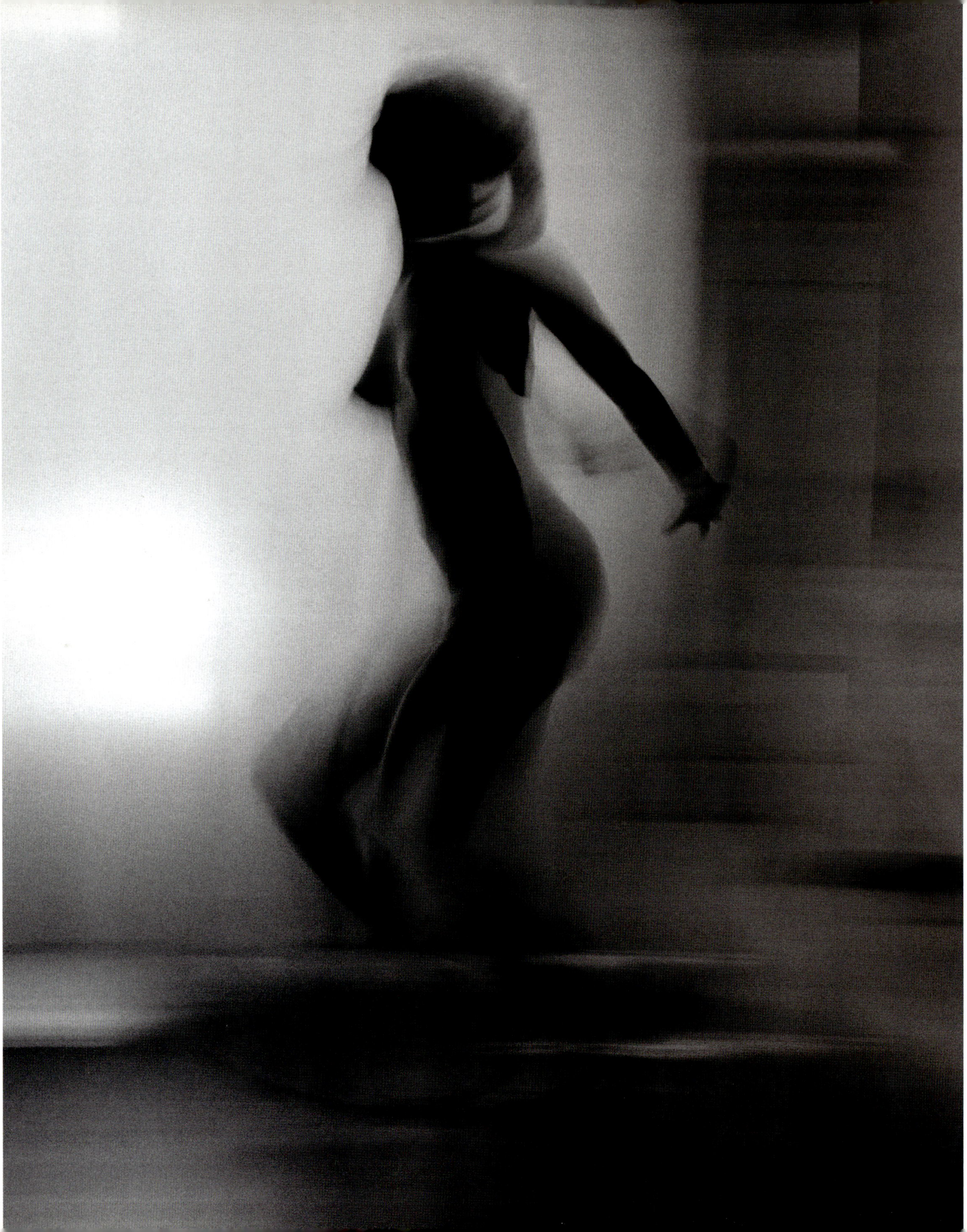

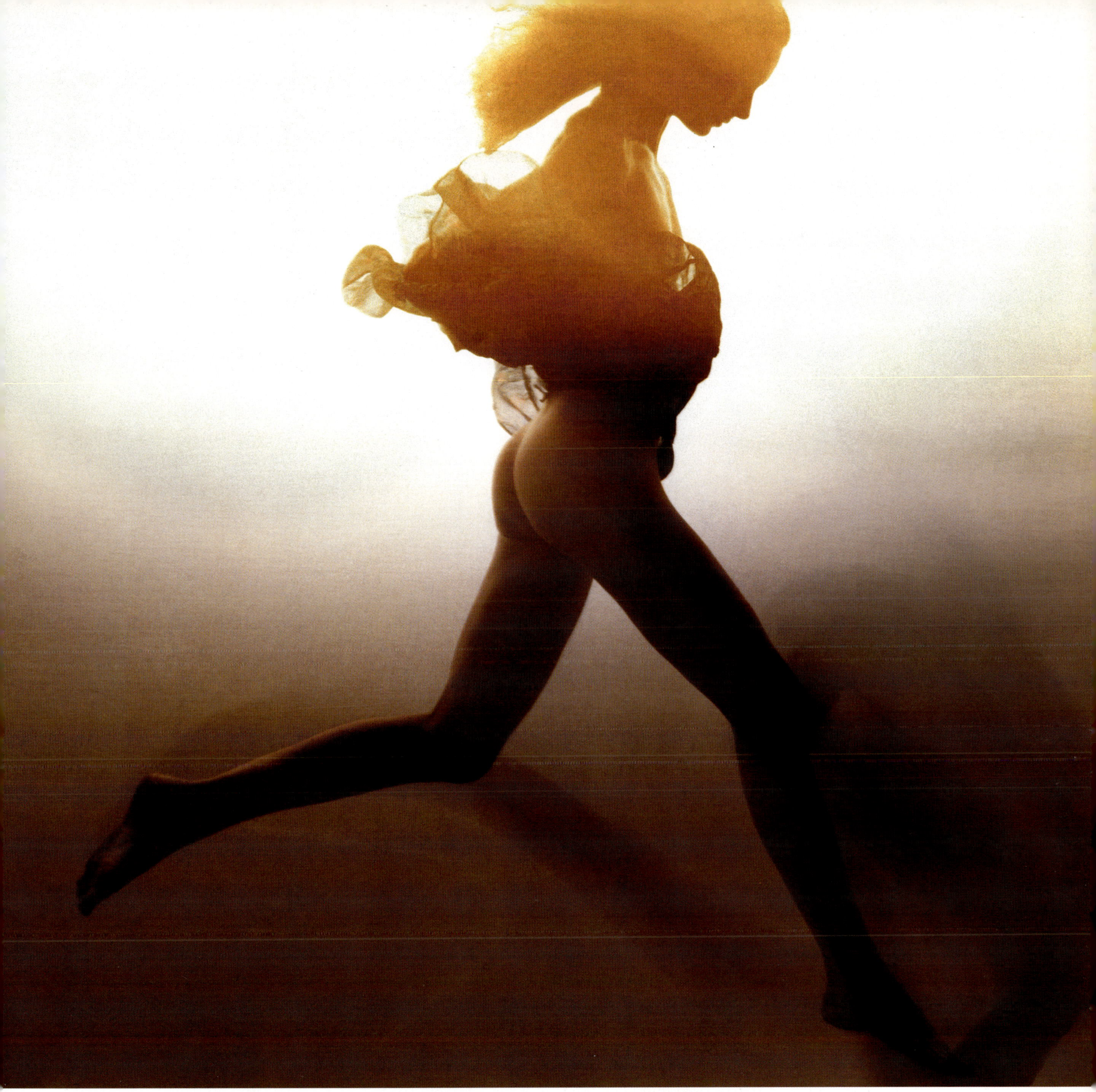

Kenro Izu

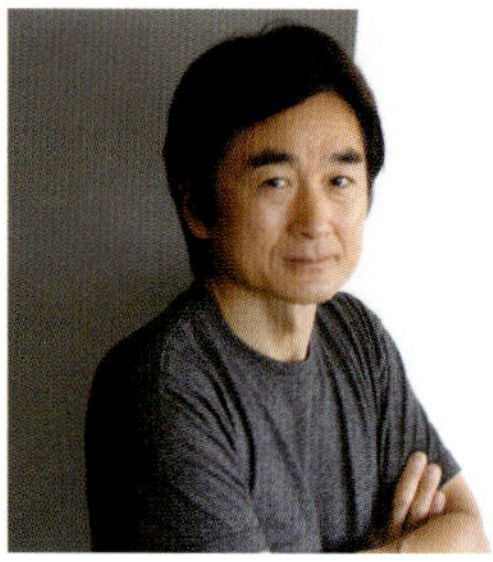

Standing in front of a Kenro Izu print in a gallery is like witnessing a miracle—like a DiMaggio swing, a Hendrix riff, or a van Gogh swirl. While the images reproduced on these pages will hopefully give you an idea of his extraordinary talent and skill as a photographer, they cannot equal the experience of gazing at a full-size print.

Izu was originally an aspiring doctor in his homeland of Japan, and his first experience in photography was capturing images through a microscope. After abandoning medicine, he began studying photography at Nihon University in 1969, before dropping out in 1971 and, against his family's wishes, moving to New York. With ¥50,000 in his pocket, he lost himself in the great metropolis, working in a restaurant, going to museums, and photographing the city by night, trying to find his vision and style.

In 1974 Izu was able to set up his own studio in Manhattan, and he began taking on regular commercial and editorial assignments. In 1983 he began using the large-format (8x10 to 14x20) and platinum printing processes that characterize his work today. His work is now included in the permanent collections of the Metropolitan Museum of Art in New York City, the San Francisco Museum of Modern Art, and the Museum of Fine Arts in Houston, Texas.

"I [first] encountered a platinum print in the early 80s, when I was searching for the right technique for my *Sacred* series," recalls Izu, referring to his project photographing sacred places and monuments around the world. "It was a Paul Strand print at an auction house in New York. I was amazed by its deep, luminous quality. I realized that I would need a large negative to contact-print. I ordered and received the 14x20 Deardorff in 1983. Since then I've used the camera and the format exclusively."

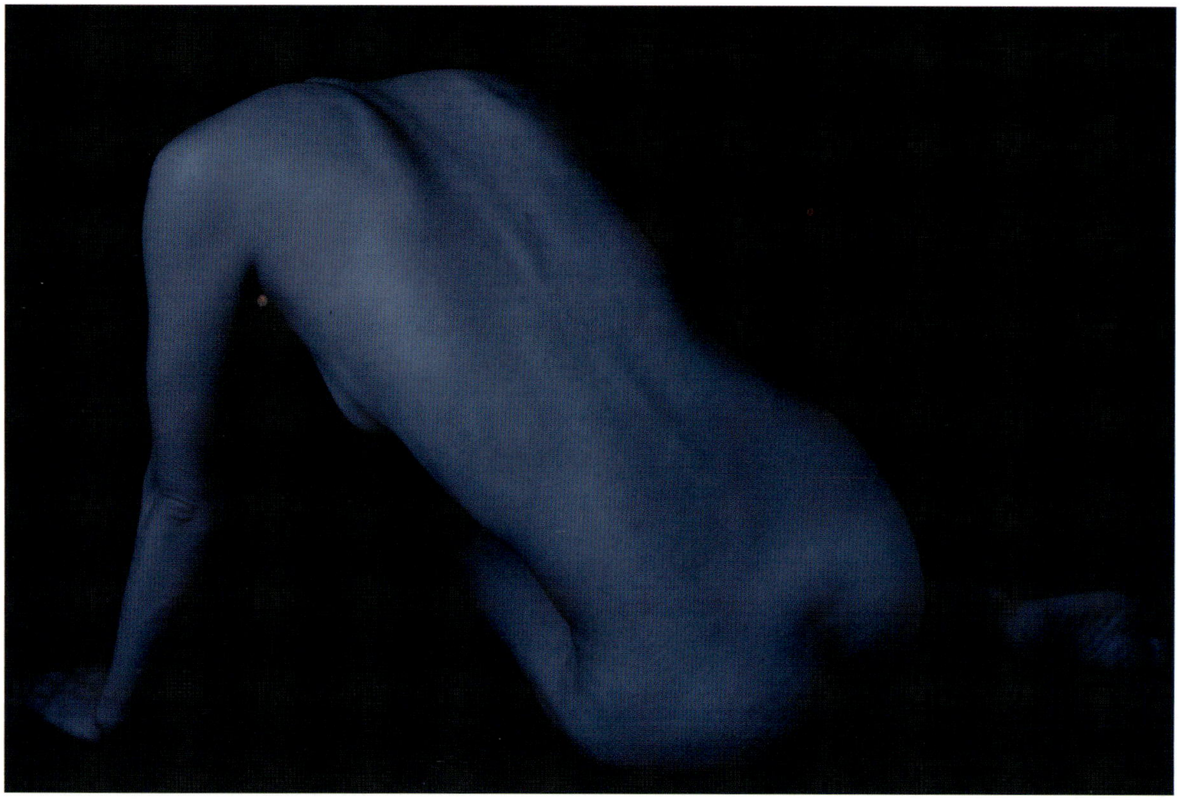

That same year, Izu started shooting a black-and-white series of flowers, titled *Still Life*. That project would continue for many years and eventually lead to a 1998 Arena Editions book of the same name that included not only the floral imagery but also a number of nudes.

The sensual flower photos combined with the nude female body were creations of stirring and intense proportions. Izu's background in documenting microorganisms found new expression in these images. His eye saw into living entities and analyzed their configurations and shapes, and his work described their contours and curves. While reflective of Edward Weston's studies of peppers and female bodies, Izu's images featured deeper blacks and lurking shadows, adding heightened eroticism, melancholy, and a sense of mortality to the photographs. The rich, platinum prints elevated the subjects to heights of divinity. *Still Life* was and remains a masterwork.

"I got the idea for the series when I started floral study," explains Izu. "When I photograph the human body, I see the body as a still life as well, in the same sense as a flower. It is a very fragile and precious life form, yet there is an existence beyond the form."

After compiling a book of his images of sacred sites (*Sacred Places*, Arena Editions, 2001) and another on Angkor, Cambodia (*Passage To Angkor*, Channel Photographics, 2003), Izu has recently turned his attention to a color that Picasso became obsessed with for many years—blue. This time, concentrating solely on the nude, Izu has developed a never-before-used method combining a platinum and cyanotype printing process. Directly printing the 14x20 negative onto a watercolor paper that has been hand-coated with platinum emulsion, he then proceeds to add up to four layers of blue cyanotype to the image.

"After numerous experiments, which included a gum bichromate process over platinum, to try to achieve deep, yet translucent blue, I have developed this method with a multilayer process," says Izu. "It is practically three to five full processes taking place in one image, which could take up to eight straight days to complete. A finished print is cold-mounted on a powder-coated aluminum sheet and float-mounted with bolts and glue on an anodized black aluminum plate."

The resulting conceptions are glorious in their depth and splendor. Swaths of outlined blue shapes swim in rich, cryptic shadows. Nude backs, legs, arms, and torsos spread across the frame. The bodies appear as dream figures—fluid and enigmatic figments of the unconscious brain. Indeed, it was a vision that Izu witnessed while in bed that led to the series. "One night I woke up and saw a vase of flowers in a full-moon light, lit in a dark blue, light-filled room, which was dreamlike," he recalls. "It was a space totally different from my usual living room, as if I was a stranger there. I could not stop thinking [about it], and comparing this with the otherworldly, tranquil, dark worship hall of a Tibetan monastery I had visited. The image, in a shadow of blue and a conviction of fragility, of substance and existence, overlapped and started to visualize [sic] in the summer of 2002."

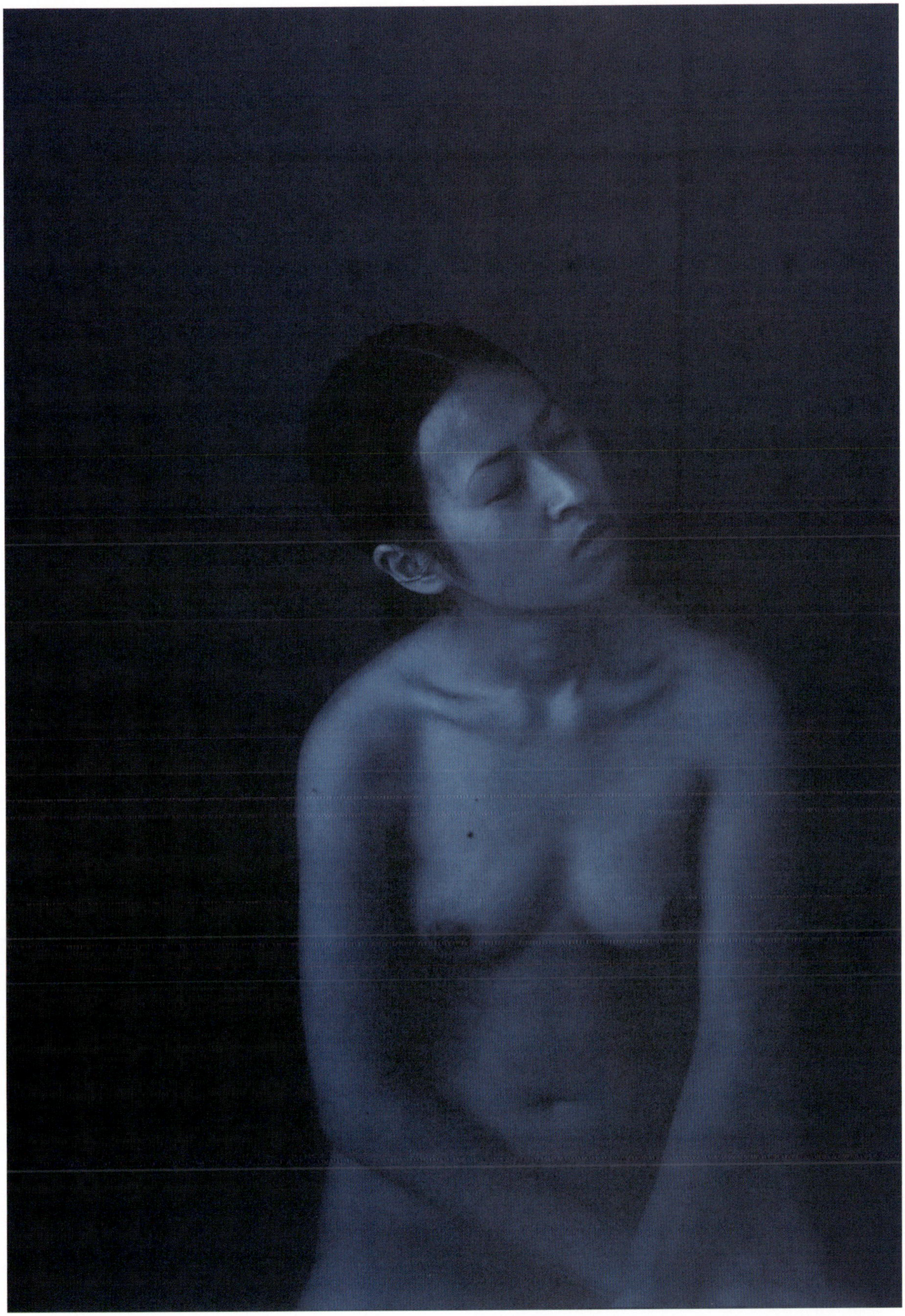

(Both images) **Untitled, 2004, from the Blue series**
"It was in the winter of early 2002 when I became interested in the darkness that embraces and absorbs everything. It began with my curious experience in a room of worship in a Tibetan monastery. Inside there was a dimly lit, gilded, holy statue, with a faint light coming from the altar. It was as if I strayed into an otherworldly space, where complete silence and timelessness reign within the atmosphere. Since then I have had the interest and desire to photograph the human body in dim lights, where the light and shadow are almost indistinguishable and the form dissolves into the shadow."

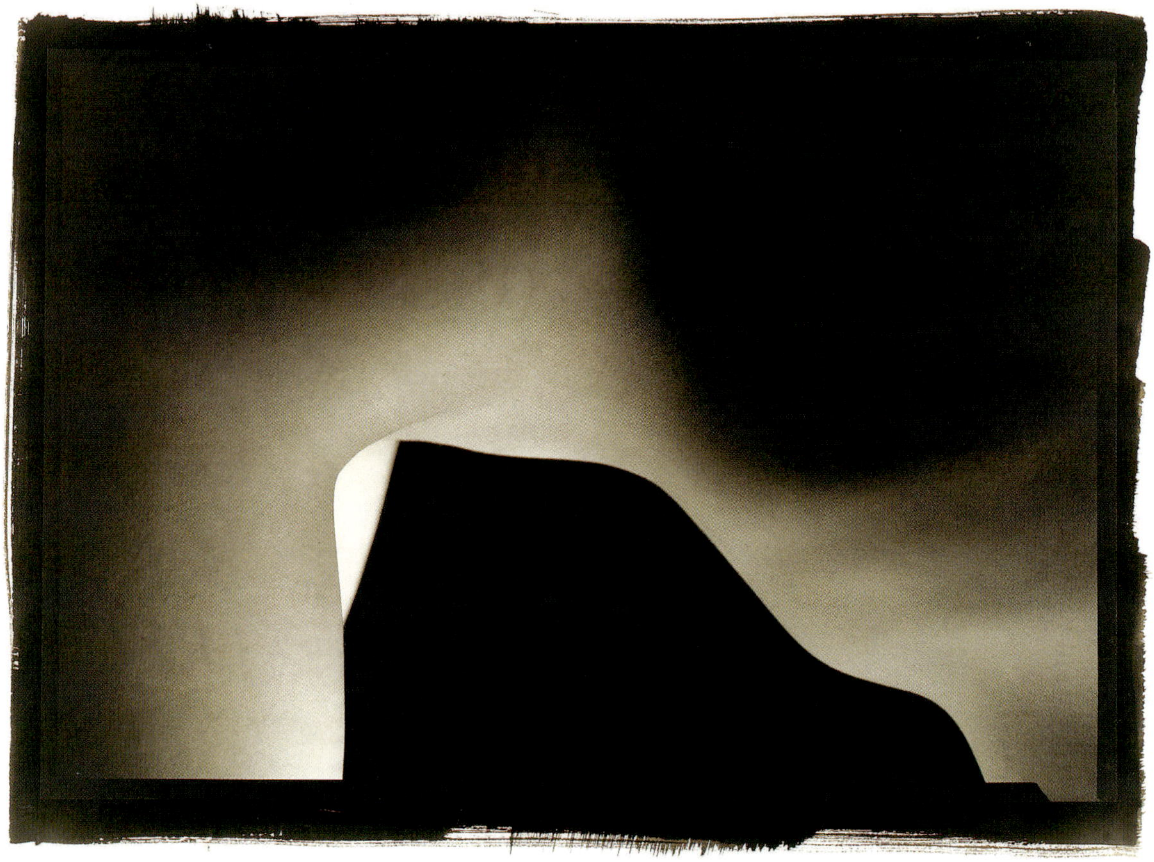

Untitled, 1998, from the Still Life series
"The human body, along with floral subjects, have been my interests since 1982. I have photographed the body and its form close-up to portray its delicate life in a light."

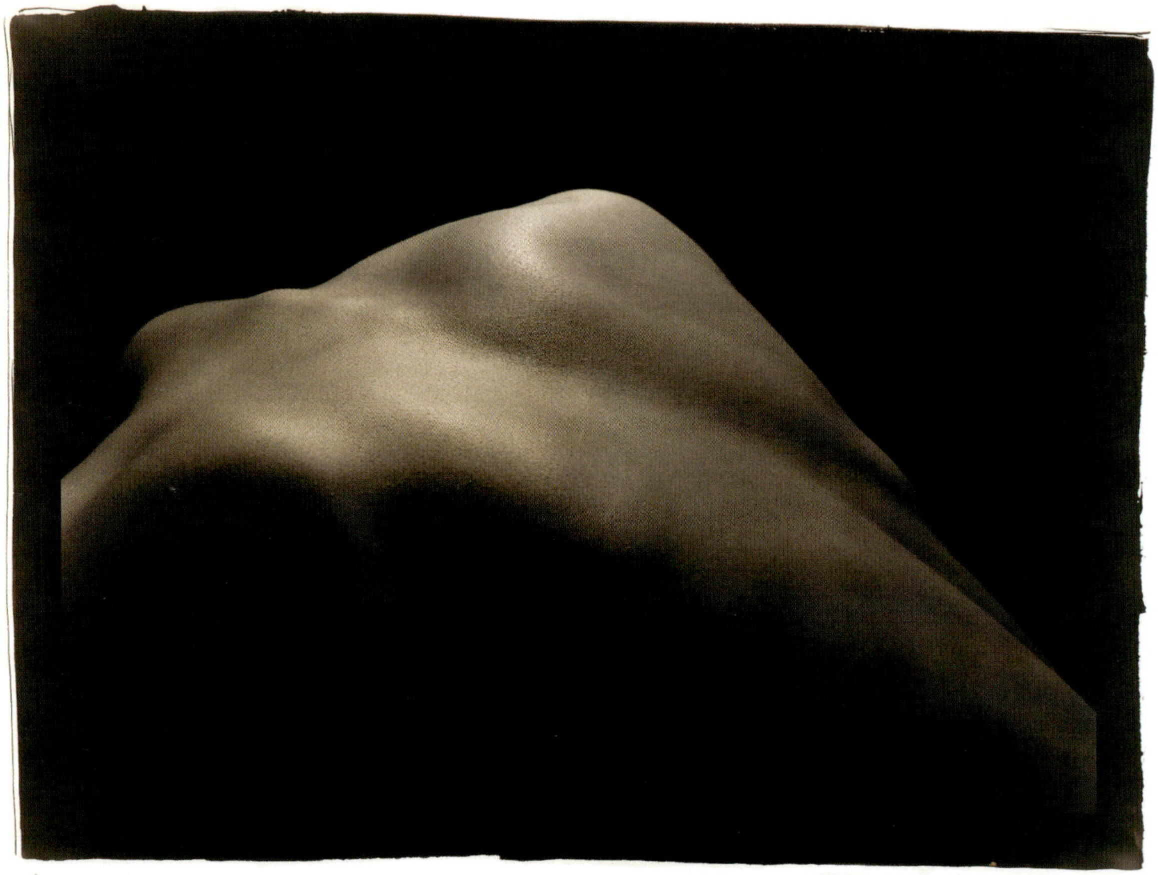

Untitled, 1994, from the Still Life series

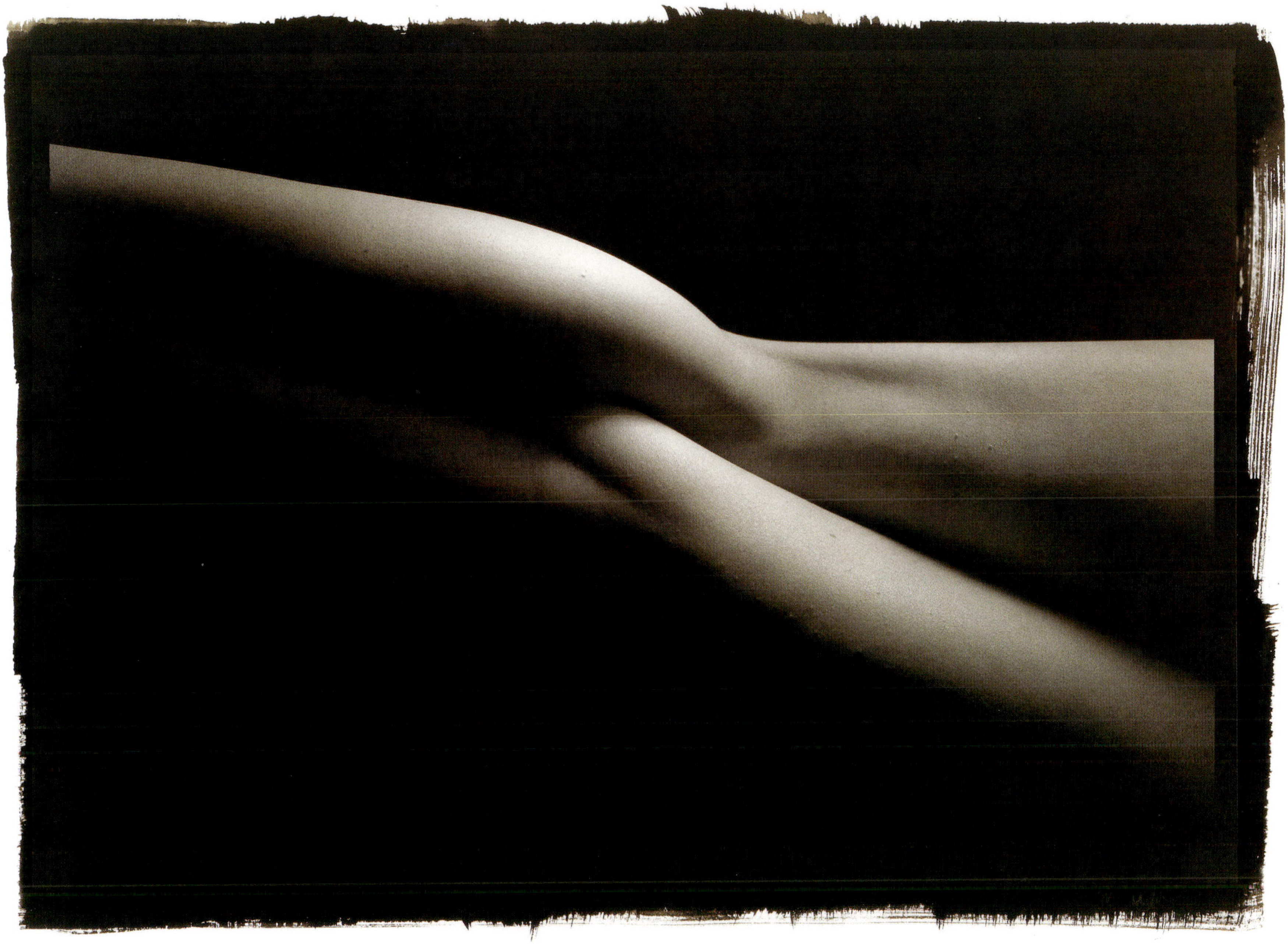

Untitled, 1998, from the
Still Life series

Mona Kuhn

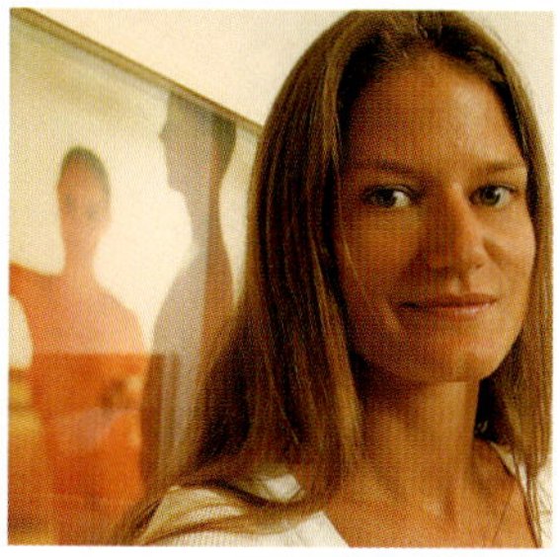

Mona Kuhn's images are saturated with the intimacy of decades of attachment. These people before us, long-time friends casting familiar glances, are captured with a profound sense of warmth and emotional closeness—so much so, that you often forget you are looking at complete strangers. When talking to Kuhn, it's not surprising to find that the subjects are, indeed, people she holds dear.

"Something in my subjects must grab my attention and give me the feeling of familiarity," she says. "In general, my subjects are people I would like to keep close to me, friends and their friends, people I admire on multiple levels."

Born in 1969 to German parents and raised in Brazil, Kuhn found herself captivated by the possibilities of charcoals and drawing at a young age. "I always liked the feel of it," she says, "its simplicity, and its unapologetic truth to gestures." It wasn't until high school, when she discovered a book of black-and-white photography, that she found her métier—a medium that she not only loved, but one that would help her while shuttling between Brazil, her parents' homeland, and then the United States, where she attended Ohio State University and the San Francisco Art Institute.

"Photography is a wonderful way of distracting yourself and escaping reality. Every time I was sad about leaving friends behind, I would simply pick up the camera and shoot. It is a wonderful tool in keeping mementos of time spent together with people you love."

Kuhn's first nude photography session was with her best friend in high school. It set a pattern that she would follow throughout her career—photographing people only after establishing a relationship of confidence. "It is a long process, which most of the time involves an initial two-year period," she explains. "Much of the trust between us comes after [the subject] has received the first batch of images and is able to see the proof sheets. We also look at them together and talk openly about anything. As time passes by, new dialogues and new proof sheets open the doors for them to familiarize themselves with my thoughts. It then slowly creates a collaborative synergy and finally an acceptance and trust of my creative process."

Containing flashes of private moments, Kuhn's photographs are bathed in natural light and shot mainly outdoors. She tends to shoot during the summer months, when, she says, "people feel comfortable in the nude." The scenarios take place in isolated communities across France, Germany, and California. Kuhn uses a Hasselblad because she believes it has a tendency to disappear between her and the subject.

In many of her photographs, the foreground presents sharp expressions and figures wrapped in the sun's rays, its light relaxing on skin, bone structures, and hair. Hands reach out as if searching, and eyes penetrate the viewer with knowing looks. Off in the background, however, torsos and limbs blend in a haze of skin and forms. People appear as remote specters, their bodies floating distantly through the scene in a marked contrast to the corporeality of the foreground—spirit versus flesh.

In some of her more recent images, Kuhn has favored color and moved indoors. These photographs capture moments of tranquil sensuality, revealing subjects cloaked in fading low light and advancing shadows.

While Kuhn mixes together men and women, she finds it to be more of a challenge shooting subjects of her own sex. "Photographing a nude woman is harder for me, because I am constantly fighting the effects of our surrounding media," she says. "Most of the time I have to ignore both the model's and my initial tendency of projecting the absorbed media representation of the female body. So I have to think a bit harder and let my own thoughts develop slowly as I get to know them better."

Exhibited all over the world, including solo shows in New York, Los Angeles, Berlin, San Francisco, Hamburg, Munich, and Atlanta, Kuhn's name is becoming known globally. But the increase in attention has not driven her away from her original principles. "You have to photograph people you admire and respect the people you photograph," she says. "You also have to trust your inner voice and embrace your passions. Everything else comes with hard work and determination."

Hannah, 2003 *(right)*
"This photograph encompasses a beautiful vocabulary present in art history: the classic reclining nude and the balance between beauty and mystery, all nearly absorbed by a dark ground. Early on, I studied painting and its shadow treatment during the baroque period. It is curious to see such elements inspiring my work again."

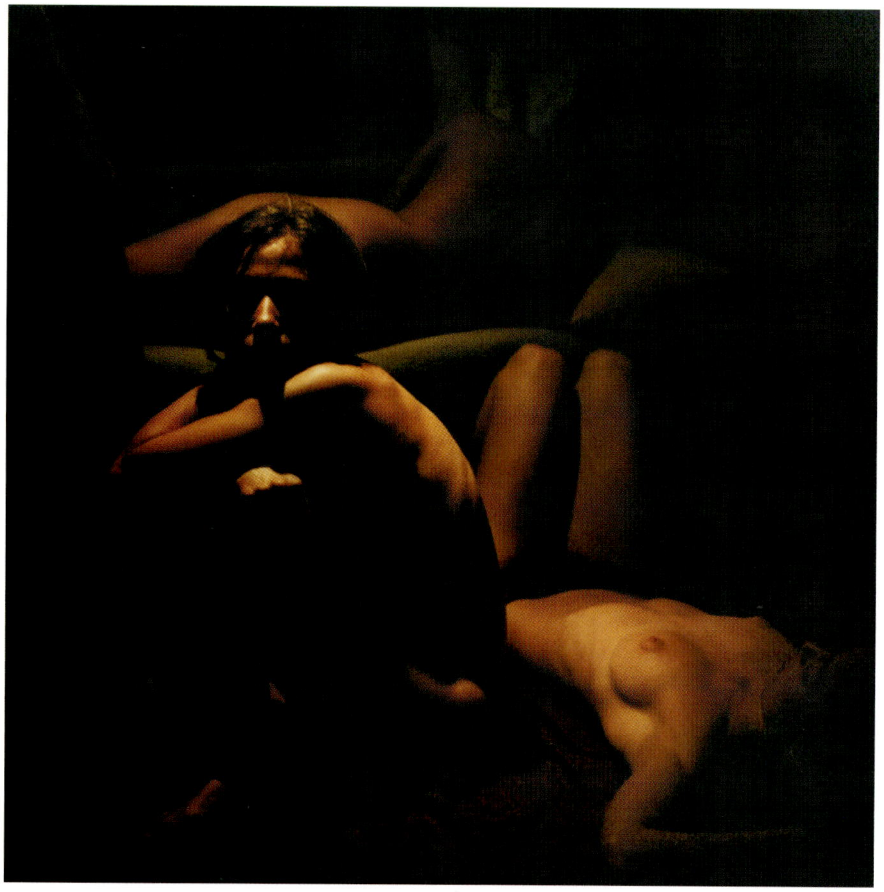

Rita, 2003 *(opposite)*
"It is an image captured at high-noon sun. Rita is stretched out by the deck, over her cardinal-red towel, while the vertical figure presents itself as a freestanding sculptural-like element centered over a white pool of reflecting light. I like to observe and recognize moments when life and art come together."

Kai and Luzia, 2003 *(page 104)*
"Their own words describe this image: 'It's a warm day, a lazy day, a day with friends. Two of us, the ones in the picture, the sisters, are especially drowsy. The coolest spot we can find is in the heart of our bungalow, on and near the green couch. We lie down and talk together, quietly, about the things we've been thinking, when Mona, our friend, comes in from the sun and discovers us.'"

Kolia, 2003 *(page 105)*
"It is a spontaneous image taken of three friends during a hot afternoon. I cherish natural and uncontrolled moments, which later affirm the initial instinct. Here, I appreciate the contrast of the reserved and melancholic beauty of a moment in unison with the incidental and playful figures by the couch. It explores our intricate emotional complexities within a playful composition."

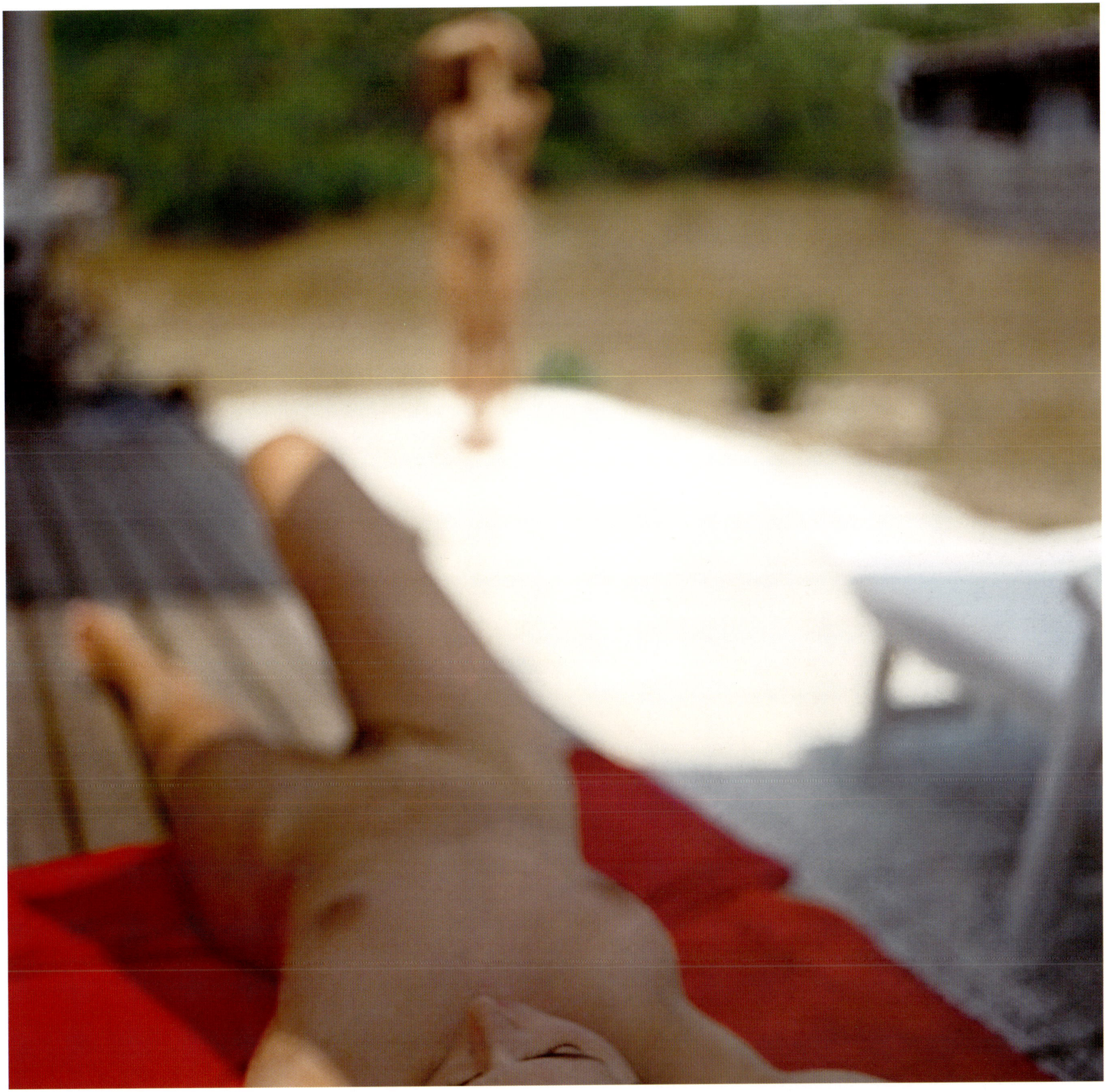

Mona Kuhn

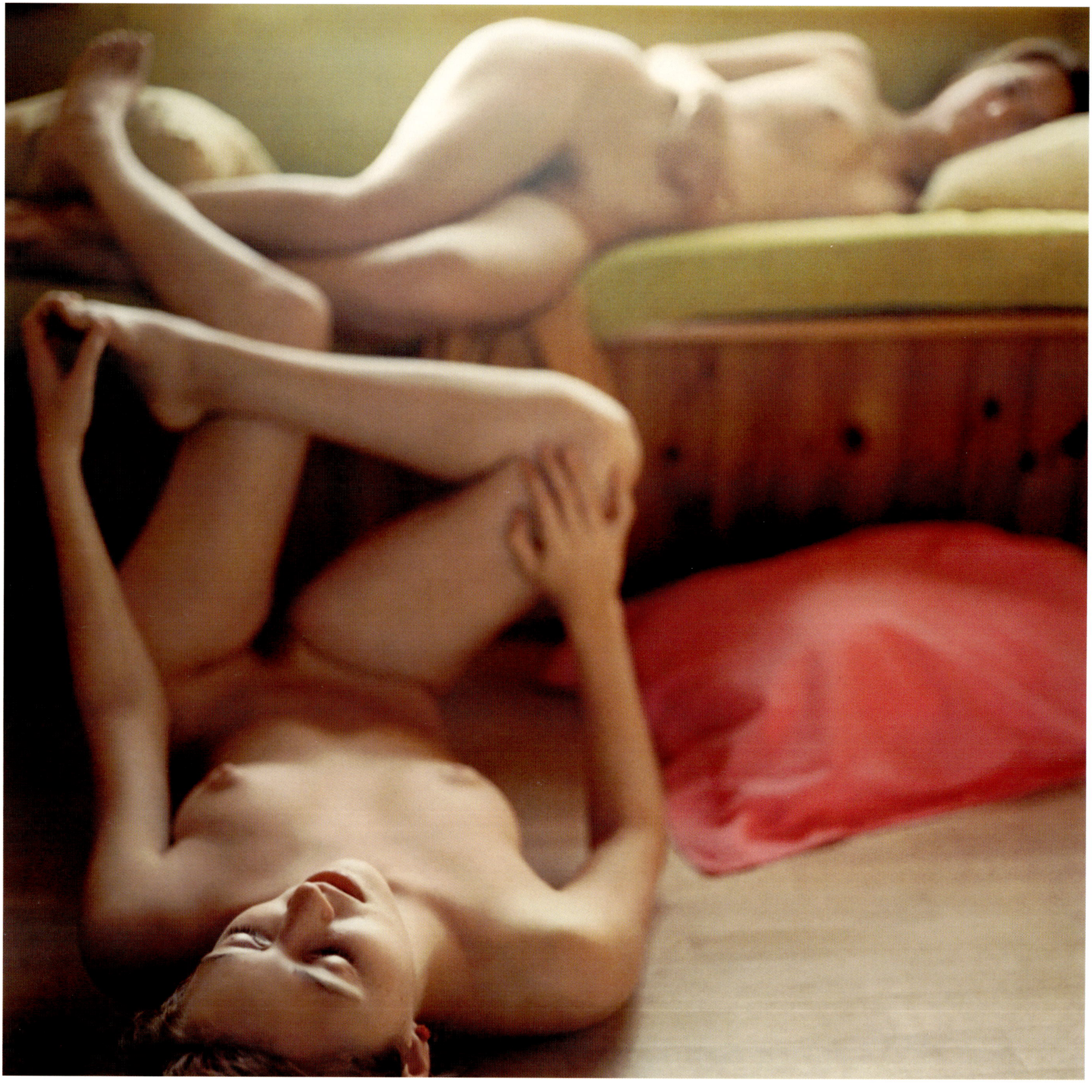

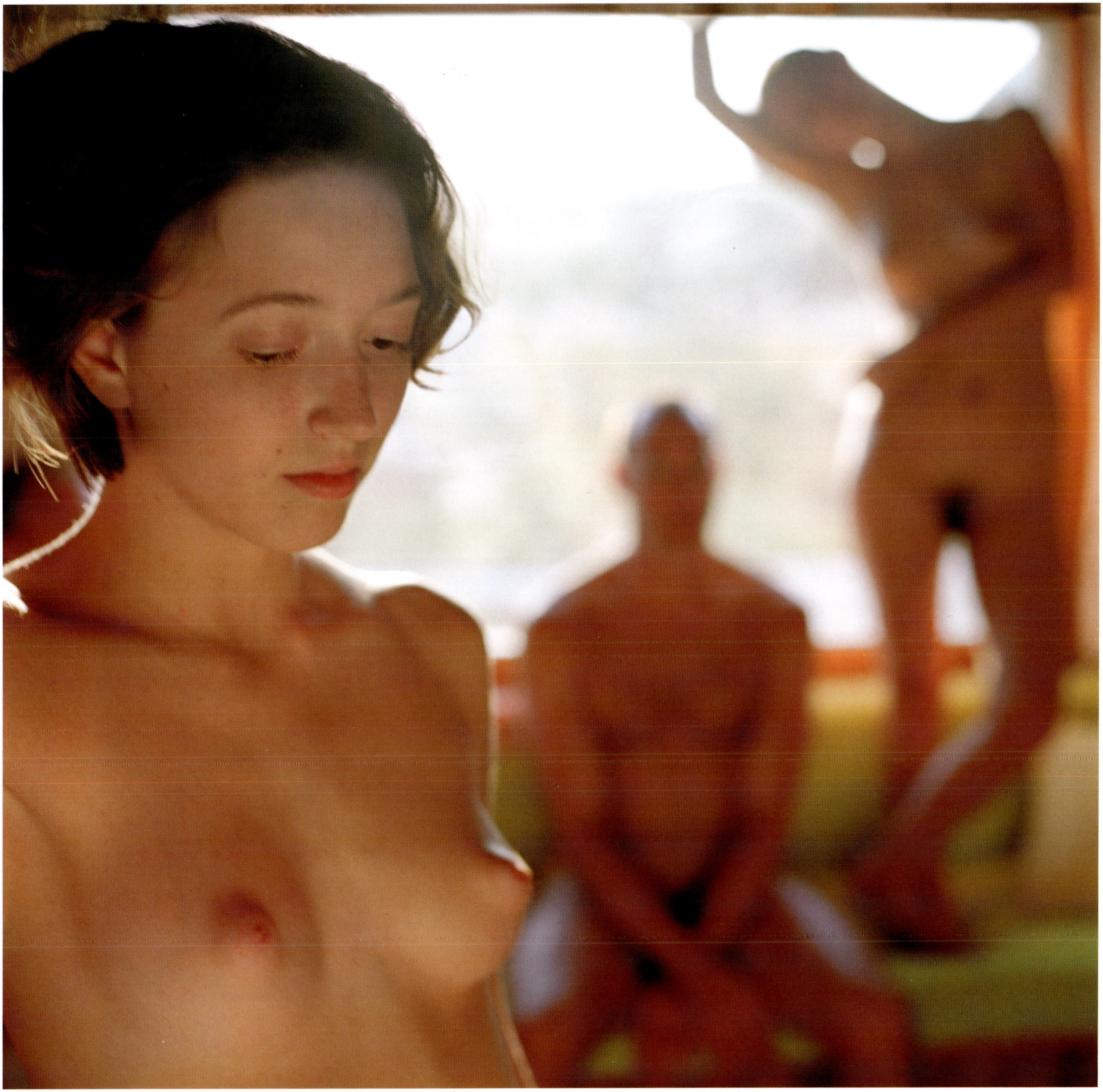

Anne Leigniel

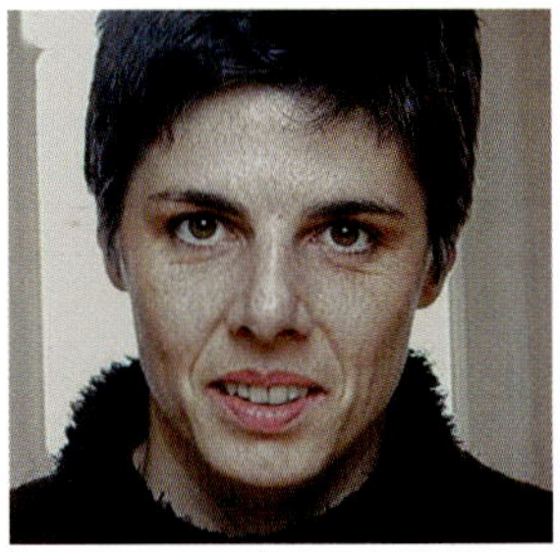

Whether they are floating apparitions in a sea of murky black, or tangles of bodies in a dusky haze, Anne Leigniel's nudes are unique visions. Born in 1963 in France, Leigniel attended the National School of Art in Cergy Pontoise, near Paris, and later received an MA in photography and advertising from the renowned London College of Printing (now London College of Communication) in 1990.

Leigniel was influenced by the writings of French literary lion Albert Camus and Polish novelist Witold Gombrowicz among other things—works by authors with a shared interest in the search for identity and meaning. She also found inspiration in the works of the French photographer Nadar. "I am fascinated by the stillness and sense of eternity radiating from his portraits," she says. "The strength of his timeless representation of the human figure is marvelous."

Leigniel's break came in the form of a solo show at the Baglama Gallery in Paris. Although her first interest lay in portraiture, Leigniel eventually found herself capturing the nude form on film. "After doing a lot of portraiture, nude felt like the natural evolution in the search for a more intimate and simple representation of a person," she explains. "At the same time, I was also getting rid of the social and cultural background conveyed by clothes and accessories."

The photographs from the series *Nudes in the Water* are an unusual and wondrous assemblage. Resembling images of a drowned Ophelia from Shakespeare's *Hamlet*, the subjects drift beneath shafts of light toward their next life, perhaps, their bodies twisted and distorted by the waves and reflections. Others from the series celebrate the joys of being immersed in water. She began the project in 1990, shooting in the River Cure in Burgundy, France. "The idea originated by swimming, and by looking at the water, looking at people swimming," says Leigniel. "It was also the direct relationship of observing others in the water and the effects of the light and water on the shape of their bodies, linked to the internal sensation of my body in the water.

"The deformation of the body in the waves was amazing," she continues. "I realized then that I could express inner feelings visually through images of the water on the skin and the rapture of the swimming experience, with the deformation created by the water's movements on the body. The feeling of fusion with the element and [the] amazing state of buoyancy was becoming visible. I carried on with the river, where I could find a wider range of effects with the trees' shadows and the clouds of mud on the body."

By comparison, Leigniel's *Dark Nudes* series unfolds like a mystery novel with no final chapter. It offers fragments of information, yet never fully reveals the details or characters. Body parts intertwine in the shadows, an intricate riddle of flesh.

These images, much like the water series, are also conceptual visions. "I have done several series of nudes [that looked] for the abstraction of the body conveyed by the position of the model," says Leigniel. "[This was inspired by] complex positions performed by athletes and dancers who were able to twist and distort their bodies easily. [Similar] abstraction and distortion comes from the water in *Nudes in the Water*, and through closeness in the *Dark Nudes* series."

For Leigniel, as for many photographers, finding her subjects is a matter of connection and captivation. "My models are people who intrigue me or simply interest me, because of the way they are, or the way they move," says Leigniel. "It is essential that I can feel we could work together, that the right chemistry is there. I show them my work, and trust is built upon a collaborative relationship between the model's confidence in the work and a desire to reach a mutual understanding of making an image. Liking the work and wanting to be part of it is halfway to establishing the trust between us."

Leigniel's work has been included in the permanent collections of the Bibliothèque Nationale in Paris, as well as the Center for Photography at Woodstock, New York. She has also been part of more than 20 exhibitions in the past 20 years, with her images appearing in the Taranto Gallery in New York, the Portfolio Gallery in London, New York's Print Space, the PABA Gallery in New Haven, Connecticut, and the Photography Festival in Arles, France.

Leigniel uses a Nikon F801, a Hasselblad, and ISO 400 film in order to have freedom in low light. She also shoots with tungsten lighting for its warm impression, and because she finds flash too intrusive in a quiet session. "I hope my images share a feeling and draw people's minds to their intimate inner world and own sensuality. It is my way to talk to people!" says Leigniel. "A successful nude photograph has the same element that makes any photograph successful: truth to itself."

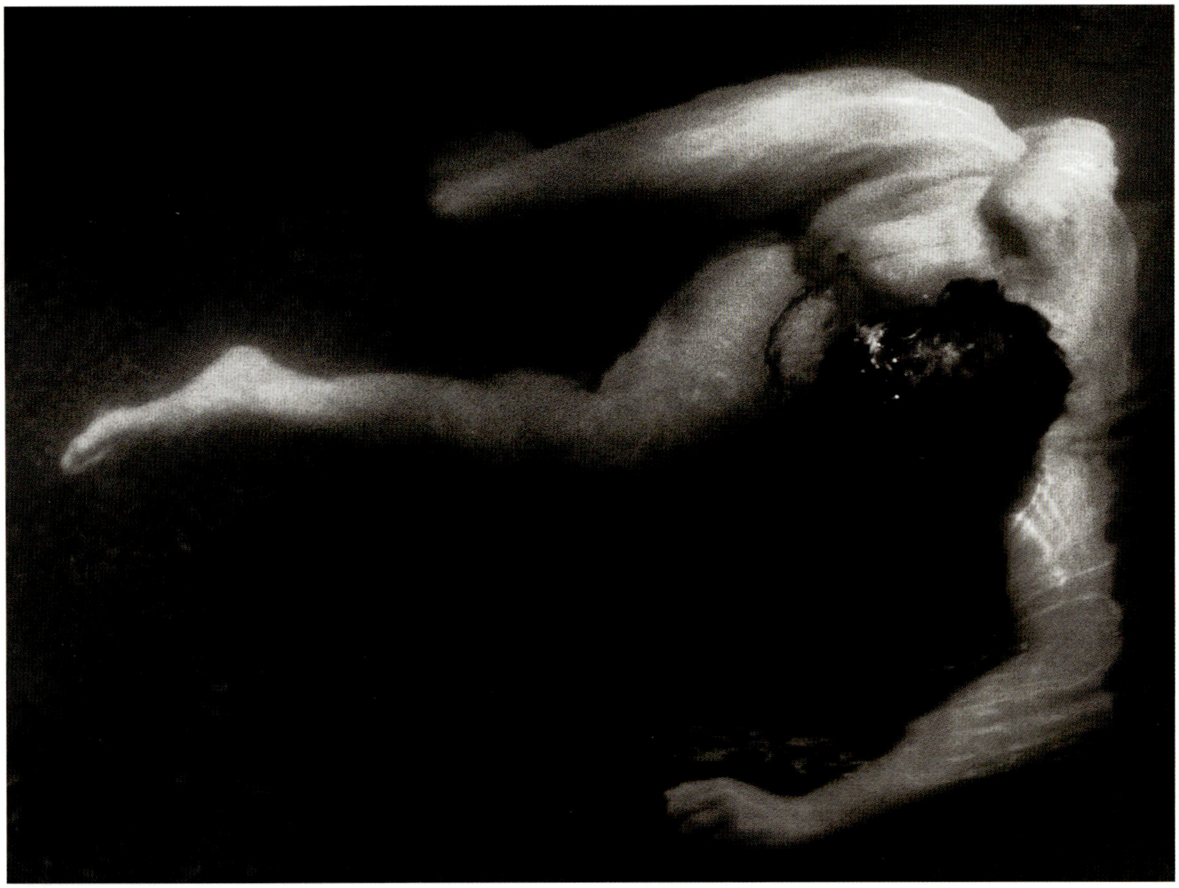

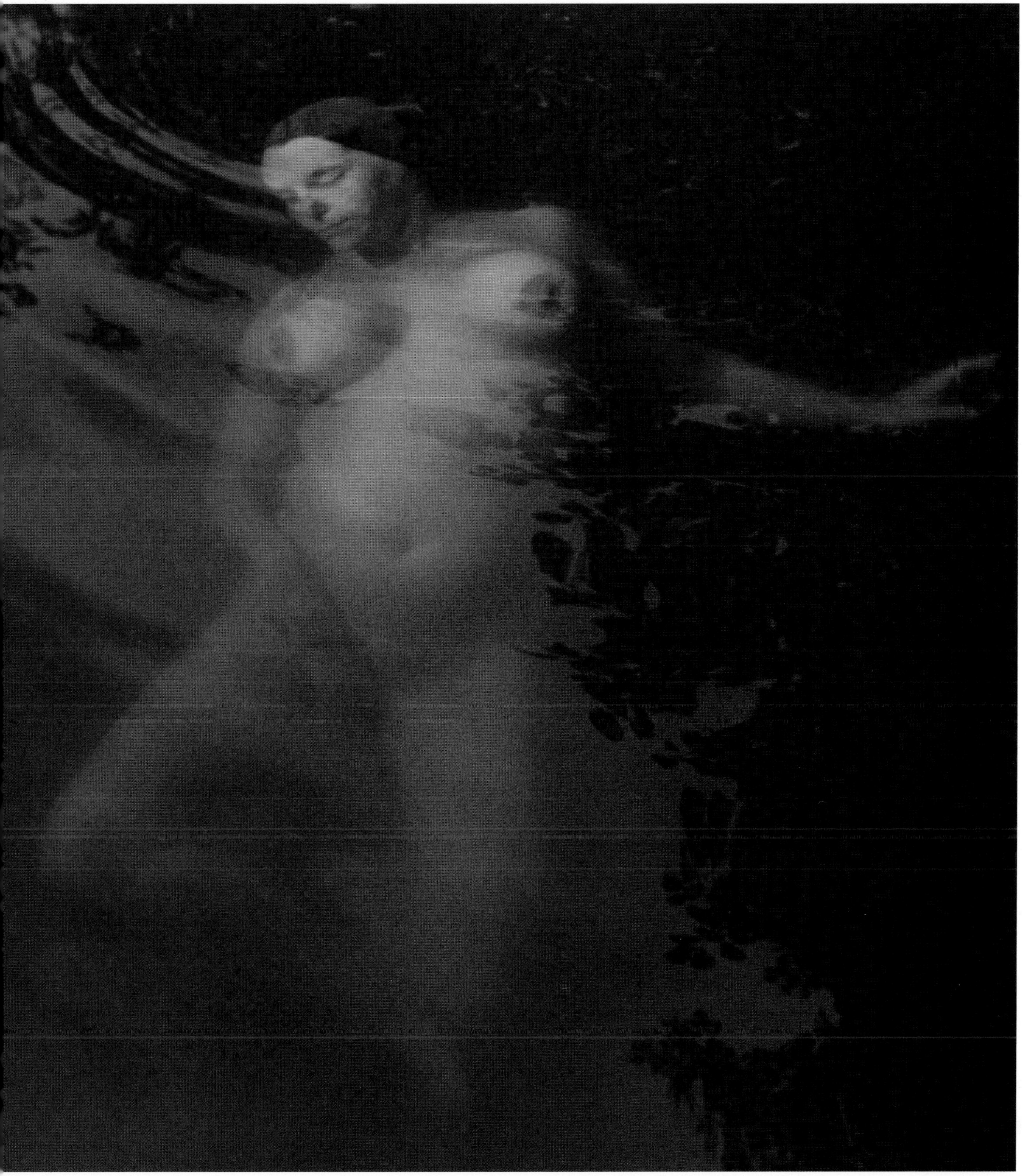

Untitled, 1996, from Nudes in the Water *(opposite)*
"I created those images in the River Cure in Burgundy, France. Waiting for the right angle of the light reaching the water is an important part of the image. I need enough reflected light to illuminate the shadows under the trees to avoid too much reflection on the water surface. The effect in the water is totally different depending on the time of the day. It becomes a medium shaping the body differently according to the quality of light."

Untitled, 1997, from Nudes in the Water *(left)*
"The sea and the body have been the two poles of my work from its beginning. I found them both equally fascinating in their ability to change and react to external influences, and in their capability to draw people's minds into their intimate, inner world and sensuality."

Untitled, 1997, from Nudes in the Water *(right)*
"The other important element is the riverbed. As soon as the model walks into the water, he or she lifts a deep cloud of mud, which darkens the water. It creates a nice effect, filtering the body parts according to its density, but it can also make it completely disappear if the mud becomes too dense. In that case we have to wait for the current to clean the set. The water series was mainly shot on 35mm with a 70/210 zoom, allowing me to follow the swimmer on a wider portion of the river without losing the subject. I am sometimes in the water, sometimes on the bank. A lot of the images have been done from above the water, from a tree or a ladder directly in the water."

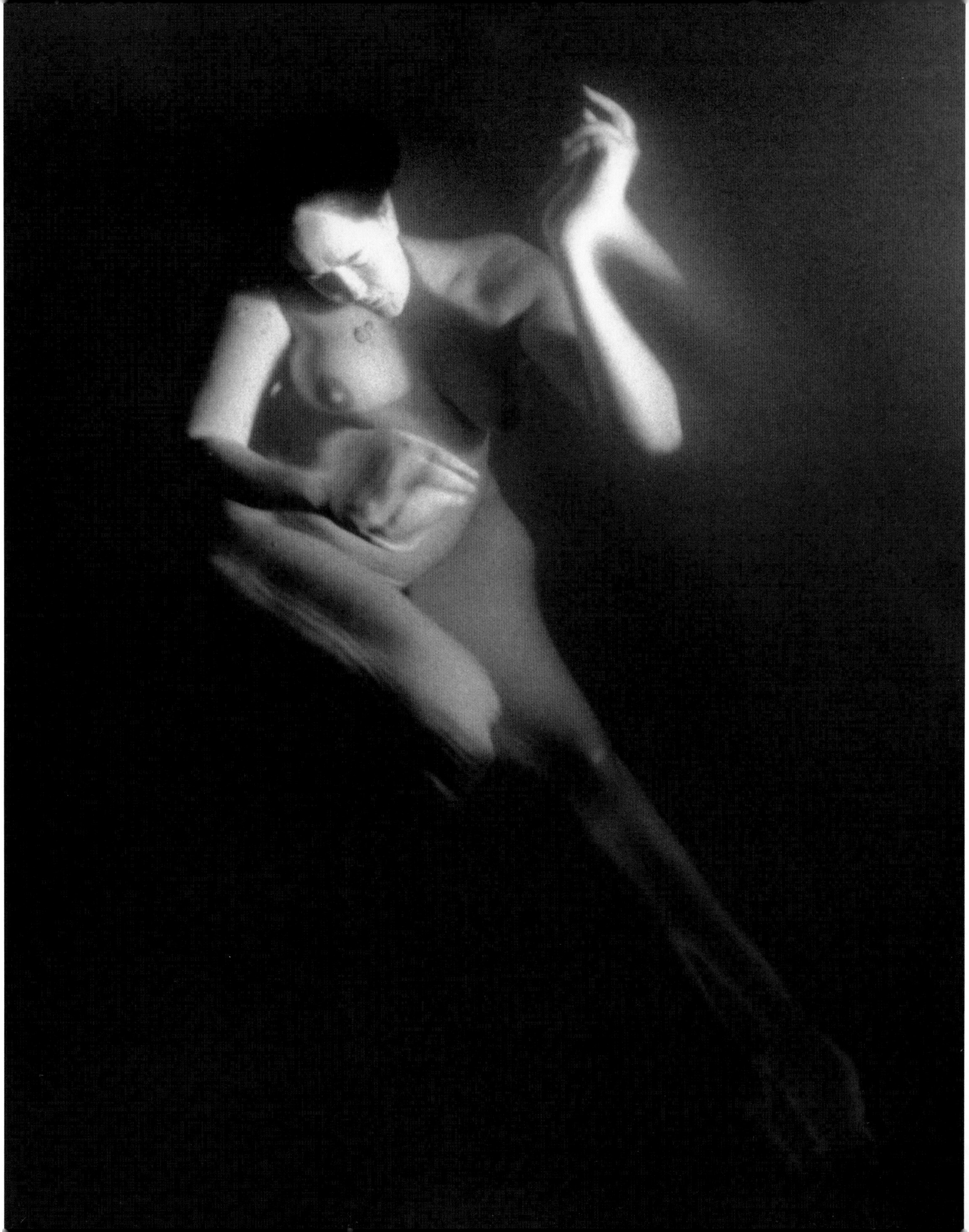

From Dark Nudes *(opposite, clockwise from top left)*
Untitled, 1998, Untitled, 1999, Untitled, 1998, Untitled, 1999
"The close-up photographs from the *Dark Nudes* series are abstract, often blurred and dark. They don't give too many clues, leaving plenty of room for interpretation. The size of the prints, 30x30, aims at immersing the viewer into a physical relationship with the image."

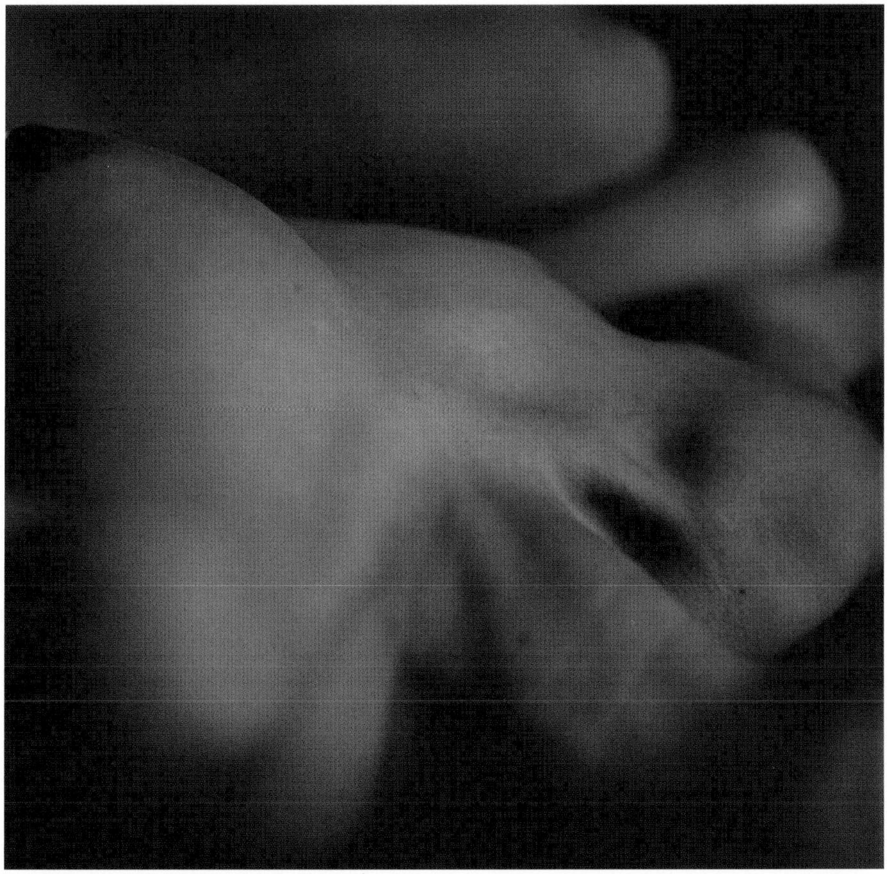
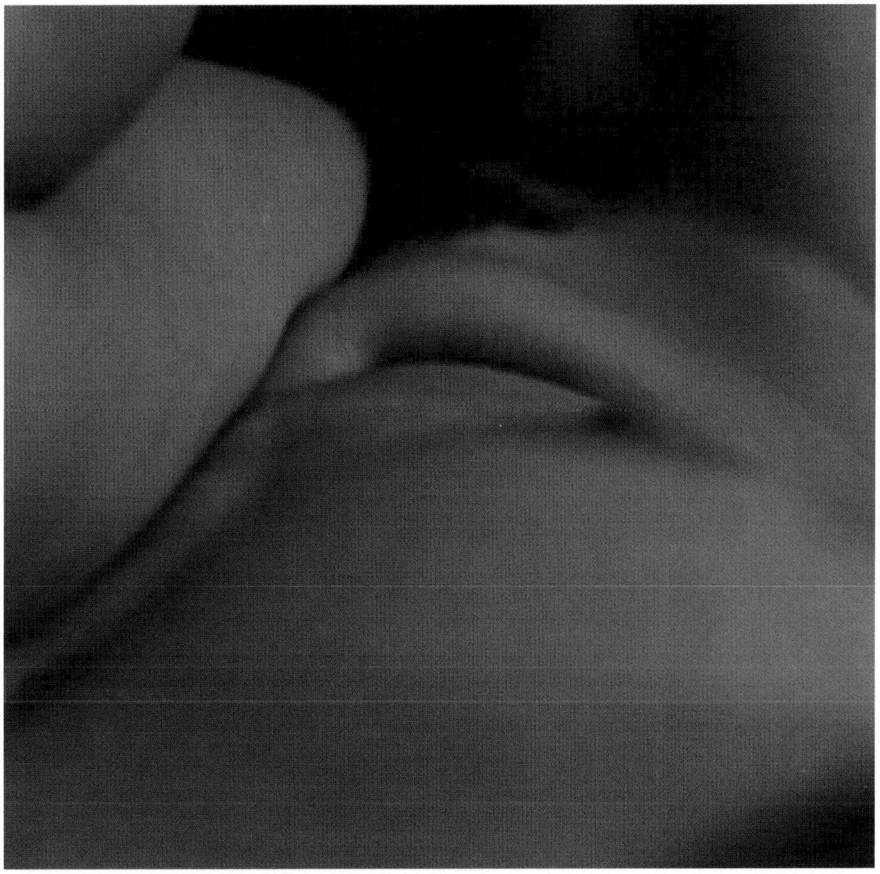
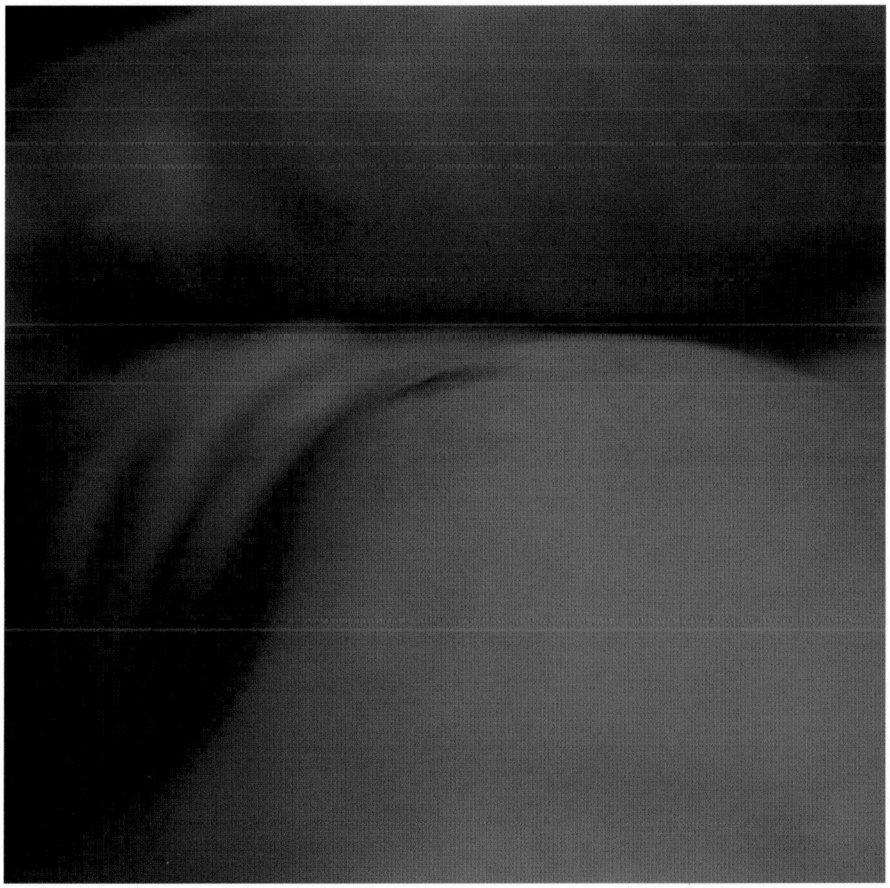
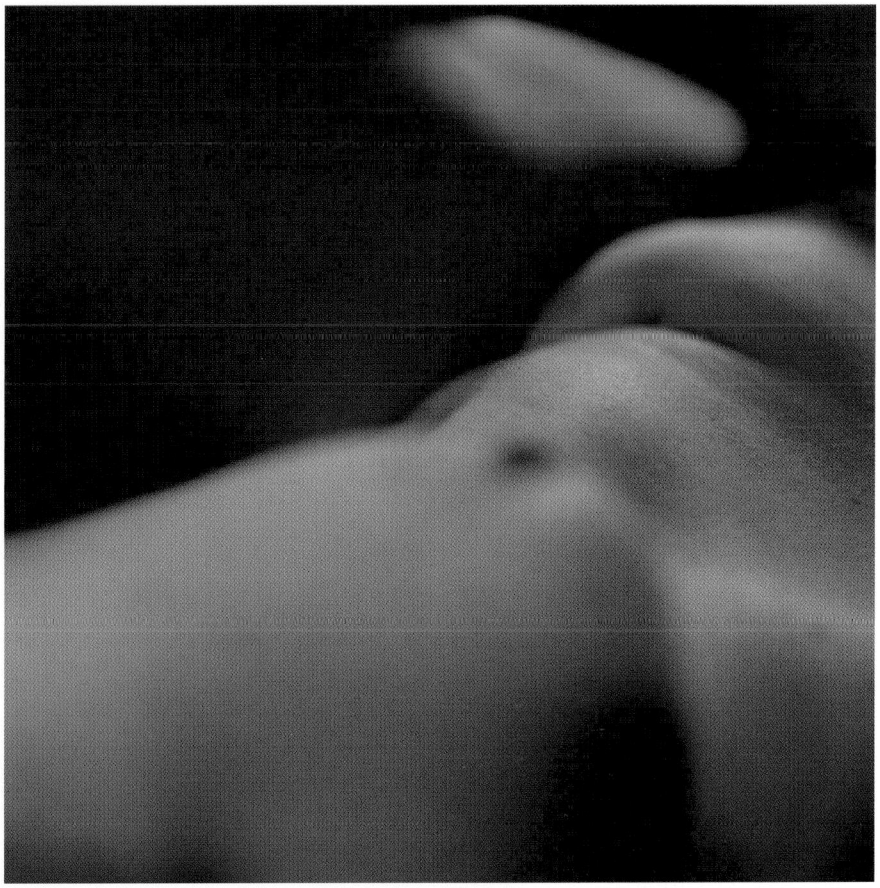

Robert Mapplethorpe

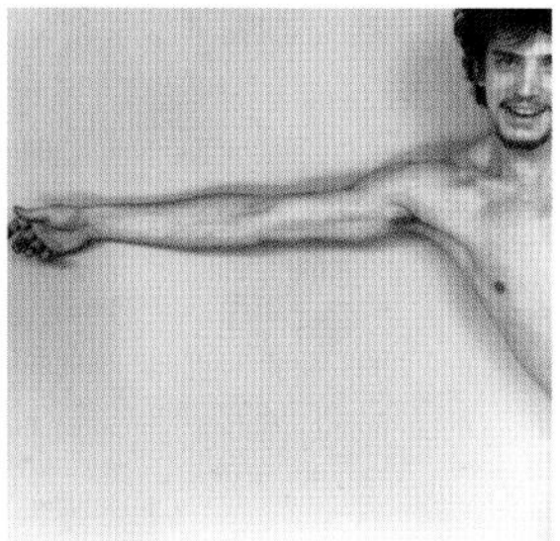

"I'm looking for the unexpected," said Robert Mapplethorpe. "I'm looking for things I've never seen before."

Mapplethorpe not only unearthed the unexpected, but he shone a spotlight on it, fearlessly pushing it into the mainstream. In the 1970s and 80s until his early death, he merged the then-unacceptable and confrontational with the conventional and the beautiful, changing attitudes to male sexuality in photography and art. Concentrating on homosexual imagery and male eroticism in many of his nudes, Mapplethorpe's images remain lightning rods for prejudice, admiration, awareness, and cultural transformation.

Born in 1946 and raised in Floral Park, New York, Mapplethorpe originally wanted to make a mark as a musician but instead found himself inside the art world, within the halls of Pratt University in Brooklyn, New York. It was there that he studied painting, drawing, and sculpture, using spray paint, masking, and cropping techniques on the ripped pages of books and magazines to create artwork.

It wasn't until the early 70s that Mapplethorpe first picked up a camera—a Polaroid—initially taking photographs of himself before turning the device on singer, poet, and close friend, Patti Smith. Mapplethorpe had no real background in the world of photography, and his work leaned more toward the realm of sculpture and traditional artwork than anything by the masters of the photography world (he often created extensive frames and encasements for his images, transforming the photograph into an *object*, more than simply an image). He was initially more inspired by the paintings and films of Andy Warhol than anything by Weston or Brandt.

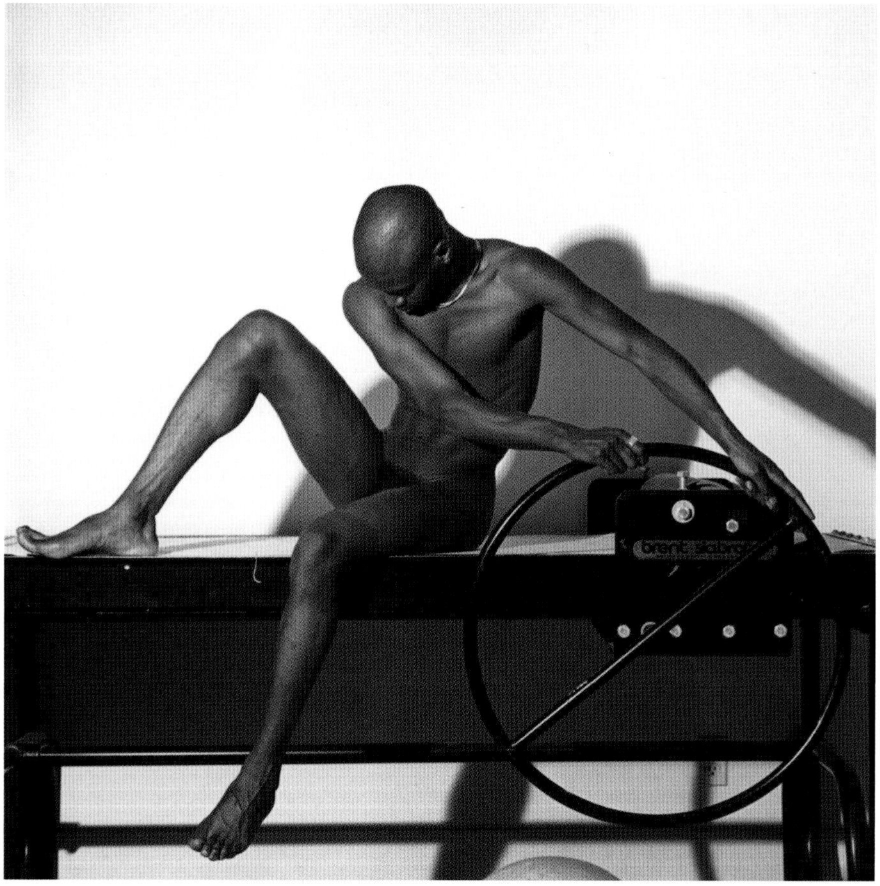

"Remember, I knew nothing about photography at that point," said Mapplethorpe in 1987. "It's interesting, because my style was developed before I knew who Steichen or Stieglitz was [sic]. It was like, I had a way of seeing and that was it. That's not to say that, over the years, having studied has not helped me define what my photography is about. I think that it was a great advantage to go into photography not knowing much about it. Not thinking. I think one of the problems with photographers today is that they never see for themselves, but just like everybody else ."

In the mid-70s, Mapplethorpe delved deeper into photography, employing a large-format camera and a Hasselblad. Along with his continuing depictions of himself and Smith, he expanded his search for subjects, gathering socialites, artists, gay men, musicians, porn stars, and members of the sadomasochist underground, among others. The candor with which Mapplethorpe presented his models, some employing props and outfits in overtly sexual ways, sent tremors through the art world and beyond. "I was in a position to take those pictures. I felt an obligation to do them," Mapplethorpe said in an *ARTnews* interview in 1988.

However, these photographs were—and remain—artistic *tours de force*. Although dealing with subjects and assemblages that were often outside of the mainstream, their strength lies in their elegant composition and technical proficiency far more than their "shock" value. Of course, it was the focus of the images that attracted greater attention and brought Mapplethorpe both fame and notoriety. "I think the pictures I take dealing with sexuality are probably the most potent of pictures that I have ever taken," he said. "They are the pictures that people remember more because they are unique. They also stand out from the rest because they somehow reflect the impact of an inner feeling of sexuality. They are more intense, though I don't think they are any more important than my other pictures. Sometimes, though, they are the only ones people remember."

In the 1980s, Mapplethorpe began expanding his experimentation with various types of camera equipment and printing processes, using photogravure, Cibachromes, color Polaroids, and dye-transfer color prints, among other methods. Within his work, he started exploring the nude in a more traditional sense, highlighting figures and geometric shapes, while also concentrating more on still lifes, especially the depiction of the flower and its elegance and erotic capacity.

In 2005, all aspects of his work were showcased in a major London exhibition, curated by artist David Hockney, which showed Mapplethorpe nudes alongside traditional portraits, formal interiors, and flower images. The exhibition was warmly received, with praise for Mapplethorpe's eye and compositional genius. The *enfant terrible* had become a master in retrospect.

"I believe in certain kinds of magic," said Mapplethorpe. "Sort of an abstract energy concept. I think there's a magic that can invest in photography sessions. It's not about the fact that I know more about photography, but that I can muster up this certain kind of thing that makes a great picture."

The quotes in this profile were taken from *Photography Speaks: 150 Photographers on Their Art* (Aperture, 2004).

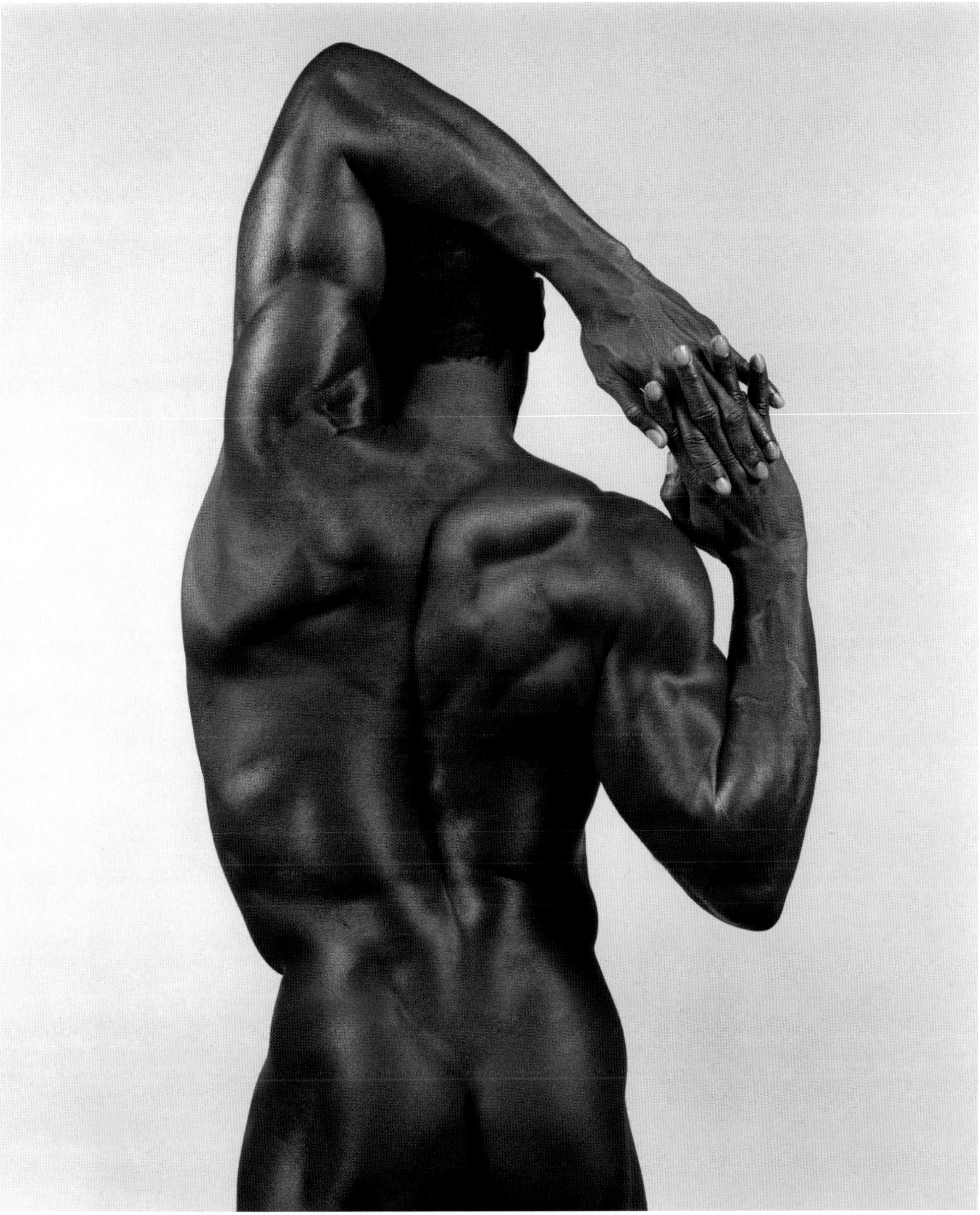

Bruce, 1980 *(opposite)*
Derrick Cross, 1983 *(left)*
As opposed to his controversial work in the previous decade, these two images represent Mapplethorpe's attraction in the 1980s toward the more subtle and classical.

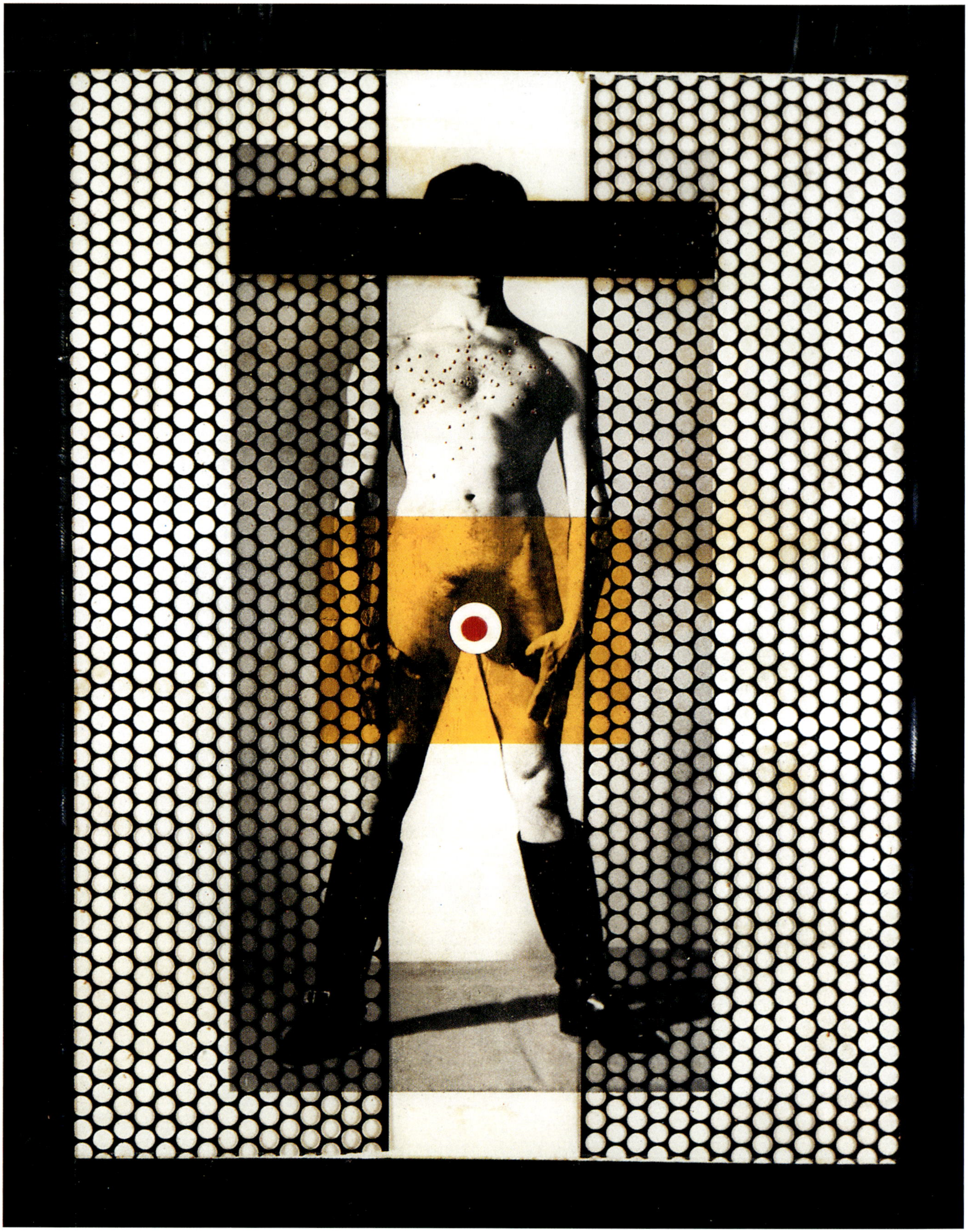

Bull's Eye, 1970
An example of Mapplethorpe's early work using masking and cropping. He began these techniques while still studying art at Pratt University in Brooklyn, New York.

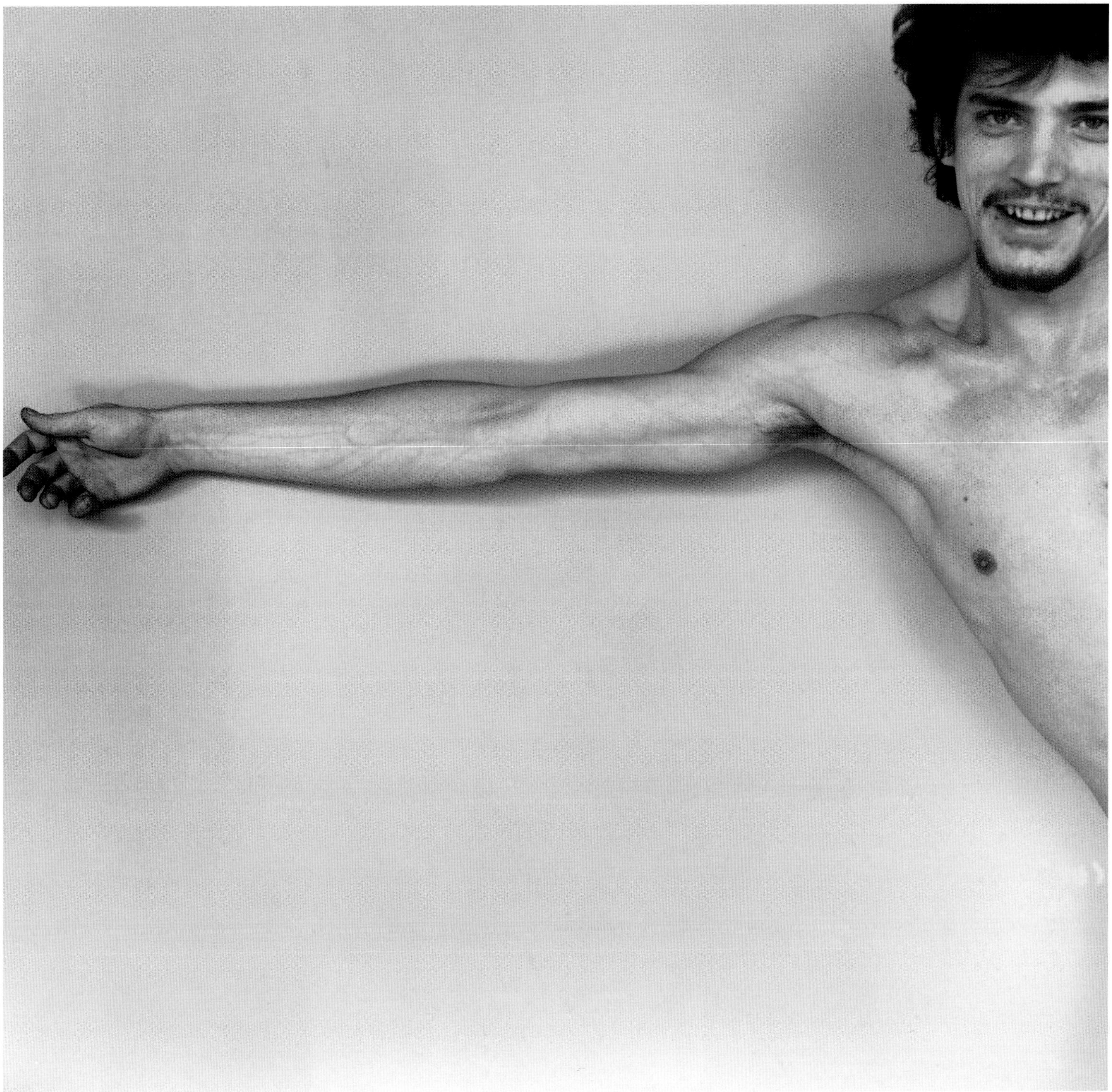

Self Portrait, 1975

Stefan May

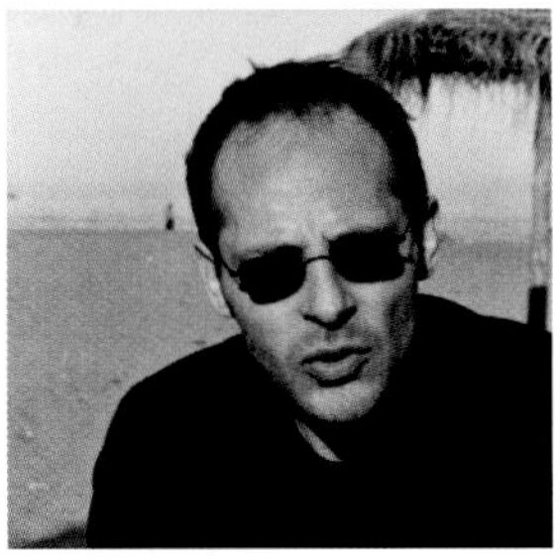

For a man whose first experience with a camera was documenting epidermal diseases for the Munich Dermatological Clinic, Stefan May has certainly transformed the way he records skin.

One of the bestselling nude photographers in the world, the German-born May has made a living from glorifying the human body. Using a keen sense of voyeurism and a proficiency for injecting verve and enthusiasm into his imagery, it's easy to see why May's books and calendars are constants in international bookstores and photography distributors.

Born in 1962, May first studied medicine and, using a Leica and a circular flash, photographed skin ailments for the archive at the Munich clinic. After deciding that he wanted to use the camera professionally, he moved to Sydney, Australia, and assisted various fashion and beauty photographers before venturing out on his own. He soon began shooting commercially, contributing to magazines that would eventually include the international editions of *FHM*, *Cosmopolitan*, *Playboy*, *Max*, *Elle*, *Stern*, and *Men's Health*. He also began a career in advertising, and his client portfolio now includes Honda, IBM, Peugeot, Puma, and United Airlines.

His career in nudes began quite unexpectedly during a fashion shoot with a genuine couple. "They were head over heels in love," says May. "Suddenly, it started to rain really heavily and we all got soaking wet—it was an outdoor shoot. The couple didn't hesitate. They got rid of their wet clothes in order to warm each other. Warm turned into hot, and I just had to pull the trigger. Voilà, my first nude shots existed."

The rainstorm was a godsend. May quickly turned his attention toward the nude body, covering the subject for years before ultimately gathering together a group of black-and-white images to produce his first book, *Couples* (teNeues, 2002). The photographs, of couples in outdoor settings and covert spaces, emanate a classic look reminiscent of Brassai and Elliott Erwitt, while also being mischievous and erotic.

"For any couple, what counts are the pheromones. Stefan May's photographs [in *Couples*] seem to exude pheromones," says Paolo Bonanni, editor in chief of *Max Italia*. "The sheer sense of movement in his photographs doesn't mean that there isn't room to reveal some hidden depth on the part of one of his subjects, even if these are men and women alone. But when they are couples, the mysterious alchemy woven by pheromones makes for an unforgettable book."

What also adds to May's allure is his talent for giving the viewer a sense of being a spectator witnessing a private moment. Various distinctive angles give you a feeling that you are there, interacting with the subject, while the piercing eyes and captivating gestures he draws from the models heighten the appeal of the images. "It's all about the so-called forbidden game," explains May, "the voyeurism every person hides, and that walk along the famous narrow border."

May's next two books focused on singular subjects. *Men* (teNeues, 2003) and *Women* (teNeues, 2004) followed the same path as his first book, maintaining his sensual, spirited, and timeless approach. Both books employed liquid—sea and sweat—as well as natural lighting to emphasize the beautiful bodies May gathered before his camera. The publications, each a tremendous success, secured May's standing as a top nude image-maker.

"The books show a collection of the best images of an entire decade," says May, who uses a Hasselblad, a Leica, and an Alpa. "Finally, to hold a book in your hands after such a long time is, in my opinion, the biggest fulfillment a photographer can find—it's like a degree, a dissertation."

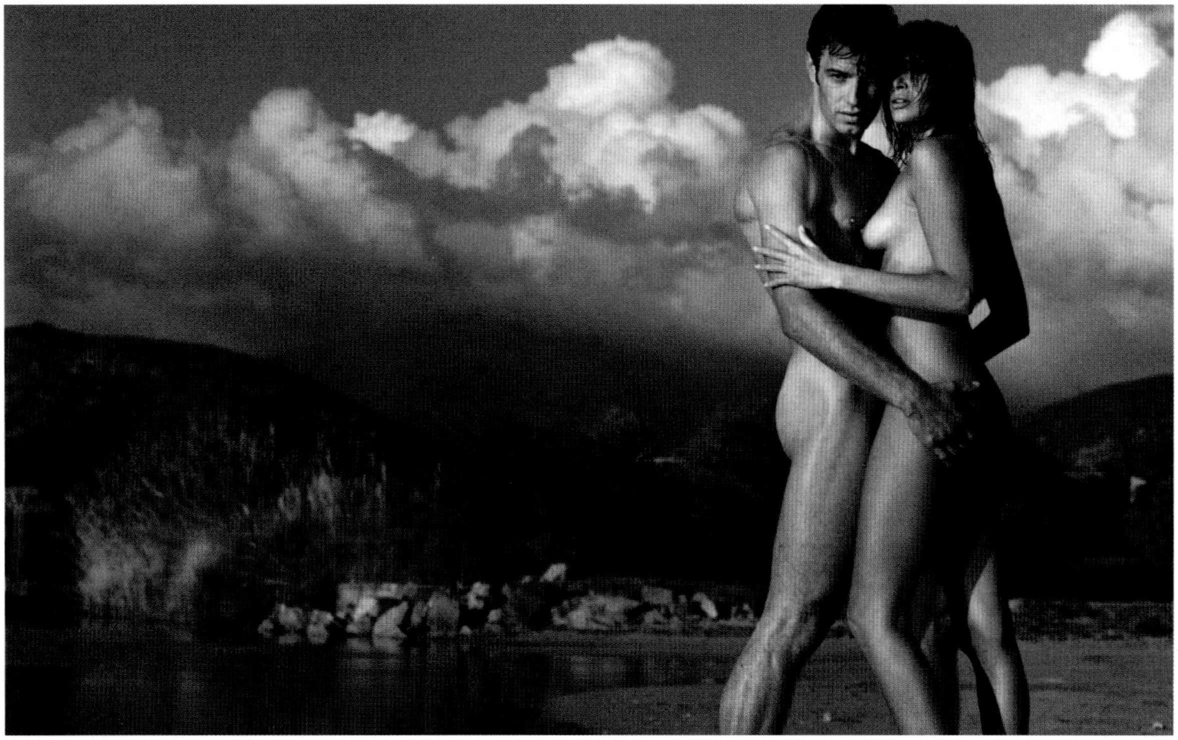

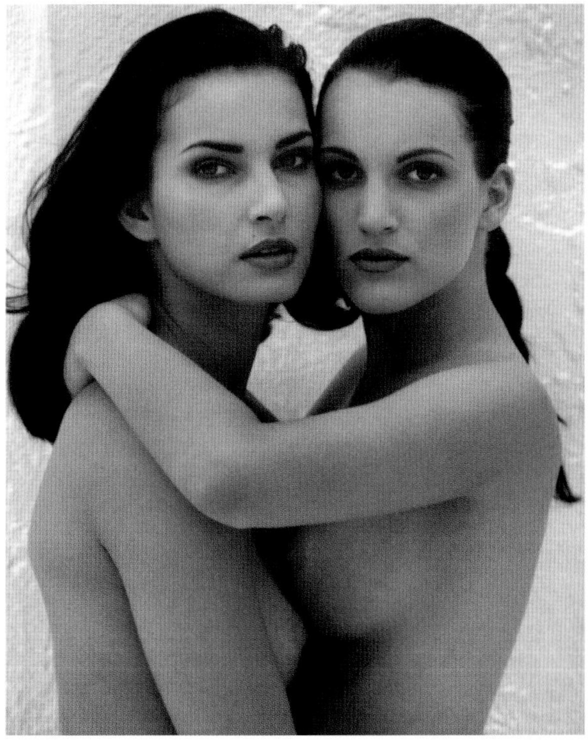

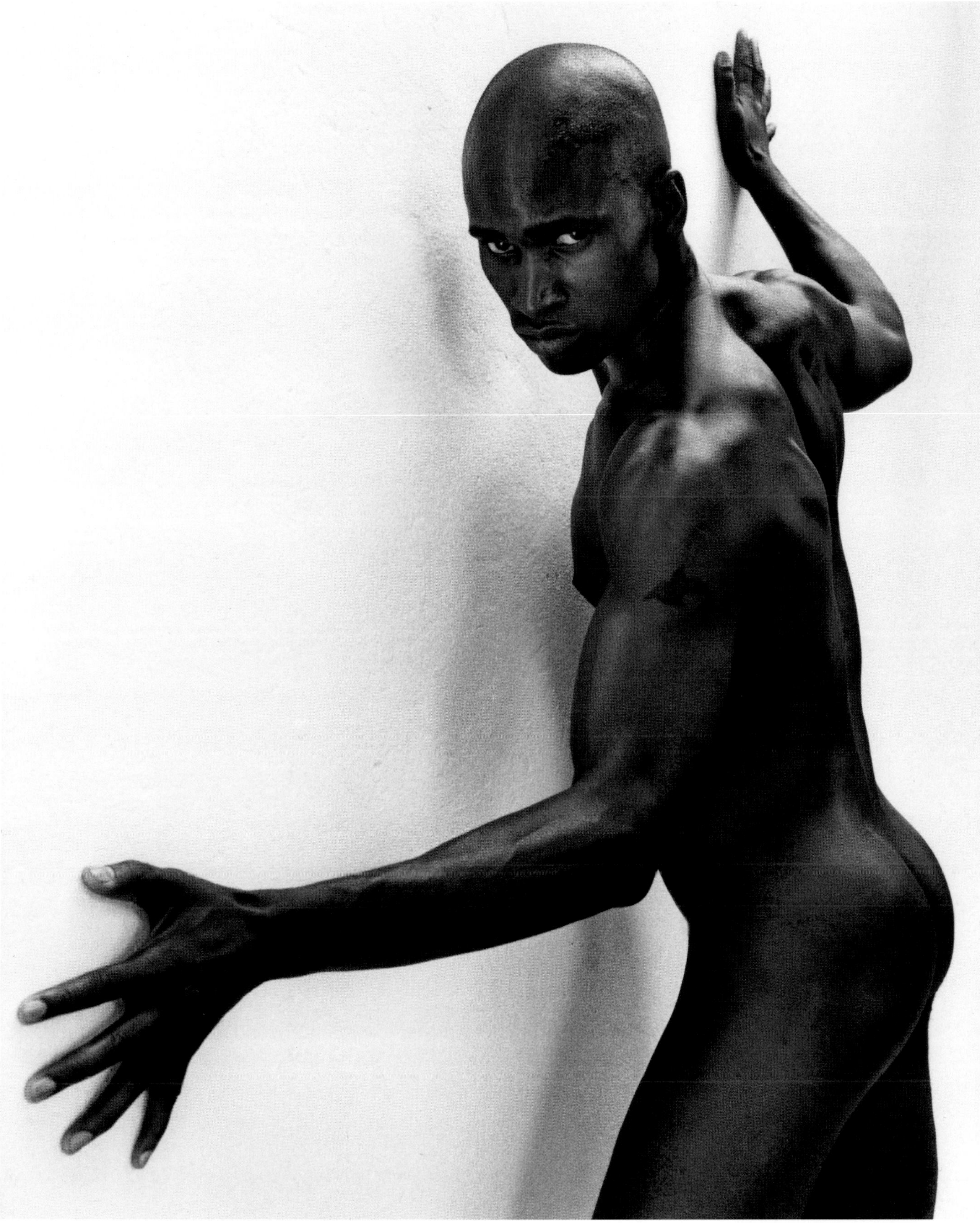

Corsican-III, 2002
(opposite left)
"A successful image must have a certain quality, of course, but a picture has to address a broad audience, too," says May. "So you have to please the average taste. 'Successful' is a very relative expression concerning photography."

Sisters, 1996 *(opposite right)*

Men Only-III, 1999

Jean-Marc Dupuis, art director for *Men's Health* in France has been using Stefan May's pictures for years. "His work fascinates me. You might think that he is talking to the models, leading them, directing. However, he is more concerned to get a feel for them, to get their scent, and to electrify them. The women in his pictures are never cold, model beauties with no imperfections. His photographs are the opposite of lethargic, aesthetic facades, which have been taken for glossy magazines. They make the bodies tangible, with the warm skin being tantalized by his light."

May's future plans include more books published under his pseudonym, Lance Lensfield—one on New York was published in 2002. But he will certainly not be abandoning the field that has brought him most acclaim. "Each task is unique and requires a different approach, although I consider nude shooting the more difficult one," says May. "But you must focus on your own ideas and deal with your own creativity in a critical manner, and don't try to copy. The only thing that counts is whether you like your results."

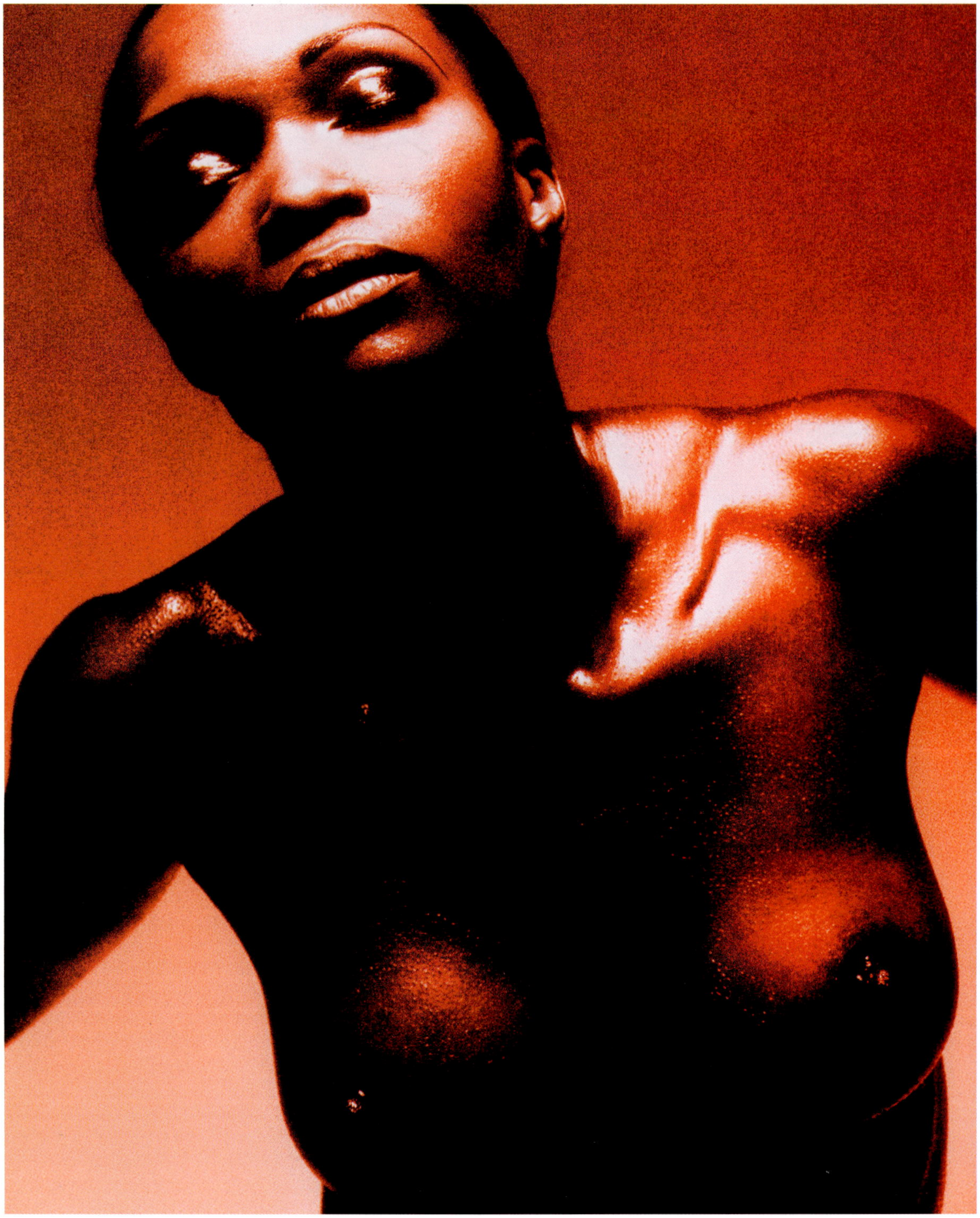

Black Color, 1998

Men!, 2004

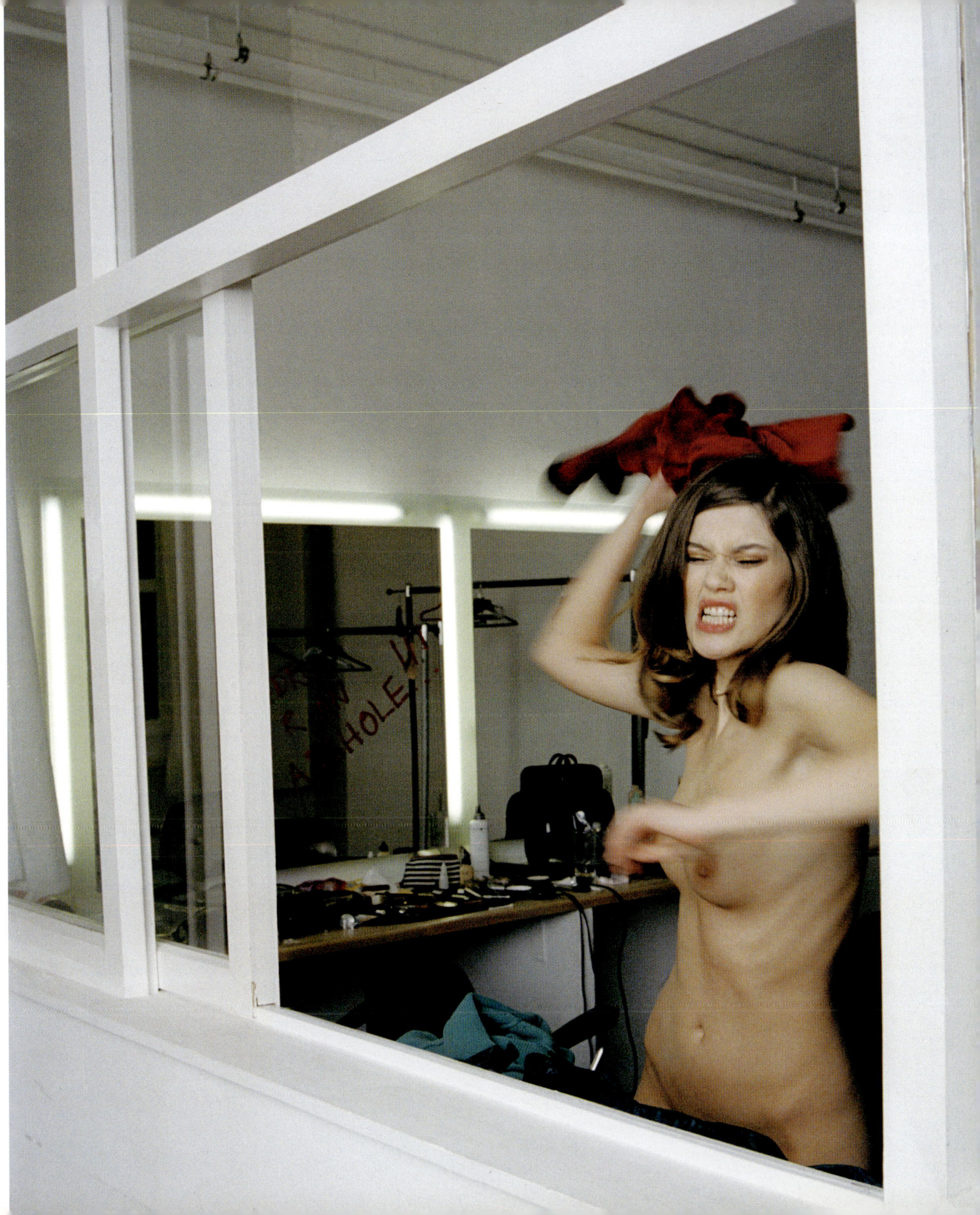

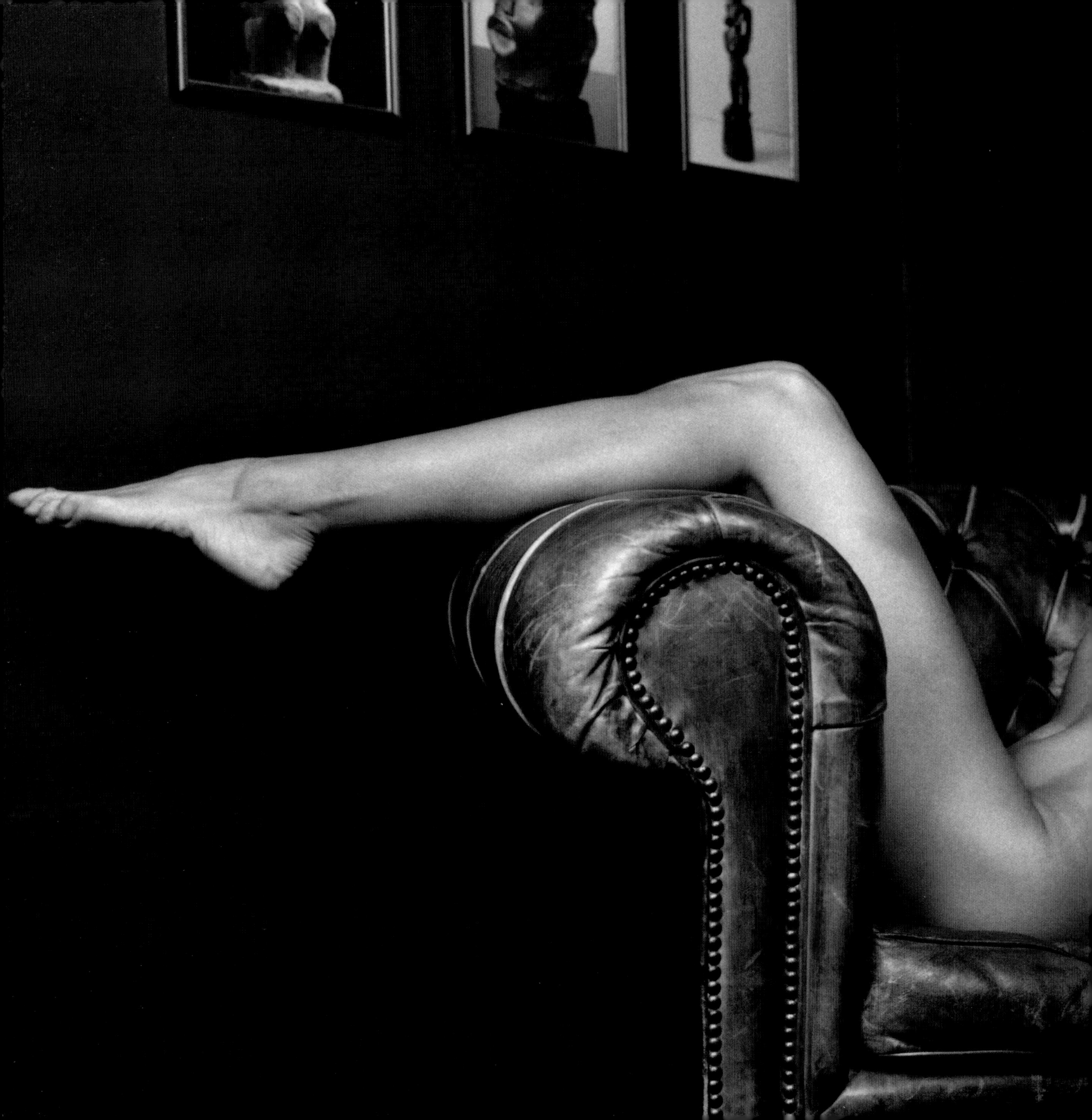

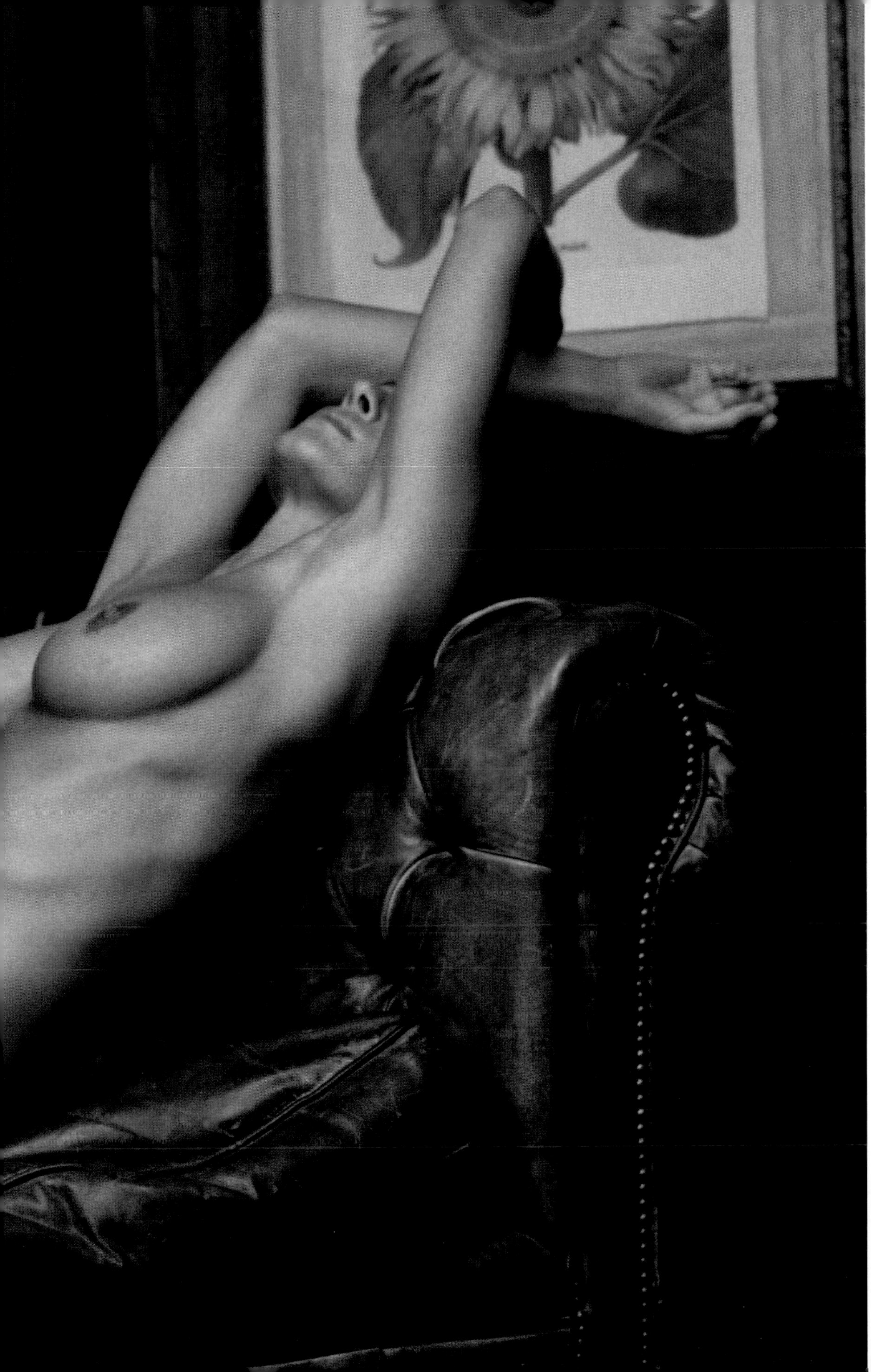

Sofa Surfer-I, 2003
"We only work together with professional models and model agencies," says May. "We get in contact with the subjects through 'go-sees,' castings, and recommendations. They have to bring along the physical premises, and we attach great importance to a personal conversation with our models."

R. J. Muna

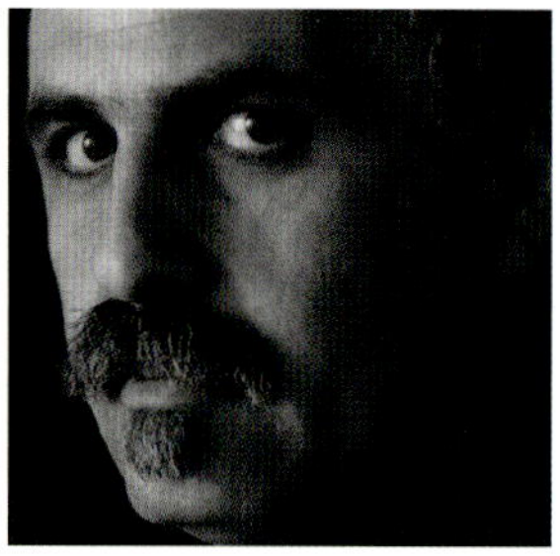

R. J. Muna thrives on movement and change. While his photography majors in the study of motion and luminosity, Muna himself has never seemed happy with the idea of focusing on a single project. Constantly leaping from idea to idea and technique to technique, Muna is a photographer who will never be caught standing still.

Well known for his car and still-life photography, as well as his nudes, Muna's work has appeared in galleries all around the United States, including the Robin Rice Gallery in New York City, the Yerba Buena Center for the Arts in San Francisco, and the G. Ray Hawkins Gallery in Los Angeles. "I've always got more than one series going on at any given moment, and several that are cooking in the background," he explains. "If those haunt me for any length of time, I will follow them and see if there is something there.

"Almost all of my work is an evolution of all that I've done in the past, so I suspect that will continue. As long as inspiration calls, I will follow. I am grateful that I have far more ideas than I could possibly bring to fruition. But then, the ideas are the best part."

Born in 1954 in San Francisco, Muna became a photographer when he was a teenager—"I had my own darkroom at the age of 13 and never looked back." He has found inspiration in another image-maker who is renowned for his ability to switch genres effortlessly, without sacrificing any quality in his work.

"I think Irving Penn has always been an icon in my mind, as I'm sure he is for many others. I find the way he conceptualizes images to be very elegant. I am always amazed at his range of subject matters and styles. He seems to be intrigued by an idea far more than a technique."

Based in San Francisco, Muna is one of the most successful commercial photographers in the United States today: he won the 2002 Infinity Award for Applied Photography and the 2003 LUCIE Award for Best Commercial Photographer. He first became interested in the nude because of its symbolism as the most elementary of subjects. "It is the one form we know from birth to death," he says. "I am amazed at how far a nude can be abstracted and still we know it's a human form. It's a sort of photographic haiku. Very pure."

The range in which Muna has presented the nude is startling. His series vary from simple representations of the unclothed body in motion, to the wonderfully intricate and evocative series, *The Apparitions*.

Some of his earlier depictions of the nude involved studies of extreme light. In *Black Nudes* and *White Nudes*, Muna created two series that experimented with bright illumination and darkness, revealing tones from both ends of the scale. Years later, Muna delved into a similar realm with *Shadow Nudes*, another series that involved the manipulation of light to create a haunting effect on the subject.

One of Muna's most memorable projects, and the one that led to his first book—*The Apparitions* (Silent Pictures Press, 2000)—is an astonishing collection of images of blurred bodies.

"The idea was based loosely on the concept of a glimpse," he recalls, "something that resides at the periphery of one's vision. And that of the many classical references to spirits, waifs, the succubus, and so on. The idea of these spirits that take form for only a moment and disappear when one tries to really stare at them."

The photographs are peculiar, beautiful, and unforgettable all at the same time. Vague impressions of pale figures drifting past the camera lens create a ghostly image of wandering souls that have found their way into the studio.

Muna remains secretive about the process by which he created these photographs, simply calling the method "involved and convoluted." And if you are hoping to figure it out through analyzing his choice of equipment, forget it. Much like his tendency to maneuver between subjects and projects, Muna also likes to employ multiple tools and schemes to fulfill his ideas.

"I have no preferences for film or digital, no special camera or light," he says. "Each idea seems to be expressed through a medium that suits it, not through some notion of fitting into

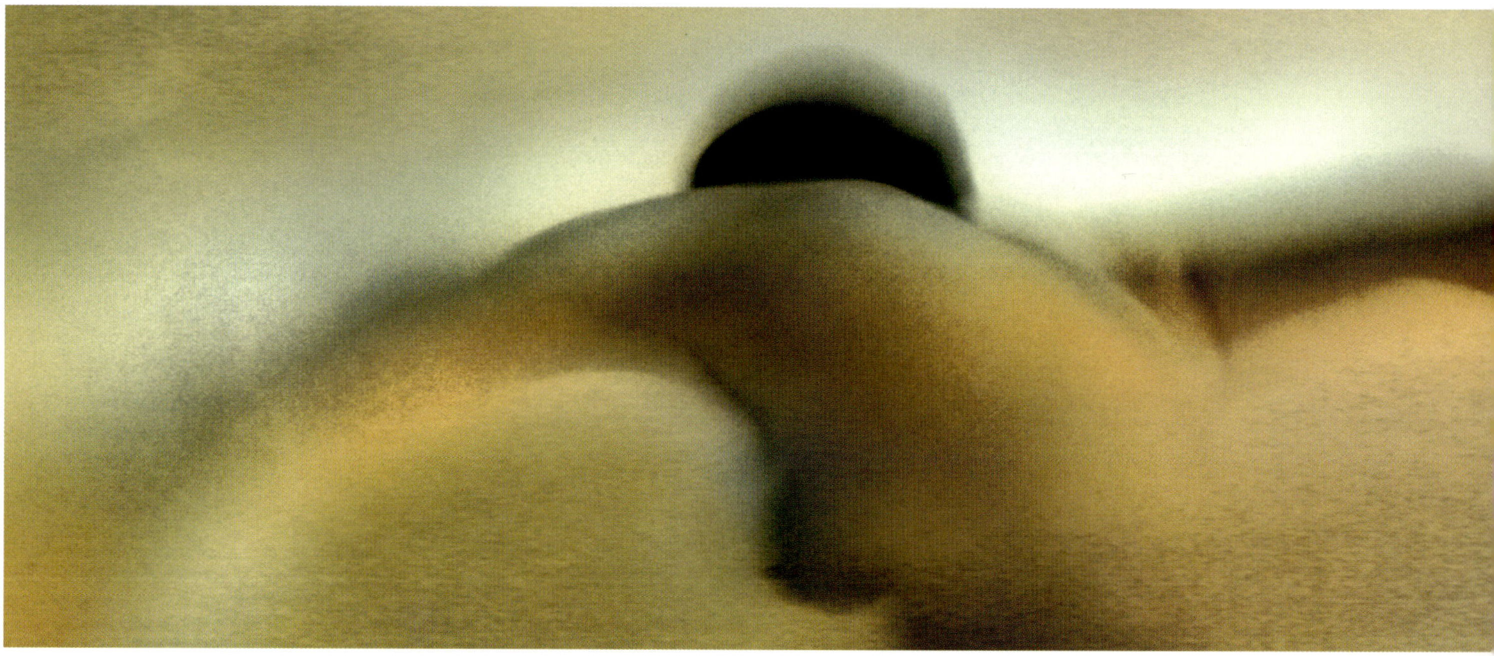

Images from The Apparitions series, 1999 *(right and opposite)*
"The process for creating them is really involved and convoluted, probably even more so than the explanation of what they are."

preconceptions. Some work is digital, some work is film-based, and some is a combination of the two."

The movement in *The Apparitions*, as well as the images in two of his other nude projects—*Physical Noise*, and *Walking Nude*—have become common in Muna's recent work and can be linked to his attachment (like some other photographers in this book) to the world of dance. He photographs the San Francisco Ballet and the ODC/San Francisco dance company, among others, and uses the performers in many of his personal series.

"I think I got into shooting dance long after I was interested in the human form," he says. "I think the dance work is an outgrowth of all the other work. I do think I'm putting a lot more motion into the work now than I was before I started shooting so much dance. It has also given me a much greater appreciation for the expression that can be drawn from the human form without words."

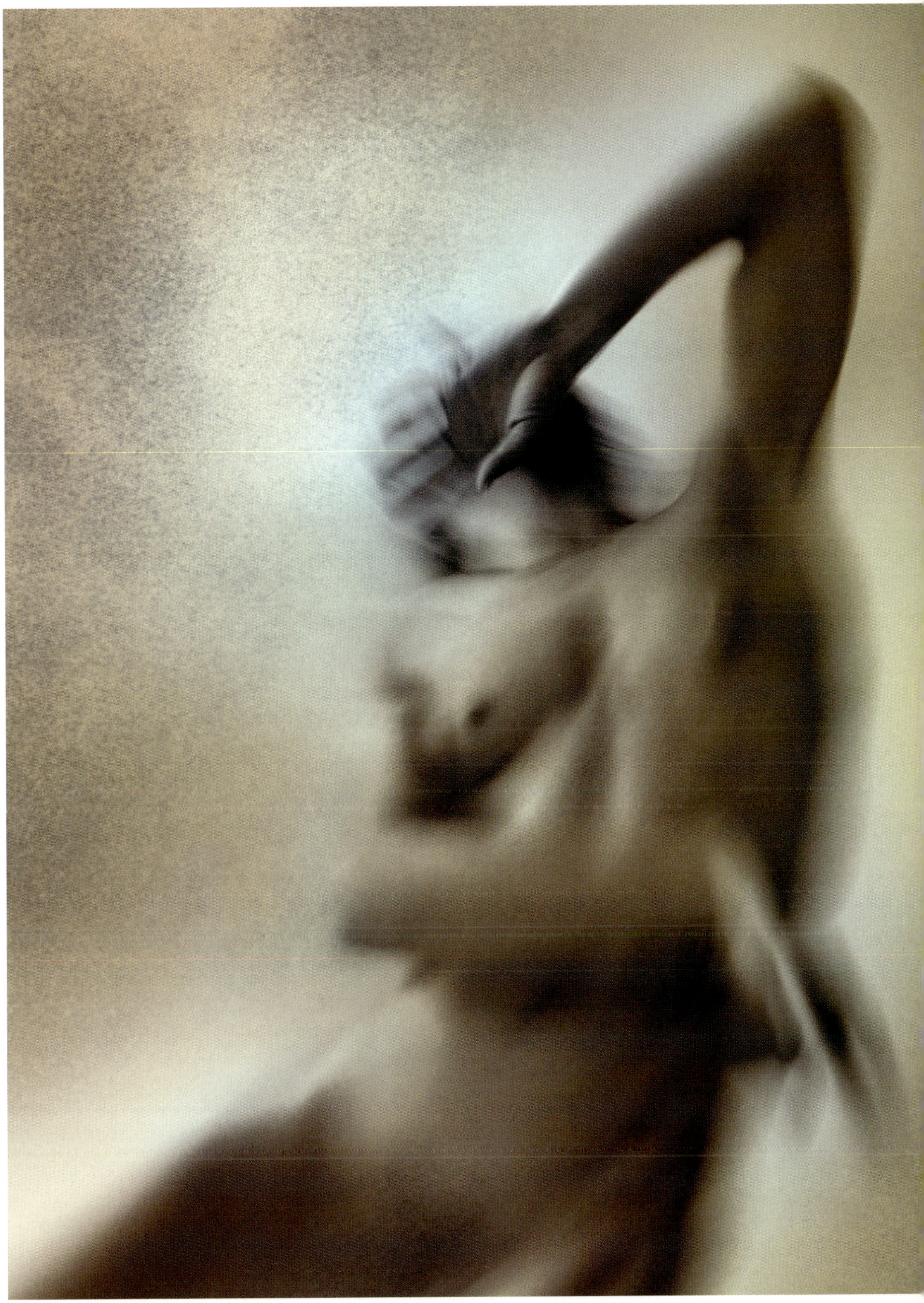

From Shadow Nudes, 2004
"The Shadow Nudes are about elemental form and line. Skin tone and detail is removed to emphasize spatial relationships. All gesture is reduced to transitional moments. They are an exercise in reduction. How much information can be removed? What new meaning can be derived from such a distillation?"

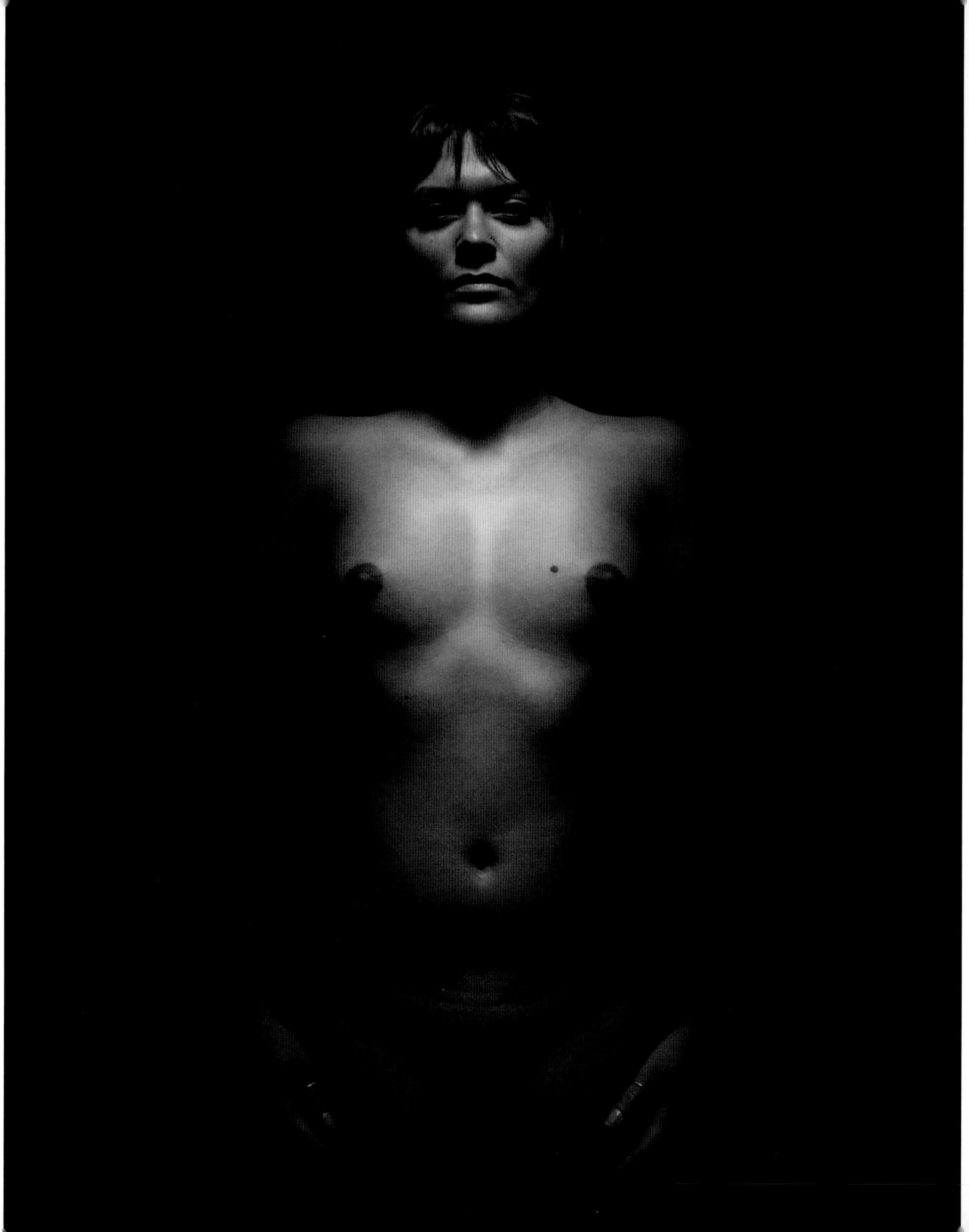

From Black Nudes *(opposite)* **and from White Nudes** *(pages 124–125)*
"This is an old series of work that came out of some experiments with light, which led to working with the ideas of light and revealing tones from either end of the scale."

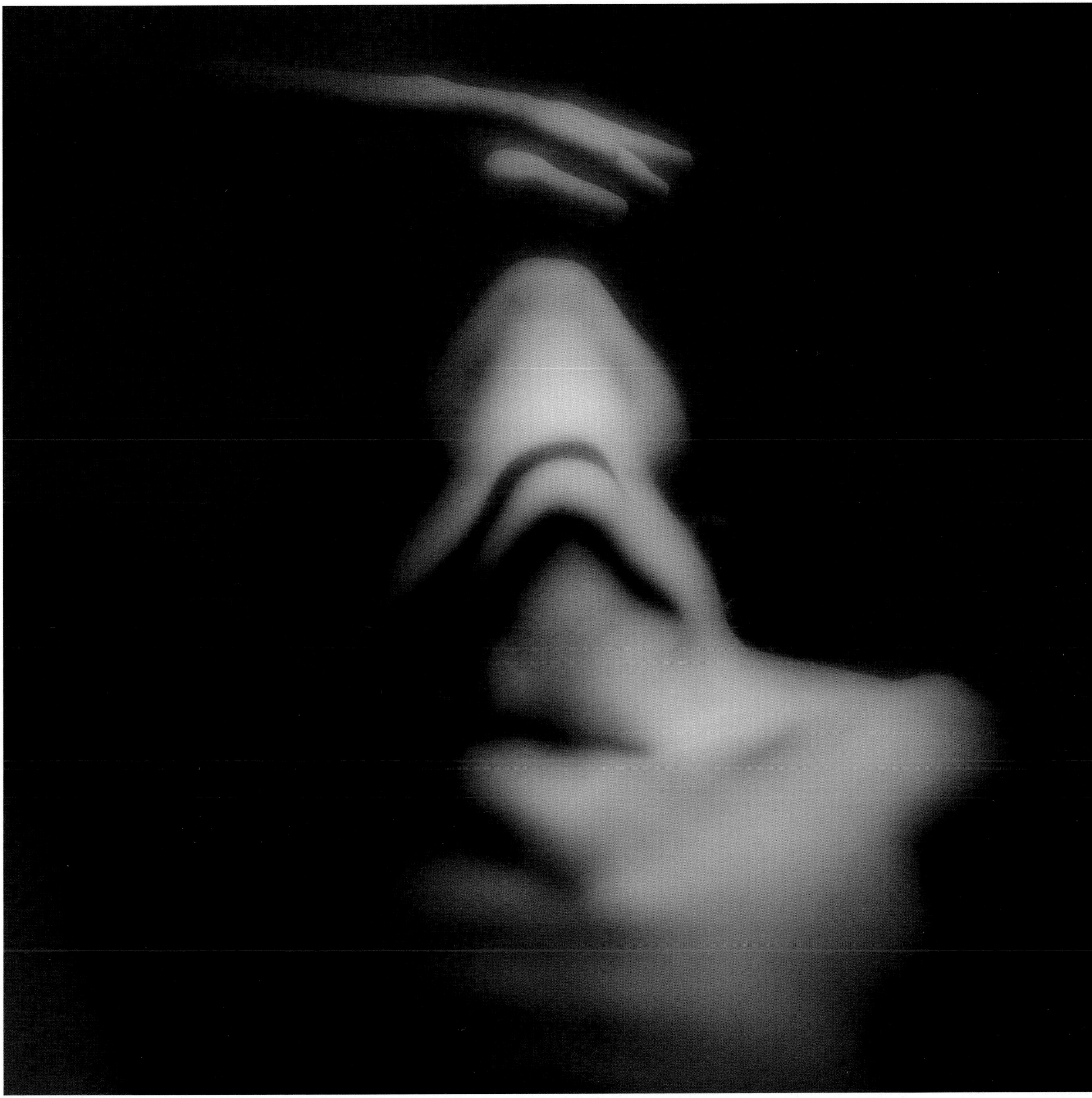

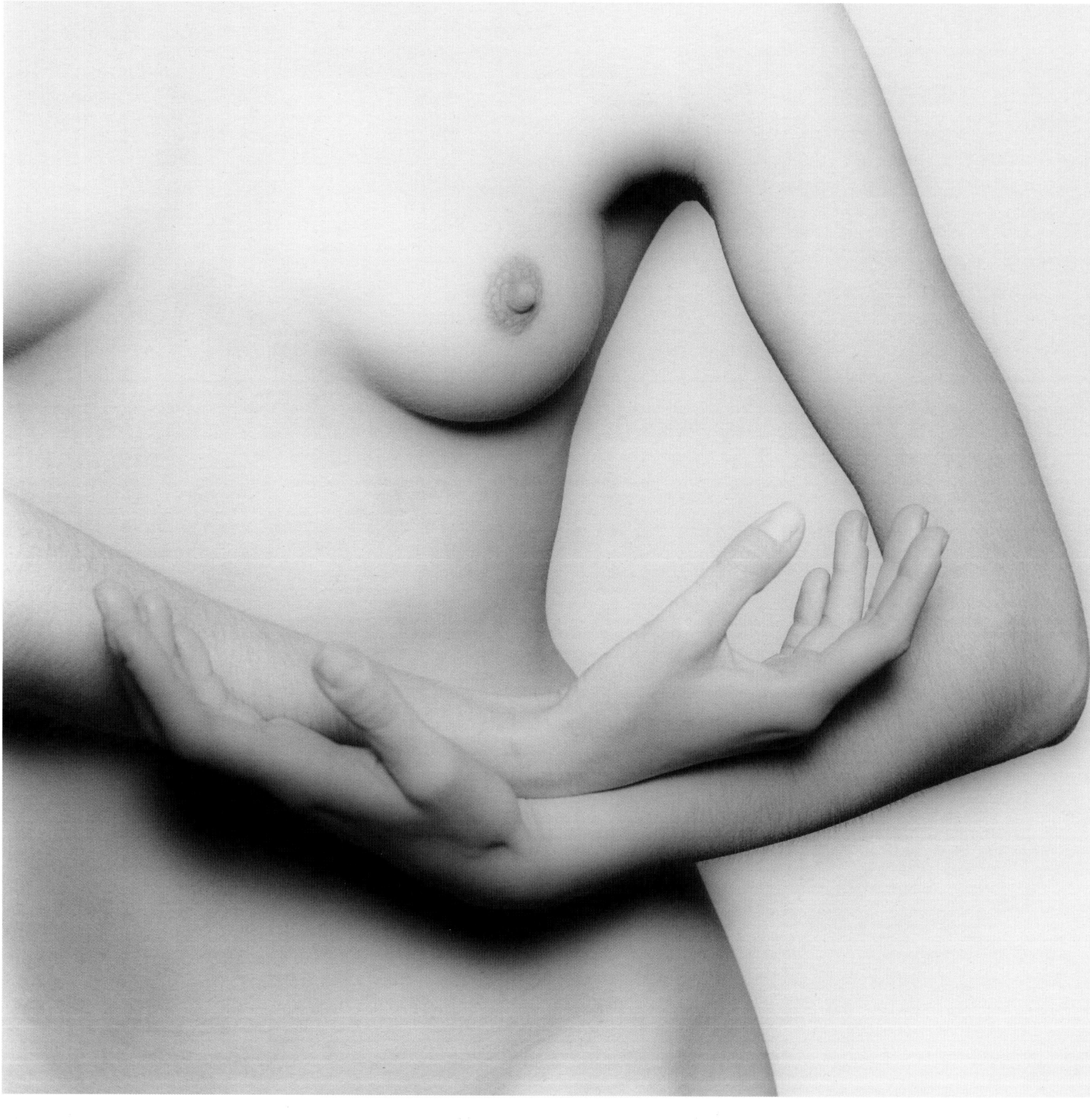

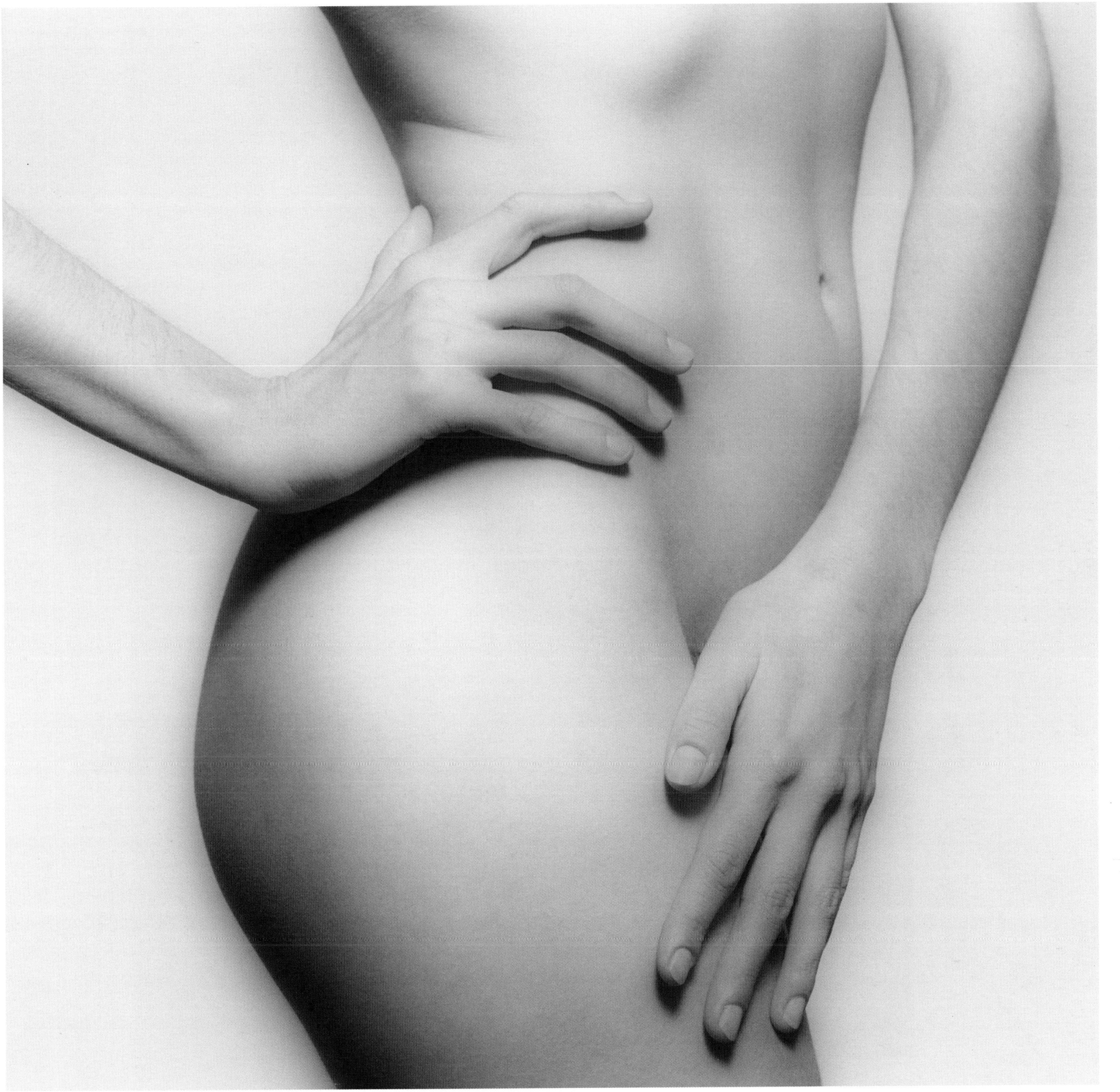

Philippe Pache

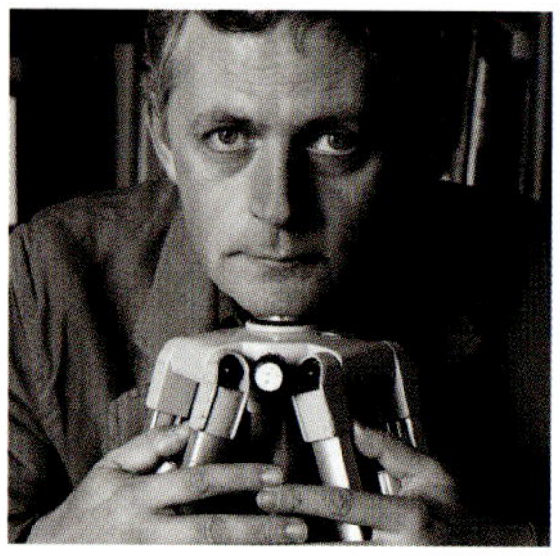

Philippe Pache's images go beyond the narrow and constantly fluctuating realm of beauty. Like misplaced stills in an old Jean-Luc Godard film, his photographs emit a cinematic intensity not found in many portfolios, books, or galleries. Not only does the loveliness of a Pache photograph strike you, but your mind is transported beyond the limits of the frame, extending toward a series of imagined previous and subsequent scenes. Pache's creations are moving images in every sense of the word.

"I love images that suggest, more than simply showing or describing the subject," says Pache.

Born in Lausanne, Switzerland, in 1961, Pache found himself attracted to photography at a very young age through the power of glossy periodicals. "When I was child I was very touched by photographs in magazines, without even thinking I would become a photographer later," he says. "When I was 15 years old I had the opportunity to learn a little with extra lessons in photography in school.

"I fell in love with photography because of the darkroom and the magic of the image appearing in the developer. Two years later I decided to be a professional photographer."

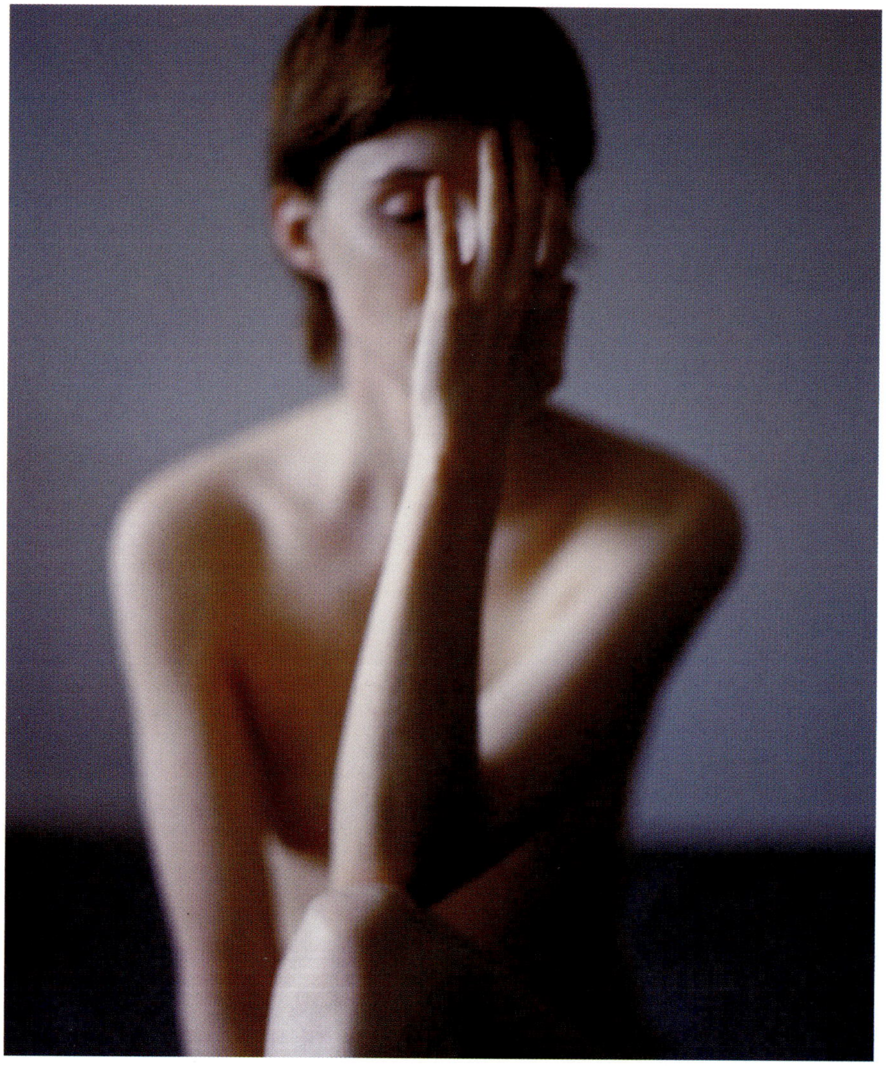

Rachel et la Main, 2001

Pache began shooting nudes not long after graduating in 1982 from the School of Applied Arts in Switzerland, and venturing into the world of portraiture. "I began with nudes, not for naked bodies, but more to avoid the anecdote of clothes," he says. "In the beginning, I was especially inspired by Jeanloup Sieff, because of the purity and elegance of the lines in his photographs, and the quality of his prints. His nudes, as well as his landscapes, touched me. When I met him for the first time in 1985, I was quite happy when he asked me to exchange two of my photographs for two of his."

Pache's early nudes are luminous black-and-white studies of willowy females. Many of the photographs are environmental portraits, highlighting the surrounding landscape and spaces as much as the model. One of his favorite and most popular images, *Rachel et les Blés* (1996), shows a woman's face and upper torso, presented prominently in the foreground, immersed in strands of light and shadow. Behind her, an infinite, sun-emblazed wall of tall grass stirs and glows.

"I think a good nude is one in which you do not think first about nudity," says Pache. "I do not like to look at nudes when you only see that the model is beautiful. I could appreciate that as a man in front of a woman, but not in an artistic or poetical vision. I hate vulgar nudes with an artistic pretentiousness. That's the worst thing for me. I prefer to see a naked woman in *Playboy* than in a pretentious artistic work. Unfortunately, we often see these kinds of nudes. A really erotic nude is more honest."

More recently, Pache has eschewed black and white in favor of color. Using retained tones, blur, indoor settings, and subtle gestures, the photographs head away from the antiquated feel of the black and whites and into a realm of heightened eroticism.

"At first I did not like color because it was too much like 'reality' for me." he says. "But now I realize that I can also dream in color. Another difference in my work is that I can use very different lighting in color. With black and white, I work with light and shadows. With color, I can work with very soft light. I still love black and white and will never give it up, but I realize that color in my work is more about a present feeling. Black and white speaks to us more about past instants. Maybe the color could be more sensual."

Pache is represented by six galleries across the world, including the Paul Kopeikin Gallery in Los Angeles, the Photo Gallery International in Tokyo, and the Photographers' Gallery in London, and his images can also be found in the public collections of the Bibliothèque Nationale in Paris, the Tokyo Metropolitan Museum of Photography, and ten other international locations.

Pache works constantly in editorial and advertising in addition to being an avid photographer of dance (he has photographed the ballet company in Lausanne, as well as being the official photographer of the Prix de Lausanne—a contest for young dancers—since 1983).

As for working with the nude, Pache's advice is simple. "Do nudes if you have something to express outside of looking at beautiful nude women, even though nobody would complain about seeing beautiful women. As Man Ray said, the paradox is that it is more difficult to take a good picture with a beautiful subject, if you want to express an emotion beyond the subject. It's exactly the same if you have to take pictures of Venice. It's not easy to show something other than the beauty of the city. But, for sure, it's a good exercise."

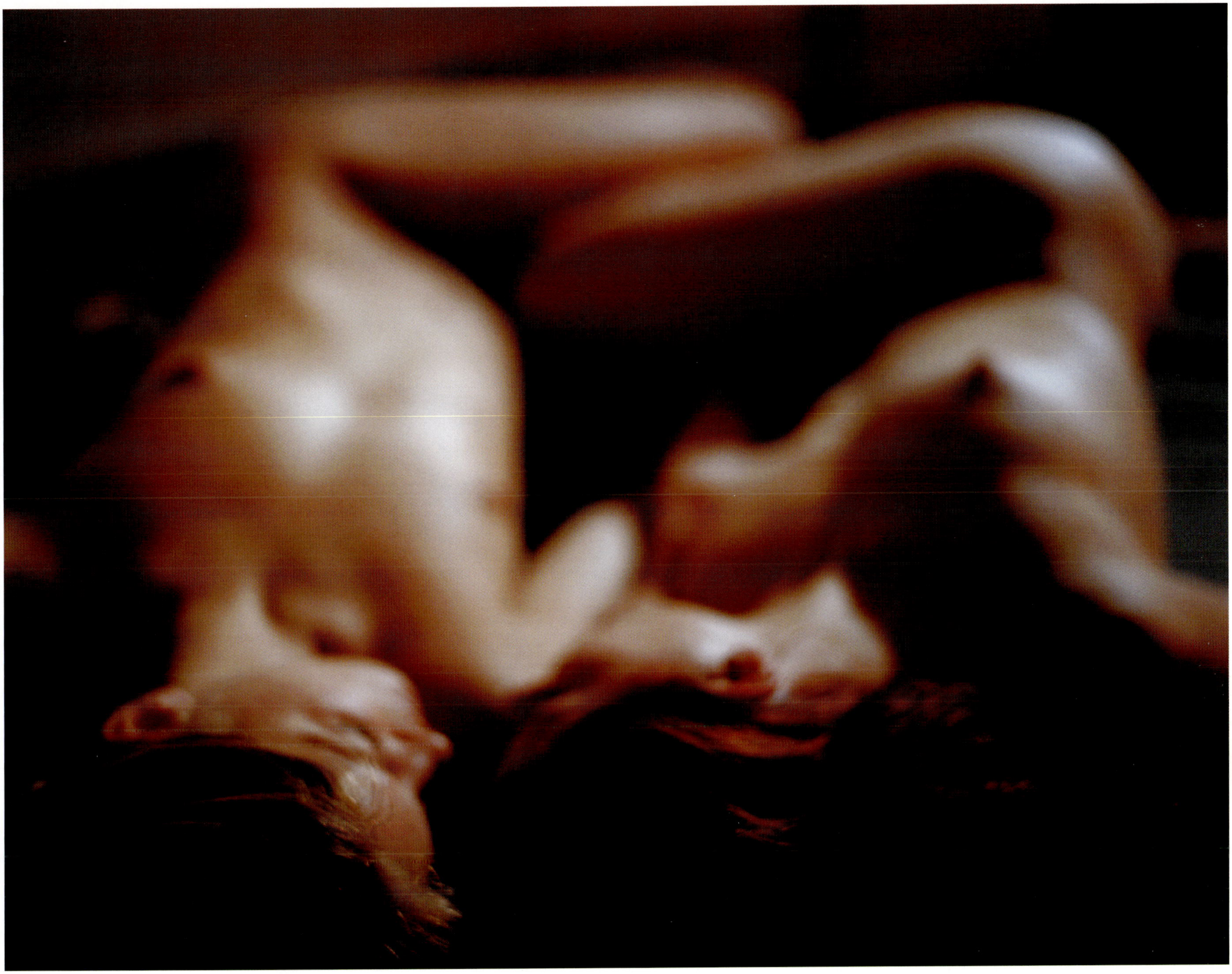

Ana and Katy, 2001
"For many years I was sure I would never work in color for my personal work, even if [I had worked with it] quite often for assignments. I was surprised by myself and quite happy to be suddenly involved in color."

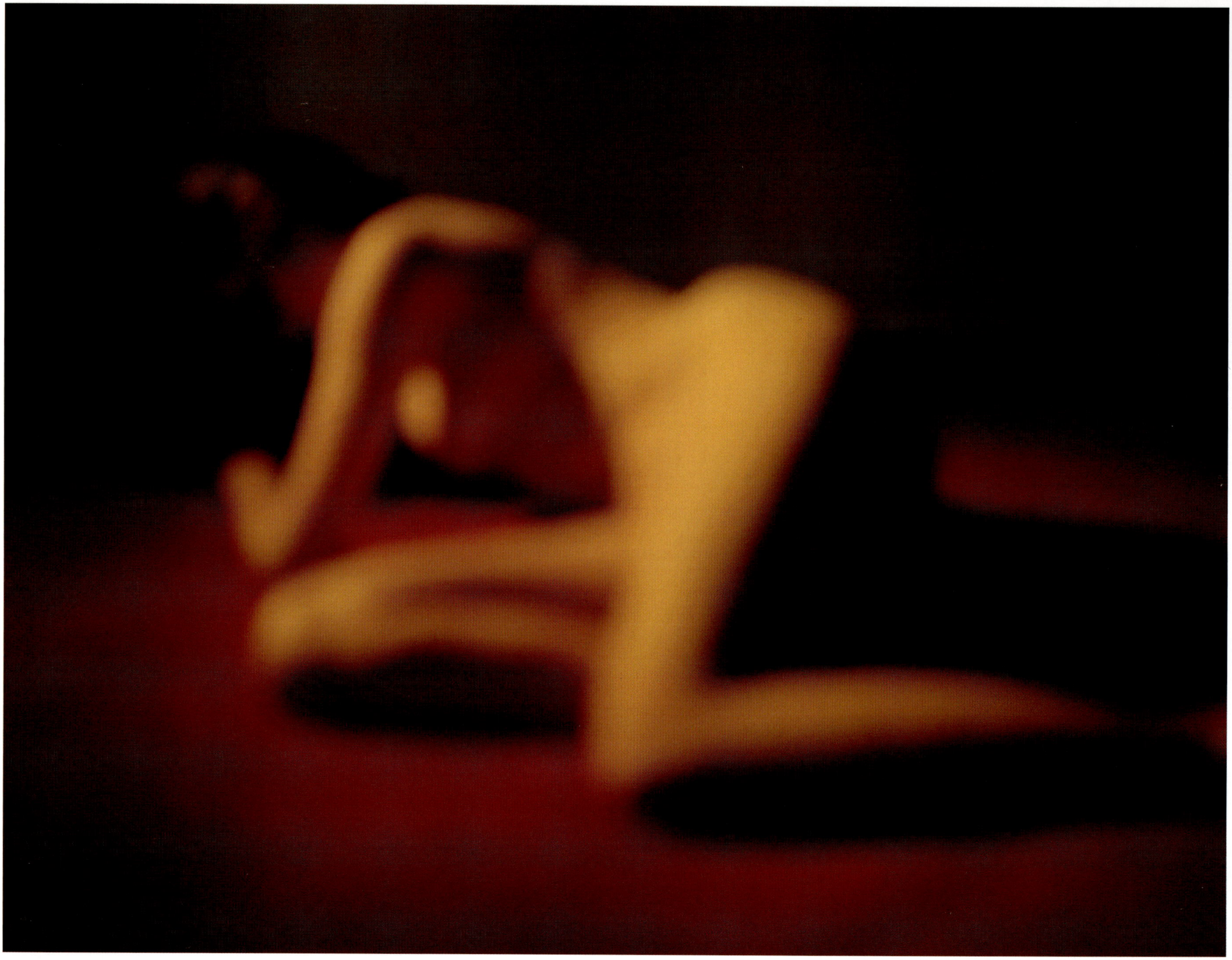

Olivia, 2000
"This image is from my first nude shoot in color. I worked here with tungsten [lighting]."

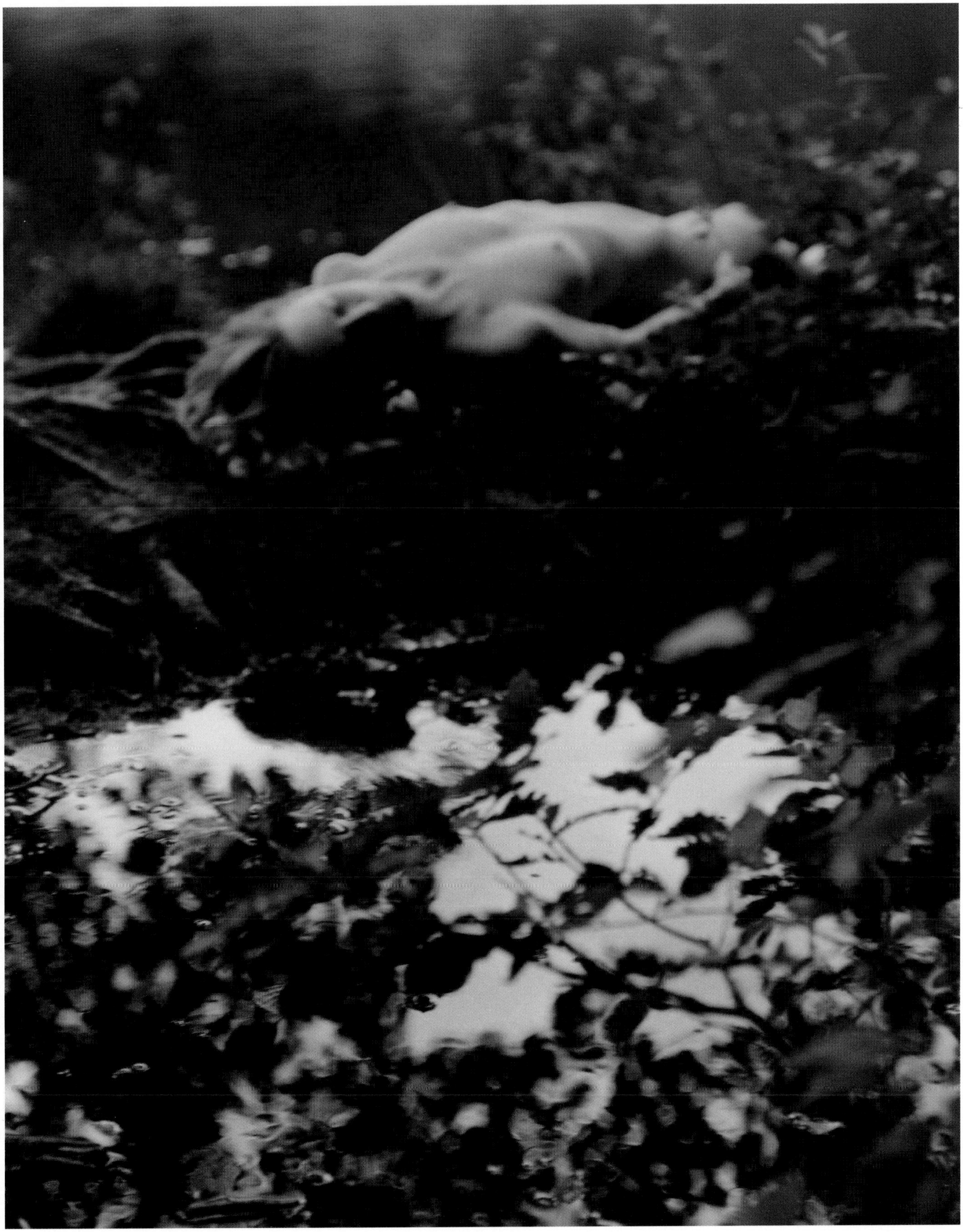

Rachel (Ophélie), 1997
"I arrived very early in the morning at this pond with Rachel, the model I have worked with the most these last years. Even if it was not on purpose, this image became like a homage to Ophelia."

David Penprase

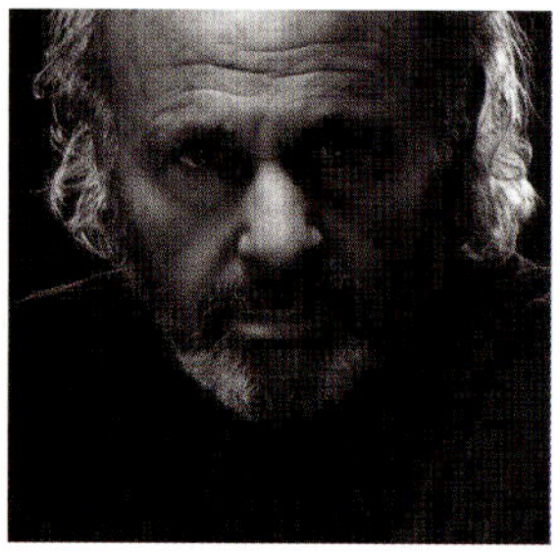

David Penprase is a Cornishman who lives and works in Porthleven, a fishing village in Mount's Bay, toward the tip of southwest England. This coast of Cornwall, known as The Lizard, is a place rich in Arthurian legend, tales of smugglers and ghost ships, ancient ruins, abandoned tin mines, and clay pits. So it is little wonder that Penprase's nudes tend to be wild creatures, at once theatrical and mythical.

The women in Penprase's wondrous yet strange photographs tend to be smeared with ash or clay and entwined in roots and branches, while the men appear to be from some Hieronymous Bosch-inspired tableau of martyrs and heroes. At times, Penprase's women seem like clay sculptures; at others, like wood nymphs and sprites captured in gritty, antique-looking prints. What this pagan and erotic fantasy world represents to the artist is anyone's guess, because Penprase isn't saying.

"It is a fantasy world," he says. "You take someone off the street, put them in this theatrical environment, and they become someone else. You can imagine what the photographer was up to, but you're probably a million miles away.

"I think the basis of my work is that I like texture and interest in a photograph. Very often there are two or three stories behind a picture. I'm asking a question of the viewer. In most cases, people have to work out what's going on in a picture. That's why I don't title it. A label immediately takes you down a particular road."

If one were to put a label on Penprase himself, however, it might be "showman." A former rock 'n' roll musician, nightclub owner, clothing-store proprietor, and "frustrated actor," Penprase uses photography much as an impresario does a stage.

Penprase was born in the Cornish industrial town of Redruth in 1942. His father worked on the roads as a laborer, his mother was a housewife, and Penprase himself was, he says, an indifferent student. "I left school with not much in the way of academic qualifications, and when my dad died I had to go to work."

Penprase's first job was as a clerk in a local clothing store, but his first love was music. When rock 'n' roll hit Redruth in the 1950s, Penprase taught himself to play guitar and embarked on a brief career as a singer. Initially, he performed solo at a local arcade under his own name, but as skiffle bands became popular all over

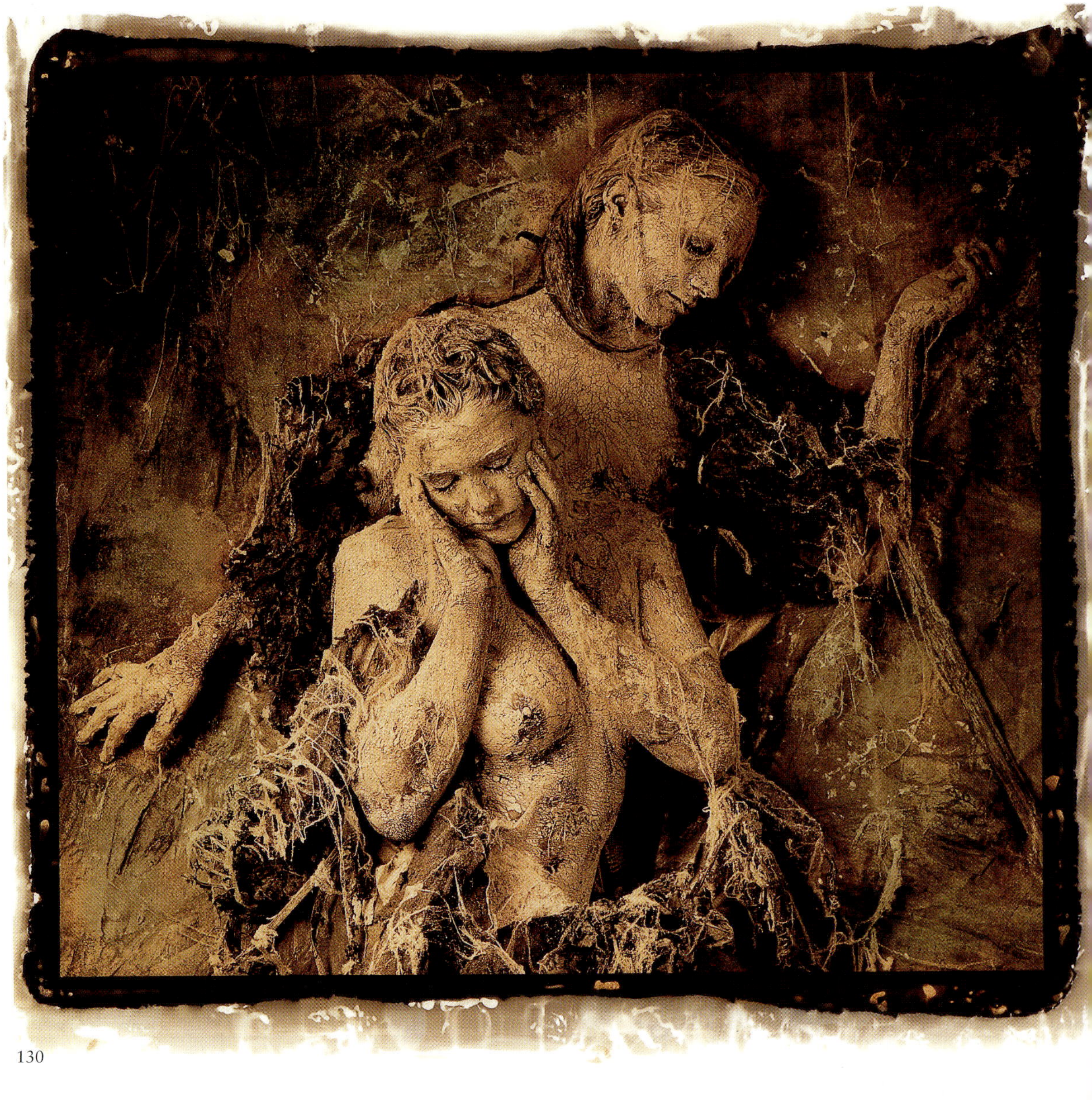

Untitled, 1999
"Both models had posed for me many times. The set I had built in preparation and the pose worked out. The difficulty, as always, is bringing some emotional content and energy into a preconceived and structured format."

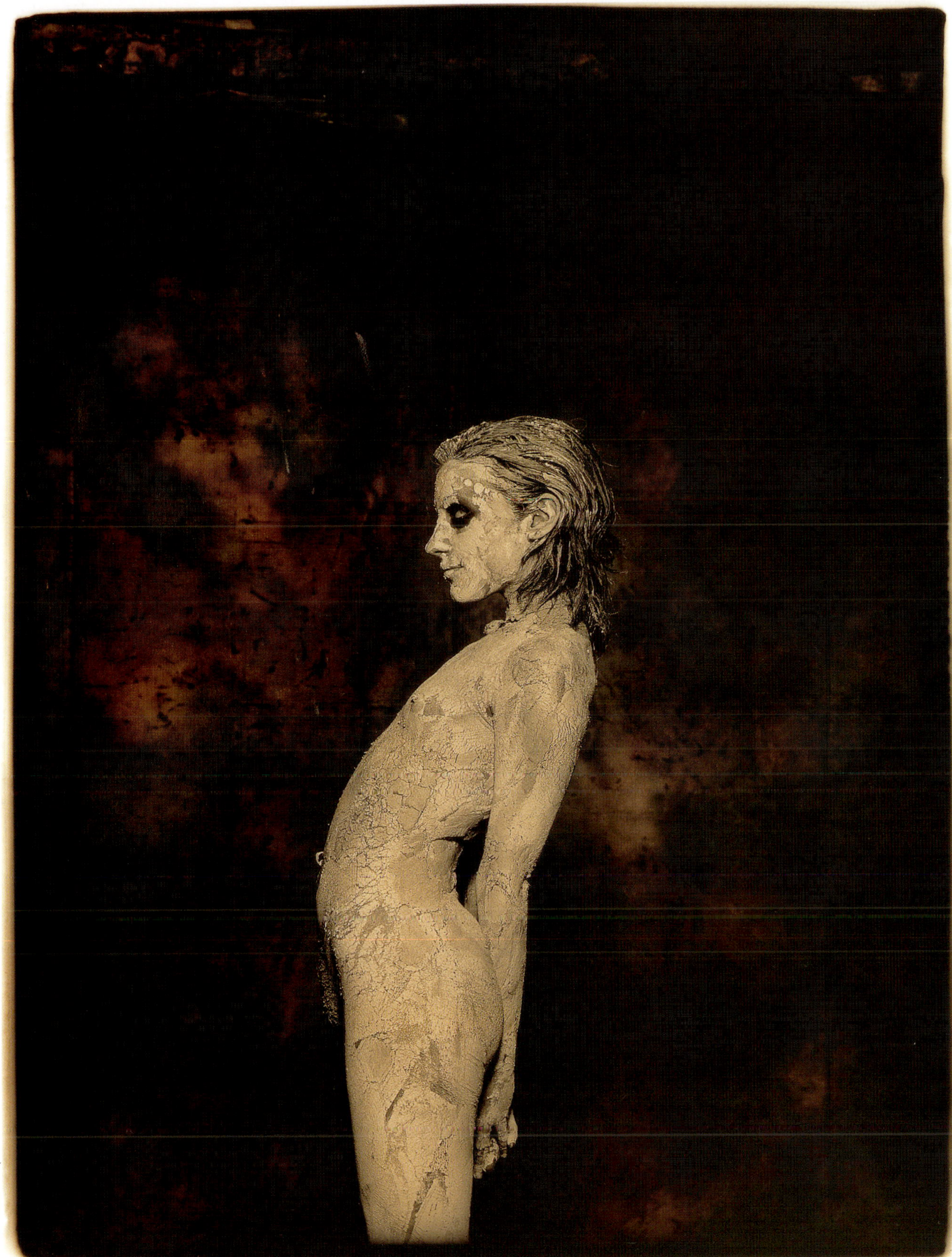

Untitled, 1998
"One of my favorite models. I photographed her over a two-year period, never failing to get the image I was after. Not what would be termed a classic beauty, but for me far more interesting. A wonderful face and bone structure, coupled with a desire to get images, gave us a real chance of getting that elusive moment."

England, he took the name Dave Lee and formed The Staggerlees, a band named after the 1959 Lloyd Price hit "Stagger Lee," a contemporaneous version of the black American legend. The band had a hit song with "Love Me" in 1963, but when Dave Lee's voice gave out while on tour in Germany, he was replaced as The Staggerlees' frontman.

Back home in Cornwall, Penprase started a disco in Truro, a folk club in Redruth, and a boutique called Togs—long since relocated to Helston, where Penprase's wife still runs it.

Compared with many of his peers, who studied art or photography from their student days, these were unlikely beginnings for an artist with such a unique and arresting style. Indeed, it wasn't until 1982, when Penprase was 40 years old, that he embarked on his new career, after a relative gave him a Canon AE-1. Weddings, portraits, and advertising provided him with work, but it was Penprase's personal photography, primarily his nudes, that gained him attention beyond Cornwall. To date, his nudes have appeared in three monographs: *Untitled* (Creative Monochrome, 1994); *Beyond the Edge* (Creative Monochrome, 1998); and *Passion, Pleasure and Pain* (D & J Publishing, 2001).

"*Untitled* was a fairly broad coverage of my work, from nudes to portraiture," he says, "but *Beyond the Edge* was quite a bit grittier, darker. By then I had started working with clay and texture on the body."

The inspiration for applying oil, soot, sand, soil, and clay to the human body came from *The Name of the Rose*, the 1986 film based on Umberto Eco's bestselling novel about a medieval monk on the trail of a murderer. "There is a scene in the film where a peasant girl seduces a young monk," Penprase explains. "She's rough and dirty, very earthy, and very, very sensual. I liked the look."

To reproduce the look, Penprase started rubbing oil and soot from his own chimney on his subjects. "I found it very beautiful," he recalls. "It's like when you meet an elderly person, wrinkled and old, and suddenly you see the beauty beneath the surface and think, 'I bet you were beautiful when you were young.' It's the inner beauty coming through."

To capture the outward texture and inner beauty of his mud-daubed models, Penprase shoots with medium-format and 5x4 cameras using Ilford SP-4 or Tri-X 400 black-and-white film and very little artificial lighting. "I've always been a simplistic worker in terms of lighting," he says. "I'm not a great technician, so I keep things as simple as I can. There's only one sun out there, and that's all I need."

Penprase says he works in "that murky area which divides erotic art from pornography," but his interest goes much deeper than mere prurience. "I like women from head to toe, but the face is my basic point of interest," he says. "It doesn't have to be beautiful, just interesting and compelling. The face and the mind. If you get someone in the studio whose head is not in it, then pack up and go home."

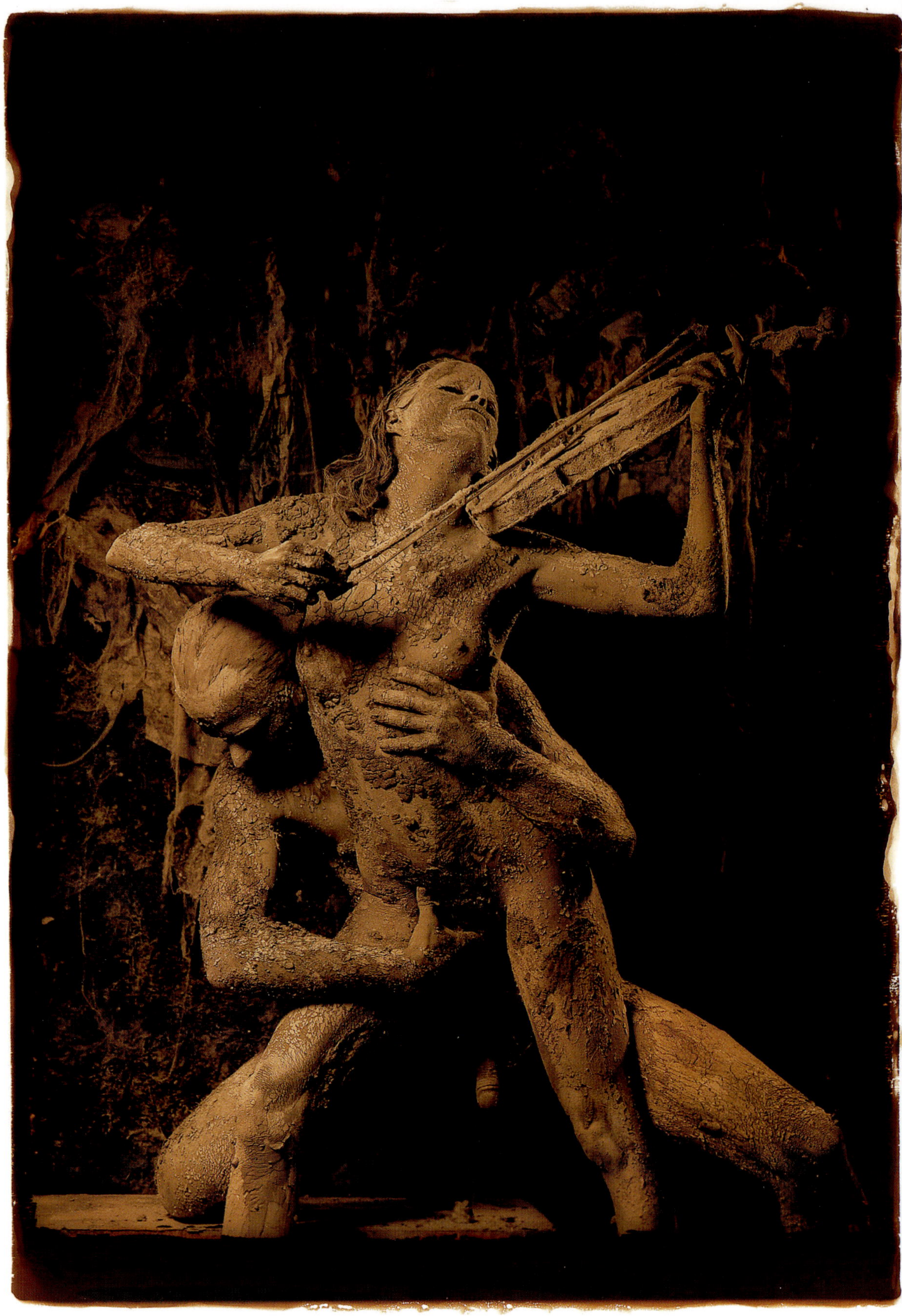

Untitled, 2002 *(left)*
"Quite an erotic image. The couple had never met before, so great care was taken to ensure that they were aware what was aimed for on the shoot. Even so, it took some time for the models to relax, and this frame was toward the end of the session."

Untitled, 2003 *(right)*
"I do have a narrative, but as with all of my work I never title, preferring the viewer to interpret and have their own 'story.' This image has everything I like to put in my work: an interesting face, hints of sexuality, and texture."

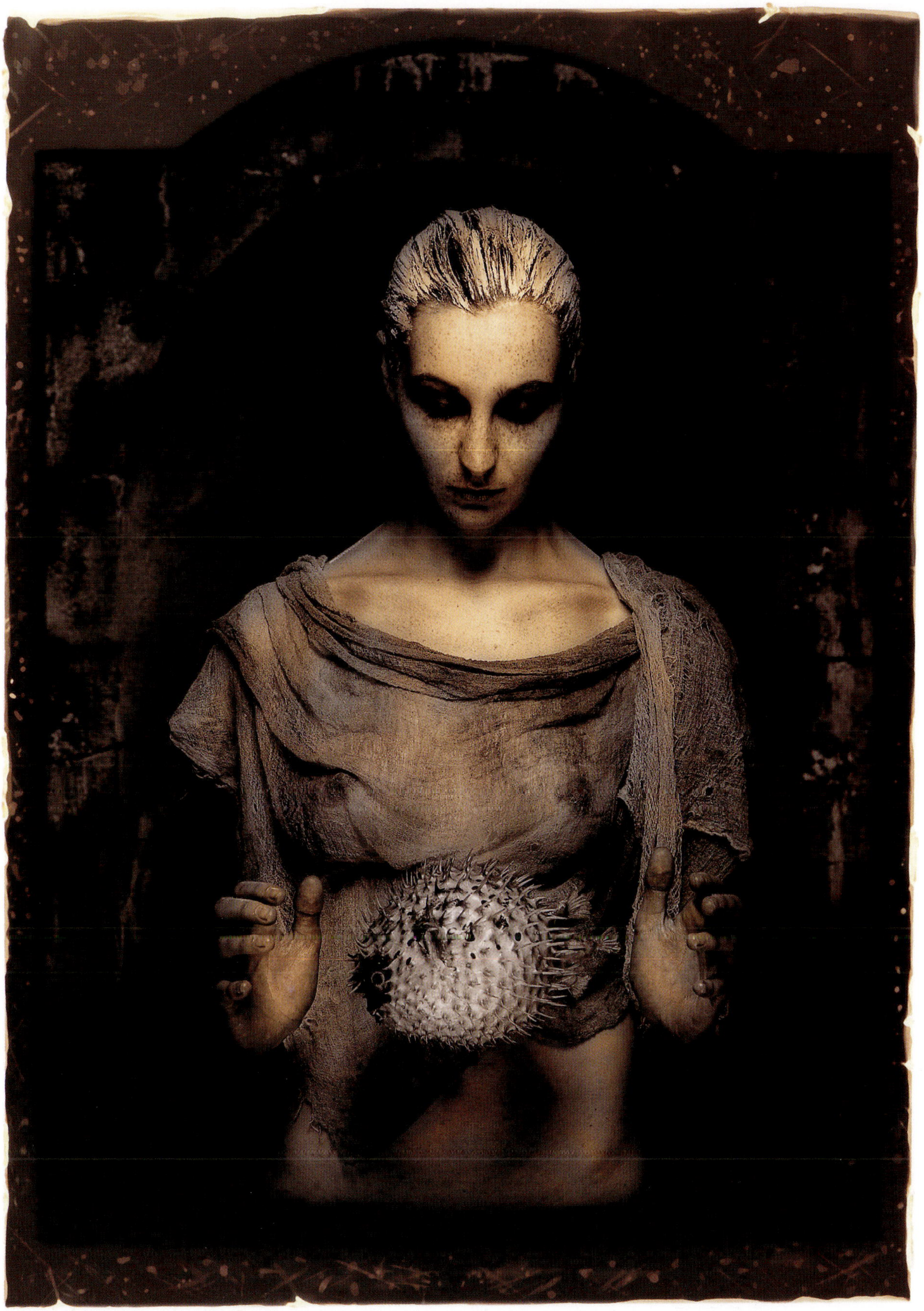

Rankin

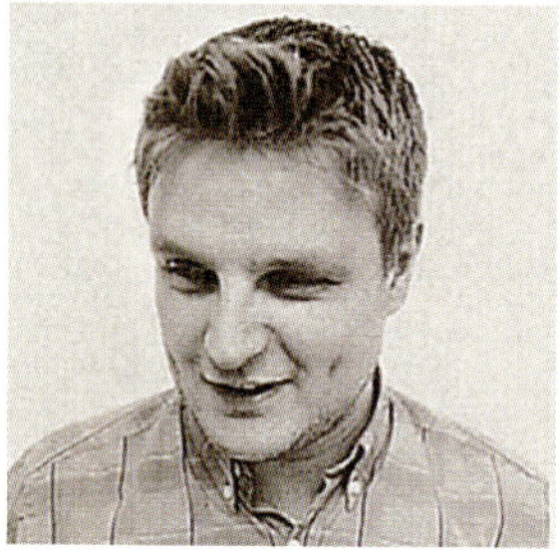

Ever since John Rankin Waddell, who uses only his middle name professionally, cofounded the hip culture magazine *Dazed & Confused* in 1991, he has been the "go-to" guy for what's hot (or cool) in British pop culture. He is the edgy bad boy of the London club scene, chronicler of the rich and famous—in short, a fin-de-siècle David Bailey. Everyone who is anyone in British society—including art star Damien Hirst, supermodel Kate Moss, designer Stella McCartney, wannabe-Brit Madonna, Prime Minister Tony Blair, and even Queen Elizabeth herself—has had a portrait made by Rankin.

Though he considers himself primarily a portrait photographer, Rankin is arguably better known for his ongoing body of nude photography, which dates back to his student days in Luton. "I'm definitely obsessed by nudity," Rankin concedes. "When I photographed the Queen, I discovered that was how people saw me. One in every two people asked me if I had photographed the Queen nude." Perish the thought! Rankin was just trying to shoot a portrait of the Queen laughing, but he confides that it did occur to him for one brief, naughty moment to hire a model with a similar body type to graft the Queen's head on.

For the most part, Rankin restricts his nude photographs to beautiful young women, both famous and not, but his first series of nudes, created as a thesis project while an art student in Luton, featured an 80-year-old life model called Dot. "They were quite shocking to a lot of people at the college," Rankin recalls. "I always told everyone she was my mother, but she wasn't. My dad came to the show and he was suitably impressed by the love/hate response it got and decided there was no mediocrity about it. So he helped me go to the London College of Printing."

Rankin was born in 1966 in Glasgow, Scotland, where his mother was an accountant and his father a sales director for an oil company. He first set out in the world to study accounting at Brighton Polytechnic, but living in a dorm full of art students convinced him he wasn't cut out for such a career. At the suggestion of a friend, Rankin took up photography and quickly shot to the head of the class of young British photographers.

At the London College of Printing, Rankin's final project was a series entitled *Canned Nudes*, which consisted of nude photographs sealed in tin cans and displayed on the shelves of a supermarket. He and *Dazed & Confused* cofounder Jefferson Hack also rocked the college community by blowing the school's entire student-publication budget on a magazine called *Eat Me*. Without bothering to graduate, Rankin left college to launch *Dazed & Confused*, and he hasn't looked back.

Nothing if not prolific, Rankin has published a steady stream of books, including *Nudes* (Rankin Photography, 1999); *Snog* (Vision On Publishing, 2000); *CeleBritation* (Vision On Publishing, 2000); *Male Nudes* (Vision On Publishing, 2001); *Sofasosexy* (Vision On Publishing, 2002), a series of female nudes posed on Rankin's own couch; *Breeding* (Vision On Publishing, 2002), a limited-edition boxed set of black-and-white photographs of androgynous models; and *Bailey & Rankin* (Rankin Photography, 2003), a pairing of David Bailey's frank photographs of female genitalia with Rankin's *Girls on Top* nude series.

Breeding was directly influenced by Bettina Rheims's androgynous nudes in *Modern Lovers*, and, like Rheims, Rankin says, "I really like to see women in positions of empowerment. I don't see nude photography as voyeuristic. It's about privilege, not control."

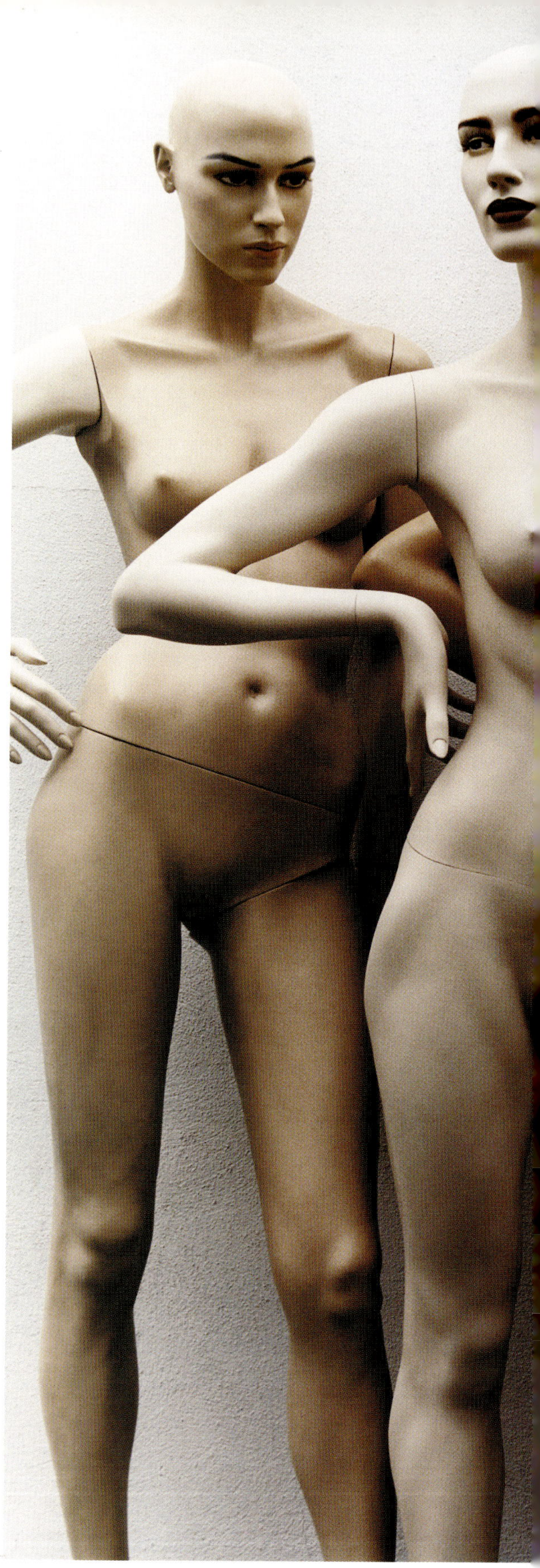

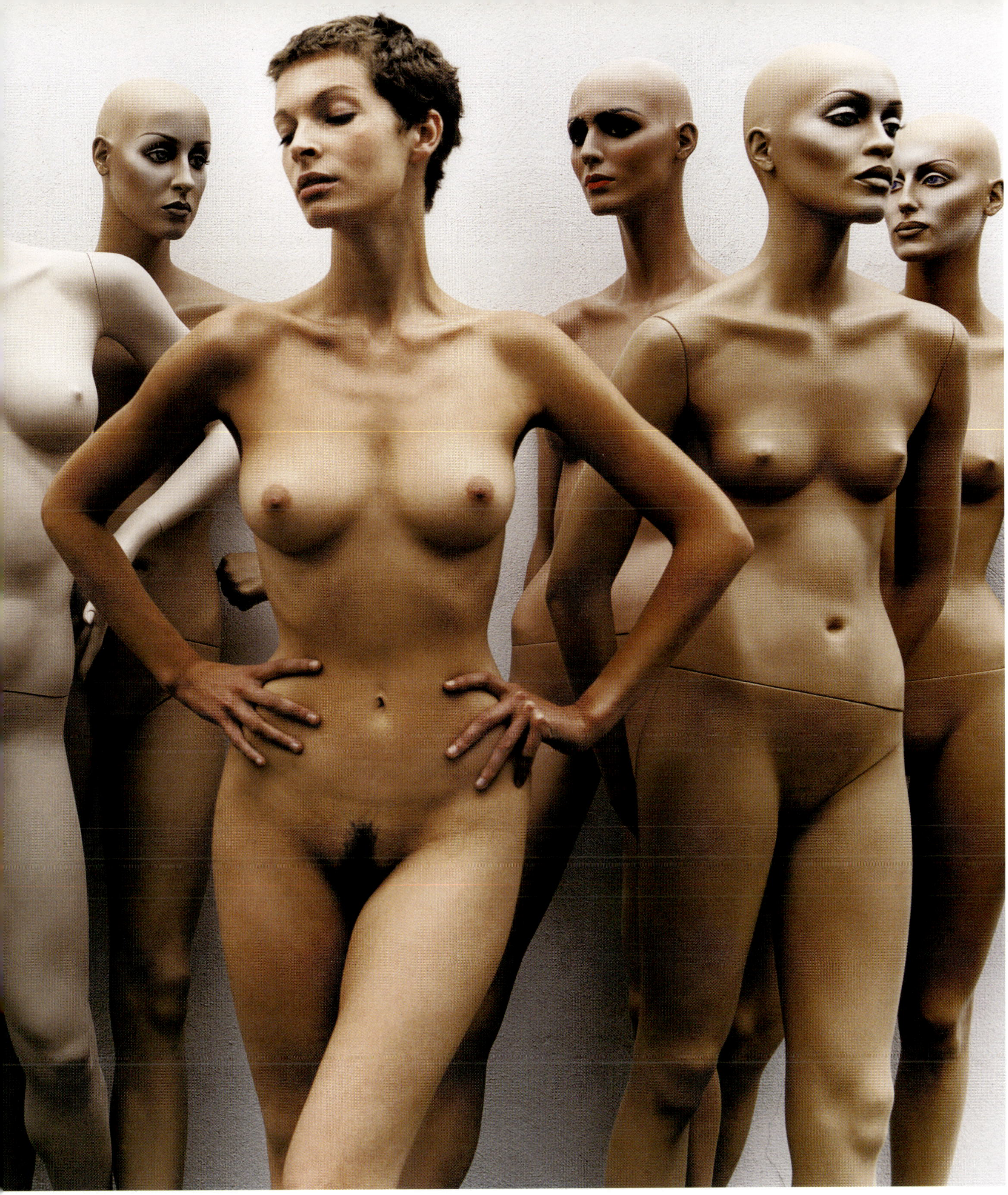

Kate Orr, 1999
"This is from my original *Nudes* project. I was trying to get girls to come up with ideas themselves, but I said to Kate, 'How about if you stand in front of mannequins with similar faces and shapes to you?' She had had a mannequin made of her, but we couldn't find it."

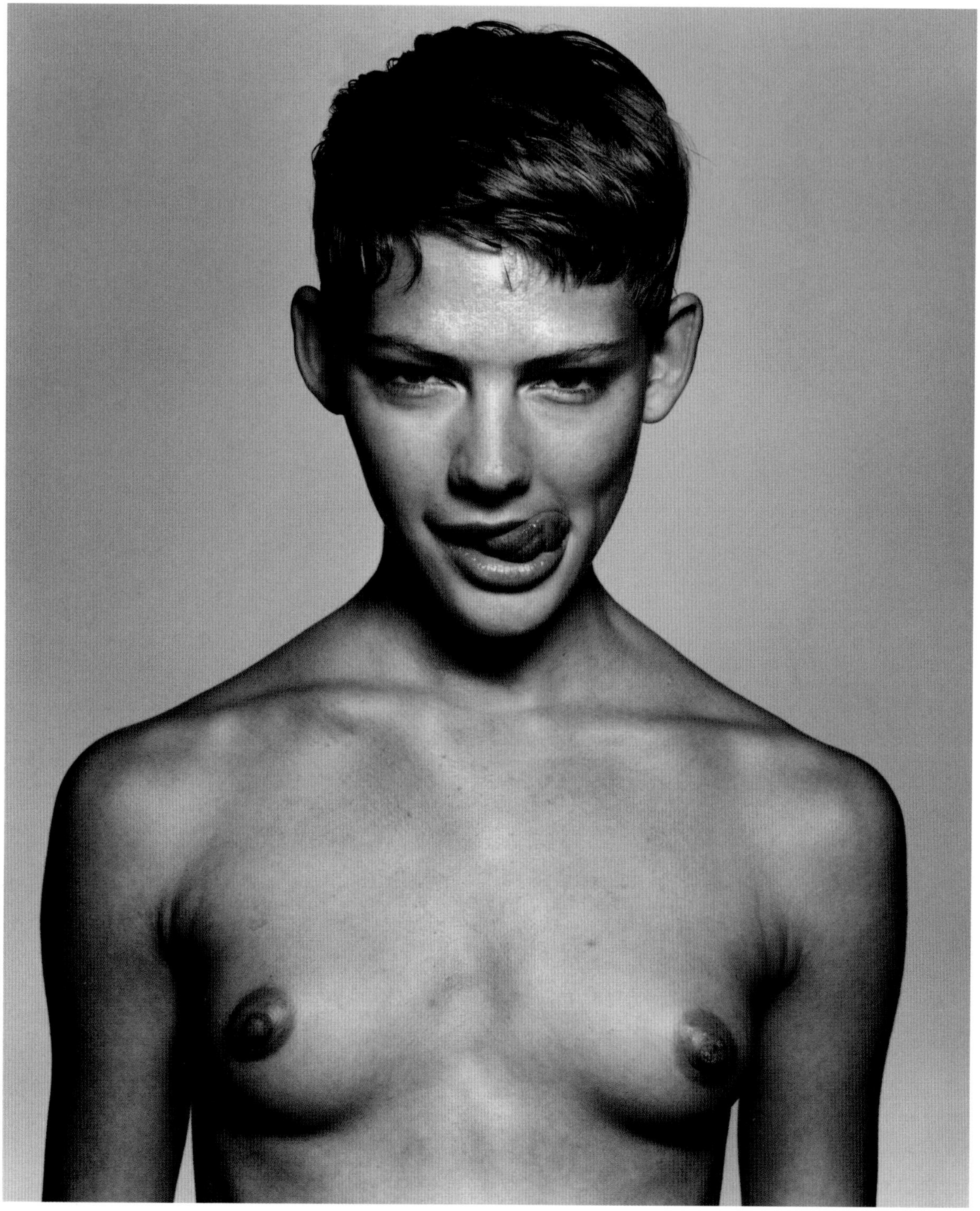

His *Girls on Top* photographs were all taken of women in the superior position, posing, teasing, writhing, bumping, and grinding on top of Rankin. The results are vertiginous high-rises of female eroticism towering above the photographer and, by extension, the viewer. "I shot it all with a Kodak digital back on a Mamiya," says Rankin. "The focal length is so tight that you get really, really close. It was a very sexual thing—the nearest you can ever get to having photographic intercourse with someone."

Far from being exploitative, Rankin says *Girls on Top* provided his models with the instant gratification of seeing each shot immediately and allowed them total control over how they would be seen. "The women were choosing the images with me," he says. "They did things I would have been too embarrassed to ask them to do."

Though he does prefer a Mamiya 6x7, Rankin insists, "A true photographer can take a good picture with any camera." He prefers to allow "a style to embrace an image," rather than making the subject conform to any Rankin style of photograph. "I'm certainly not stylistically stuck to one way of making images. I jump around. It's not just one camera, not just soft porn or high art. I like to jump around with styles. Otherwise I get bored."

Acknowledging the inspiration and influence of, among others, photographers David Bailey, Bettina Rheims, and Helmut Newton, Rankin says, "The next time I come back to nudes, they will be very much me, not influenced by anyone else. I'm still finding where I fit into the world of photography."

Emily, from Breeding, ongoing works in progress
"Even though she's boyish, she's incredibly attractive. With *Breeding*, I was interested in the strange gene all models seem to have, how their eyes are farther apart, something that makes them very beautiful to other people. If you took out the breasts, you wouldn't be 100 percent sure she was a girl."

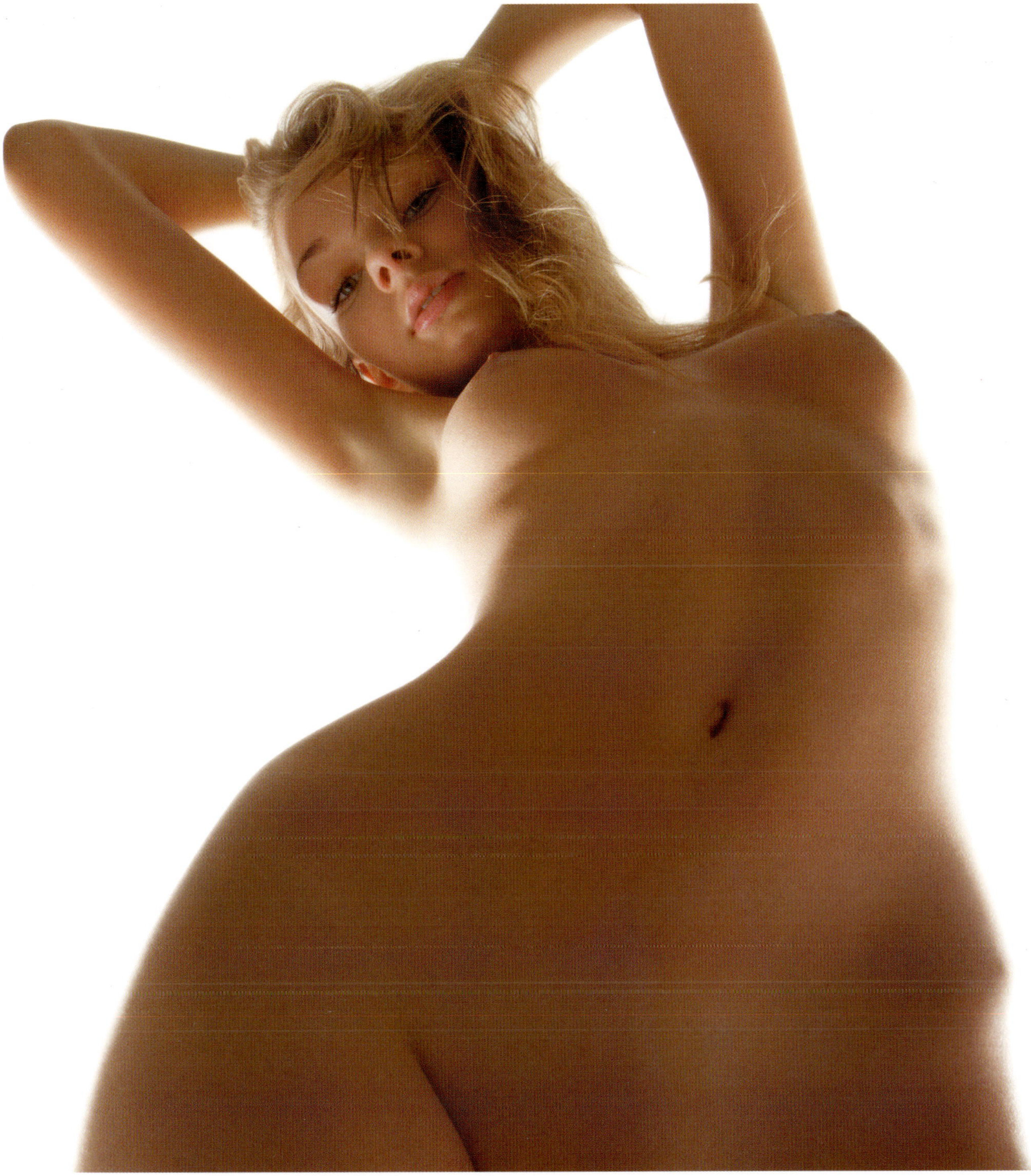

Anna, date unknown
"This is in *Girls on Top*. I remember the girl being incredibly sexual. This is actually quite erotic, as was the reality of doing it. She really took the bull by the horns."

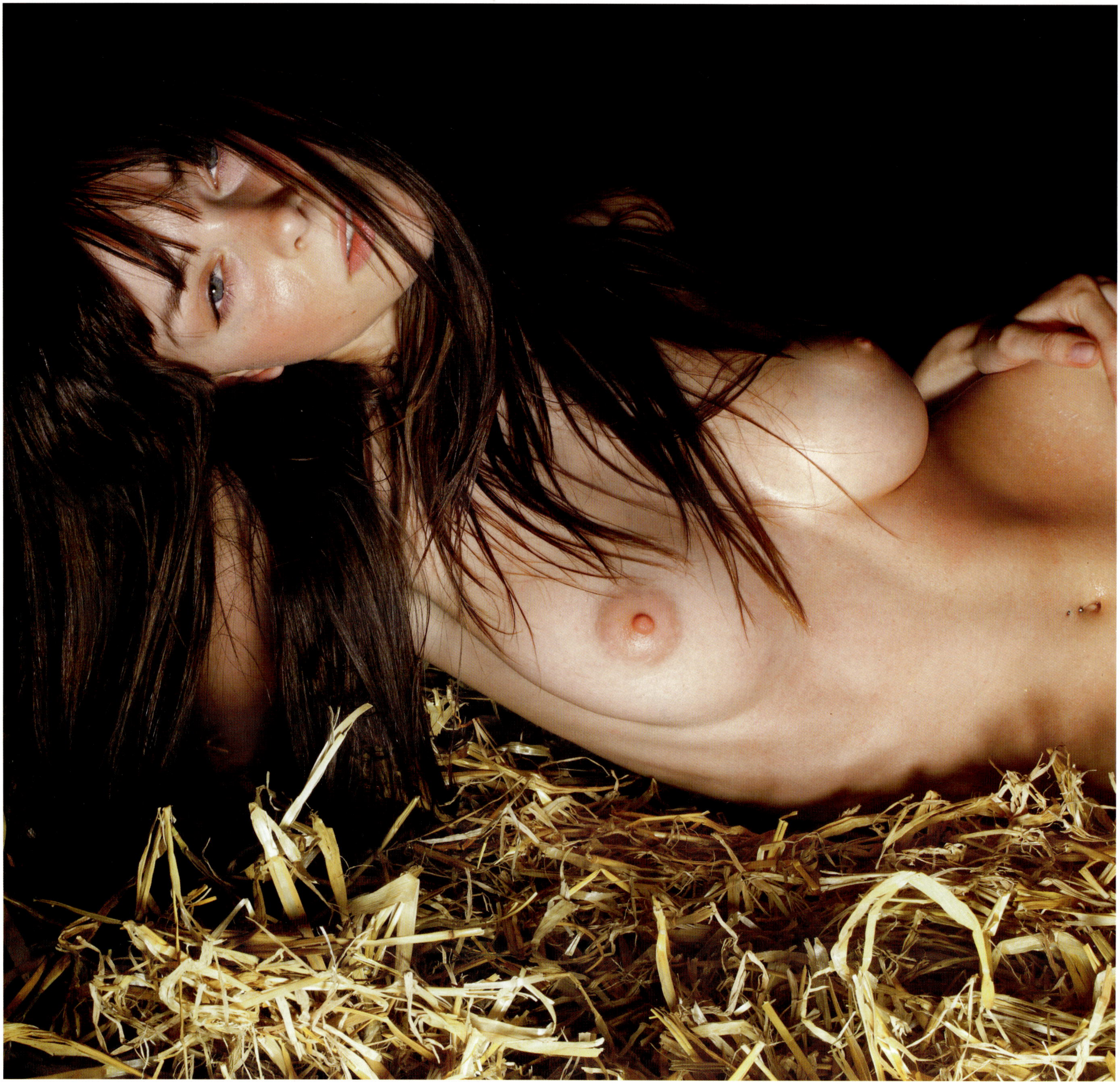

Zoe Havler, date unknown (*left*)
"This was from a project for *Arena* magazine. The idea was to do elements—snow, water, earth, land, straw. It's a purely erotic fantasy image for me that I did for them. It was quite easy really, because she was unbelievably beautiful."

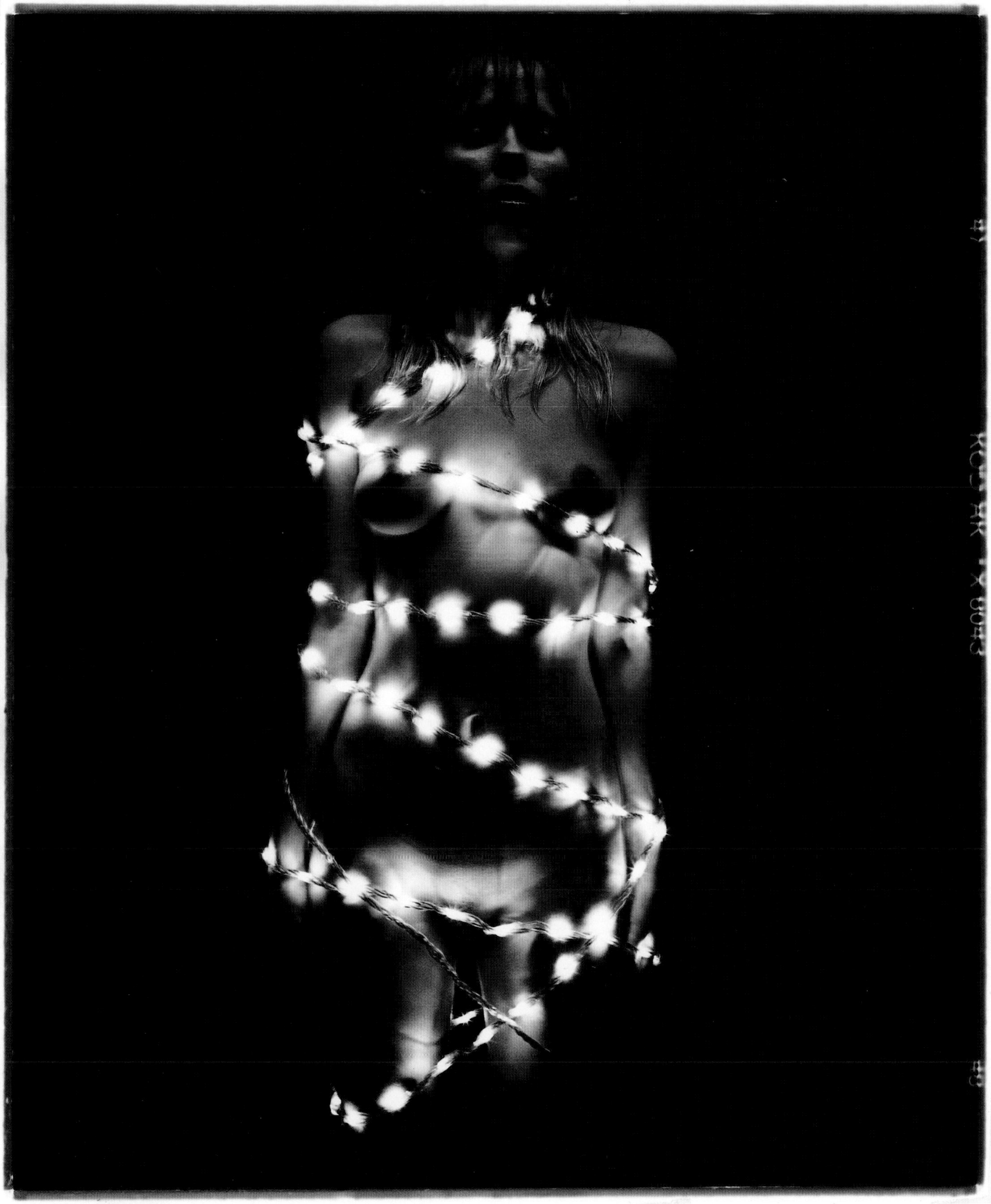

Sanna, 1999 (*right*)
"Sometimes I see images in my head. I just imagined a girl covered with Christmas lights. If you can describe a photograph, you can take it. This was for a fashion shoot called 'Turn the Dark Off' involving light for *Dazed & Confused* [magazine]."

Bettina Rheims

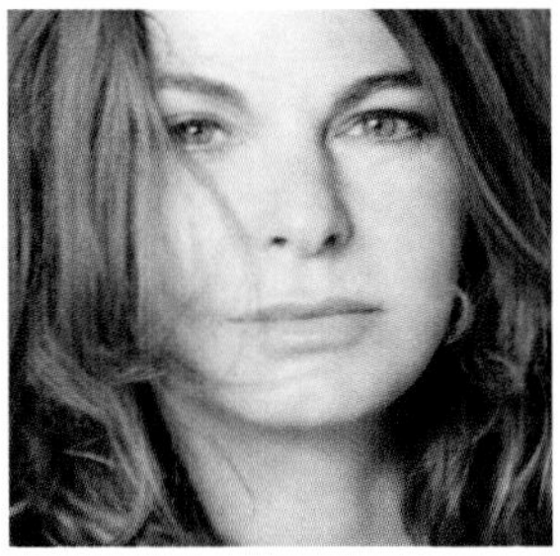

"Taking off your clothes is, for me, a way of stripping down to your soul," says Bettina Rheims. "It's not about tits and butts. It's more about leaving social status in the makeup room."

Bettina Rheims is one of France's most celebrated photographers, having emerged in the late 1970s with a series of photographs of strippers and acrobats published in Nicole Wisniak's cutting-edge *Egoiste* magazine. Since that time, Rheims has consistently pushed the boundaries of nude and erotic photography with provocative images that explore female sexuality in some of its most daring dimensions.

Female Trouble (Schirmer/Mosel, 1989) was a groundbreaking book of portraits of strong, independent women ranging from celebrities such as Anouk Aimée, Lauren Bacall, and Naomi Campbell, to friends, strangers, and circus performers. *Modern Lovers* (Edition Braus, 1990) explored adolescent sexuality in a series of photographs of androgynous teenagers who seemed almost angelic in their naked innocence. *Chambre Close* (Kehayoff Verlag, 1992), Rheims's first book in color, was a collaborative work of voyeuristic fiction with writer Serge Bramley, for which Rheims took photographs of women cavorting in cheap hotel rooms.

INRI (Monacelli Press, 1998) was an elaborate restaging of the life of Christ for which Rheims, a Jew, was accused of blasphemy when she photographed a nude female Christ on the cross. For *X'mas* (Kehayoff Verlag, 2000), Rheims photographed teenage girls discovering the manipulative power of sexuality. Works from these books and more were published in 2004 in *Bettina Rheims: Retrospective* (Schirmer/Mosel).

Born in Paris in 1952, Bettina Rheims now lives and works in the Marais district of the city, but she actually began her career in New York on the other side of the camera. "I was 18 years old and didn't know what to do in life. I had no studies, so I moved to New York," says Rheims of her brief modeling career. "I was never a great model. I was always too short and my nose was not straight, but I worked for three or four years. I never liked being in front of the camera. I never liked people to look at me. If I walk around to the other side and use a large enough camera I can hide."

Having been overweight as a child may have made Rheims sensitive to issues of body image, but, whatever the reason, in her work she became obsessed with the female body. As a woman photographing female nudes, Rheims essentially returns the male gaze through surrogates. Her early photographs of professional exhibitionists, such as striptease artists, established Rheims as an artist willing to explore social taboos, but she insists she never intended to be provocative.

"Provocation has never been for me a goal or an issue," Rheims says. "I seek after questions and try to find answers. I use the camera to try to understand things about life and about myself that are not clear. I don't even like the word 'provocation.' But people asking questions through my work is one of my desires."

Rheims believes that her work sometimes causes strong reactions simply because it is ahead of the times. "When I did *Chambre Close*, at the time you could not deal with sex as an artist," she says. "It was the same when we did *INRI*, the project about the life of Christ. Religion and art were separate. You could not be an artist and be talking about religion."

Rheims says her *INRI* photographs were only considered blasphemous in France, again insisting that she had no intention of being controversial. "It is a very serious work," she says. "It is not satirical. It is a revisitation of the Bible with a modern medium: photography. How would you express it in a modern way? I had no idea of offending."

Rheims's most explicitly sexual photographs to date are from a recent series entitled *Morceaux Choisis*, which depicts women making love to women, but she tends to downplay their importance in the overall body of her work. "It was a day and a night in a studio with four girls, a commission project," she says. "We got two porn stars and two not. It was quite quickly boring."

She points out that a recent book, a travel diary entitled *Shanghai* (powerHouse Books, 2004), contains very few nudes. "Women are the basis of my work," Rheims says, "but I do much less nudity than most of my fashion-photographer colleagues." And there is laughter in her voice when she notes that her most popular book is *Animal* (ArtData, 1998), a series of photographs of stuffed animals. "It's sold out 60 times."

Having emerged as an artist from the field of fashion photography, Rheims tends to take a directorial approach to shoots, staging and lighting shots with a stylist's eyes. But she professes very little interest in the technology of photography. "I use 6x6 and 6x7 cameras, all sorts. I use everything I can lay my hands on," she says. "Even outside I use lights. Everything is relit. Living in Paris, a dull, dark city in terms of weather, I can never depend on the light, so I use strobes, movie lights, amateur flashes, both directly and indirectly. But I don't have a system. I believe in no system. I use simple things very precisely and I know what I want. I'm known for being very fast. I'm very impatient."

What you see in many of Rheims's best photographs are women acting out, exposing themselves in unexpected and sometimes humorous ways. There is an obvious rapport between the photographer and her subjects, almost a sense of conspiracy to flout convention. "I do think of myself as a feminist, but not in a radical sense," says Rheims of her artistic intent. "I can never keep away from my mind that I am a woman. I think I've helped a lot of women in a funny sense. I've helped the women I've photographed like themselves more. I'd call it 'feminist on the light side.'"

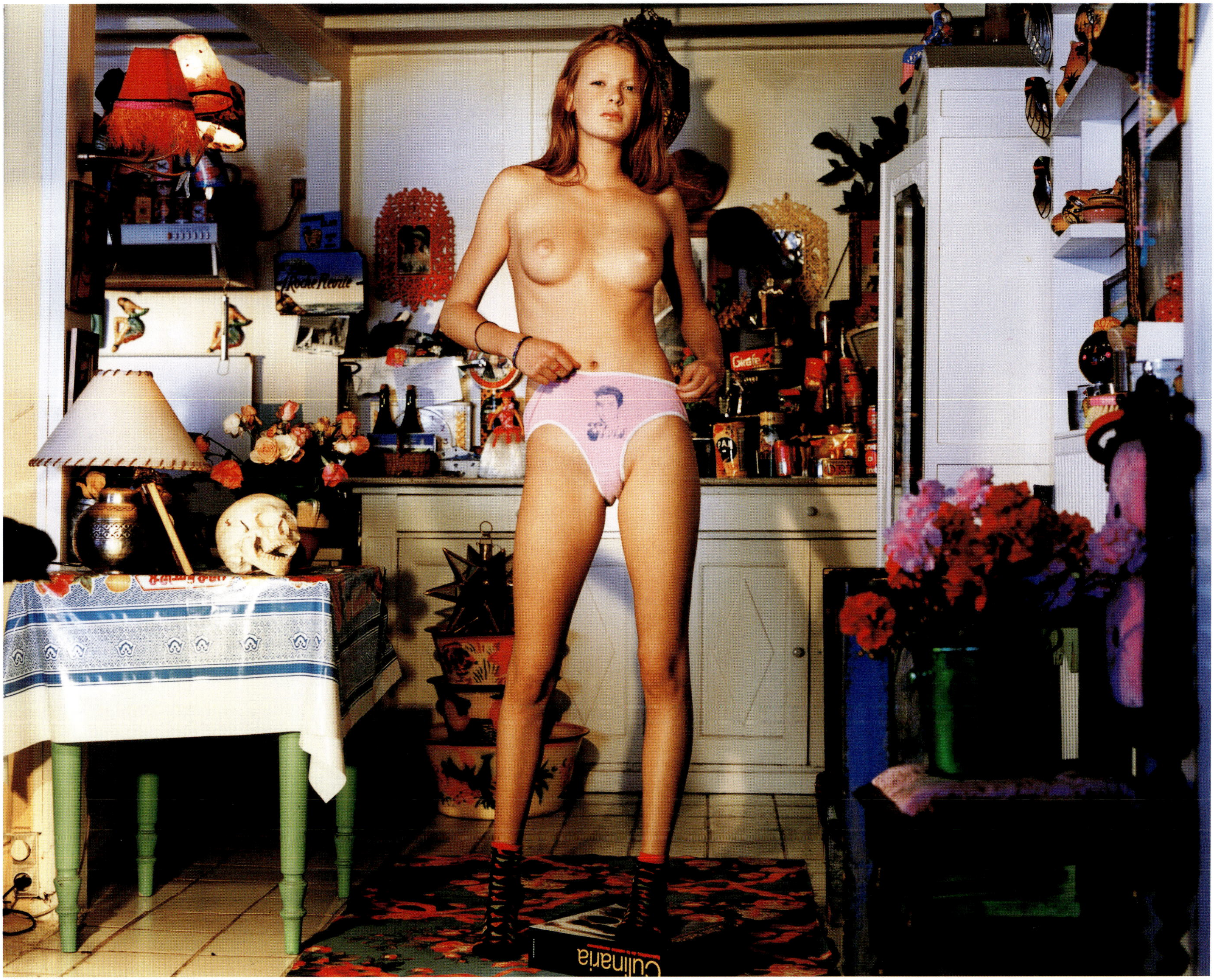

X'mas I, Private Property, 1999
"The whole *X'mas* series came about from seeing Stanley Kubrick's *Eyes Wide Shut*. There was this strange scene where Tom Cruise goes to a costume store to rent a costume. There is a little girl you understand to be the daughter of the owner. She's wearing underpants and a bra. Then there's a scream from a closet and there are two dirty little Japanese men in there. You think it's a poor girl being sold by her father for some dirty sexual things, but then it becomes clear that she is running the game. She's probably forcing her father to sell her. I was interested in this image of a teenage girl in underpants in the middle of the night being so much in control of her life. I photographed about 100 teenage girls, inventing scenes like that, where they were in control of their destinies."

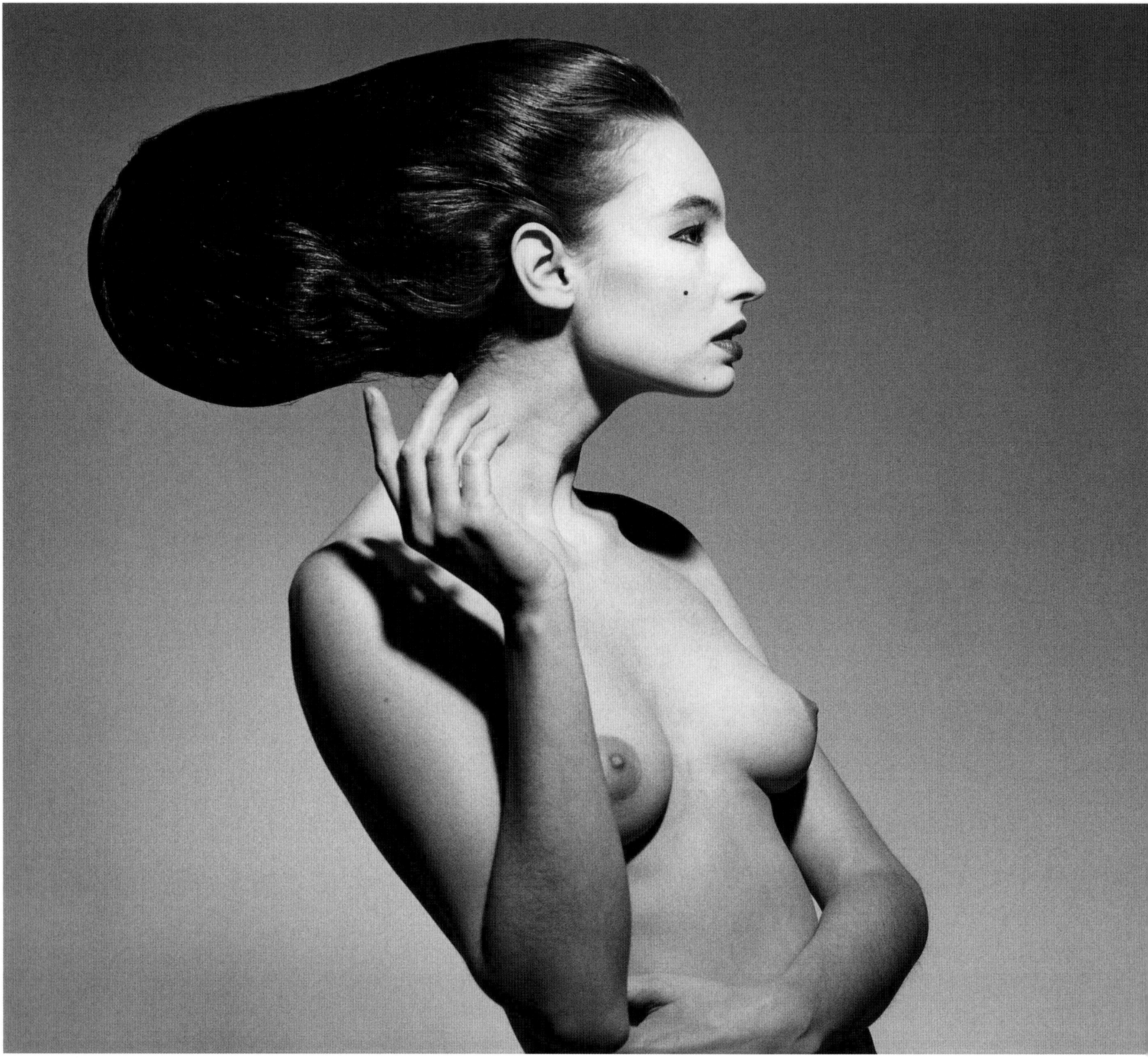

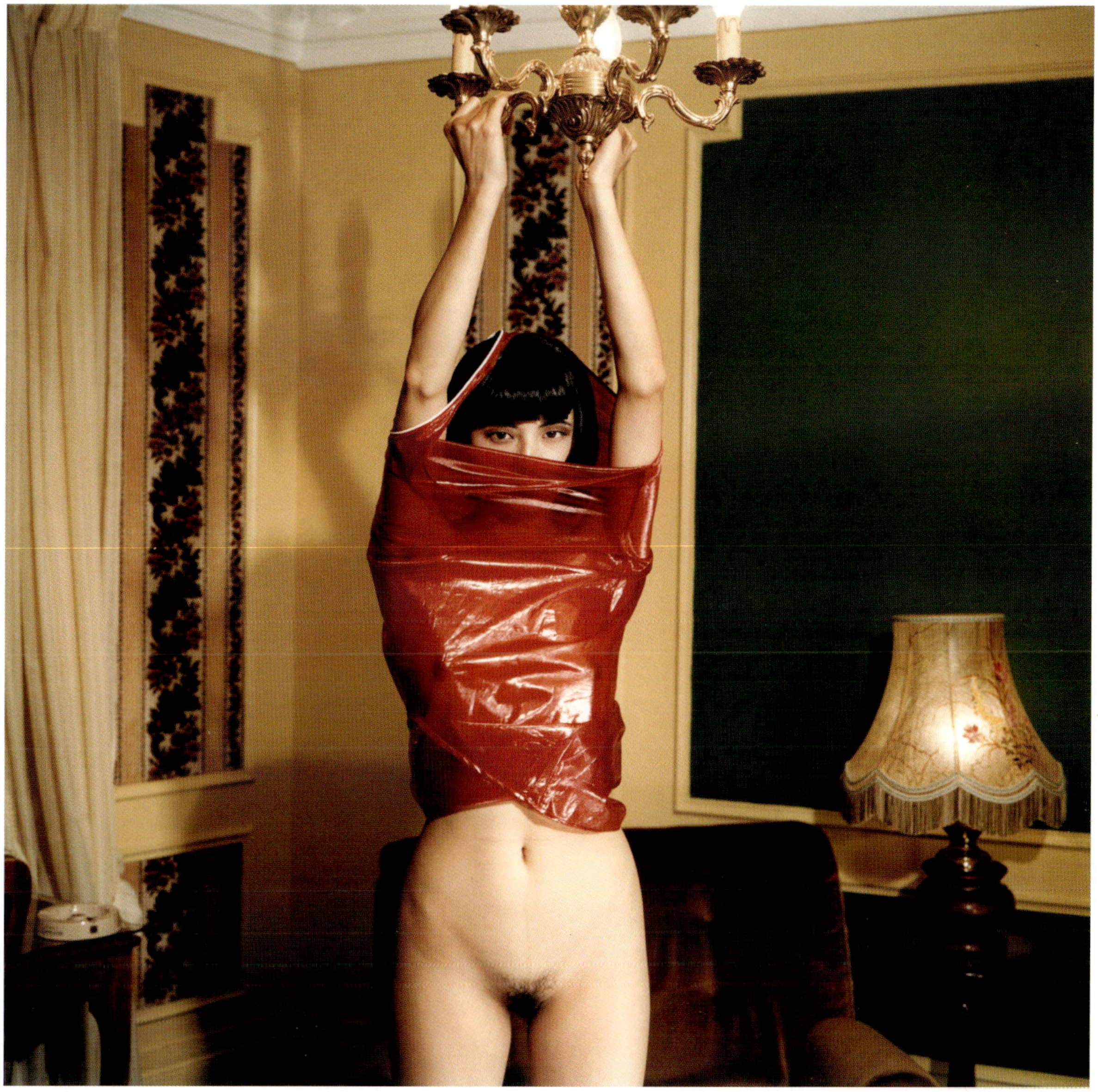

Terry pour Christian Lacroix, 1987, Paris (*left*)
"It was done for the French magazine, *Egoiste*, very big black and white. Richard Avedon and Helmut Newton published in it. This was for one of the first issues. Christian Lacroix was doing his first collection as a young designer, and I was a young photographer. He had this strange hairdo that he wanted, but the one thing missing was the dress. The dress never showed up. I didn't mean it to be a nude, but I told Christian the hairstyle looks like you and the girl looks like you."

26 août, Paris, 1991 (*above*)
"This was taken a few years after *Chambre Close* was released. It was my biggest selling book, so every time a new edition came out I would change a few images. A Japanese collector came to me and asked if I would photograph five or six Japanese women, like in *Chambre Close*. I accepted. The pose I can't really talk about. It just happened like that."

All images from *Retrospective*, by Bettina Rheims (Schirmer/Mosel, 2004). Bettina Rheims, courtesy Galerie Jérôme de Noirmont, Paris, and Schirmer/Mosel, München.

Ernestine Ruben

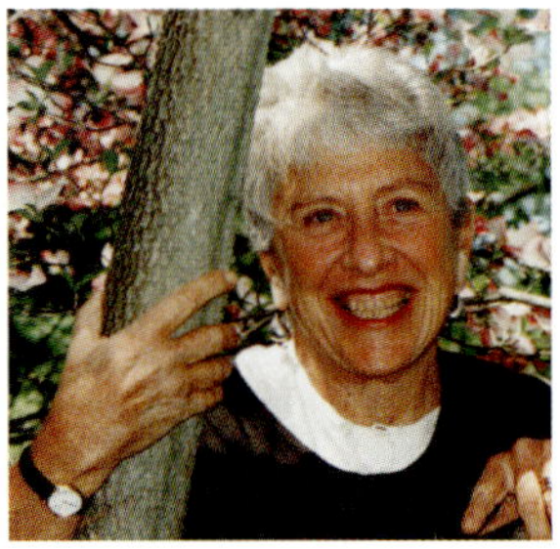

Ernestine Ruben does not simply take photographs—she creates living, breathing visions full of sweeping movement and, often, remarkable color. Using dozens of methods and materials to produce her unpredictable images, Ruben is an artist who is impulsive and endeavors to remain original.

"I am always striving to transcend what the camera sees and what we expect," she says. "Sometimes this even involves rendering an experience somewhat abstract. I cannot simply record. I absolutely must rebel against that which is given to me by the camera."

While Ruben has covered subjects such as landscapes, both natural and manmade, during her career, it is the human body that has fascinated her for decades. Her images of the nude have appeared in dozens of books and numerous solo publications, including *Entre Deux* (Paris Audiovisuel, 1987); *Ernestine Ruben Photographs* (Edition Stemmle, 1989); *Ernestine Ruben: Forms and Feelings* (Audiovisuel, 1990); and *In Human Touch: Photographs by Ernestine Ruben* (Nazraeli Press, 2001). Her photographs of fragments of Rodin's sculptures are equally mesmerizing studies of the body. While they are not images of living flesh, they appear to be breaking free of their stone casts.

"I hear all the time that people want to see how the body is translated into feelings, and that viewers are hungry for the less obvious, the less dogmatic. We all have a body, and many of us want to see, in an image, what we need to see, often reflecting ourselves," she says.

Ruben now lives in New Jersey and New York but was born in Detroit, Michigan, in 1931. She received a BA in art history at the University of Michigan in 1953 and an MA in art education at Wayne State University in 1956. After being a reporter for various newspapers during her school days, she didn't pick up the camera professionally until she was 48 years old—and after that it was nonstop commitment. The John Stevenson Gallery in New York and the Galerie Baudoin Lebon in Paris now represent her.

Ruben says she was inspired by Bill Brandt and Frantisek Drtikol, by sculpture, and painters in the futurism, pre-impressionism, and Hudson Valley School movements. Her work was eventually "discovered" in the 1980s by Jean-Claude Lemagny, director of photography at the Bibliothèque Nationale in Paris. She went on to have shows all over the world, while her images found their way into the collections of 19 international museums and institutes, including the Musée de l'Elysée in Switzerland, the Museum of Modern Art in Paris, the Philadelphia Museum of Art, and the Museum of Fine Arts in Houston, Texas.

Her interest in the nude started at a young age, when she began drawing the human figure, even taking a life-drawing class in fifth grade. Her black-and-white studies reflect an attraction to dance, with bodies closely cropped and captured in moments

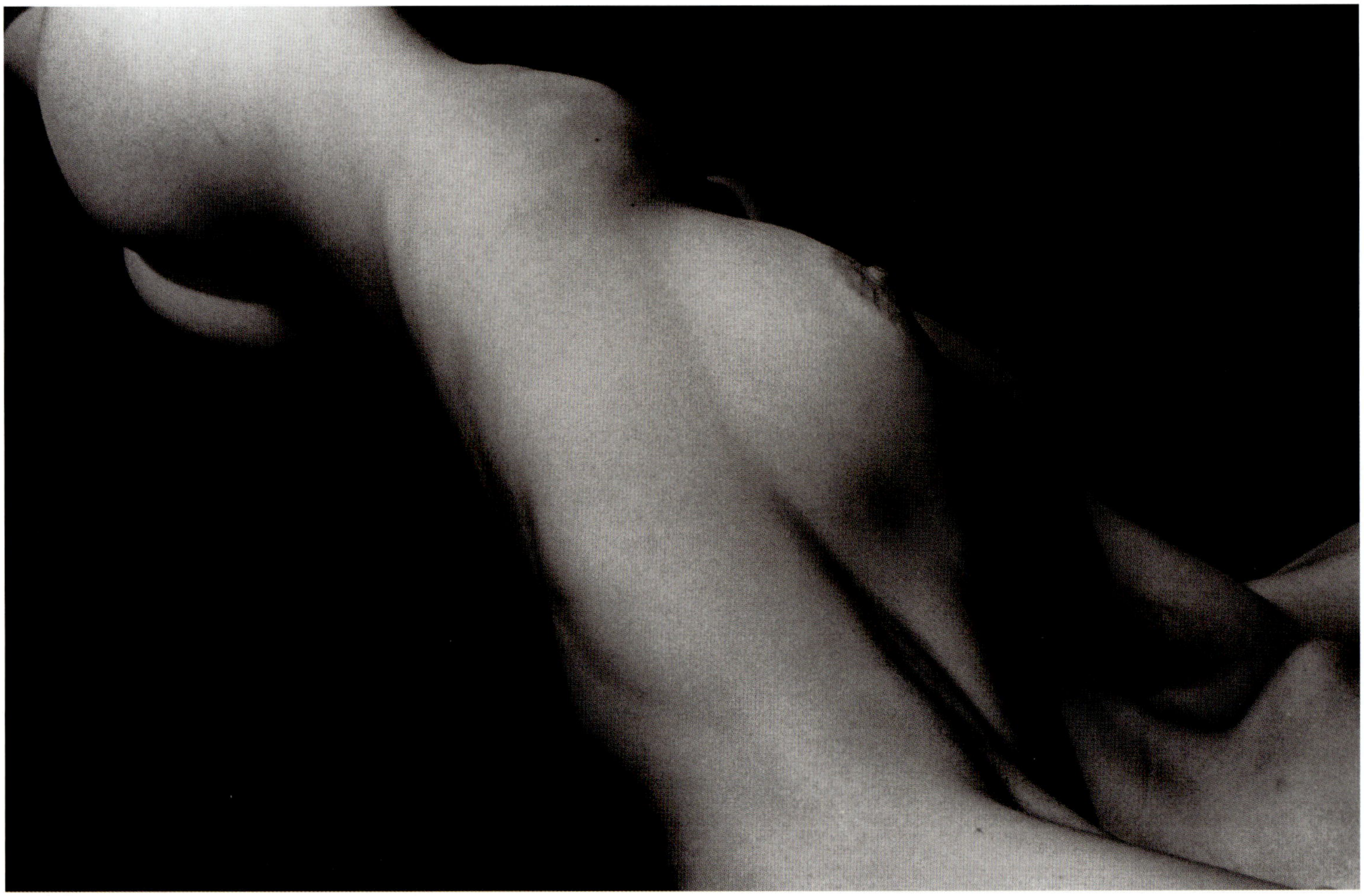

Upside Down, 1981
"This image is part of the series called 'Athlete.'"

of activity: torsos extend, muscles tighten, necks strain, and shadows cling to bodies that appear more like slivers of marble than flesh.

Ruben's color images show a completely different world. While her black-and-white photographs are mainly printed with silver and platinum finishes, her color work explores the now rarely used gum-dichromate technique. One of photography's earliest ways of producing an image, gum printing entails coating paper with a solution of gum arabic, potassium dichromate, and a water-soluble pigment.

"I experiment constantly because life changes, feelings change, models change, and therefore so must the approach change in order to keep images alive," says Ruben. "Also, my training has been pretty extensive in many art forms."

Within her color work, nude forms emerge from a cloud of washed-out pastels. Some figures are difficult to discern through the haze. Others, hidden beneath a metallic, copperlike finish, are beautifully realized renderings of the body. Her subjects include both men and women, mainly captured in the natural landscape. "I try to work with people involved in the arts, who are sensitive, imaginative, and communicative," says Ruben. "These qualities are, for me, more important than the actual type of body. The fact that I am a female and a grandmother helps me to gain the confidence of my subjects," she continues. "I also show the models my work before beginning, and as I work we maintain a dialogue. Most importantly, I tell them exactly what and why I am photographing. That way, they are part of the creative process."

As a teacher at the Detroit Institute of the Arts and various other schools in Michigan, New York, and New Jersey, Ruben recommends using workshops to master the art of photographing the nude. "In my opinion, the nude is probably the most difficult thing to photograph," she says. "It must be compositionally strong, and must invite the viewer's participation. For me, a successful nude photograph is full of life, questions, and mystery."

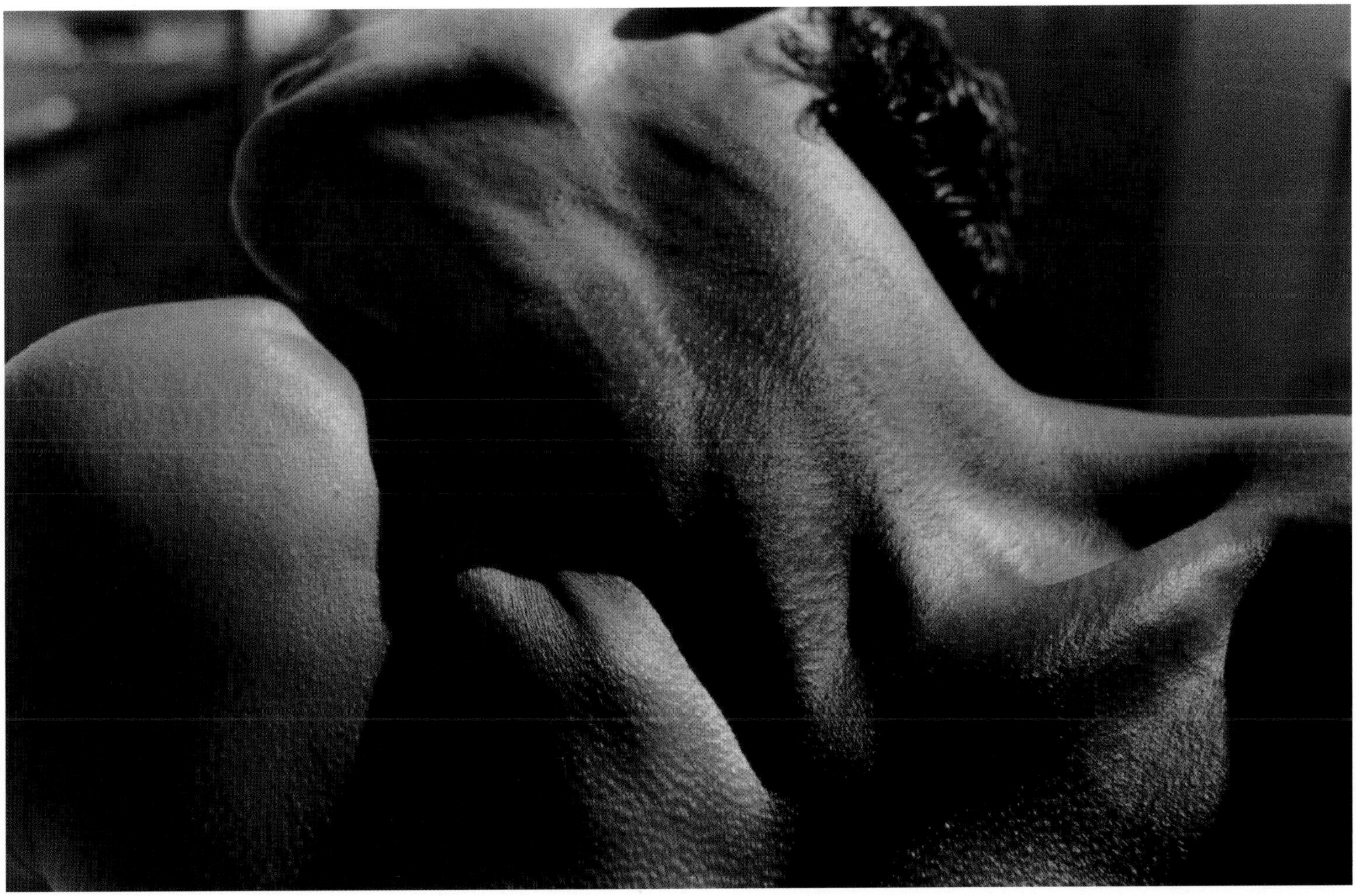

Side Neck, 1981
"An early image that interrupts our visual expectations. The model, while using much bodily tension, creates new muscular pockets and shadows."

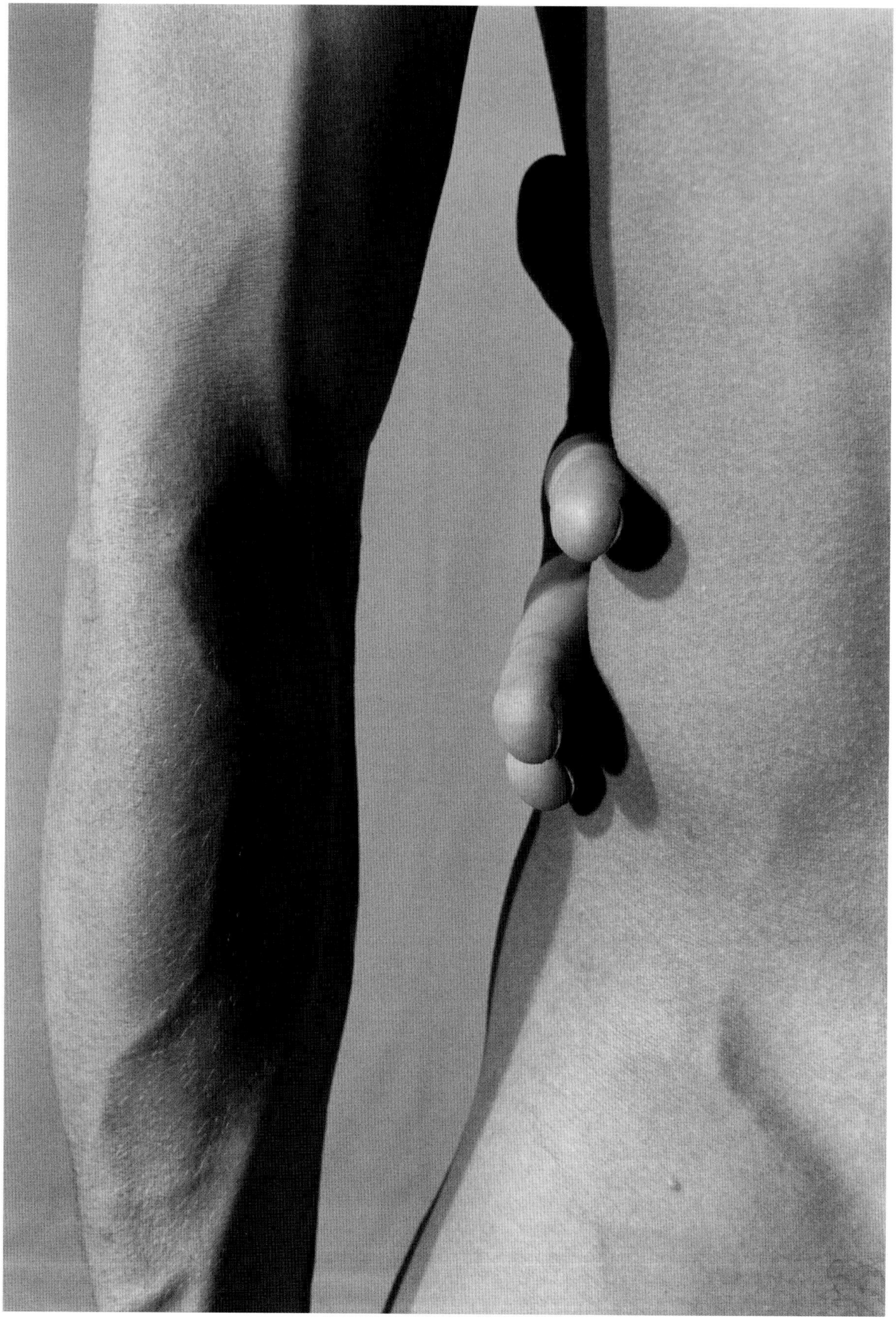

Peek-a-boo Fingers, 1987
"Frequently I work with the 'unseen.' I try to imagine what is happening behind the model, behind the photograph. Is there life beyond what we see?"

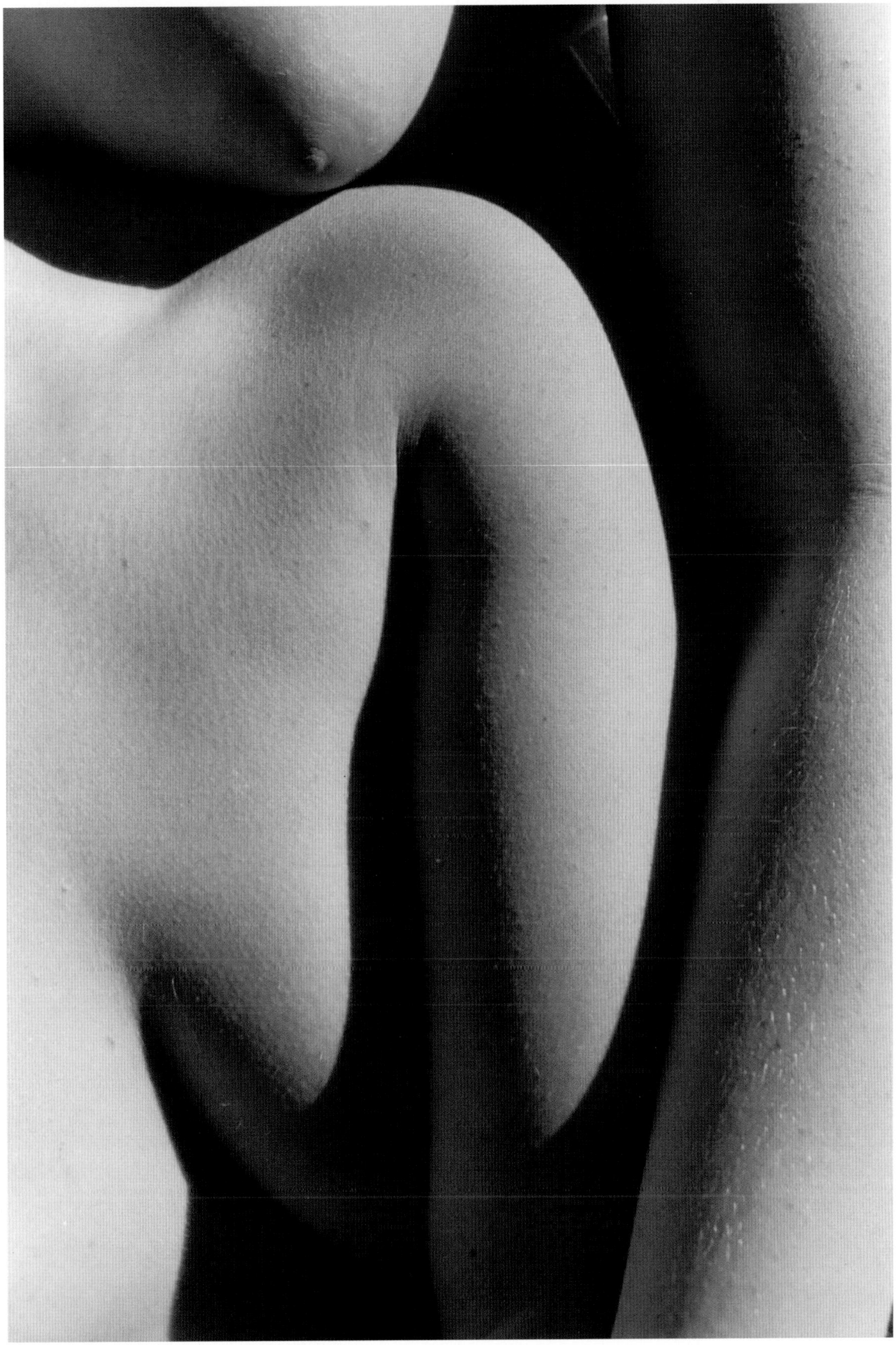

Teenage Arms, 1981
"This was one of the first images I ever did using multiple bodies together, resulting in abstractions in such a way as to create new bodies. I have always been intrigued by the negative spaces and the mysteries in the shadows."

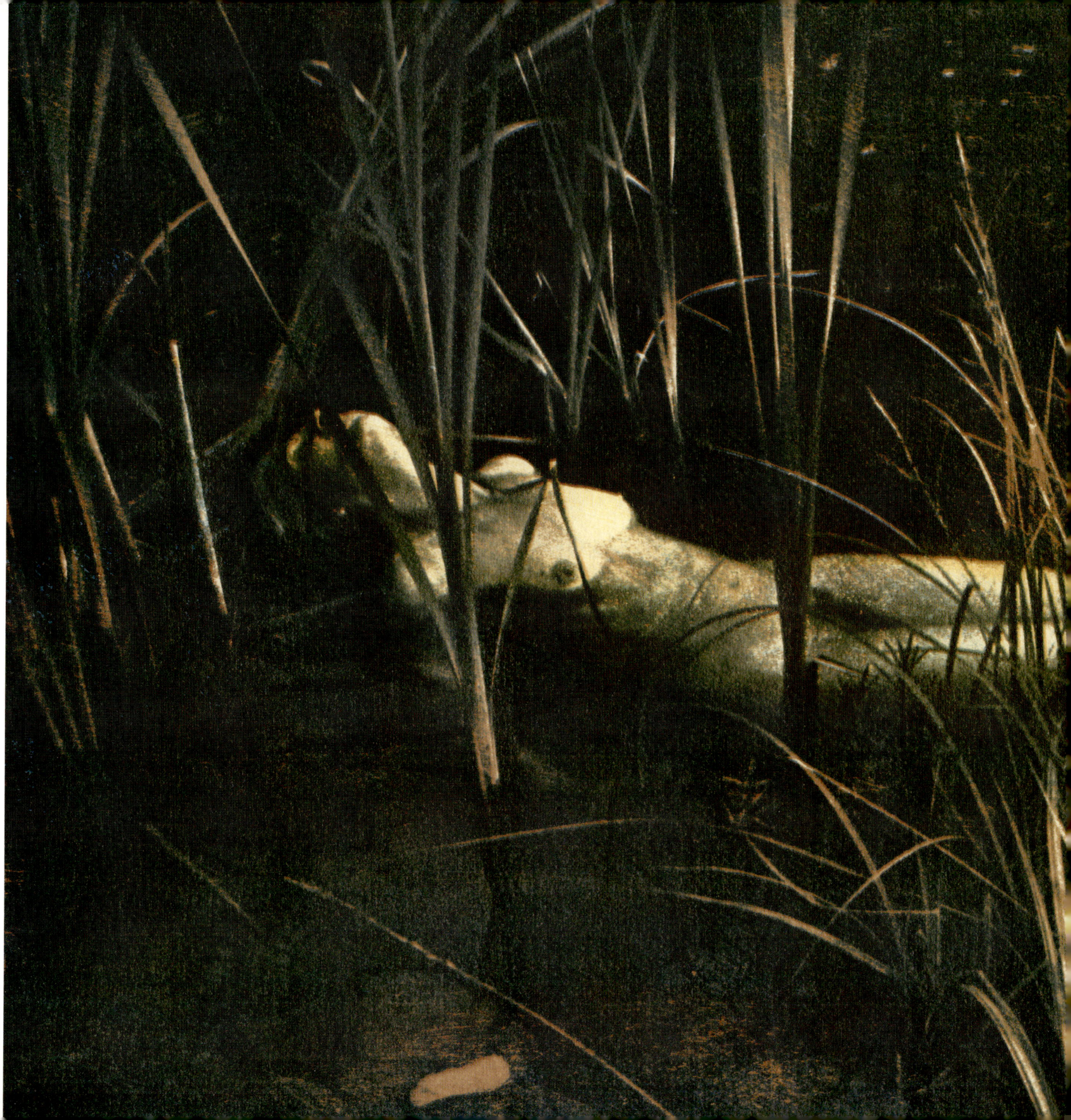

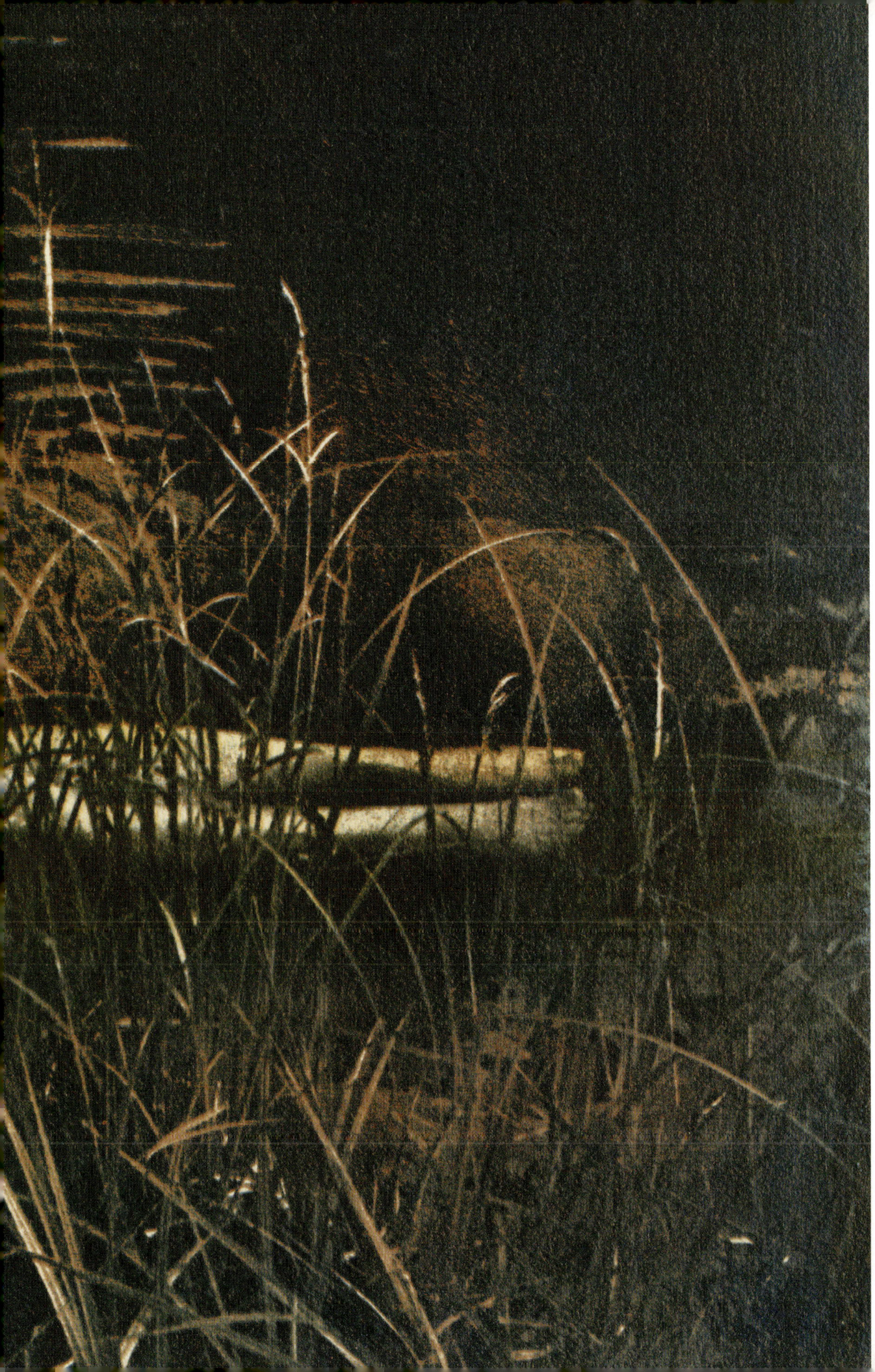

Ophelia, 2003
"[This was] photographed in Innsbruck, Austria, during a workshop about 'The Body in Landscape.' The use of texture in gum is important and fun to achieve." (Gum-dichromate print from a 35mm black-and-white negative.)

Robert Stivers

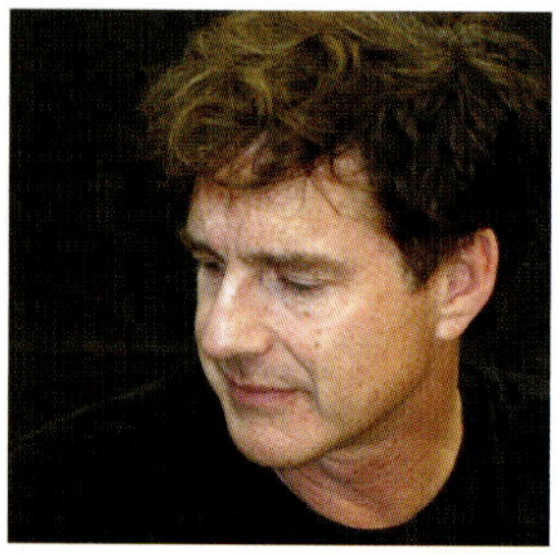

The photographs of Robert Stivers rarely seem like images captured through a lens. They appear more like stills beamed directly from his subconscious, revealing hints and identities from his memories, and from the edges of his dreams.

A former dancer, Stivers reveals his past in his images. But whereas some photographers' work represents an affinity with the classical lines and forms of dance, Stivers's images hide his affection behind blurred, often haunting compositions.

"My negatives are sharp, but I throw the image out of focus in the darkroom in an effort to discover 'something' hidden from the casual or specific observance," he says. "I have been enjoying the mystery that out-of-focus imagery evokes." Indeed, his creations represent everything photographers such as Edward Weston and Walker Evans rallied against, gravitating more toward the pictorialist style that was so prominent around the end of the 19th century.

Born in Palo Alto, California, in 1953, Stivers received a BA in history from the University of California, Irvine, before attending the graduate program at New York University. After a traumatic back injury curtailed his dancing career, Stivers went on to become a choreographer, before turning to photography. At first he tried his hand at being an artist representative in Los Angeles. However, a photography course at the University of California, Los Angeles, hooked him on the idea of being behind the camera himself. After dabbling in editorial images, he shifted toward more personal work and has stayed there ever since.

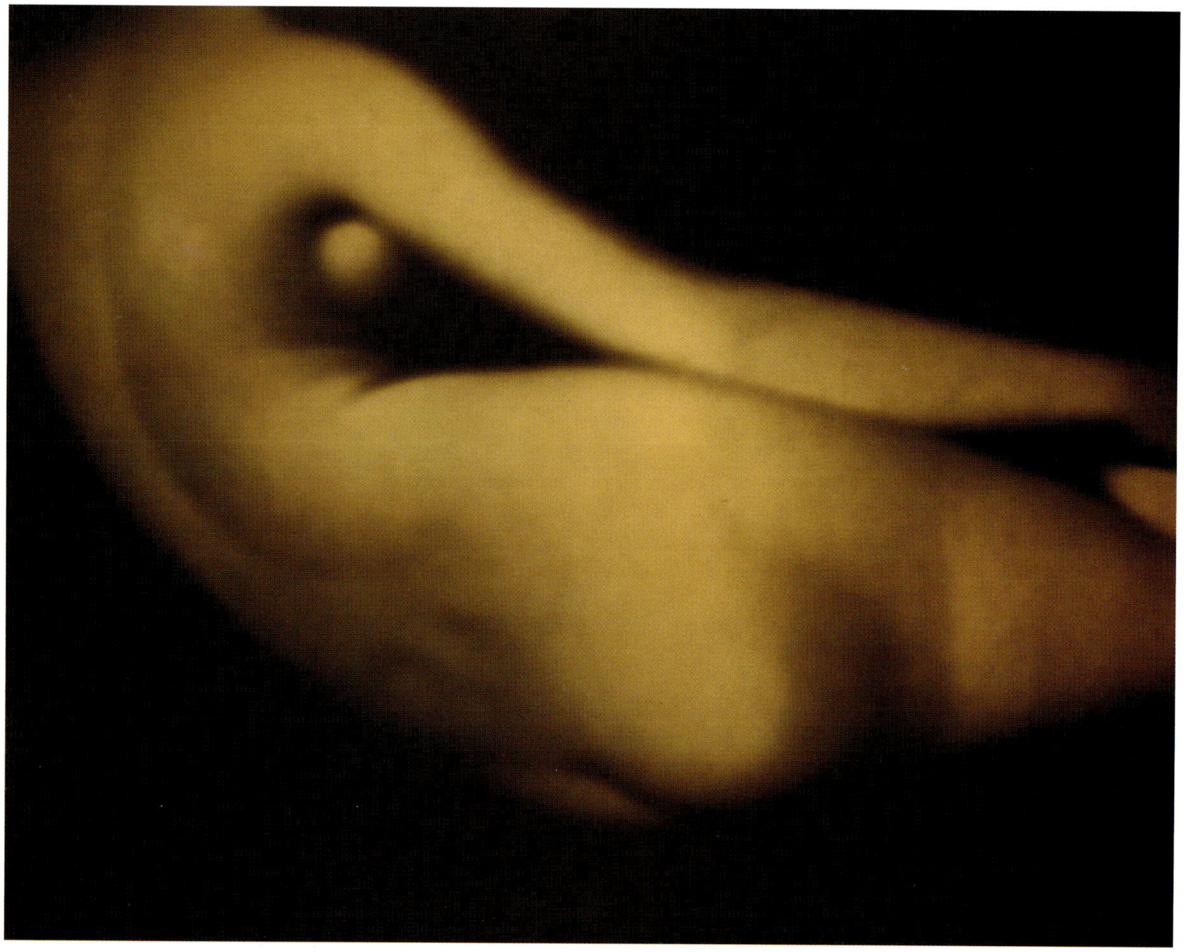

His break came with the publishing of his first book, *Robert Stivers: Photographs* (Arena Editions, 1997). Its spectral, David Lynch-like imagery was, and remains, instantly memorable. Foreboding faces and full bodies hover within dark spaces. Yet, blended into the murkiness, there is a feeling of dark sexuality concealed in the unlit regions. "I love the human form," says Stivers. "It elicits eroticism, desire, fear, temptation, guilt, confusion, and lust. I like the ambivalence."

Two Seated Figures, one of Stivers's favorite images, is a perfect example of mystification in a Stivers nude. It displays a couple, their pale, gray torsos intertwined like a tree trunk, while their heads and arms are lost in the shadows. "My nudes are not merely about form—although form and light play an integral part," explains Stivers. "My intention is to elicit feelings of vulnerability, tenderness, and discomfort while also not offering a clear message. Historically, I have liked to challenge our notions of beauty and sexuality. I have always liked a sense of the macabre."

His next book, *Listening to Cement* (Arena Editions, 2000), featured architectural forms as well as human bodies, layering each image with a seemingly ancient glaze. Stivers's most recent book, *Sestina* (Channel Photographics, 2004), builds on his fixation with the arcane and the antique, while adding sharpness and a tendency toward a slightly more, as he puts it, "romantic, less edgy" style. Named after a French poetic form that deals with repetition, the images appear like forgotten, early 20th-century daguerreotypes discovered in a dusty box in an attic somewhere.

"As a former dancer, choreographer, and short-filmmaker," says James Crump, Stivers's former editor at Arena Editions, "Stivers builds erotic tableaux that play off movement and juxtaposition, while also revealing the subtle balance of intimate rapport and autocratic stage direction. The best Stivers nudes underscore a gothic, film-noirish sensibility that often casts these pictures in shockingly unique and individualistic terms in a genre overcrowded with pastiche and numbing quotation."

Stivers's unique look is achieved with a 20-year-old Hasselblad 50cm, along with an 80mm lens and Plus X film. His studio lighting is kept simple, he uses one strobe, and most of his image manipulation is done in the darkroom. A calculated mesh of black and white and color also adds to his look.

Since 1993, Stivers has had solo exhibitions all over the United States, including shows at the Paul Kopeikin Gallery in Los Angeles, the Yancey Richardson Gallery in New York, the Fahey/Klein Gallery in Los Angeles, the Catherine Edelman Gallery in Chicago, and, most recently, the Rivera Yates Gallery in Santa Fe. His images are also part of the permanent collections in more than 20 museums and institutions.

"The bulk of my work is black and white, or toned black and white. When I shoot color, I am most often 'rephotographing' a black-and-white print, so the color is uniform," says Stivers. "I like to choose colors that are 'otherworldly' so the resulting image appears dreamlike, mysterious, haunting."

After Ingres, 2000 *(opposite)*
"This was born out of fear, vulnerability, and ecstasy."

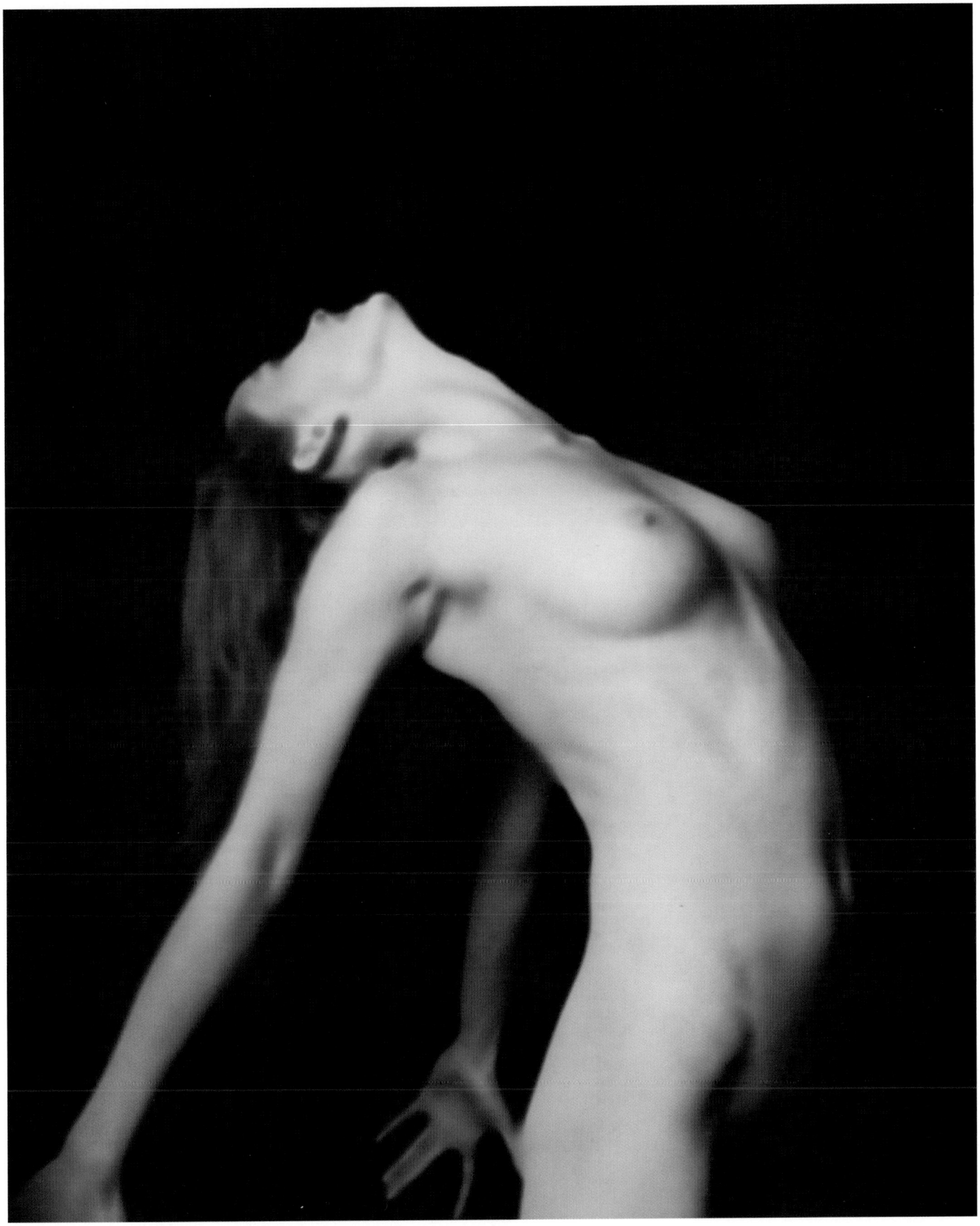

Arched Woman, 1996 *(left)*
"Admittedly, I am reluctant to describe my images in text. Although technique—in other words, lighting, proper exposure, darkroom ability (and not digital knowledge)—is required, the images are born out of the psyche and intuition. They, the images, manifest most often during the printing process when I am alone and unfettered by the 'distractions' of 'taking the picture.' Oddly, sometimes the model is simply a means of exploring the themes of memory, love and loss, and one's identity."

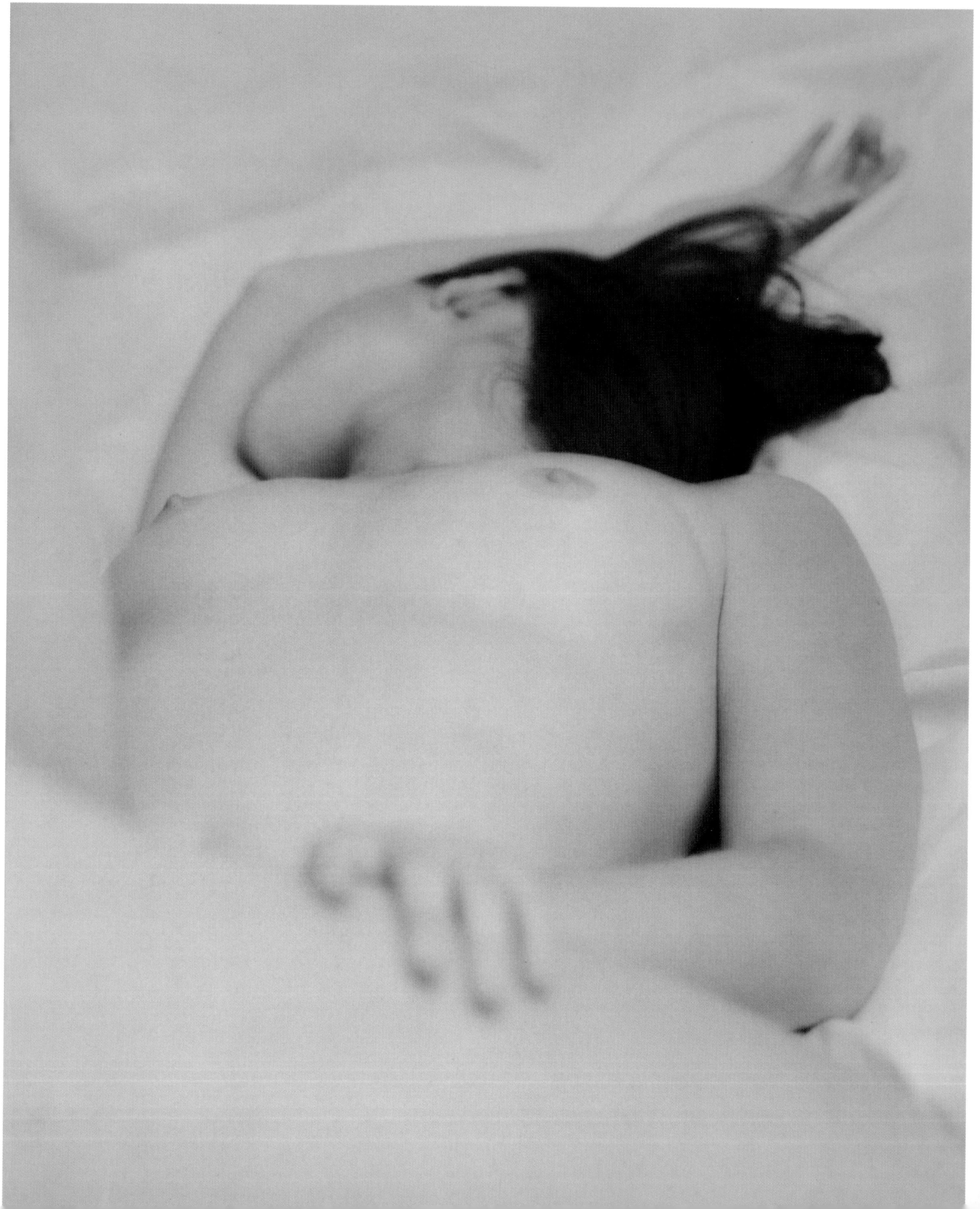

Female Nude, 2002
"This concerns refection, solemnity, and/or quiet sensuality."

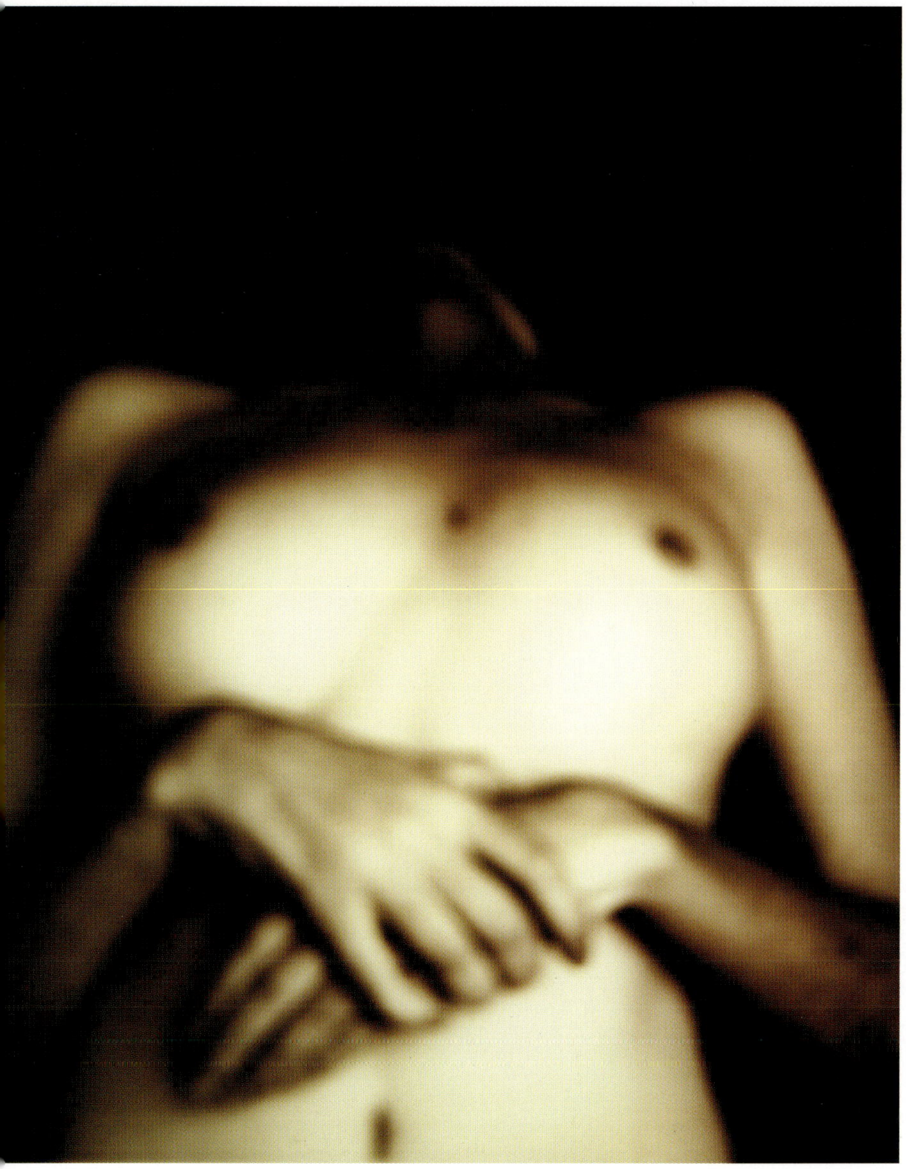

Female with Crossed Hands, 1998
"This explores the tension between repose and death."

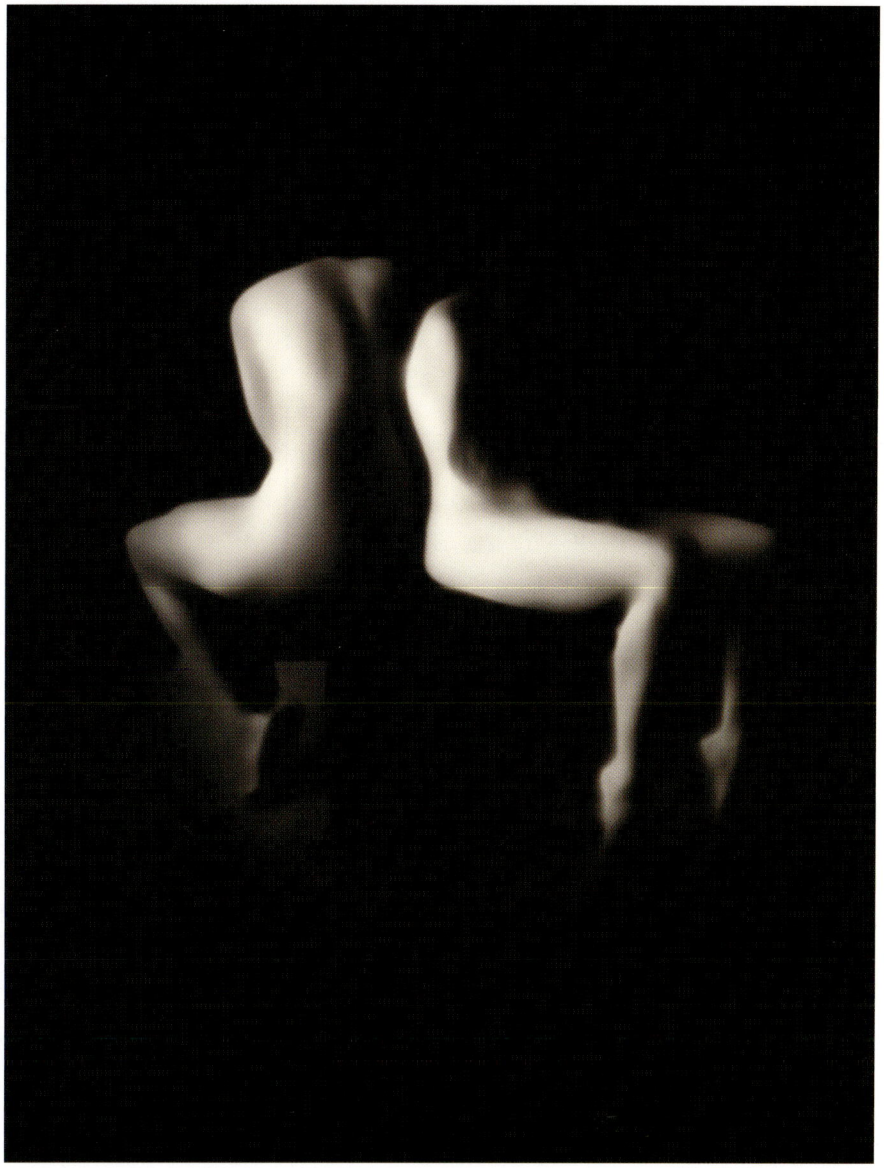

Two Seated Figures, 1994
"This investigates notions of abstraction and isolation."

Arthur Tress

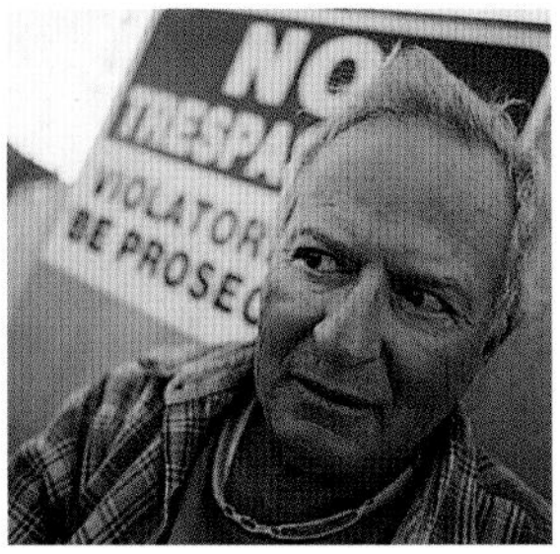

One of the world's consummate photographers of the male nude, Arthur Tress identifies one source of the power in his work as a curiosity about social taboos that has been with him since childhood. As a boy, Tress confesses, he sometimes crept into the bedrooms of his friends' parents and went through their drawers, irresistibly drawn to that which was secret, private, and hidden.

"If you're lucky, you're able to follow some of your childhood instincts," says Tress. "People like myself and Duane Michaels made a point of following our inner drives and yearnings, going into forbidden territory and getting our hands slapped by society."

Working in timeless black and white, Tress typically portrays the male nude in dramatic, often symbolic poses that are inspired by dreams, myths, and fantasies: a young man huddled on the shore covers his head against an approaching storm; in a bleak city, a figure struggles to free himself. The sense of struggle and torment in Tress's work is informed by homosexuality—his own and that of his subjects. "Being a gay man photographing gay men," he says, "my sensitivity, my desire, my emotional insights are into the male nude."

Since 1991, Tress has been living and working in the Big Sur, California, but he was born in Brooklyn, New York, in 1940. There, as a sensitive child, he took refuge from the harsher realities of the city by escaping into the cultural treasure houses of the Brooklyn Public Library and, most importantly, the Brooklyn Museum, with its collection of ethnographic artifacts. Years later, Tress's art draws heavily on primitive myths and rituals to explore gay subculture.

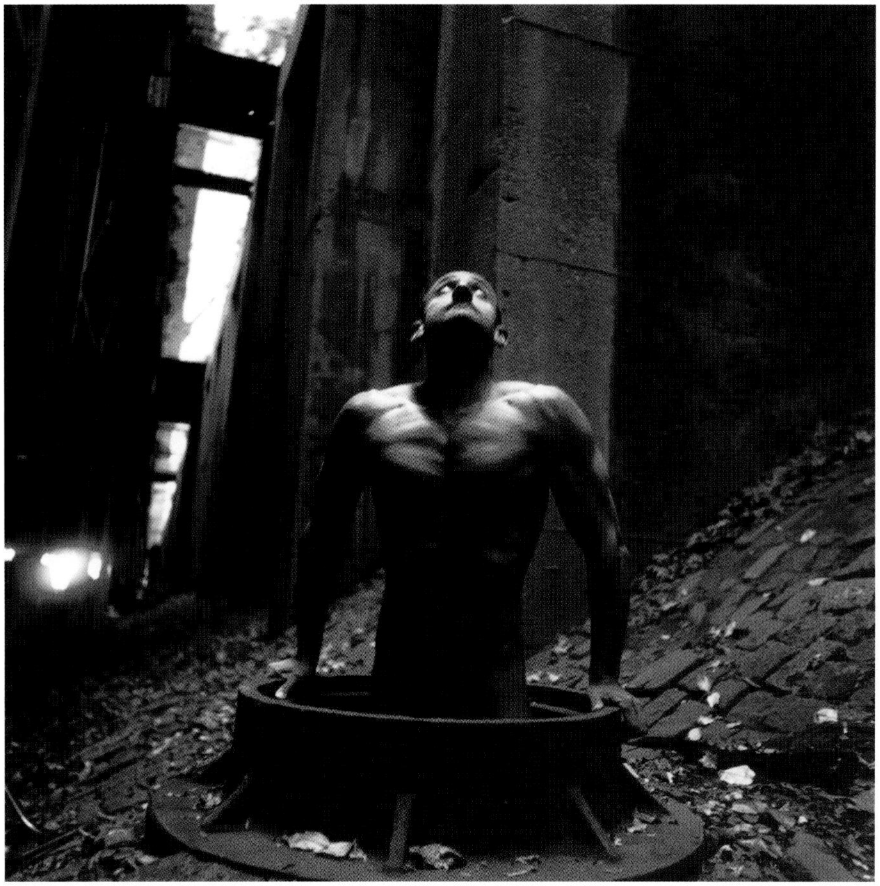

The Minotaur, New York, 1994 *(right)*
"This was done right in the area under the West Side Highway, where there's an old railroad tunnel. It has shafts of light. I took the model down underneath to have him looking up toward the light. He's Arabic, so he has an interesting kind of face. To me, he seemed like a genie."

Stormy Weather, California, 1995 *(opposite)*
"This was done in Palm Springs. Again, the spontaneous element was the storm coming in as we were about to do the shoot. It's a sculptural pose with the weather threatening and he's protecting his head. And he has an incredibly beautiful body. It's like in an Indian miniature erotic painting where a coming storm means the heating up of the kundalini. It's my bestseller."

Tress took up photography as a teenager, photographing abandoned mansions at Sands Point in Nassau County and the forlorn precincts of Coney Island. After graduating from Bard College in 1962, he traveled extensively in Europe, Mexico, Japan, India, and Africa before returning to New York in 1968. There he began photographing the gay pickup scene. "All along the West Side of Manhattan there were dozens of abandoned piers, docks, and warehouses that became the great playground jungle of the sexual revolution for gay men," says Tress. "People cruised day and night on the piers. Part of my first approach to the male nude was photographing on those piers and docks."

Initially, Tress found work in New York illustrating articles and stories for gay magazines. Where Robert Mapplethorpe elevated his homoerotic photographs through sheer artistry, Tress performed this transcendence by bringing his metaphysical interests, in particular a study of the archetypes of psychologist Carl Jung, to bear on his subjects. In a 1973 photograph entitled *Hermaphrodite, East Hampton, New York*, for example, a muscular young man stands in a formal garden between statues of Venus and Mercury with his penis tucked between his legs.

Tress's early nudes were published in 1980 in *Arthur Tress: Facing Up* (St. Martin's Press), but the male nude was never Tress's only photographic interest. He made more straightforward documentary images of open spaces in New York City and spent 1969–70 photographing Appalachia as a VISTA (Volunteers in Service to America) volunteer. In a more surrealist vein, he recreated dream imagery described to him by children in *Arthur Tress: The Dream Collector* (Avon Publishing, 1971), and made pioneering staged photographs for *Theater of the Mind* (Morgan & Morgan, 1976). Much of this work was collected in a major retrospective at the Corcoran Gallery of Art in Washington, D.C., in 2001 as *Arthur Tress: Fantastic Voyage*.

Although he shoots male nudes exclusively in black and white using Tri-X film and a Hasselblad with a 50mmm lens, Tress has also created several garishly colorful fantasy series, among them *The Teapot Opera* (Abbeville Press, 1999), and *The Fish Tank Sonata* (Bulfinch Press, 2001). In these fanciful images, Tress makes a fetish of an object rather than a figure.

Tress says he is not interested in presenting nude male figures as "idealized Adonises." What he is after is "an investigation of the dark sides of homosexuality." As such, his nudes possess a primal quality, images tense with anxiety and desire. "The male nude makes people nervous, especially men," says Tress. "No advertisers would use male figures. The art world has dealt with that very well, but the political right is going after any kind of sexual imagery under the guise of protecting children. I'm afraid there's going to be a big repression coming soon."

His most recent book of nudes, *Male of the Species* (Fotofactory Press, 1999), features four decades of male nudes, including the more naturalistic photographs Tress has taken since moving to California. "I'm older," he says of his later, more mature nudes, "so maybe I'm trying for more spiritual photographs. What I'm doing now is nude portraits where the emphasis is not on the body so much as the soulful expressions of the face."

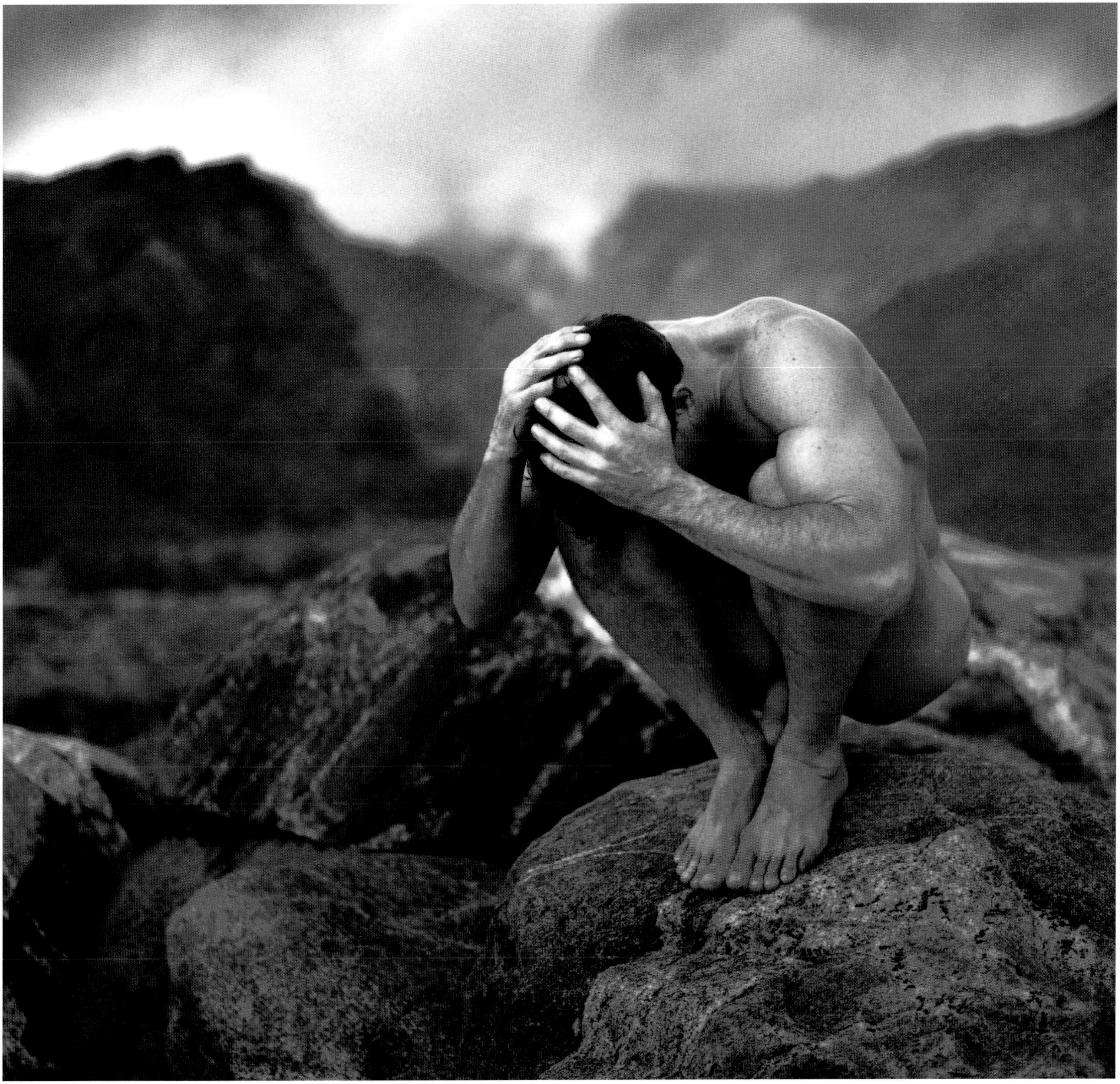

Arthur Tress

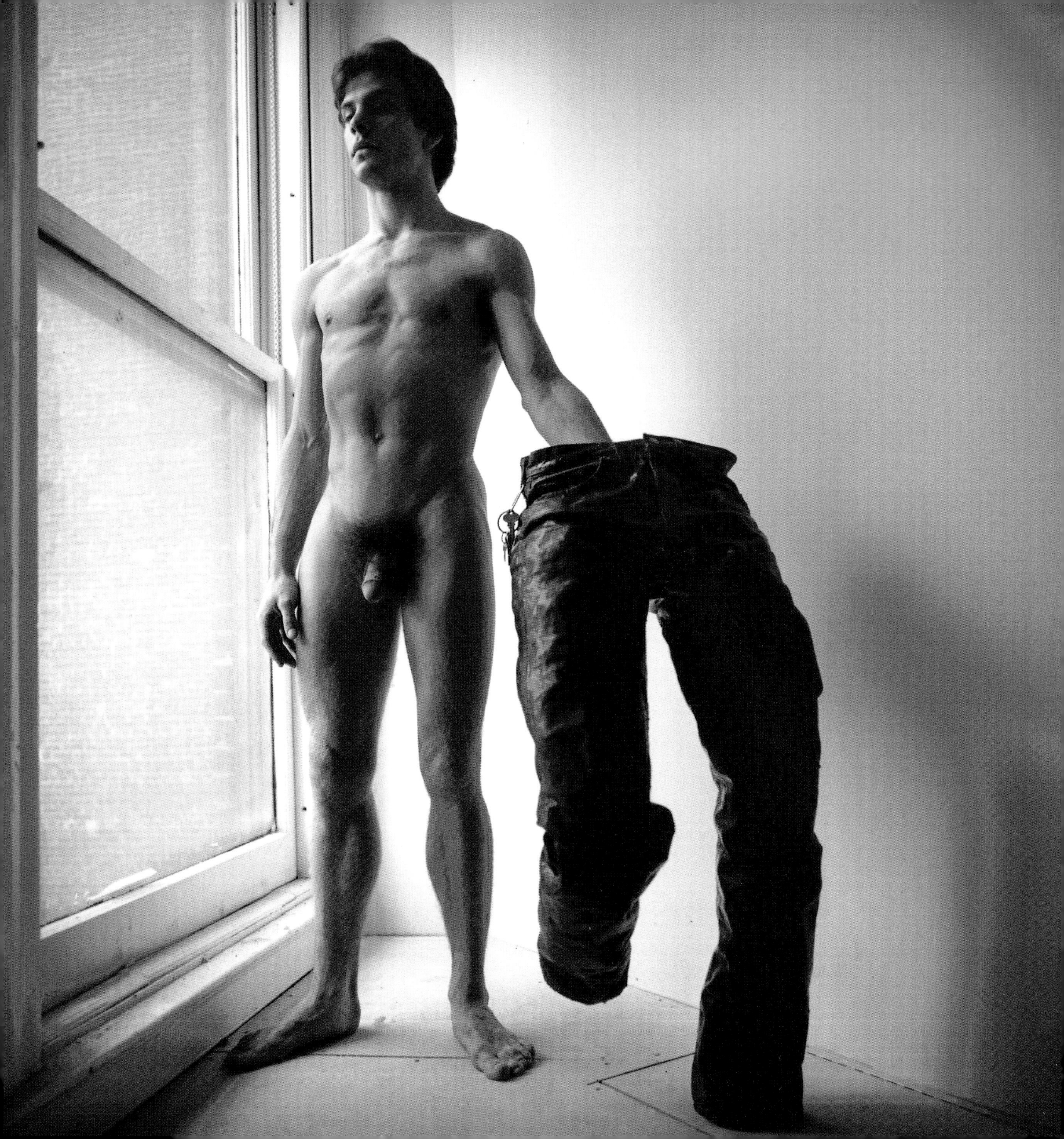

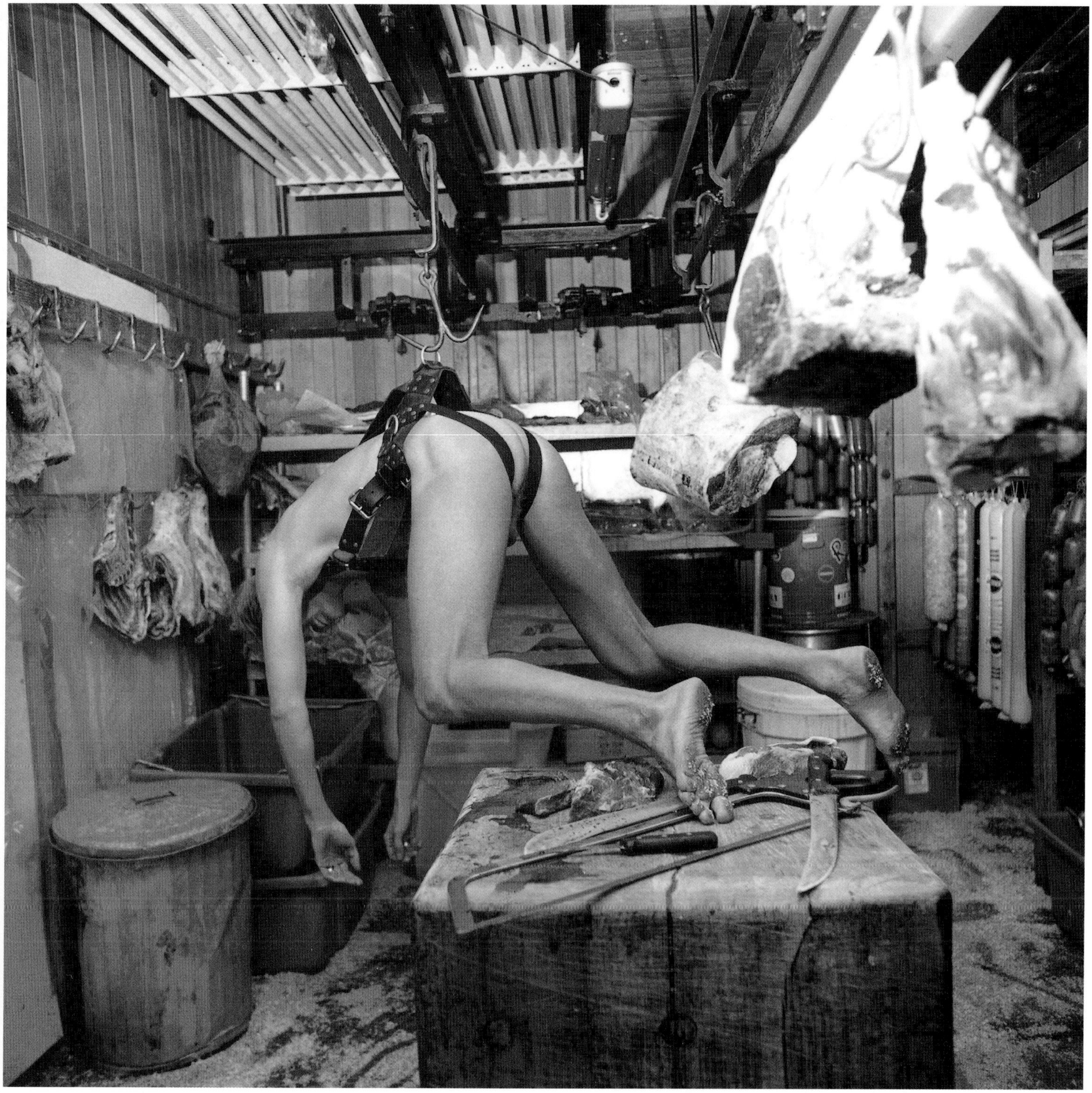

Man with Plaster Pants, 1979 *(left)*
"Peter Reed was a modern dancer with a superb body who had been photographed by Robert Mapplethorpe. It was taken in the loft he shared with his lover, an artist who had made the plaster blue jeans as a personal project. The hand reaching inside the pants and the model's averted eyes seem to me to symbolize the irresistible urge for genital contact, and the guilt associated with that universal gesture of desire."

Butcher Fantasy, New York, 1979 *(above)*
"I had met a gay butcher at a party and he offered his shop as a location for a shoot. In my study of homosexual slang I came across the use of the phrase 'He's a great piece of meat,' as well as the 'Meat Rack,' a place in New York City where hustlers used to hang out in Washington Square Park at night. I thought illustrating these phrases in their most extreme form would make them disturbing and surreal."

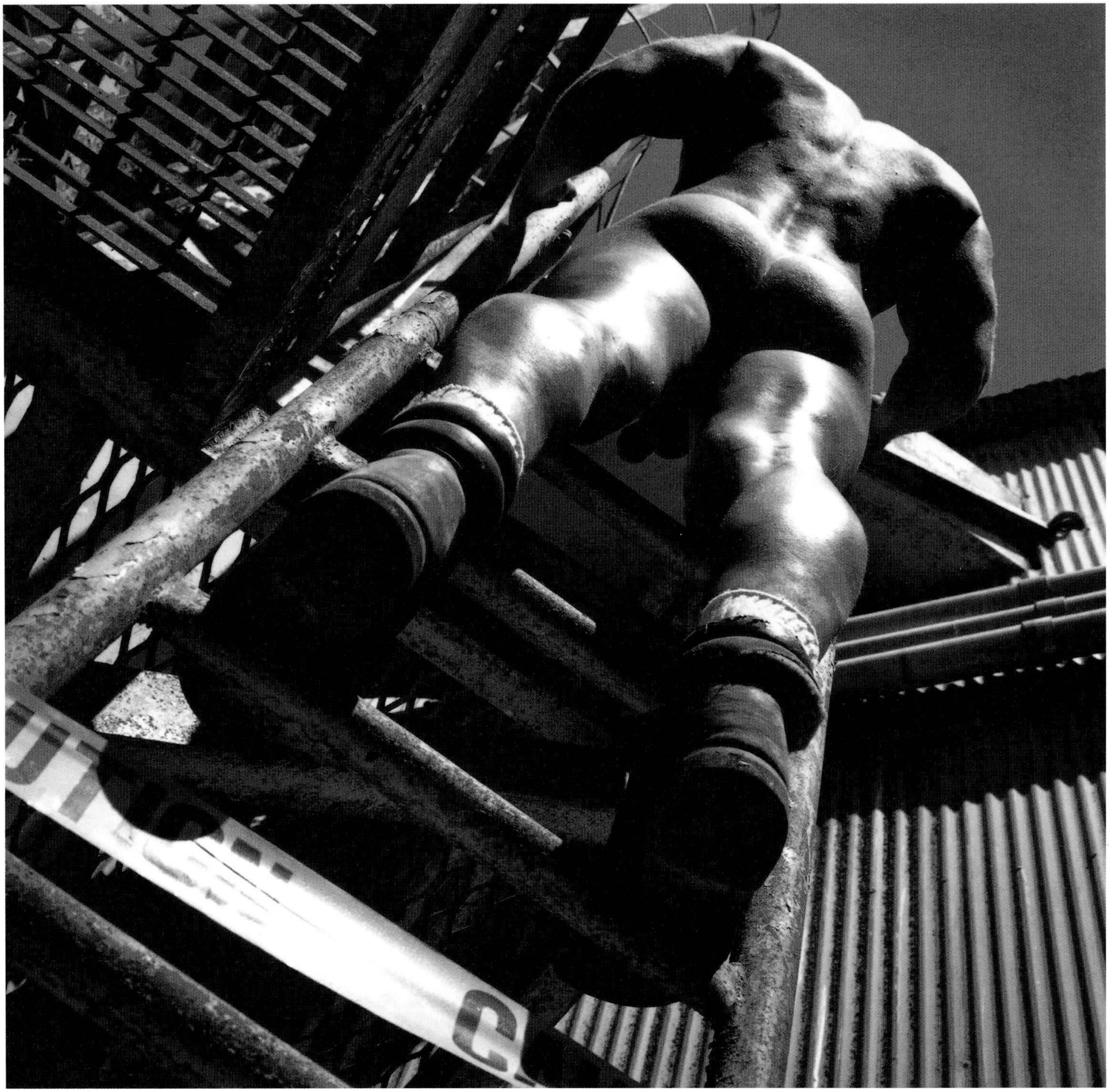

Caution: Man at Work, California, 1995
"This photo was taken in a closed sugar refinery in Guadelupe, California. The model worked at the nearby Vandenburg airforce base. The photo, with its extreme, tilted angle is a play on the Russian hero workers propaganda posters done by the constructivists Alexander Rodchenko and El Lissitsky in the 1920s."

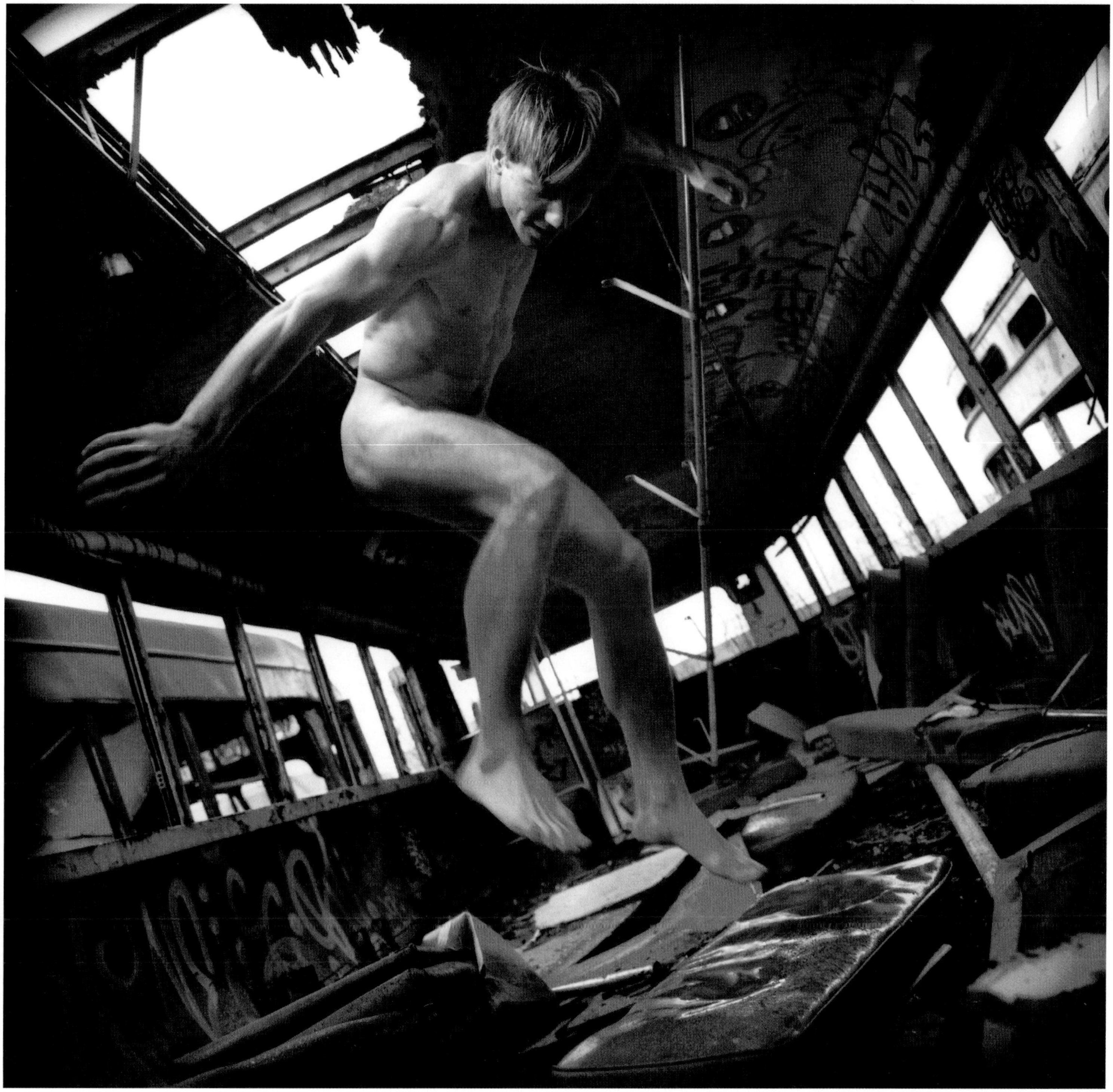

Boarding the Bus, California, 1997
"The locale is a group of abandoned muni trolley cars on the shutdown piers of South San Francisco. I encouraged the model, who is a surfer and skateboarder, to do an improvised riff as though he was on a moving board, giving a sense of a dreamlike action by using a slow shutter speed."

Nic Tucker

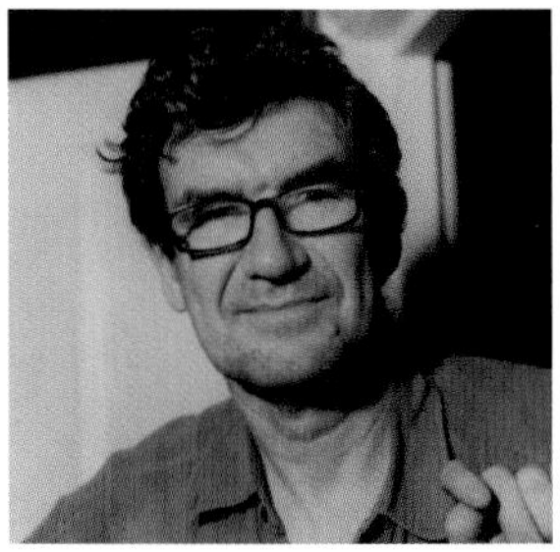

Generations of artists have made the portrayal of the nude a convention of fine art in the name of everything from the search for the ideal human form, to investigations of social mores, personal truths, or the promotion of sexual liberation. London-based photographer Nic Tucker, however, has no truck with such highfalutin notions. "You don't need much of a reason when you're taking girls' clothes off, to be honest," says Tucker. "Of course, it's voyeurism."

Tucker's refreshing candor reflects the straightforward honesty of his approach to photographing the nude. He sees the female nude not as an abstraction, a symbol, or a statement, but as "the most wondrous thing in the world."

The women in a Tucker photograph have a sense of casual reality, even sheer normality, about them. They appear approachable, because they are not professional models wearing masks of style, but friends and lovers willing to grant the artist the privilege of just looking. This intimacy sometimes has the charged, flirtatious look of seduction, but more often than not Tucker's women friends are simply lolling about in apartments and studios as languid as house cats, striking poses that amuse them, or feigning indifference. "I like photographing girls I like. Girls you can talk to and have a good laugh with," says Tucker.

Tucker was born in 1948 in the small Devon town of Topsham, where his father was a banker. He discovered photography as a young teenager, but it was the process of developing film in his attic that captivated him at first, not taking pictures. When he finished his schooling, he went to London intending to enroll at the (then) London College of Printing, but when the grant he was counting on failed to come through, he took a job "doing slave work" for an advertising photographer. In the late 1970s, after eight years working as an assistant, Tucker went out on his own.

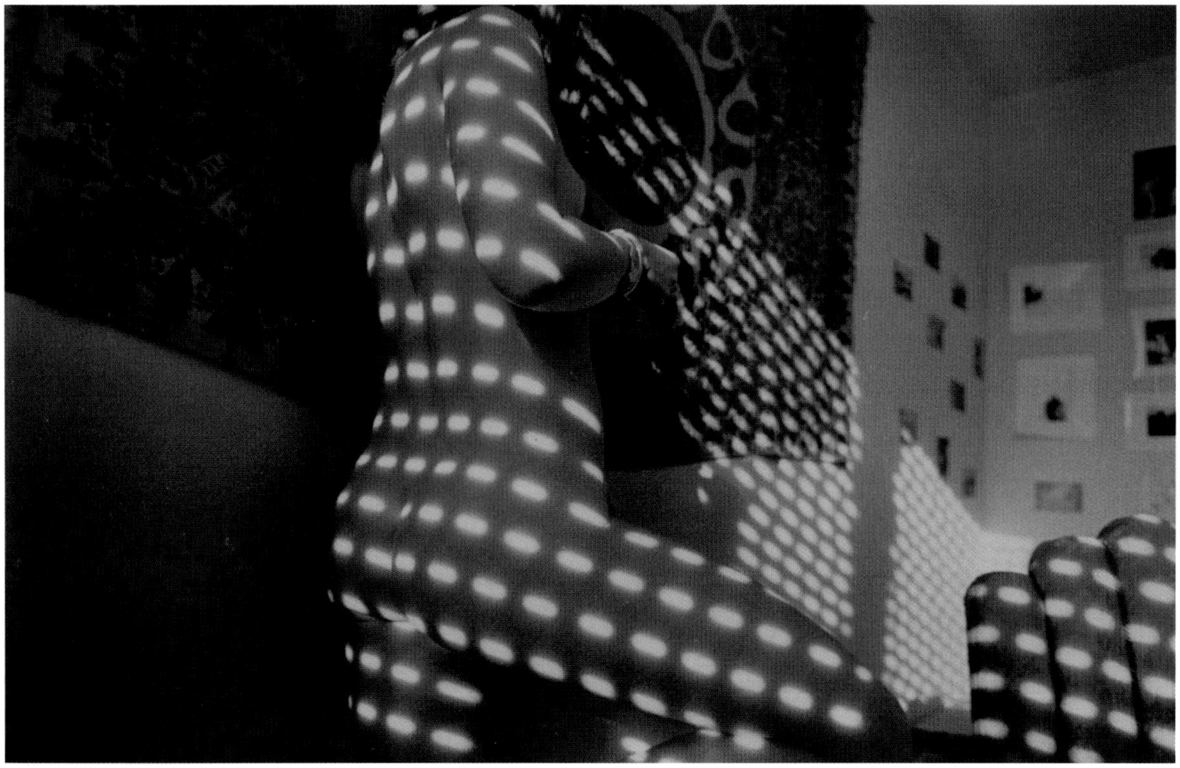

By the early 1980s, his travel photographs, portraits, and nudes had established him as one of Britain's leading photographers, his work appearing in such publications as *Harpers & Queen* and *Vogue*. His travels took him to such far-flung places as Cambodia, Chile, China, Russia, Spain, and Vietnam. Some of his best-known portraits are of such photographic greats as Ansel Adams, Bill Brandt, Manuel Bravo, and Aaron Siskind. He never did manage to photograph the photographers he liked best, however.

"I think originally it was probably Harry Callahan. I don't know why. I admired his pictures for being incredibly calm," says Tucker, whose work has been included in the permanent collections of the Museum of Modern Art (MOMA) in New York, the Victoria & Albert Museum in London, and the Bibliothèque Nationale in Paris. "And then there was Edward Weston, of course. Everyone [likes him], don't they?"

A denizen of the venerable Chelsea Arts Club, Tucker lives and works in a four-story home he shares with his wife, prominent attorney Victoria Younghusband. He describes himself as "the token Bohemian artist" in a Chelsea neighborhood once known as a Bohemian hotspot.

When not traveling on assignment, Tucker enjoys adding to his impressive collection of nudes. "I do like girls without their clothes on," he admits, "but that's not very unusual. If I can persuade them to get their kit off, I'll do a photograph."

Tucker says approaching a woman about photographing her can be a delicate transaction, but he finds that many women enjoy the idea of preserving their beauty for posterity. Typically, Tucker simply shows potential subjects his work and asks them if they would like to be photographed themselves. "People you'd think would never agree are very often the ones who will," he says.

Tucker shoots mainly with a handheld 35mm Nikon or a Mamiya 6x7, finding black-and-white photographs that he prints himself "more satisfying" than color images. He occasionally uses tungsten lighting, but he much prefers available daylight. Indeed, if there is a defining characteristic to Nic Tucker's work it is his distinctive use of shadows. Quite often his photographs wrap women in webs of shadow, creating a casual yet complex interplay between the female form and the light that illuminates it. Not surprisingly, Tucker has two books at the developmental stage, one on the nude and the other on shadows.

"Shadows mostly come about because I use daylight through windows," he explains. "It started some years ago, and I find it becoming a kind of theme."

Yes, Tucker's images are voyeurism, but a Tucker nude is also a private moment in which the photographer, and by extension the viewer, has been given permission to look. "I'm trying to make a decent picture, nothing more serious than that," says Tucker. "I find them inspirational, I suppose. I hang them on the wall and when I walk by I think, 'Oh god, she's lovely.' It makes you feel better just looking at it."

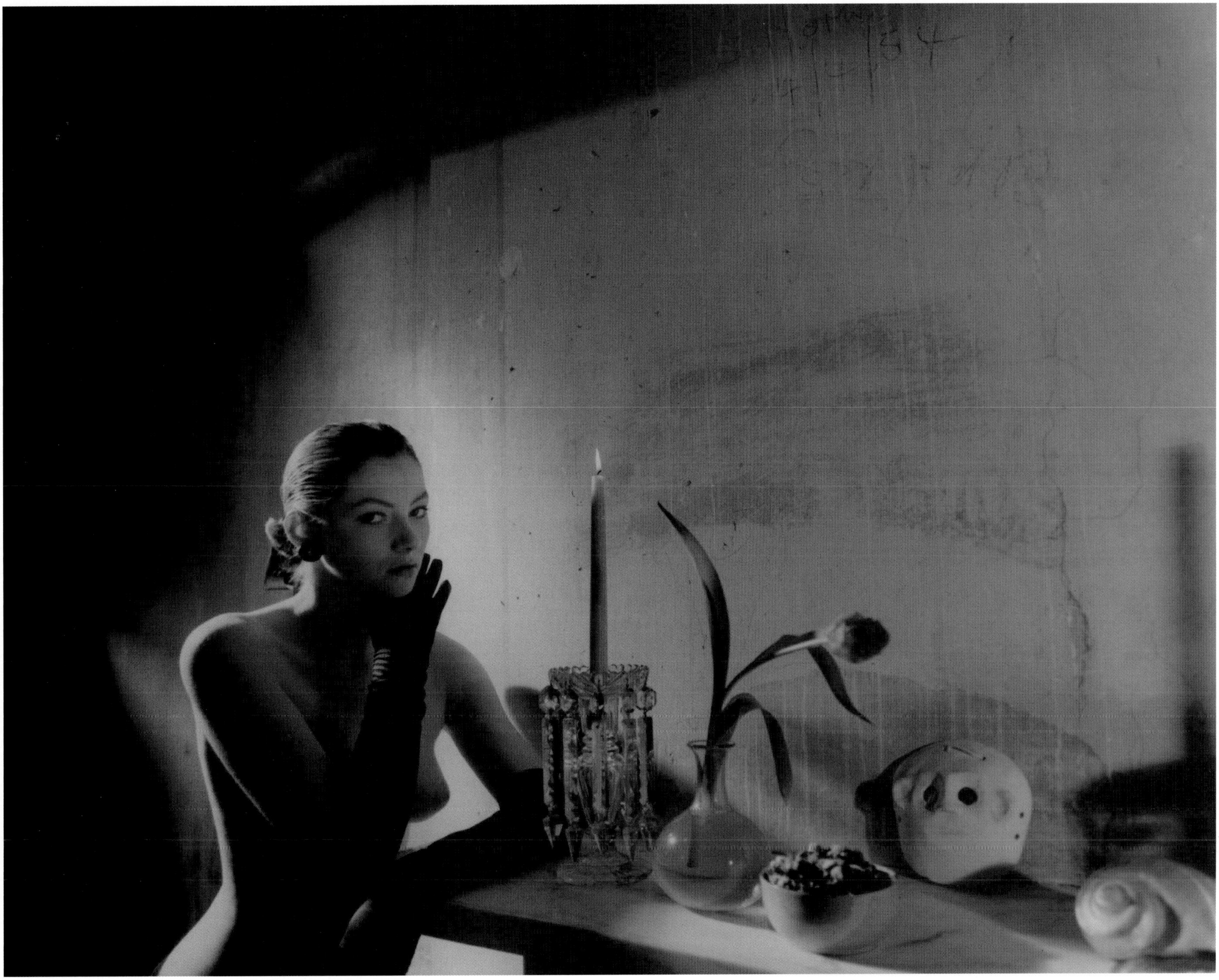

Fairlie in Sabadell, 1977 *(left)*
"Sabadell is a small industrial town in Spain, near Barcelona. My girlfriend at the time had just taken a job teaching English there. I went out to see her. It was taken in her flat in a little high-rise block—not a very attractive apartment really. It was four or five o'clock in the afternoon, and the sun coming in through the metal blinds made that effect when they weren't quite closed."

Mantelpiece, 1986 (*above*)
"This was taken at the home of an artist friend who I had worked with at *Harpers and Queen*. The girl, Deborah, wanted some photos for a portfolio, and I had to be careful of the crop as I had only persuaded her to take half her clothes off."

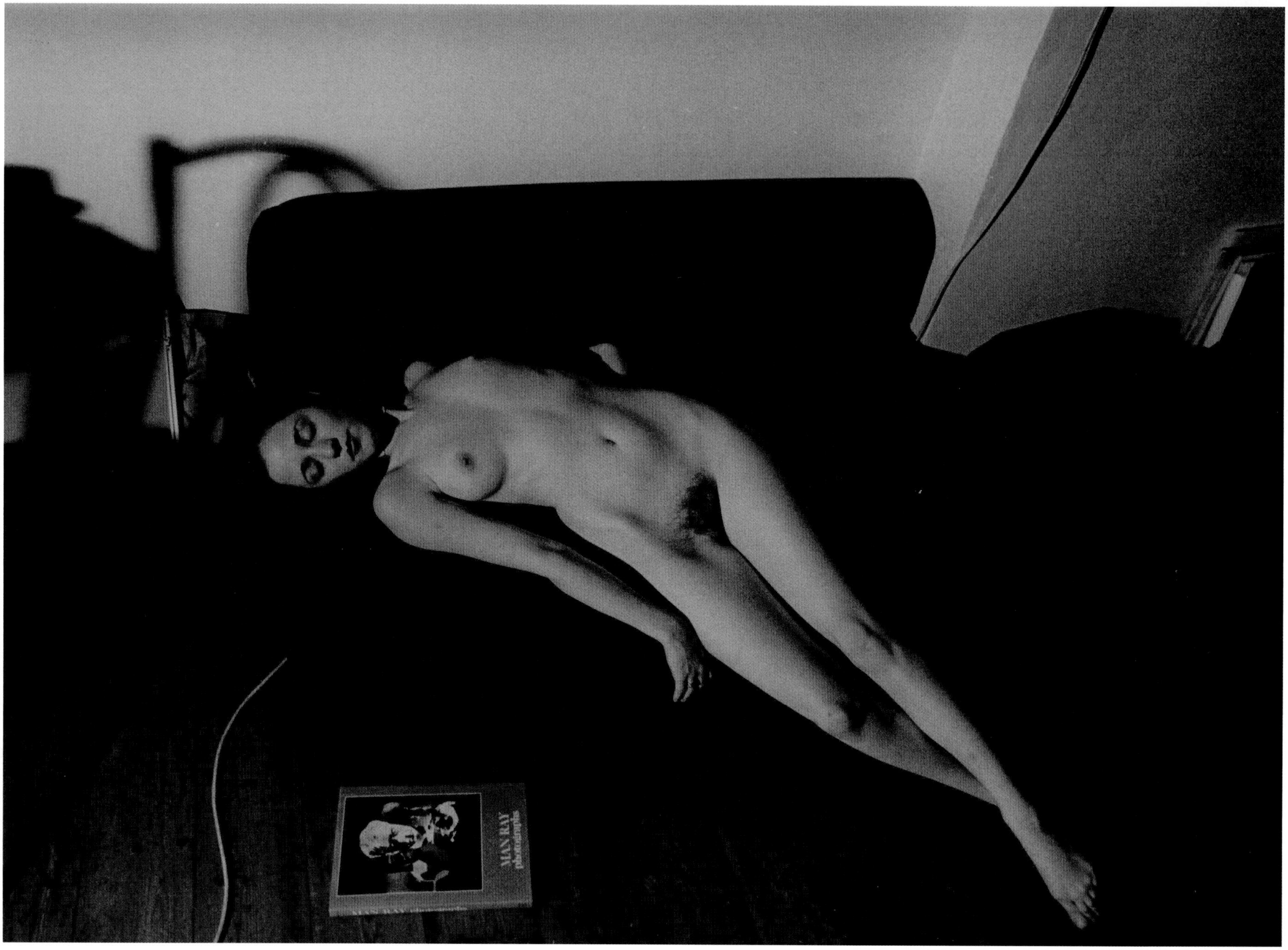

Joanna, 1980
"The Man Ray book was a coincidence. It wasn't intended. While I took pictures, she started reading the book. It was taken in another photographer's studio, a friend of mine, but I had a key. He was surprised and delighted when he came back and found a naked girl there."

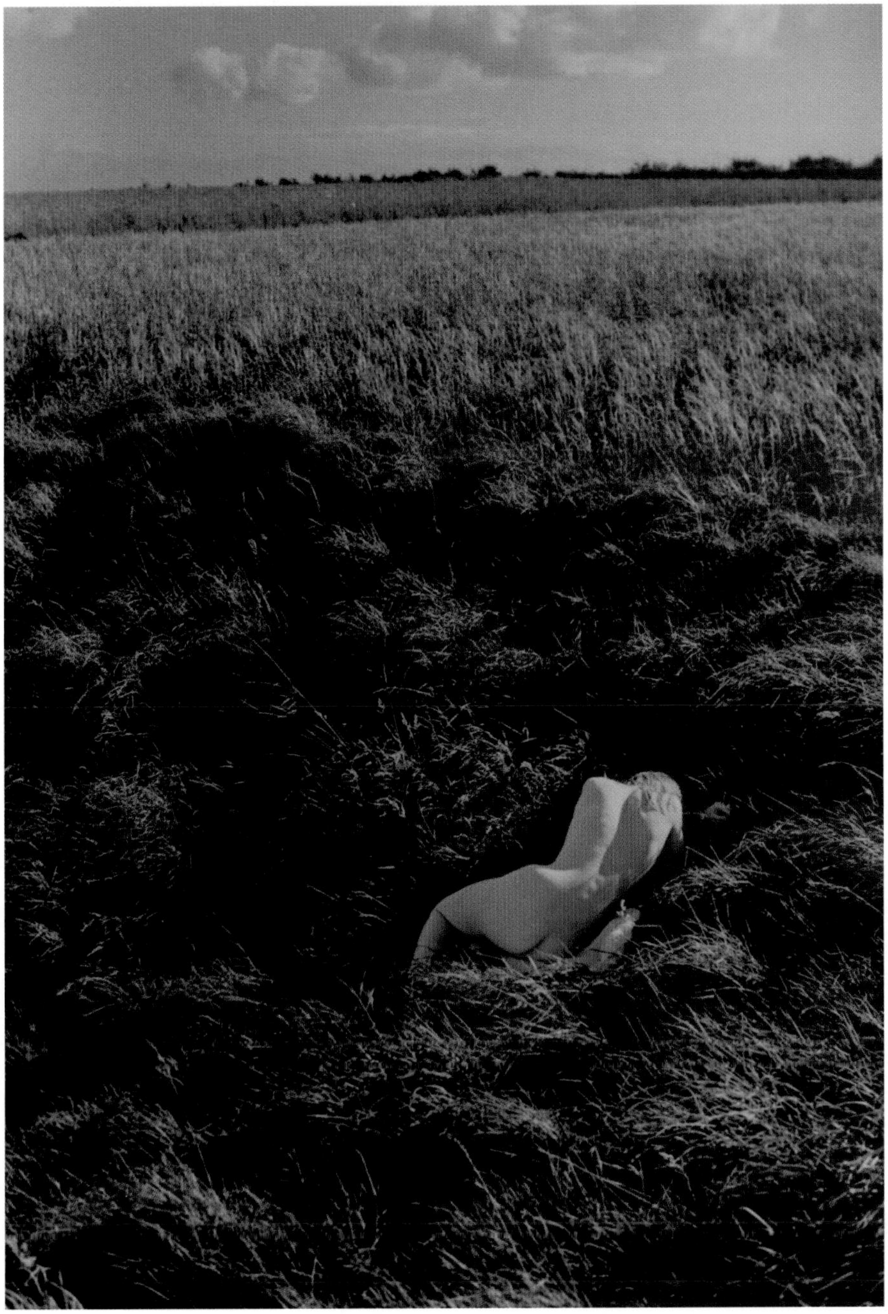

Dorset, 1970
"There was almost a deep hole in this field. We had been to the country to see my parents, and as we went by we stopped here for a walk and thought to take some photos. It amused people driving by."

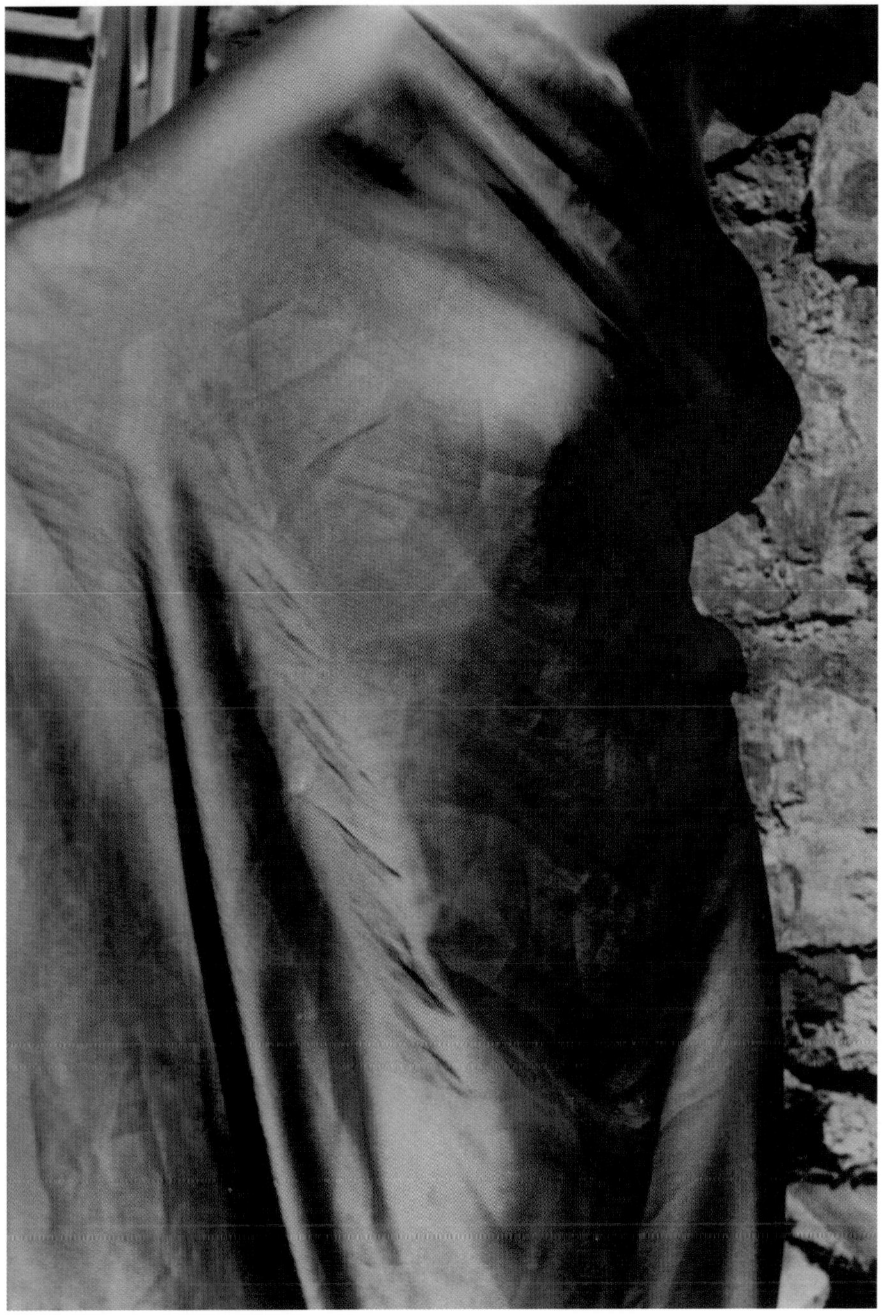

Emily in Garden, 1999
"I met Emily through a friend at the Colony Club, a notorious drinking club in London. She came around a couple of times, and she was one of those girls who had ideas of her own. She was good fun and extremely pretty. She decided she'd go into the garden with that stuff on her. I followed dutifully with the camera."

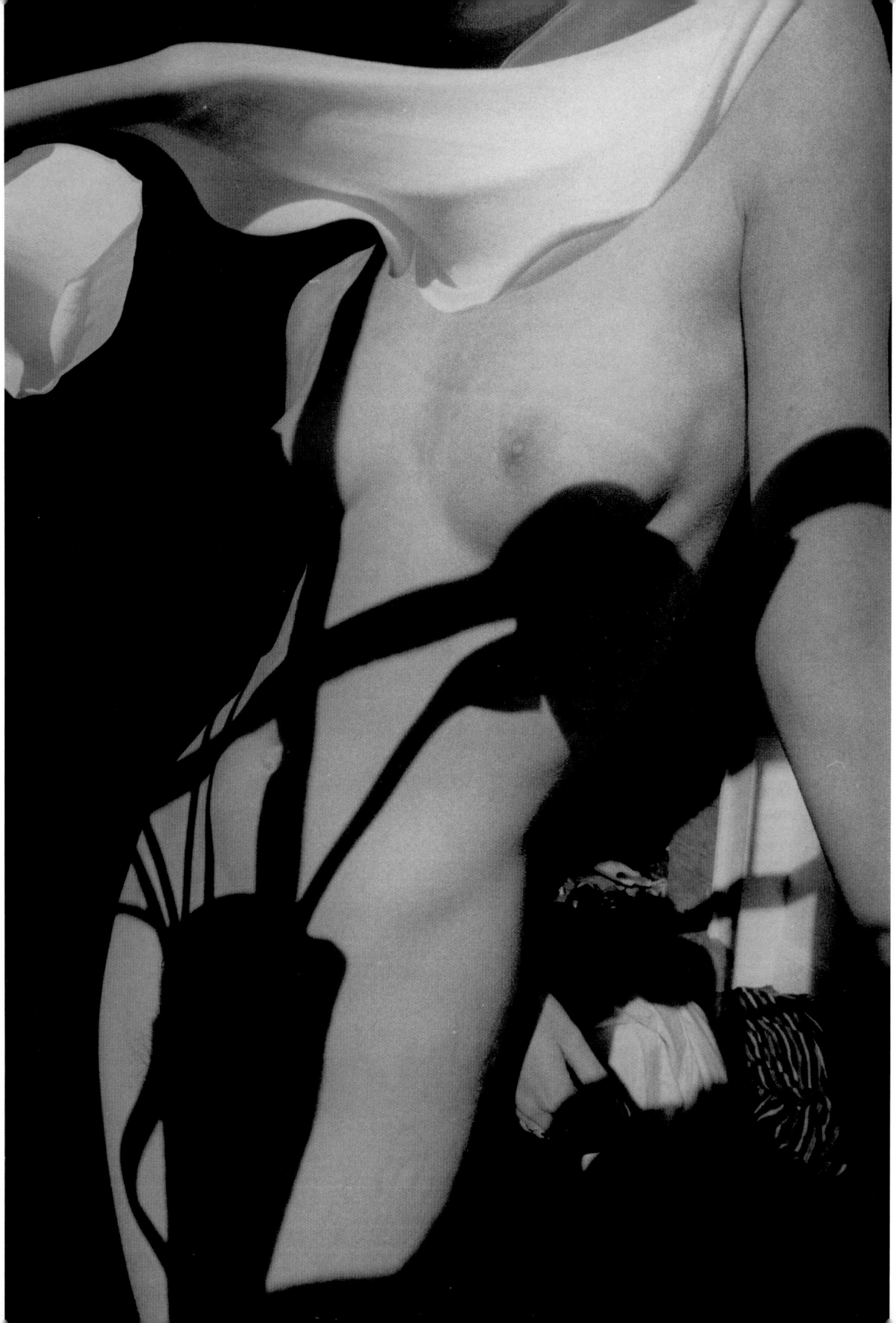

Calla Lilies, 1987
"The girl in the picture had just come back from Morocco, where she had had extreme food poisoning. She'd lost a lot of weight. It was taken in a friend's flat sometime in the early 1980s. Just for fun, I took the lilies along. I do like shadows. When I was learning about photography, I was working in the film business using a lot of lighting, but I didn't use any lights in this one. It's daylight."

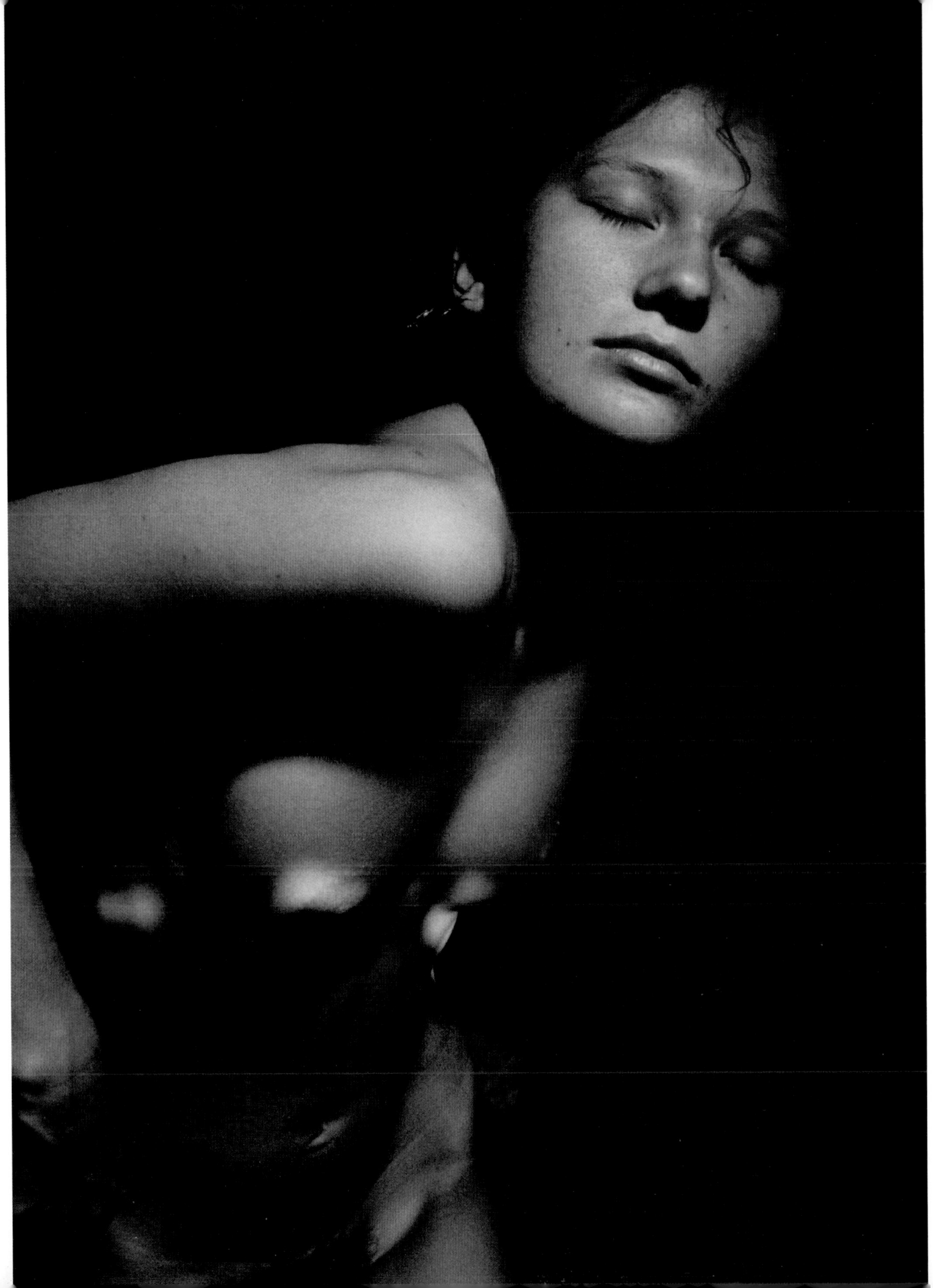

Tanya Twist, 1984
"We were lucky in that we had good weather, a certain amount of sunshine. While you can create almost anything with artificial light, you cannot create the uncertainty of nature."

Christian Vogt

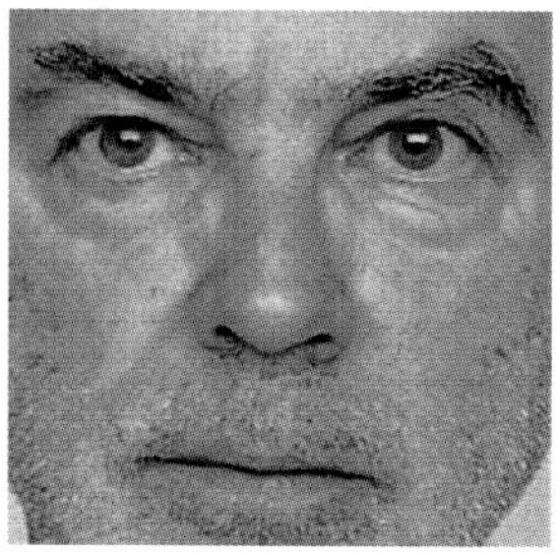

All images untitled and undated.

(*Below*) "I'm often shaky. Sometimes that's good, sometimes that's bad."

(*Opposite*) "My work has a lot to do with observation—human and otherwise. I think this is well represented in my series *Photographic Notes*, from which this selection is taken."

While looking through the images of Christian Vogt, you get the feeling that the Swiss photographer would be the perfect person to liven up a party full of pompous bores. Much of Vogt's nude photography can be described as instantaneous injections of exuberance. They are curious, inventive, ironic, and mischievous—like the creations of a teenager who has got hold of his parent's camera for a weekend. With an ingenious sense of humor, an inventive eye, and the audacity to test the boundaries of photography and its traditions, Vogt is regarded as one of the most unique photographers in the industry.

Vogt was born in 1946 in Basle, Switzerland, and a "keen interest in visual arts and the desire to make images" led him to study photography from 1964 to 1967 at the famous Allgemeine Gewerbeschule School of Design in his hometown.

After assisting American photographer Will McBride in Munich, Germany, Vogt went on to open his own studio in 1970. Two years later, he was freelancing for a number of magazines, including *Playboy*, *Du*, and *Camera*.

His interest in the nude began with one distinct emotion: "It was curiosity," he says. "I was a teenager in the 50s. [If you wanted] to see a nude, there were only Botticellis or Rubens in the museum. When one was lucky, one could see a breast in a copy of *Playboy*. At that time, pubic hair was considered pornography, and *verboten* [forbidden]."

That curiosity, coupled with Vogt's expansive imagination, led him to explore projects outside of his editorial career. "I had always been doing my own personal work. In Europe, in the early 70s, this was unusual," says Vogt. "Other than reportage photography, there was hardly anyone working 'creatively' with the medium. 'Creative photography' gained in interest, and this is when my work was first looked at seriously."

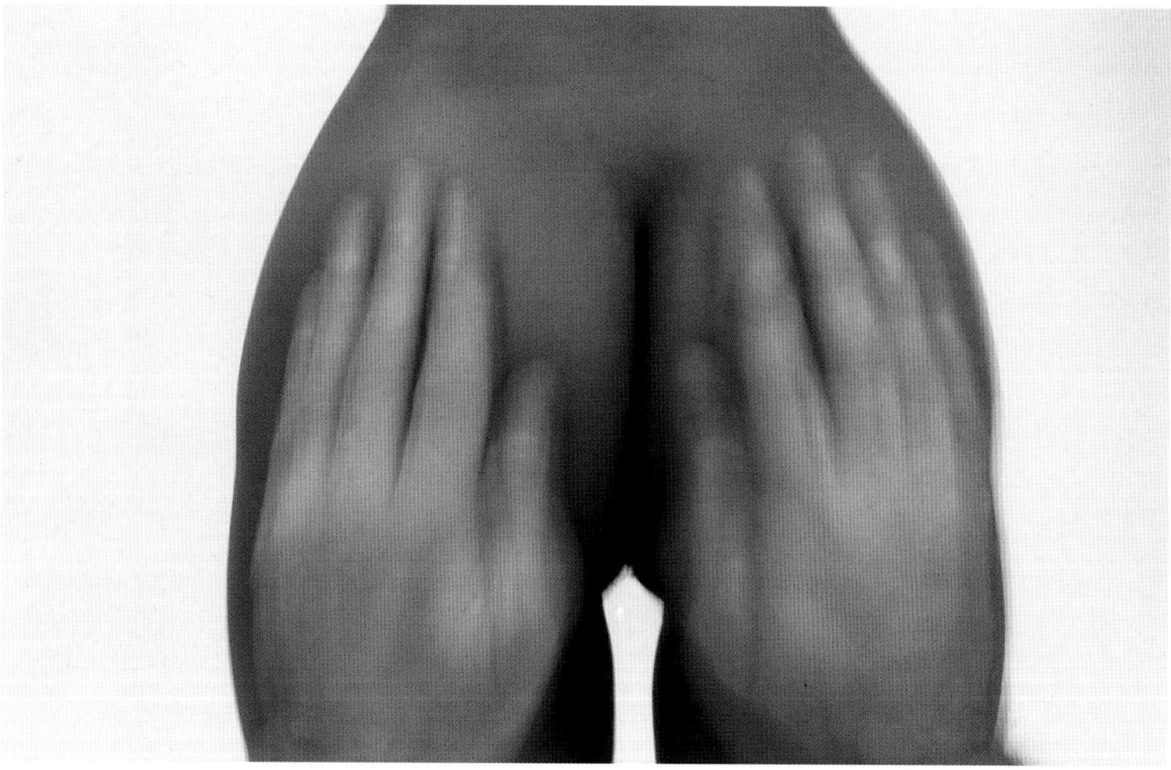

In the decades since then, his work has been exhibited in almost every renowned international museum or gallery, including the Museum of Modern Art (MOMA) in New York, the Photographers' Gallery in London, and the Tel Aviv Museum of Art in Israel.

In 1979, Vogt began work on a series of images that would eventually be published in the book, *In Camera* (RotoVision, 1982). Vogt's second monograph (his first was a self-titled 1980 publication) not only provided viewers with a sense of his lyrical, evocative imagery, but it was also immediately distinctive due to Vogt allowing the models to select and design the complete setup of each photograph. The book featured a set of photographs involving nude women, a single wooden crate, and various other props, such as fabrics, mirrors, paper, and even dogs. Like an erotic, adult version of a minimalist Dr. Seuss tale, models climb in and out of, and around, the box. The resulting photographs engage the viewer with ingenious meditations on space, shape, conjecture, and the use of concealment as an artistic device. "I love secrets," Vogt once said. "I like to leave things open. I like the things behind things." The 82 images that appeared in the book are among Vogt's best known, and many have gone on to become icons in the realm of nude photography.

This affection for the enigmatic and the thought-provoking would continue throughout Vogt's career. In 1998, Edition Stemmle published Vogt's *Photographic Notes: Everything Is Important—Nothing Is Important*, a captivating book of nudes, still lifes, and landscapes that were combined with cryptic, ironic text. Vogt's somewhat ambiguous messages next to the already offbeat photography made the entire experience both bizarre and amusing.

One image—a photograph that displays a brightly lit white woman riding the back of another bright-white torso at the extreme left side of the frame—carries this text below its border: "they would talk about anything to anybody but never with each other." Another, featuring an image of a woman hanging upside-down wearing only a black mask, a black brassiere, and a wide grin, includes these words: "Roberta acted the way she thought she was." *Photographic Notes* was like a private scrapbook of friends, lovers, and adventures that let you in on the party.

In addition to his nude work, Vogt has covered a large number of topics in the photography world. In 1991 he ventured into areas of Switzerland, Italy, and France to capture images of ancient battlefields. Ten years later, in a series titled *Prodigal Fathers*, Vogt and writer Martin Dean explored the effects on people growing up without a natural father, only to have him to come into their lives when they were older.

In recent years he has collaborated on a number of books highlighting the creations of the famous architect of spaces, landscape designer Dieter Kienast. His most recent work has integrated many of these themes, including nude imagery. "A successful image for me is when things come together—when 'how,' 'when,' and 'what' come together—in photography and in life," says Vogt. "I look forward to what presents itself to me, and seeing how I respond."

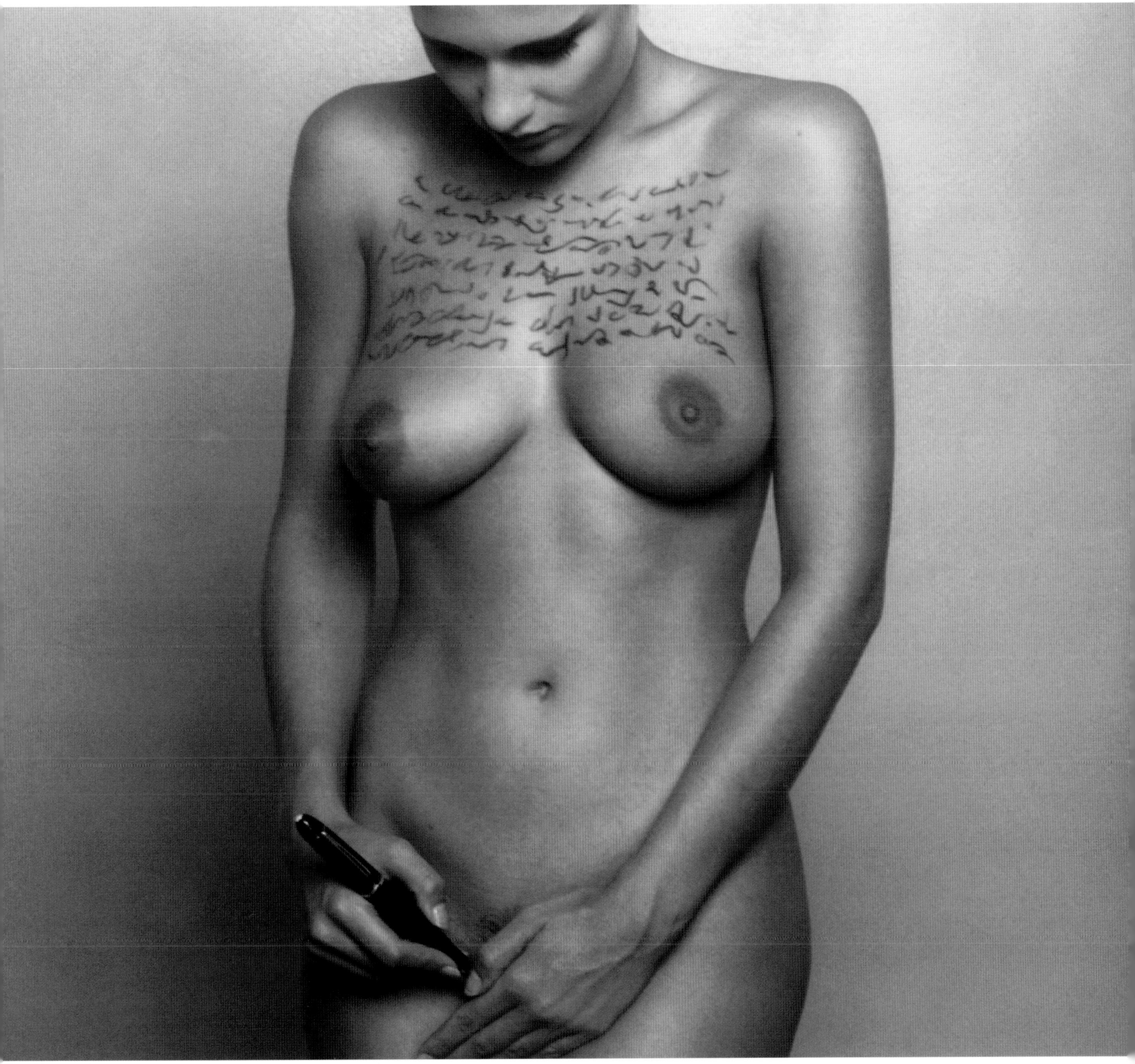

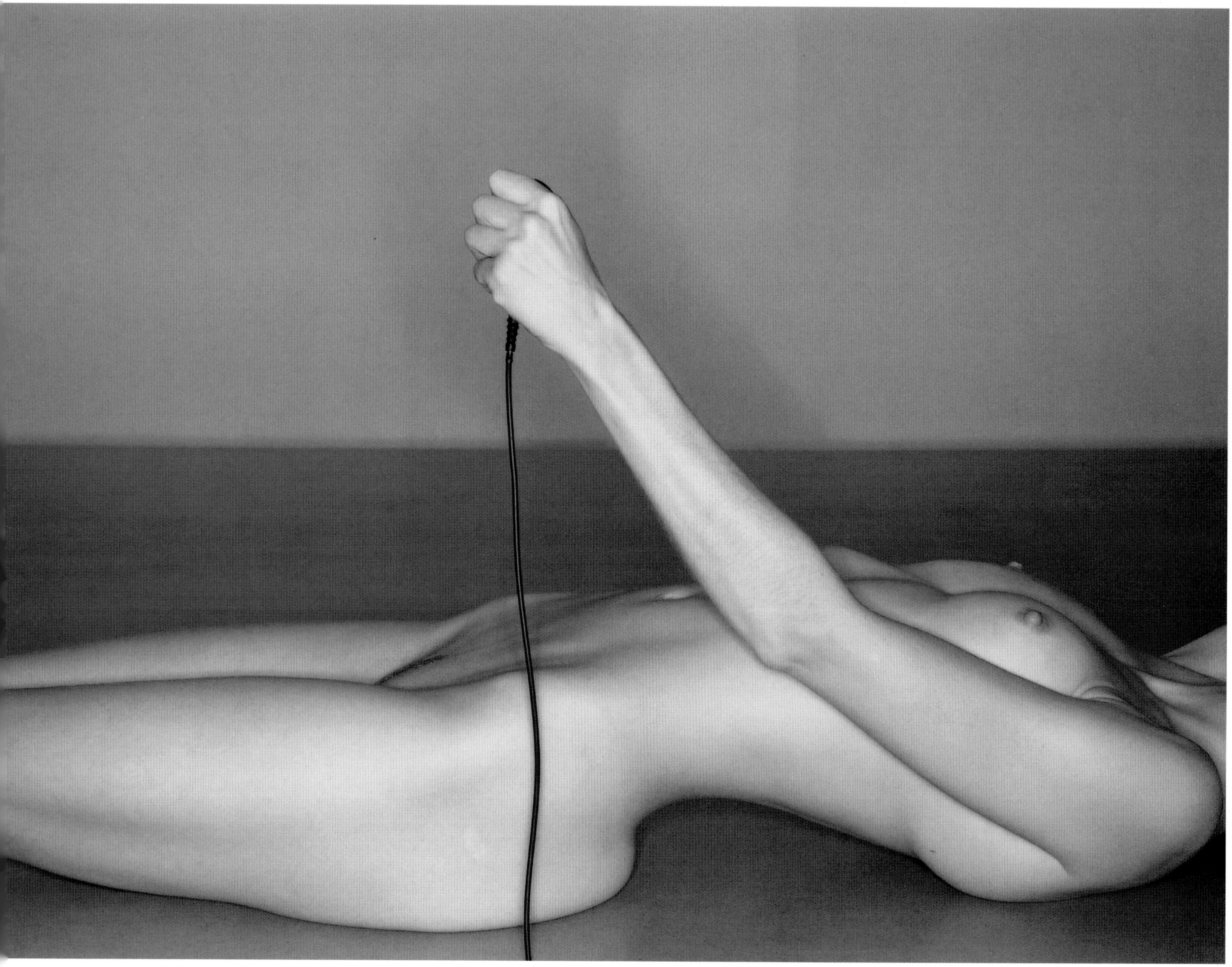

“The question in my work is not the subject, but rather what am I doing with it—be it a nude, a landscape, an animal, or a building. It is not about the ‘what,’ but about the ‘how.’”

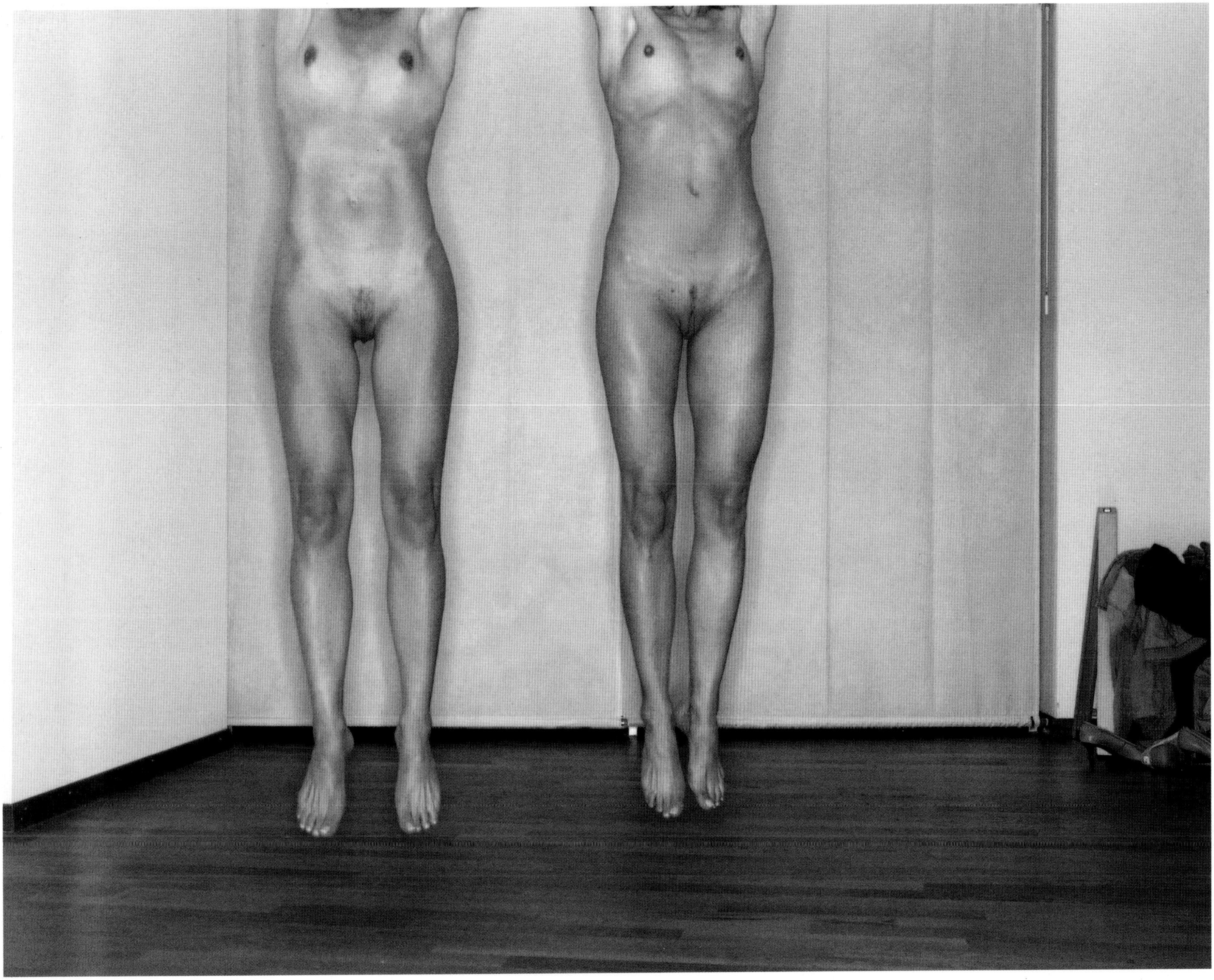

“and again Paul was confronted
with the fact that he was unable
to appreciate what he couldn’t
comprehend”

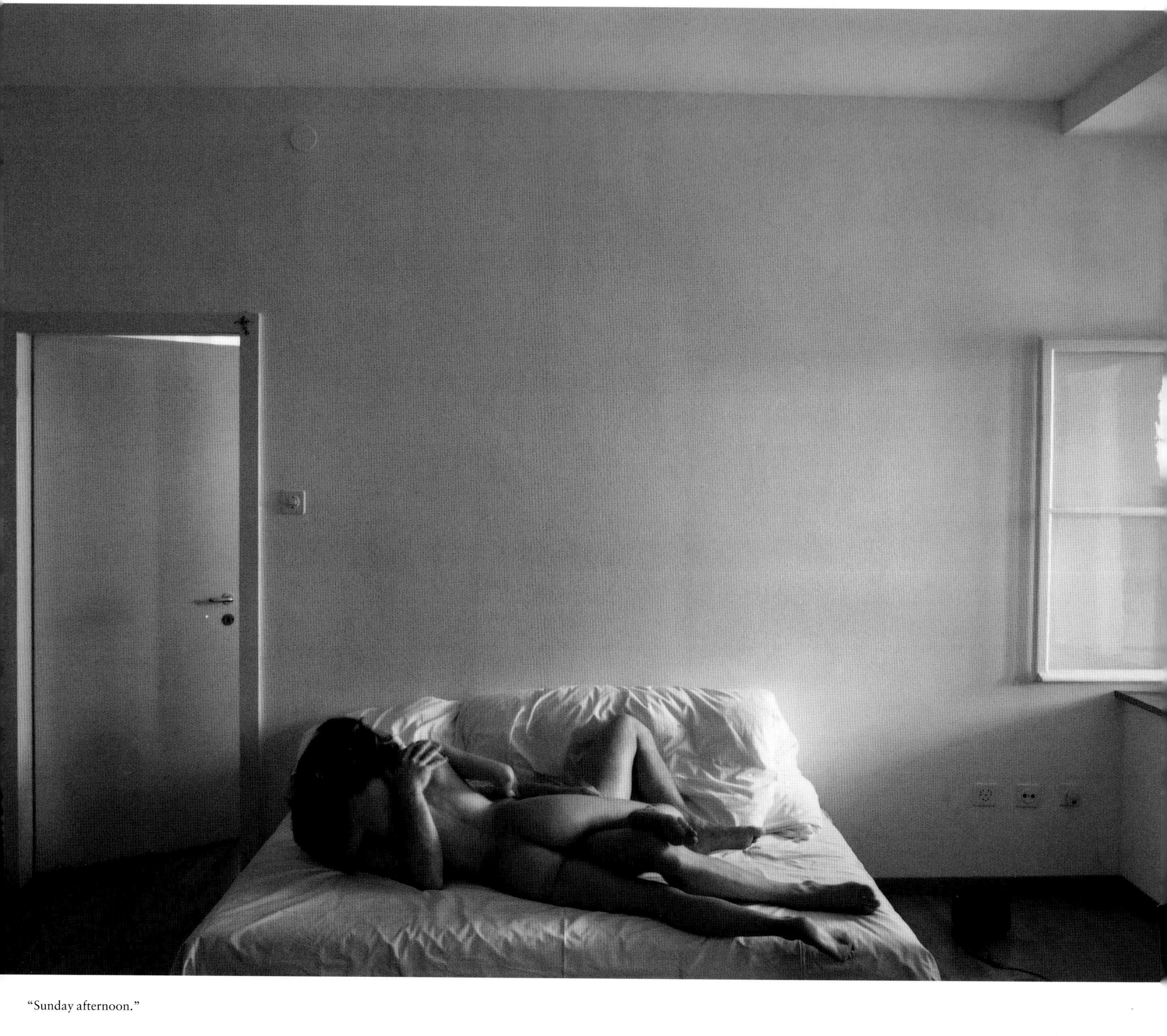

"Sunday afternoon."

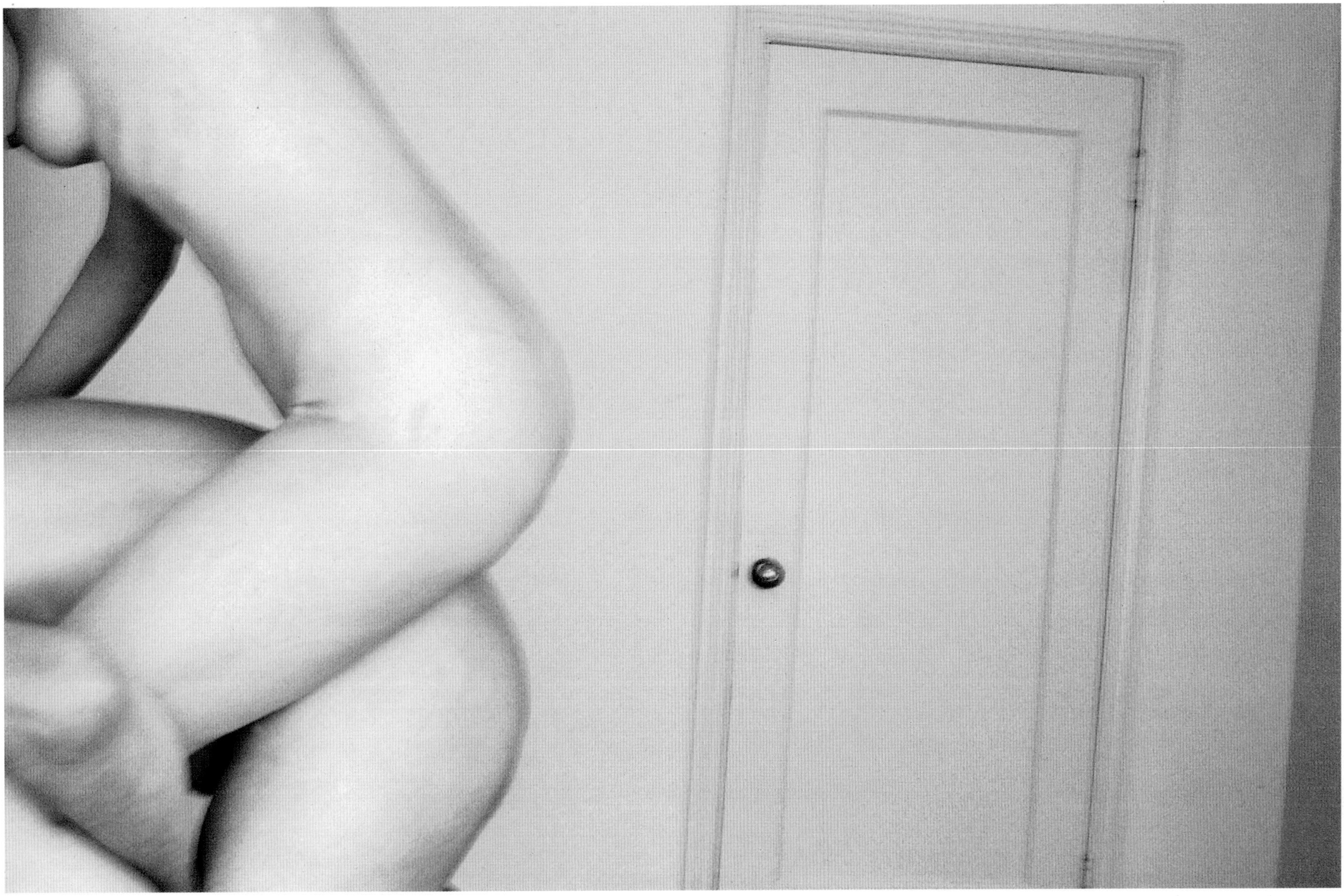

“they would talk about
anything to anybody but never
with each other”

Directory

Guido Argentini
www.guidoargentini.com
Agent:
BLOB Creative Group
Via Tertulliano, 56
20137 Milan
Italy
Telephone: +39 02 54 00 17 01.

Marc Atkins
www.marcatkins.com

Marc Baptiste
www.marcbaptiste.com
Agent
Vernon Jolly
180 Varick Street #912
New York
NY 10014
USA
Telephone: +1 212 989-0800.

Andreas H. Bitesnich
www.bitesnich.com
Agent
BLOB Creative Group
Via Tertulliano, 56
20137 Milan
Italy
Telephone: +39 02 54 00 17 01.

Sylvie Blum
www.sylvie-blum.de

Barbara Bordnick
www.barbarabordnick.com

Guy Bourdin
www.artandcommerce.com
Estate represented by:
Art+Commerce
755 Washington Street
New York
NY 100014
USA
Telephone: +1 212 206-0737

Gallery: Fahey Klein Gallery
148 North La Brea
Los Angeles
CA 90036
USA
Telephone: +1 323 934-2250.

Bob Carlos Clarke
www.panicpictures.net
Agent:
Ghislain Pascal
6a Kings Avenue
London SW4 8BD
UK
Telephone: 020 7498 3350

Gallery: Eyestorm
547 West 27th Street
Second Floor
New York
NY 10001
USA
Telephone: +1 212 226-1000.

Regina DeLuise
Gallery:
Bonni Benrubi Gallery
41 East 57th Street
13th Floor
New York
NY 10022
USA
Telephone: +1 212 888-6007.

Yuri Dojc
www.yuridojc.com
Agent:
Nicki Peters & Associates
187 Fulton Avenue
Toronto
Ontario
Canada
Telephone: +1 416 603-0300

Robert Farber
www.farber.com
Agent:
Elaine Korn Associates
372 5th Avenue #2E
New York
NY 10018
USA
Telephone: +1 212 760-0057

Gallery: G. Ray Hawkins Gallery
300 North Crescent Heights
Boulevard
Los Angeles
CA 90048
USA
Telephone: +1 323 655-4180.

Greg Friedler
www.gregfriedler.com

Ralph Gibson
www.ralphgibson.com
Gallery:
Howard Greenberg Gallery
41 East 57th Street
New York
NY 10022
USA
Telephone: +1 212 334-0010.

Greg Gorman
www.gormanphotography.com
Agent:
Trish Swords
8275 Beverly Boulevard
Los Angeles
CA 90048
USA
Telephone: +1 323 782-1870

Gallery:
Fahey Klein Gallery
148 North La Brea
Los Angeles
CA 90036
Telephone: +1 323 934-2250.

Peter Gorman
www.petergorman.com

Katy Grannan
www.katygrannan.com
Agent:
Bill Charles Representatives
116 Elizabeth Street
New York
NY 10013
USA
Telephone: +1 212 965-1465

Gallery:
Artemis Greenberg Van Doren Gallery
730 5th Avenue
New York
NY 10019
USA
Telephone: +1 212 445-0444.

Mark Edward Harris
www.markedwardharris.com
Agent:
Apex Fine Art
152 North La Brea
Los Angeles
CA 90036
USA
Telephone: +1 323 634-7887

Sam Haskins
www.haskins.com
Agent:
The Katy Barker Agency
208 West 11th Street
New York
NY 10014
USA
Telephone: +1 212 627-2558.

Kenro Izu
www.kenroizu.com
Gallery:
Howard Greenberg Gallery
41 East 57th Street
New York
NY 10022
USA
Telephone: +1 212 334-0010.

Mona Kuhn
www.monakuhn.com
Agent:
Tidepool Reps
1459 18th Street #109
San Francisco
CA 94107
USA
Telephone: +1 415 643-1231

Gallery:
Fahey Klein Gallery
148 North La Brea
Los Angeles
CA 90036
Telephone: +1 323 934-2250.

Anne Leigniel
www.anneleigniel.com
Gallery:
The Photographers' Gallery
5 & 8 Great Newport Street
London WC2H 7HY
UK
Telephone: +44 020 7831 1772.

Robert Mapplethorpe
www.artandcommerce.com
Estate represented by:
Art+Commerce
755 Washington Street
New York
NY 100014
USA
Telephone: +1 212 206-0737

Gallery: Fahey Klein Gallery
148 North La Brea
Los Angeles
CA 90036
USA
Telephone: +1 323 934-2250.

Stefan May
www.stefanmay.com

R. J. Muna
www.rjmuna.com
Agent:
Marianne Campbell Associates
840 Fell Street
San Francisco
CA 94117
USA
Telephone: +1 415 433-0353

Gallery:
San Francisco Camerawork
1246 Folsom Street
San Francisco
CA 94103
USA
Telephone: +1 415 863-1001.

Philippe Pache
www.philippepache.com
Agent:
Olivier Ripoll
82 Rue Marcadet
75018 Paris
France
Telephone: +33 6 74 89 46 88

Gallery:
The Photographers' Gallery
5 & 8 Great Newport Street
London WC2H 7HY
Telephone: +44 020 7831 1772.

David Penprase
www.davidpenprase.co.uk

Rankin
www.rankin.co.uk
Agent:
Montage Photographic
119 North Larchmont Boulevard
Suite 1
Los Angeles
CA 90004
USA
Telephone: +1 323 769 0600.

Bettina Rheims
Agent:
Jed Root
61a Walker Street
New York
NY 10013
USA
Telephone: +1 212 226-6600

Gallery:
Eyestorm
547 West 27th Street, Second Floor
New York
NY 10001
USA
Telephone: +1 212 226-1000

Ernestine Ruben
www.ernestineruben.com
Agent:
Mason Vickers Productions
117 Van Dyke Road
Hopewell
New Jersey
USA
Telephone: +1 609 466-0911

Gallery:
The John Stevenson Gallery
338 West 23rd Street
New York
NY 10011
USA
Telephone: +1 212 352-0070.

Robert Stivers
www.robertstivers.com
Gallery:
Riva Yares Gallery
123 Grant Avenue
Santa Fe
New Mexico 87501
USA
Telephone: +1 505 984-0330.

Arthur Tress
www.arthurtress.com
Gallery:
The Vault Gallery
2289 Main Street
Cambria
CA 93428
USA
Telephone: +1 805 927-0300

Nic Tucker
www.nictucker.com

Christian Vogt
www.christianvogt.com
Gallery:
Galerie zur Stockeregg
Stockerstr. 33
Ch-8022
Zurich
Switzerland
Telephone: +41 1 202 69 25.

Acknowledgments
Many thanks go out to all the people who contributed to this book. To Edgar Allen Beem, who contributed magnificent text and service. To Reuel Golden for the opportunity to take on this project. To Chris Middleton and April Sankey at RotoVision for all their help. To Darren Ching and Jane Helmick for their technical assistance. To Whitney Lawson, James Crump, Zachary Buchanan, and all the other people in the photography industry who presented their assistance. To all the photographers who graciously offered their inspirational images and words. And to Mom, Dad, Barbara, Alicia, Steven, Andrew, and Miana for all their continuing support.
—Anthony LaSala, 2005

Picture Credits
All photographs are the copyright of the photographer or their estate unless otherwise stated, and are reproduced courtesy of the photographer, or with the permission of the photographer's estate.

Photographs by Marc Atkins
© Marc Atkins / www.marcatkins.com

Photographs by Guy Bourdin
Guy Bourdin/Art+Commerce Anthology

Photographs by Bob Carlos Clarke
© Bob Carlos Clarke / bobcarlosclarke.com

Photographs by Regina DeLuise
Regina DeLuise and the Bonni Ben Rubi Gallery

Photographs by Kenro Izu
Kenro Izu/Courtesy Howard Greenberg Gallery, NYC

Photographs by Robert Mapplethorpe
Robert Mapplethorpe/Art+Commerce Anthology

Photographs by Stefan May
© Stefan May / stefanmay.com
All rights reserved

Photographs by Bettina Rheims
© Bettina Rheims, courtesy of Galerie Jérôme de Noirment, Paris, and Schirmer / Mosel, München

Photographs by Ernestine Ruben
Ernestine Ruben Photography

Photographs by Nic Tucker
© Nicolas Tucker

Photographs by Christian Vogt
from the series *Photographic Notes*
© Christian Vogt